MASS MEDIA AND THE LAW

Freedom and Restraint

Edited by DAVID G. CLARK and EARL R. HUTCHISON

A volume in the *Wiley Series* on *Government and Communication,* edited by Ray E. Hiebert

The First Amendment to the Constitution reads in part, "Congress shall make no law...abridging the freedom of speech, or of the press...." yet there are numerous legal restrictions and regulations on the press, radio, television, literature and the film. At the same time, there are complaints from the media about "access" to news, credibility gaps, official government secrecy, the bar association's efforts to restrict news about criminal trials, and censorship of questionable material dealing with sex or religion.

MASS MEDIA AND THE LAW amplifies these and other issues, and shows how laws (or the absence of laws) bearing on the mass media, affect our lives. The topics dealt with by the contributors to this volume are of interest not only to students of the mass media, but to everyone. The dual nature of law as a defender of expression, and as a restrainer of expression, is the basic theme of this book. While the articles in this volume do not always prescribe remedies for the increasing conflict between law and freedom, they do present sufficient evidence to enable the reader to form his own conclusions about specific problems and ways of dealing with them.

AND THE LAW

WILEY SERIES ON GOVERNMENT AND COMMUNICATION

Edited by Ray Eldon Hiebert

MASS MEDIA AND THE LAW

Freedom and Restraint

EDITED BY

DAVID G. CLARK

AND

EARL R. HUTCHISON

WILEY-INTERSCIENCE,

a Division of John Wiley & Sons

NEW YORK · LONDON · SYDNEY · TORONTO

Library of Congress Catalogue Card Number: 76-115653

ISBN 0 471 15851 8

Printed in the United States of America

10 9 8 7 6 5 4 3 2 1

To the Students

Series Preface

In a democratic society there is no more important principle than the people's right to know about their government and its obligation to keep the people informed. The role of the press and communication in the governing process has been important since the earliest days of the nation.

In the modern mass society of an international power, communication between government and people through a complex and often instantaneous means of transmission has vital implications and consequences. The explosive impact of the mass media on the political and governmental process has brought about changes in politics, public administration, and international relations.

The interrelationship between government and communication has many new dimensions that must be explored and understood. The "Wiley Series on Government and Communication" was conceived to probe and provide greater understanding of those new dimensions.

Some of the books in the series deal with the way in which governments (local, national, and international) communicate with the people, either directly or through the press and mass media.

Other books in the series discuss the way in which the people, usually through the press and mass media, obtain information from government.

Finally, some of the series books treat problems that arise at that intersection of society at which government and people meet through the media. These are problems of the social, economic, legal, and political implications of the communication process when dealing with government, the problems of restriction and censorship, of distortion and propaganda, of freedom and national security, and of organization and technology.

Certainly the future of democracy may depend to a large extent on the success with which we understand and meet the problems created by the relationship between government and communication in a new age.

RAY ELDON HIEBERT
Series Editor

Preface

With the exception of college professors, reviewers, and a few students, hardly anyone reads a preface. With this in mind, we resolutely make a brief comment.

We consider the students of mass communications our colleagues. We believe we have common goals. And although we are over 30 years old, we hope that these students will not distrust us because of differences in age.

This book is dedicated to the students and has been carefully edited with the student of mass communications in mind. We feel strongly that our mass communications system is entering a highly critical stage. If, in the next few years, the restraints in our communications cancel out the freedoms, if secrecy in government proliferates, if the flow of ideas is dammed by media barons, and if the right of access to media is denied to minority groups, then an irreversible trend may be set toward a monolithic, totalitarian state.

We also believe that the future of this country rests in the hands of the persons who are now under 30 years of age. Their idealism is the stuff that the United States was founded on. A contagion of their idealism is what America now needs to give it a moral sense of purpose. The whole world *is* watching them by virtue of our mass communications system. And these students should be watching the whole world. Most important, they should keep a careful eye on the spectacles through which they are being observed and through which they, in turn, observe. These students should be aware of the very few people in the mass communications industry who share their ideals; and they should be especially aware of the many people in positions of power in this industry who have lost sight of the true meaning of the Constitution and its amendments. How else, except through clear and keen vision are students to know the United States and the world that they wish to change? How else can they expect to bring about their aims and goals intelligently and efficiently?

Only through the smooth and proper functioning of its mass communications system can a democracy such as ours continue as a democratic society. This is what is so disturbing about the present Administration's attempt (though officials and Vice-President Spiro Agnew's attack on the television networks) to curb and intimidate its critics. Such serious problems continually blight the mass communications arena and, consequently, that arena requires a constant vigil.

For these reasons we commend the country's mass communications to the students' study. We need, and want, their help.

The flavor and excitement of the mass communications arena has been distilled (we hope) in this book. As students, we suffered through texts that ignored many of the major problems plaguing the industry and, instead, concentrated on major court cases and their discussion. However, we believe that students using this book may want to complement it with study of pertinent cases in the law library or in those books composed of major court cases. For their convenience, a list of the most important court cases follows each chapter, along with a selected bibliography for further study.

DAVID G. CLARK
E. R. HUTCHISON

Madison, Wisconsin
Nashville, Tennessee
January 1970

Acknowledgments

To the people who helped to make this book possible, we express our appreciation.

To the ones who contributed original articles, we owe a debt that can never be fully paid. Among this group are the distinguished Chicago attorney Elmer Gertz, Brian K. Williams, and Mrs. Ann Varnum Commons. We are also grateful to those whose articles, although not included in the final version of this book, nevertheless provided stimulating insight and whose omission can only be counted as our loss: Victor Weybright, David Kaser, Richard Doherty, Richard A. Peterson, David Berger, William A. Hachten, Federal Communications Commissioner Kenneth A. Cox, Justice William J. Brennan, Jr., and the late Carl E. Lindstrom.

Among those from whose writings we have included selections, we particularly thank Commissioner Nicholas Johnson of the Federal Communications Commission, John Kittross, Judge Edward J. Devitt of the U.S. District Court for Minnesota, Ben W. Holman of the U.S. Department of Justice, and Thomas I. Emerson of Yale University.

We are grateful to Don Hyndman, director of public relations for the American Bar Association, and Larson M. Powell, Vice-President of Moody's Investors Services, Professor Phillips Brooks and Miss Darlene Helm, both former students at George Peabody College, whose good efforts improved our work considerably.

Allen Deutsch and Mr. Steve Klitzman, formerly graduate students at Stanford University, were extremely helpful in educating one of us (D.G.C.) to problems raised by the U.S. Customs Service and by the lack of diversity in the marketplace of ideas. Professor Lyman Ray Patterson of Vanderbilt University read the chapter on copyright and kindly offered suggestions and criticism.

We also express our appreciation to John Sullivan, formerly of Wiley, for his help in the early stages of this project, and to Ray E. Hiebert, series editor and head of journalism at the University of Maryland, for his many good suggestions and for seeing us through some troubled times.

Finally, we thank Mrs. Aline Walton, of Wiley, for the book's design and Malcolm Easterlin, of Wiley, for the editing.

D. G. C.

E. R. H.

Contents

xiii

MASS MEDIA AND THE LAW

Introduction

DAVID CLARK

E. R. HUTCHISON

W HEN most people think about law and the mass media in the same context, they probably consider only a few areas, and even these in limited ways. There is the First Amendment to the Constitution, which reads in part: "Congress shall make no law . . . abridging the freedom of speech, or of the press; . . . ." Does not this mean that there are no legal restrictions on the press? But a Federal Communications Commission exists, and it "regulates" radio and television. And they are part of the "press" too, are they not? At least, television talks a lot about how important it is in keeping us informed. The thought of any contradiction between the concept of the First Amendment and that of the FCC may not occur to most of us.

But everyone is aware of the various laws that are frequently proposed—usually around election time, it seems—dealing with pornography and the problem of keeping it out of the reach of children. The citizen feels obliged to support these laws in principle, although he sometimes votes against them. He has never seen any "hard core" pornography, nor have his children (at least, they won't admit that they have), nor have any of his friends' children. Nevertheless, these laws are aimed only at smut peddlers, not at reputable publishers—isn't that right?

Also there are the complaints appearing in the media about "access" to news, about credibility gaps that the Administration creates by its insistence on keeping secret certain of its dealings. Less often there are similar complaints about local governmental bodies. And, sometimes, there are stories about libel suits; and, perhaps once in a while, an editorial is published contending that the bar association's efforts to restrict news about criminal trials is really an effort to jeopardize the public's right to know how justice is meted out.

The purpose of this book is to amplify these and other issues, and to show how law (or the absence of law), bearing on the mass media, affects our lives. We think that the topics presented are of interest and concern not only to persons involved in or contemplating careers in the mass media but also to well-informed citizens in every walk of life. For the media touch on our everyday affairs—not just when we're interested in news, entertainment, and advertising but frequently in totally unsuspected ways:

3

Envision a young man at college. He is awakened one morning by his clock radio, which is tuned to a station playing a Bob Dylan record. After listening to the CBS World News Roundup, he dresses and goes downstairs to breakfast, where the talk, as usual, centers on sports. Perhaps the baseball season is underway, and the young man defends the showing of *his* team: the New York Yankees. After breakfast, he has a few minutes before class. He goes back to his room and brings out his electric guitar for practice (*sans* amplifier) on the new chords in order to be ready for a session later in the week. At his first class—music appreciation—the professor plays a recording of Leonard Bernstein and the New York Philharmonic. Next, he attends a class called "Introduction to the Mass Media" in which the professor, after making a reading assignment in the textbook, asks his students to describe (in five minutes) the ways in which the mass media affect their lives. The young man thinks a minute, then jots down that the media provide news and entertainment (in that order, because the professor is a serious fellow). As an afterthought, he adds that, of course, the media also carry a lot of advertising, which he personally ignores, but which helps to drive up the prices of goods like cars and soap (and vodka, he adds to himself).

But the young man did not know that each one of his activities on this day involved not just the "mass media" but *one* corporation in the mass media: the Columbia Broadcasting System. Bob Dylan's record was made by Epic, a company set up by Columbia to tap the expanding teenage market. The radio station that played the record was a CBS affiliate, which means that it had contractual agreements with the network. (If the young man had been listening in any of seven cities, he would have heard the record played on a CBS-owned station.) The New York Yankees were owned by CBS. So was Fender Electrical Instruments, the company that made the electric guitar that he was so proud of. The Leonard Bernstein recording was made by still another subsidiary of CBS, and the textbook in the class on the mass media was published by a company merged by CBS.

The problems created by this bigness are numerous. In the conglomerations that are CBS, the Radio Corporation of America, Time, Inc., Metromedia, or a dozen other communications giants, who is really responsible for what is made available to the public? Who really makes the decisions, and what frames of reference are used? What motives lie behind these decisions? What legal checks work to represent the public interest? And what is the public interest?

This book attempts to clarify the relevance of these problems to the average person. We point out how the law works, and does not work, to protect the public from the results of a monopoly of voices in the marketplace of ideas. We show how laws, drafted in the early years of this century (or even earlier, and modified only slightly since), have little application to the kinds of problems created by trends of the past twelve or fifteen years.

The thread of law as defender of freedom of expression, and as restrainer of expression, striates this book. After all, law is the manifestation of the people's desire for a system of ethical behavior. And the clash of opinions about how to define and achieve ethical behavior, historically, has produced laws that clash with one another in philosophy as well as in practical application. We illustrate some of these clashes today. For instance, the Supreme Court, more than thirty years ago, outlawed the restraint of expression before publication. And yet this same court and other legal bodies consistently have sustained certain forms of prior restraint (in motion pictures and in broadcasting, most frequently). Moreover, laws preventing formal censorship sometimes stimulate attempts by certain persons to evade the spirit of the law by establishing extralegal (or informal) censorship. Although the First Amendment to the Constitution forbids Congress to abridge the freedom of the press, the press itself has made implicit agreements with government to prevent the public from hearing news. Sometimes these agreements, usually described as self-regulation, have produced some good; they are always well-intended. But when the news media voluntarily agree to withhold from the public news of racial disturbances, for example, the ends (not to mention the means) seem highly dubious in a society that supposedly places a premium on free exchange of ideas.

But even if the concept of restraint prior to publication should be firmly outlawed, there remains the problem of access to information. It has become increasingly clear that if anything that is known may be published, the way to avoid embarrassing publicity is to find ways of making certain that secrecy prevails at the source. Therefore, we have included a section showing the various relationships of government and the media, through law, on this issue. Government, at all levels, may facilitate and restrain the public's awareness of public business. We show how it seeks to accomplish these ends.

The Constitution seems to allow for freedom and restraint of the press. At least, in these modern days, problems created by the apparent conflict inherent in the freedom-of-the-press amendment (the First Amendment) and the fair-trial amendment (the Sixth Amendment) are very much to the fore. And yet, attempts to clarify and resolve the problem seem to lead to confusion and further misunderstandings. Some segments of the press seem to want to sensationalize criminal trials for profit, out of habit, and through a misguided conception of what is important; and some lawyers, for their own convenience, would restrict the press, while others would use the press to win in appeals courts what they cannot win in trial courts. We include a section devoted to this conflict.

In addition, there are numerous examples of citizens, individually and in groups, working today to achieve suppression of hated opinions or speech, apparently in blissful ignorance that the machinery they desire to use against others might someday be turned against themselves. Public servants vaguely threaten legal action to force citizens to conform to the public servants' personal ideas of morality. We believe that these are important issues now. They have always been and will probably continue to be.

Also there are examples of media going so far as to ruin reputations, to violate privacy, and to threaten life.

Because of our issue-oriented approach, we have not proceeded as a law professor might. We have not organized our book according to various divisions of law (such as torts or administrative law), since we are not attempting to make lawyers of our readers. We are attempting to make readers aware of the ways in which these issues are being confronted—by the media, legal scholars, other experts, and, sometimes, laymen. These are matters that

concern all responsible citizens in a free society, not merely citizens with vested interests or those charged with administering
the law.

Sometimes these issues are simple. More often they are complex
—perhaps so complex as to be basically insoluble. Sometimes the
selfish interest is so transparently obvious that it is funny. More
often there is a genuine conflict of principles, which have long
been revered in our system of life.

What, then, should be the role of law in assuring that freedom
of the press continues to be a term of real meaning in our society?
Serious thinkers have grappled with this question, in one form
or another, ever since there have been governments, laws, and
notions of free speech. Phrasing the question in the above words
presupposes several assumptions with which we are in accord:
(1) law does have a role in assuring freedom of the press; (2)
freedom of the press does exist, in great measure, in this country
but might be greatly extended; (3) both law and freedom are
essential to a democratic society; and (4) conflicts that involve the
concepts of freedom of the press and the concepts of business,
individual, or governmental rights should be resolved according
to a philosophy that does not seek to restrict the press but seeks
to serve society's needs.

Of course, it is a good deal easier to declare these assumptions
than to prescribe specific courses of action to assure that the aims
they embody are fully realized. But if we cannot always prescribe
remedies, we can present sufficient evidence to enable the reader
to form his own conclusions about what should be done. And
this, we submit, is reason enough for this book.

Prior Restraint: Keeping Ideas Out of Print

THE legal doctrine of prior restraint (or formal censorship before publication) is probably the oldest form of press control. Certainly it is one of the most efficient, since one censor, working in the watershed, can create a drought of information and ideas long before they reach the fertile plain of people's minds. In the United States, the doctrine of prior restraint has been firmly opposed by the First Amendment to the Constitution, and by the Supreme Court, perhaps most notably in the case of *Near v. Minnesota,* decided in 1931. But the philosophy behind that doctrine lives zestfully on, and shows no signs of the infirmities of age.

Prior restraint, whether it takes the form of prepublication censorship, or licensing, or whether it has the extralegal shape of codes of conduct and self-restraint under pressure from power sources, has a deceptively simple rationale: certain facts or ideas are, in themselves, so dangerous that if they are published, evils will result which society has the right to prevent. Such reasoning has never endured, even in the most authoritarian societies, since ideas and their advocates eventually find ways of evading censorship. But censorship has an insidious appeal at times of stress, no matter how firmly a society feels itself committed to ideals of free expression.

In recent years, some form of prior restraint has been applied in almost every area of public concern, but politics, war, and sex continue to be the areas in which censorship is most consistently applied. Lately, however, there have been cries for, and movement toward, prior restraint in the coverage of certain of the racial disturbances that have swept the country.

The first article in this chapter, by James Russell Wiggins, who has had many opportunities to battle censorship during his tenure as editor of the *Washington Post,* traces the history of prior restraint and points out an important communications medium—broadcasting—which is still subject to a variation of that form of control. And not only has broadcasting never been included in the protection extended by the *Near* decision but another form of mass communication—motion pictures—has been consistently subjected to stringent prior restraint in many localities. In the form of state and municipal licensing and

11

review boards, movie censorship thrived until the mid-1960s. Even today, when all state boards have been declared unconstitutional, the Supreme Court has refused to declare itself unalterably opposed to the licensing of movies. In the 1968 case of *Teitel Film Corporation v. Cusack,* even as the Court voided the City of Chicago's motion picture censorship ordinance, it issued, in effect, an invitation to the censors to try again with an ordinance providing "procedural safeguards designed to obviate the dangers of a censorship system." These safeguards, said the Court, would include prompt judicial review of a decision not to grant a film license for public exhibition.

The second selection, written by E. R. Hutchison, one of the editors of this book, documents a case study of how informal, extralegal censorship works, while the public, lulled by the fact that the Constitution assures freedom of the press, does not realize that part of its potential reading matter is eliminated from the marketplace by the self-appointed.

Aside from formal regulation, or illegal informal censorship by the official acting beyond his authority, there is a third form of prior restraint. This is self-regulation through adherence to an ethical standard or voluntary code of conduct. In some cases, such as Vietnam war coverage, these codes operate in the shadow of formal machinery which already exists and may be called into play if the codes fail to work. Hence an axe hangs over the extended neck of reporters, whose misbehavior in the eye of authority might result in the institution of formal control. In other cases (such as the new movie code, advertising, and news coverage of explosive events), voluntary codes seem to come into existence out of fear of possible government intervention otherwise. Although the objectives of these voluntary codes may be considered as positive by the majority, the effect of such prior restraint is the same as that of formal censorship: ideas and messages are suppressed.

The remaining selections in this chapter illustrate these codes —and their weaknesses—in action.

The Right To Print Without Prior Restraint

JAMES RUSSELL WIGGINS

*And though all the winds of doctrine were let loose to play upon the earth,
so Truth be in the field, we do injuriously by licensing and prohibiting to
misdoubt her strength.*

Milton, Areopagitica

From 1538 to 1695 the struggle for freedom of the press, in
England, was largely a struggle against licensing.

The proclamation of 1538, issued by Henry VIII, put the
whole press under a licensing system. All who sought to publish
were required to submit their intended works, prior to publication, for official approval and censorship. Religious works were
scrutinized by the clergy; political works by the government, at
first. For intervals, heresy and treason were almost indistinguishable crimes.

The freedom of the press lay under this burden, in various
forms, until the lapse of the last licensing act in 1695.

It is not remarkable that a struggle which cost so many
lives and extended over so many years put so great an emphasis

---

upon the importance of licensing as to cause many to believe that the freedom from prior restraint, the escape from censorship, and the emergence from licensing constituted the whole of press freedom.

Hallam's *Constitutional History of England* declares that "Liberty of the press consists, in a strict sense, merely in an exemption from the superintendence of a licenser."

Sir William Blackstone declared: "The liberty of the press is indeed essential to the nature of a free state; but this consists in laying no previous restraints upon publications. . . ."

This is by no means all there is to freedom of the press. Zechariah Chafee, Jr., has pointed out that this Blackstonian definition is not an interpretation of the American Constitution, but a statement of English law at the time, and one out of harmony with English law of the last 125 years. He has described the theory of Blackstone as "inconsistent with eighteenth-century history . . . contrary to modern decisions, thoroughly artificial, and wholly out of accord with a common-sense view of the relations of state and citizen."

Our First Amendment, Cooley has pointed out, was intended to do much more than merely secure the press against licensing.

The evils to be prevented were not the censorship of the press merely, but any action of the government by means of which it might prevent such free and general discussion of public matters as seems absolutely essential to prepare the people for an intelligent exercise of their rights as citizens.

In the catalog of those rights essential to a free press, none probably is less vulnerable to frontal attack. The most indifferent citizens would hardly be likely to view lightly legislation or executive order imposing a universal censorship or setting up a system of press licensing.

If this one of our press freedoms has been made relatively secure by the long struggle through which it was established, by its conspicuous place in the history of our institutions, by the ease with which formal licensing and censorship can be identified, it still is by no means utterly safe.

It is not safe because there are means of requiring prior

restraint in less obvious ways than those employed from Henry VIII to Queen Elizabeth. There are means of imposing censorship not so conspicuous as licensing acts.

To say that the freedom from prior restraint is not all there is to freedom of the press is not to say that it is unimportant to freedom of the press. It is vitally and indispensably important. We must be constantly on the alert to detect impairment of this freedom, however subtle.

Americans have been justifiably disquieted by experiments in this direction. The approach to press licensing under the National Industrial Recovery Act of the first administration of Franklin Roosevelt deserved the resistance that was encountered. Concern has been created by the enactment of Public Law 557, which became effective on 29 July 1954, and under which organizations required to register under the Internal Security Act of 1950 must register all equipment in their possession, custody, or control for printing or publishing any printed matter.

This law is a good illustration of the difficulty of deciding at precisely what point a fundamental freedom is menaced. Few citizens are likely to be alarmed by restraints laid upon political groups with which the overwhelming majority is so completely out of sympathy. The risk, of course, is that once having allowed registration of the presses in the hands of certain unpopular groups, what is to prevent Congress from requiring registration of the presses of additional groups?

It is not easy, either, to decide at what point mere registration becomes equal to licensing. The Swedish constitution, which has so many excellent provisions on press freedom, requires the registration of a printing establishment in the county in which it is located, at least two weeks prior to the first print issued.

In the context of the liberal Swedish constitution, it may be doubted that this simple act of registration is a serious menace to freedom of the press.

However, in other climates and under constitutions not otherwise so clear, it might well be fatal to press freedom. Operation of a secret press, to which so many peoples in so many lands have at various times been indebted for the preservation of their liberties, would be rendered infinitely more precarious under such a statute. In a country, and under a government, hostile to all press criticism, the very act of registration would constitute a disclosure fatal to freedom of the press.

The risks involved presently in Public Law 557 may not appear alarming. Yet, it could be extended by statute, or even by construction of the law requiring registration of subversive groups, so as to embrace not only Communist and like subversive organization presses, but the presses of others desiring to express dissent of a wholly different sort.

Is the danger which this law attempts to reach worth the risks that it involves? In measuring both the danger and the risks, we need to consider the future as well as the present. The question is not only: What is the risk today? We must ask: What will be the risk at some future date when this law is at hand for a government determined to crush all press opposition?

In spite of our relative security against direct licensing, it is evident that something very close to licensing has been enacted, with very little public notice. If it is not licensing, it is the closest thing to it that has been seen since the adoption of the Constitution. Whether or not it is consistent with the First Amendment is for the United States Supreme Court to say.

In spite of the First Amendment's ban on prior restraint of the press, censorship of the press has been frequent in American history.

In wartime the government has imposed censorship in combat theaters, and in World War I and World War II it operated censorship in the zone of the interior. These lapses from the full enforcement of the First Amendment have been countenanced under the liberal construction of the emergency powers required to save the country—powers of self-preservation that seem inherent in sovereignty.

Operation under the Atomic Energy Act also has involved a kind of prior restraint and advance censorship. This has grown out of the fact that the law precludes the publication of information on nuclear science not cleared for publication by the Atomic Energy Commission. In order to find out what has been cleared, newspapers have frequently found it advisable to submit to the Atomic Energy Commission material intended for publication, before printing it. The Act reversed the conventional military theory under which the press was permitted to publish anything not proscribed, and applied the rule that nothing was to be published unless cleared. Here again there had to be a weighing of risks and dangers. No doubt national opinion once supported, and it may still support, this policy, preferring the dangers of censorship to the risks of compromising atomic secrets. The dangers are minimized here by the closely specified area to which censorship is confined; but it must be acknowledged that Congress has passed and the country has acquiesced in a plain exception to the First Amendment's ban on prior restraint.

This ban may be interfering with the country's rapid utilization of atomic energy for peaceful uses. It has piled up in the classified envelopes of AEC some eighty million documents already, and experts engaged in declassification find it difficult to keep up with the flood of material. Information on the construction of power reactors has been released and declassified so that private industry is able to proceed on contracts for their construction. What industry cannot know, and what it has not been told, however, is whether or not the AEC retains under classification information on more efficient and effective reactors. Industry knows how to build one type of reactor. Are there other, cheaper, and better types? And may information about them be released and declassified after plants have been built according to plans presently declassified?

This ignorance and doubt produces a state of insecurity for the few large firms capable of financing such construction. In such uncertainty, it is not easy to interest responsible company directors in ventures running into costs of millions of dollars.

More and more personnel are being put to work by AEC on the task of declassification.

As long as the present law is in effect, however, there always will be some brake on peacetime uses of atomic energy. New information automatically falls under classification, wherever it is originated. The process of its accumulation will be swifter each year and it will be progressively more difficult for declassifying operations to keep up with it. This will impose a lag on private utilization of atomic information. It is difficult to estimate the seriousness of this lag. When we find out how serious it is, we may be far behind countries that have handled the matter differently. Curiously enough, we may lag behind both the countries with less secrecy and greater private access and behind those (such as Soviet Russia) with greater secrecy and no private access whatever. In the case of the latter, of course, the fullest construction does not have to await private investors' confidence or their full information.

The real risks in the censorship imposed by the military authorities in combat areas and on military installations and that enforced by the Atomic Energy Commission lie in the temptation to push the censorship beyond allowable boundaries. It is not always easy for untrained personnel to distinguish between material that endangers security and that which only threatens to embarrass.

Recently, an officer in the Pentagon who asked to see photographs of the restaurant operation in that building, before their publication, urged the omission of photographs that showed the wall menu, including prices. Not the slightest element of security was involved, but it is not always easy to distinguish between policy and security. Once the right to censor for security reasons has been acknowledged, it is no longer as easy to maintain the same solid resistance to censorship of any kind.

The Constitution may protect against the exercise of prior restraint on publication by congressional enactment, but what about prior restraint employed by executive agencies with the consent of the press? Many publications feared this might be involved in the Office of Strategic Information set up in the Commerce Department in 1954 for the purpose of diminishing the flow of technical information that might be of use to an enemy. A government bureau, without a single statute to support it, in a time of fear and panic, no doubt could get nearly all publications to submit to restraints on publication of prescribed data. A press that would tamely submit to censorship and prior restraint would not deserve many tears. However, the constitutional immunity to prior restraint was not devised for the benefit of newspapers but for the information of the people.

Such a consent to prior restraint would imperil their access to information as much as a legally enforceable censorship.

The authors of the Bill of Rights were clearly trying to protect citizens against a system under which the information permitted to them might fall under the control of government. It is doubtful if they would find censorship enforced by a conspiracy of office holders and editors any less offensive than one enforced by Congress.

This is an aspect of freedom that ought to be kept in mind by newspaper editors and reporters when they are brought into a degree of collaboration with officials. There is a very fine line indeed separating this kind of co-operation from prior restraint under law.

This sort of "co-operation" can be made to sound very palatable and reasonable. Arias Delgado of the Spanish Ministry of Information has explained that in Spain, "previous consultation" is only a "preventive function of harmonious co-operation and tutelage for the common good."

Conscientious publications, anxious to avoid breaches of security, in recent years have developed a practice of "clearing" matter of questionable safety with government agencies involved. This is an inescapable necessity so far as atomic matter is concerned. It may be advisable where editors are in doubt about other security material. It is easy to move from here, however, into clearance for policy considerations. Government officials consulted on security matters find it difficult to restrain an impulse to suggest changes that will put an agency in a better public light, a temptation to put forward alterations that will soften an adverse opinion or put an official in a more favorable posture. This is fine for relations between government and press but it may deprive the public of the sort of critical appraisal that the authors of the Bill of Rights were trying to preserve.

When Jefferson said that no government ought to be without a critic and that none would be as long as the press was free, he had in mind a press that did not have to "clear" its views on government with the very departments and agencies being criticized.

The sudden emergence of radio broadcasting as a means of

communication presented the government with problems the solution of which was not to be found in past experience with the press. The flat and explicit ban of the Constitution on licensing and prior censorship posed no insoluble practical problems. The country never reached the point of saturation in the number of presses at which their operation interfered with each other. Many European critics of the American press thought that newspapers were so numerous, in the nineteenth century, as to lower the quality of all of them. No one ever suggested that government reduce the number by licensing. The number of presses was unlimited and competition could be left to diminish the ranks of the newspapers.

Radio had differences instantly apparent. The number of channels was limited. They had to be allocated. Once allocated, it was necessary that the stations be required to stay on their authorized channels and utilize authorized power. The alternative was a chaos of conflicting signals in which none of the stations could have been heard. Obviously no private power was equal to the task of allocation or enforcement. Government assumption of the obligation was inevitable. This meant, inescapably, government licensing of a media differing from the press only in the mechanical device employed to disseminate information. Government was thus propelled into a sort of licensing which every constitutional authority until the advent of radio would have described as unconstitutional.

The Communications Act of 1934 authorized the Federal Communications Commission to make rules and regulations required by public convenience, interest, or necessity "not inconsistent with law."

The programs of stations, the information and entertainment that they dispensed, quickly and perhaps inevitably became an element in the decisions of public necessity. And as soon as the programs of the stations came under the purview of the Commission, and entered into judgments involving the issuance and extension of licenses, government found itself knee-deep in an enterprise that surely would have been abhorrent to every one of the founding fathers.

The Mayflower opinion of 1941 illuminated the dangers in-

volved. The Commission reproached Station WAAB for broadcasting editorials urging the election of various candidates for
political office. It stated flatly that "a truly free radio cannot be
used to advocate the causes of the licensee. It cannot be used to
support the candidates of his friends. It cannot be used to support the principles he happens to regard most favorably. . . .
These requirements are inherent in the conception of public interest set up by the Communications Act as the criterion of regulation."

The radio station committed itself not to editorialize in the
future and on this promise its license was renewed. The Commission thereby bluntly exercised governmental power to restrain
future utterance or "publication" in the precise manner the First
Amendment was intended to restrain.

The principles which governed the Communications Commission in this proceeding and those which governed the United
States Supreme Court in Near *v.* Minnesota on 1 June 1931 are
simply irreconcilable. They were separated in point of time by
only a decade; they are a world apart in philosophy.

A Minnesota statute provided for the abatement, as a public
nuisance, of a "malicious, scandalous, and defamatory" newspaper, magazine, or other periodical, and also of obscene periodicals. Courts were empowered to issue injunctions stopping
the convicted newspapers entirely. The law was invoked against
the *Saturday Press,* charged by the county attorney with being
largely devoted to "malicious, scandalous, and defamatory articles." The paper was closed by the courts. Near, the manager,
lost in an appeal to the state supreme court. The case was then
carried to the United States Supreme Court.

The case of the *Saturday Press,* of course, was a much worse
case than that of the Mayflower Broadcasting Company. No one
had charged the Mayflower Broadcasting Company with being
"malicious, scandalous, and defamatory." It was only accused of
being "editorial" or "partisan."

The United States Supreme Court found the Minnesota gag
law repugnant to the First Amendment. An opinion, written by
the Chief Justice, bluntly described it as "the essence of censorship." The Court pointed out that "the general conception of

liberty of the press, historically considered and taken up by the Federal Constitution, has meant principally although not exclusively, immunity from previous restraints or censorship. The conception of the liberty of the press in this country had broadened with the exigencies of the colonial period and with the efforts to secure freedom from oppressive administration. That liberty was especially cherished for the immunity it afforded from previous restraint of the publication of censure of public officers and charges of official misconduct."

The Court concluded:

The fact that for approximately one hundred and fifty years there has been almost an entire absence of attempts to impose previous restraints upon publications relating to the malfeasance of public officers is significant of the deep-seated conviction that such restraints would violate constitutional right. Public officers whose character and conduct remain open to debate and free discussion in the press find their remedies for false accusations in actions under libel laws providing for redress and punishment, and not in proceedings to restrain the publication of newspapers and periodicals.

Of this decision and opinion Zechariah Chafee wrote:

Its strong hostility to previous restraints against the expression of ideas may conceivably be applied to quite different forms of censorship, affecting other media of communication besides the press. Newspapers, books, pamphlets, and large meetings were for many centuries the only means of public discussion, so that the need for their protection has been generally realized. On the other hand, when additional methods for spreading facts and ideas were introduced or greatly improved by modern inventions, writers and judges had not got into the habit of being solicitous about guarding their freedom. And so we have tolerated censorship of the mails, the importation of foreign books, the stage, the motion picture, and the radio. In an age when the film and broadcasting station have become rivals of the newspaper for the transmission of news, the new judicial attitude evidenced in Near v. Minnesota may have important consequences.

Up to the present time, there has been no real opportunity for the United States Supreme Court to apply to radio and television the plain principles of Near *v.* Minnesota. Those who remain in business at the precarious pleasure of the licenser have not dared push a challenge to the highest court, apparently. So we have the curious paradox of a Supreme Court opinion stating that government may not stop a newspaper, even if it is or has been "defamatory," while an agency of government threatens to stop a radio station for statements merely "editorial" and not even alleged to be defamatory.

It was evident, from the beginning, that the very exercise of licensing power ran the risk of this kind of censorship. The most apprehensive thought that such censorship, although never publicly professed or openly asserted, would so influence the licensing decisions of the Commission. Even the most fearful did not anticipate in 1934 that the Commission by 1941 would be openly asserting not only the right to reproach a licensee for past utterance but the authority to govern his future utterance.

Is such authority inseparable from licensing? So the advocates of a free press, as it is conceived in our Constitution, have thought for 150 years. It will be a real test of political ingenuity to discover some system by which order can be maintained on the air without the risk of censorship.

Such flagrancies as the Mayflower case probably do not represent the commonest danger. The criticism that it provoked, and the reaction later to the Federal Communication Commission's blue book, suggest that formal assertion of authority over programs may be more infrequent in the future than in the past. Yet, the shadow of the Commission's authority lies over all radio and television stations, inhibiting their comment on political issues to whatever degree the individual station management may fear that what is uttered over the station may jeopardize the renewal of his license.

Perhaps this fear is a minimal factor in the decisions of stations in the hands of rich and powerful individuals or corporations. The First Amendment was devised to protect, not only the liberty of the rich and the powerful, but that of the lowliest citizen. To make the radio really free, some means must be found by which the FCC can be divested of the power to withhold licenses for engaging in precisely the sort of political comment and criticism that the framers of the First Amendment wished to preserve.

The controversy over pay television has served to emphasize how inconsistent and improper is the government's relation to broadcasting. Only time will prove whether it is or is not feasible to charge users for television programs. Government, however, ought to be no more involved in this decision than it has been involved in the past in the decision of the press on the same question. Newspapers and periodicals have come to their several, differing choices on whether to put their reliance upon the payments of the subscribers or those of the advertisers. Government intervention in the decision would have been spurned by the press, denounced by the people, and refused by the courts. Whether *Reader's Digest* chooses to get all or part of its revenue from readers, or all or part of it from advertisers, is a decision for *Reader's Digest*. Whether television is to be supported by advertising or admissions ought to be a decision for television. If government stood apart from the issue, competition would decide it sooner or later and probably in somewhat the same fashion that competition has made a like decision in the publications field.

The impropriety of life-or-death control by government of a press intended to be the critic and censor of that same government is so obvious that the point did not have to be argued in our courts for 125 years. The impropriety of the same sort of control over radio and television, which ought to be the same sort of censor and critic of government, is equally obvious. Plain as it is, that control seems to continue without much challenge, either from the broadcasters or from the public.

Few situations better illustrate the difficulty of making any freedom forever secure against encroachment, by constitutional or legislative devices.

The first Congress of the United States must have felt, when it completed the First Amendment, that it had made freedom of the press and freedom of speech as secure against future encroachment as human devices and institutions could make them. It would be difficult to devise plainer language than "Congress shall make no law . . ." From that day until this there has been no assertion, by Congress or by the courts, to deny that "censorship and prior restraint" are comprehended within the objects of that prohibition.

Still, such are the differences of opinion on what constitutes censorship and on what constitutes prior restraint that executive agencies, under the sanction of Congress, have trespassed even here.

And of all these trespasses, the Communications Act of 1934 most fully vindicates the judgment of Alexander Hamilton, who wrote in *The Federalist:*

> What signifies a declaration, that "the liberty of the press shall be inviolably preserved?" What is the liberty of the press? Who can give it any definition which would not leave the utmost latitude for evasion? I hold it to be impracticable; and from this I infer, that its security, whatever fine declarations may be inserted in any constitution respecting it, must altogether depend on public opinion, and on the general spirit of the people and of the government.

In the light of our history, few would be willing to abandon the practical protection of freedom of the press that has been conferred upon the American people by the First Amendment. At the same time, it is possible to wish for a public opinion, a "general spirit of the people and of the government," more alert to and alarmed by the stealthy erosions of long-established rights.

Guardians at Work

E. R. HUTCHISON

Author's Note. Over the years, as the courts have given our society increased protection against prior restraint of expression, would-be censors have responded by adopting some rather subtle techniques. The following selection shows how subtly censorship is exercised in a large Wisconsin city. Perhaps the most disturbing of many unsettling facts that the reader will encounter here will be how secretively the restraint is applied and how aware the censor is that he is acting extralegally.

Just before *Tropic of Cancer* directly encountered Milwaukee's "program of guardianship," the *Milwaukee Journal* on May 11, 1960, reported that Assistant District Attorney Surges had told the Citizens for Decent Literature of Greater Milwaukee at the Knights of Columbus Building that he was forming a literary review board (a literary commission) which would seek the "co-operation" of publishers and distributors to keep objectionable material off newsstands. Surges said that this was his private idea and that he would pick members of the review board personally. The members, he said, would be a dealer in books, a distributor, a police officer and a university professor. *Publishers' Weekly* reported on January 16, 1961, that a review board for obscene publications had indeed been created in Milwaukee.

The day before legal action was taken against *Cancer* in Mil-

---

Abridgment of a chapter in *Tropic of Cancer on Trial: A Case History of Censorship* (Grove Press, 1968). Reprinted by permission.

waukee, District Attorney McCauley and Professor David R. Host, who once again headed the new Milwaukee County Literary Commission, explained the commission to the *Milwaukee Sentinel.* It was "purely advisory . . . but so far its recommendations to remove certain books . . . have generally been complied with."

From the talk Surges gave to the CDL, one could gather that he was beginning to get interested in the obscenity side of the District Attorney's Office. Surges came to the District Attorney's Office in 1957, and was promoted to First District Attorney about 1962. By the time *Cancer* was published, he was generally recognized as the obscenity expert in Wisconsin. His "program of guardianship" for Milwaukee was in full swing, and apparently he had relieved McCauley of the worries attending the curbing of obscene literature in Milwaukee. The ardor and the zeal with which Surges embraced his duties make McCauley seem like a patron of the arts. But Surges is probably not atypical of district attorneys or of other official but still somewhat self-appointed censors whose professional occupations are tracking down smut.

Richard Surges is a Catholic. In 1962 he was the father of five children. A fellow lawyer in Milwaukee has described him as "a very ardent crusader entirely dedicated to his Church and to whatever the Church stands for." That he is a zealot in his pursuit of questionable literature there is little doubt. The chairman of the Milwaukee unit of the ACLU wrote me that "our local district attorney's office has . . . been a leader among the censoring groups." (McCauley, also, was a Catholic.) Robert Hess, who defended *Candy* in Milwaukee, wrote that he also felt that the District Attorney's Office stirred up censorship groups. Leonard Zubrensky noted that Surges is very pleased with the censorship situation in Milwaukee. He is reluctant to allow questionable books to be sold, and "any telephone call to him will cause a book to be removed."

One of the difficulties with governmental censorship in the area of morality is that the official connected with the job is no better equipped than the butcher and/or the baker to make precise moral judgments. Today's censor is no more discriminating than his predecessors. Lockhart and McClure point out:

The same ignorance or disregard of the literary and other values of a book marks the censor's activities today as it has in the past, and the reasons for this are not hard to find. For the censor is seldom a person who appreciates esthetic values or understands the nature and function of imaginative literature. His interests lie elsewhere. Often an emotionally disturbed person, he sets out to look for smut and consequently finds it almost everywhere, oblivious of the context and the values of the book in which he finds what he seeks. His one-track interest often is reinforced when his smut-snuffling becomes a professional occupation.

In the light of these comments let us examine Surges' thoughts on obscenity and literature and the Supreme Court decisions involving them. Through a letter and an interview, and Surges' public testimony on these matters during the *Cancer* litigation, we are able to glimpse all these things as they seem to appear to him.

This Wisconsin obscenity expert commented freely on the *Ulysses* decision in a letter to me in December 1961. "The noteworthy aspect of the *Ulysses* decision," Surges wrote, "was that the test of obscenity was changed, to substitute the 'average, normal, healthy human being' for the person most susceptible to corruption, as a standard." Surges neglects to mention that portion of the decision treating the dominant effect of the work as a whole, for one reason or another. That it is through ignorance will be apparent from his statements later in connection with the banning of *Cancer*. In a later interview he admitted that he had not read *Ulysses*.

Of erotic realism in literature Surges wrote:

With regard to your question as to whether an author is pandering to prurient interest, when coincidental to his intent to portray realism, and the subject stirs sexual emotions, my spontaneous response would be, an unqualified "no," if I were to answer the question in the form presented. Whether or not the subject matter stirs sexual emotions, is not the question involved in determining whether or not such subject matter is, or is not obscene. Frankly, as you may well know, sexual emotions can be stirred in different individuals by as many things as exist in this world.

Elaborating upon prurient interests, Surges also touches upon "community standards," something he bases his later legal arguments upon in the *Cancer* litigation:

It is most important to recognize that there exists in each individual, a prurient interest, and this pruriency is somehow intermingled with the individual's animalistic beginnings, and functions. I stated that pruriency exists in every person, and it is controlled or not controlled in varying degrees, depending on the environment, education, culture, and in some instances, the mental capacity of an individual. If, therefore, written or printed or photographic matter appeals to this pruriency which exists in everyone, and in descriptions and representations of these things (sex, nudity, or excretion) goes beyond the customary limits of candor, it is obscene. It must be apparent that within the meaning of the term custom, or customary, there is encompassed, standards of a particular community, and the essence of candor also involves the standards of a community with reference to morals, customs, etc.

Surges will be quoted at length here and elsewhere because it is important for us to know as much as possible about a typically official censor's attitude toward such matters as literature and prurient interest, and because Surges is the key figure in the whole Milwaukee censorship story.

The reasons for Surges' actions against obscenity are outlined in the next paragraph, along with his attitude toward the nature and function of imaginative literature:

A rather underlying premise involved in legal actions against literature, or against persons, for the sale of literature considered to be obscene, is that we consider that people do not exist for the sake of literature. On the contrary. Literature exists for the sake of people. People do not exist to give an author fame, the publisher wealth, or a book a market. . . . [Literature] exists to increase a man's interest in the world, his joy of living, his sympathy and understanding of all men in all walks of life. It exists to refresh, to console, to please, and enhearten. So that people do not lose their faith and confidence in the written word, it is necessary to protect the manner in which the printed word is used by persons only interested in commercial or other extremely selfish considerations in its use.

Later, in public testimony, Surges was to tell a Wisconsin legis-lative committee that some of our best-known authors are writers of pornography.

Most persons engaged in the suppression of obscenity strongly assert they are immune to its influence. But Surges does not feel this way. In an interview in his Milwaukee office, Surges declared that you "could be 'hooked' by obscene literature," and that it destroys your control. He admitted to going to confession two or three times a week to help keep him from becoming "ad-dicted." Obscenity, Surges said, is like narcotics.

However, the Wisconsin civil libertarian Theodore Schroeder has said that psychologists have found that "to exhibit great touchiness about obscenity indicates mental inflammation over sex."

Elaborating upon his "addiction" statement, Surges gave an example. If there were a window cut into this wall here, he said, indicating the wall above his office desk, and there were a man and a woman in bed on the other side having sexual intercourse and you and I knew it, we would feel "compelled," drawn to the window, to watch them.

Surges told about a case that involved a man who used porno-graphic pictures to seduce his small niece and nephew. Then he said, "Let me show you what we've collected." Surges opened his office closet and pulled out a cardboard box full of photographs and girlie magazines. Then came a most startling performance. Holding them close to the red vest he was wearing at the time of the interview, Surges thumbed through the examples, showing them to me. And as he did so, he made small throat-clearing noises. At that time, my business concluded, I quickly ended the interview.

Surges explained how his "program of guardianship" operated, in part, in this paragraph of his letter to me:

Within the Vice Squad of the Milwaukee Police Department, there are several men, who have been trained and instructed in the manner in which to proceed in dealing with questioned magazines, books, rec-ords, pictures, etc. I have worked with them for well over a year, and as a result, they are fairly well acquainted with what type of matter will offend the current legislative prohibitions. Even if these men are certain that the material is obscene, according to current definitions, they do not seize the material, but purchase the material, and bring it to the District Attorney's Office for review. In this way, we have taken more than just the necessary precautions in protecting the rights of individuals and the printed word.

This method of procedure, with the help of many druggists and book stores, whose cooperation I am pleased to say we have, has developed into a community-wide interest in advancing the position of good literature, by removing slowly but surely, pornographic literature from the shelves. The awareness of this effort has also had the effect of controlling the amount of "junk" that would normally appear on the newsstands and shelves. Consequently, we do not consider ours a program of censorship, but rather a program of guardianship.

What actually happens when the bookseller is selling questionable material and it is bought by the vice squad members was related by Surges in the interview. The bookseller is asked to appear at Surges' office. He is shown the material, or pages in the book or magazine, and asked if he knew he was selling such material. According to Surges, "Nine out of ten booksellers 'cooperate,' " and remove the objectionable material.

But many of the booksellers never make it to Surges' office to be intimidated by the grandeur of the Milwaukee County Building. Two members of the vice squad, James Donnelley and Robert Gaurke, admitted that they "nudged bookdealers and the distributors," and that 99 per cent of the booksellers took the "nudge," and removed the material. Distributor William Aschmann said police were "continually going through my literature." The vice squad men are self-educated. They have read *Cancer, Lady Chatterley's Lover,* and the Kronhausens' *Pornography and the Law.* They have not read *Ulysses.* Surges described them later to a legislative committee as men who

worked very closely and hard, both during working hours and after working hours, on obscene literature, [and they] became well known [versed?] in the field of obscene literature because of their studies in it.

Everyone acquainted with the obscenity problem in Milwaukee, from legislators to newspapermen, seemed to know that the policemen and Surges operated as they did. . . .

When Surges was present at the meetings of the Wisconsin

joint Legislative Obscene Literature Commission, State Senator John Potter deferred to him in such a way that Surges dominated them. Certainly from the public transcripts it appears to be Surges' show.

In another way, too, it was Surges' show, as we are able to see from the testimony that opened with Milwaukee distributor Aschmann. Queried by Assemblyman Adrian J. Manders at the September 23 public hearing, Aschmann admitted that through

a great amount of effort *we* have eliminated *a tremendous amount of titles*. And I have in front of me—it is not—I won't use this as a rule of thumb, but *we have here an N.O.D.L. list* which I think we distribute approximately 22 per cent of, and included in this are titles such as "Sexology," which has already gone through the courts, and some men's adventure-type merchandise which, I agree, if you asked me, have no basic value except that there are certain elements of people that read it. But if I come down to the girlie titles, we are talking about somewhere in the realm of 10 or 12 titles. I assure you that *Fling* will never get distribution through our area, but that is the only specific way that I can eliminate them if I get some kind of action against them. I am not a censor, and I don't ever and I never will contend to be a censor.

"I only wish," Aschmann told the committee, "Mr. Surges would write me a letter and say 'Don't carry these 12 titles.' "

Throughout Aschmann's testimony, though he may be ungrammatical and ambiguous at times, he rarely forgets to include Surges as a party and a motivating force to what he is doing. Notice the *"we"* in the first line of the preceding quote. . . .

Despite Aschmann's declarations of not being a censor and not engaging in prior censorship, the following exchange took place. Surges asks the questions:

Q. Mr. Aschmann . . . when you get your shipments in, on many occasions you have conferred with me on the quality of some of the things that you consider questionable; is that correct?

A. We certainly have, and one of which was *Tropic of Cancer,* and I got nothing but trouble on that one, and—

Q. (interrupting) But even on magazines you have done that?

A. Oh, yes. Well, our last occasion was but a few weeks—well, I guess it was last week, and we have eliminated titles and there have been many magazines, one of which I predominantly, I mean, I specifically

think of is with the last issue of *Nugget*. You and I sat on that one
there for about an hour one morning discussing it.

Q. And you sent a letter then to the publisher?

A. I didn't put it out. [The magazine.]

Q. But, and in addition to that, Mr. Aschmann, you have called
to our, the Office of District Attorney, and asked for opinions on titles;
is that correct, and magazines, before you circulated them? Is that
correct?

A. Absolutely, and I feel that I have every right to. I am a taxpayer
and I am asking you for help, too, Dick.

Q. Right.

And so does Surges reassure Aschmann. But to reassure himself,
Aschmann continues, "Just the situation is so great that I just
don't know which way to turn, but I feel that the direction I'm
going in is absolutely correct."

Surges believes the direction Aschmann is taking is correct
too. Either unaware that he is engaging in extralegal pressures,
or not caring that he is, Surges displays his "program" for the
edification of the committee members. Here is a solution to the
obscenity problem, says Surges, for the state, and, through
Aschmann, for the nation. Aschmann sometimes wavers and
questions the whole process, but whenever he does, he is always
reassured by Surges.

Aschmann sees a public spiritedness behind the "program,"
and uses this to rationalize his actions:

A. Milwaukee is a tremendous, tremendously fine reading town, and
they deserve to have good merchandise, and I try to get them as many
as I can.

Q. [Still by Surges.] Now, after there has been some complaint about
particular titles, in what manner do you operate then, Mr. Aschmann?

A. There I use more of an affirmative or a direct approach. Now,
I don't know if you recall, Mr. Surges, that during the course of one
of our meetings several years ago we thought this title was objectionable. I don't think any legal action was taken against it, but I wrote to
the publisher, and since then he has been sending me a copy of the
title each and every month, and as yet I have not personally even felt
that the thing is capable or within the program which we are trying
to talk about, and I would not take it down before Mr. Surges. . . .
So this is the format we are running, if that is what you mean.

Q. Then your procedure is that if—if an issue of a particular . . . magazine, has been determined to be beneath the standards of this community, you then ask them to show that they are improving their quality or their format; is that correct?

A. That is correct. And some of them have improved, and then some I have shown you that they have made improvement, and I think you will agree.

Q. I can recall one, as a matter of fact, was *Swank,* is that correct, that had improved their format?

A. Yes, sir.

Q. And another one was *Cavalier;* is that correct?

Aschmann, of course, agreed:

A. . . . they came well within the scope of being of some value. If I recall, *Cavalier* went out and hired some very fine national writers and improved the scope of the book. There was some merit to the book itself.

Q. In conjunction with your effort and the efforts of our office to exterminate this type of material, you have withheld many titles from distribution in this community?

A. Oh, yes, without even—well, Dick, you are such a busy man, I know what kind of, more or less in the format, and without even second question I have sent back many tons of mechandise that I don't put out.

Q. You refuse to distribute?

A. Yes, sir.

Q. As a matter of fact, you just recently made out a list for me; is that correct?

A. Yes, sir.

That list Surges refers to is not of Aschmann's *own* doing, however. As Aschmann makes clear in the next few sentences:

Q. Would you like to refer to that list?

A. Yes, I could, but these titles are specific titles which *you and I* acted upon in one way or the other.

Referring, once again, to the list, Surges asks:

Q. Specifically you have taken off these titles without the requirement of actual Court action; is that correct?

A. Yes, *and more,* as you say.

When asked to read the list of titles taken off the newsstands, Aschmann is careful, once again, to include Surges as a partner in removing the magazines from the stands:

A. These titles were *quietly* cut off the newsstand distribution *through efforts on your part and my part* after feeling that they had no basis or value to the area of Milwaukee, and they are as follows: *Ace, Bachelor, Bachelor's Best, Black Lace, Bode, Caper, Carnival, Casanova, Dare, Debonair, Don Juan, Exposé for Men, Fizeek,* both annually and quarterly; *Fling, Follies, Futurama, Fotorama, Frolic, Furry, Gala, Gentleman, Glance, Grecian Guide Pictorial, He, Hi-Life, Jem, Joy, Manorama, Manual, Mars, Men's Digest.* The tabloid newspaper *Midnight. Mister, Monsieur, Ogle, Pose, Rascal, Rat Fink, Real Life Guide, Scamp, Scene, She, Sir,* an annual. *Topper, Trim, Vim, Vue,* and *Zest.* And I believe the last one was *Fling.* However, I would like to say this: That this might be a rule and guide which we first worked on with—through Mr. Surges' office, but—and I can go right down our, which I have either withheld or cut off or refused to handle, and if you will notice all these blank spots—I notice you have such a list—and it deals in *many, many hundreds of titles because now we have a format, we have a basis for working* which we, without going through your office, we did not handle or care to handle.

For many years publishers submitted texts to the postal officials, in advance of mailing, for their advice on whether they were mailable. "Postmaster General Frank C. Walker regarded this as censorship . . . and notified publishers this would not be done any more." According to one astute newspaperman, this practice "had every appearance of the kind of prior restraint plainly offensive to the First Amendment." Milwaukee's Aschmann, and other distributors, are carrying on in the manner of the publishers. Surges, meanwhile—unlike some district attorneys in recent years, who in the role of extralegal literary censors have issued blacklists to local dealers of titles of books and magazines never condemned by a court—engages in a different kind of illegal prior restraint. With the prestige and backing of his legal office, he coerces distributors to make out a list *for* him. But actually, as Aschmann time and time again makes plain, Surges is not only consulted, Surges guides the distributor's blue pencil as it crosses off objectionable titles.

Aschmann is a key figure in Surges' "program of guardianship" for Milwaukee. The owner of the Milwaukee News Company at this time was Victor Ottenstein, who lived in Washington, D.C. Ottenstein gave Aschmann permission to take all objectionable material from his warehouse. Distributing 95 per cent of all printed matter in the community, the Milwaukee News Company is in a virtually monopolistic position. How Aschmann came to be so completely under the control of Surges and the District Attorney's Office is not known, but Walter Gellhorn has explained how intolerable pressure can be exerted upon persons in Aschmann's position by law-enforcement officials:

Application of pressure is especially easy in the case of paperbound books. In few cities are they distributed by more than two wholesalers, whose trucks also deliver magazines and comic books to news dealers and other retailers. [Aschmann's delivers paper-bound books and news-stand material.] The police need not attack upon a broad front, but can entirely control the situation by squeezing this narrow bottleneck. Truck operators are usually heavily dependent on police tolerance of brief violations of parking regulations, during unloading operations; wholesalers' warehouses are subject to being especially closely examined by building, fire, and health inspectors. Moreover, the retailers may be municipal licensees. Both wholesalers and retailers (who often combine ignorance of their rights with a disinclination to defend those of which they are aware) are therefore readily influenced by police "suggestions" that particular books be suppressed.

Aschmann no doubt was aware of how unpleasant things could be made for him if he didn't "cooperate." That he was under some emotional strain seems obvious from his sometimes vague, ambiguous, and sometimes just plain incoherent ramblings about the operation he is running. His speech difficulties occur many times in the following extensive testimony when he is discussing the "agreement" that he has entered into with Surges and the District Attorney's Office. He admits to a fear possessing him when he entered into the agreement, he confesses to uncertainties about the program, and then embraces it too wholeheartedly. But listen to the exchange between Surges and Aschmann. Surges has just asked Aschmann why he doesn't carry certain titles which are carried in nearby Madison—titles which Aschmann has just expressed a thorough disapproval of:

A. Because you and I have talked it over, and we felt, through our so-called unofficial committee, that had no basis or value for the—we in general are trying to increase the reading, the betterment of the reading habits in the City of Milwaukee, not through censorship, but we feel we just needed the titles.

Q. Now, "agreement" is a term you mentioned sometime, did you not?

A. Absolutely.

Q. What do you mean by "agreement" and how? I think the members of this committee would be interested in understanding the manner in which you think that this entire problem of the dissemination of smutty literature can best be controlled in this state, and, as a matter of fact, since we don't publish it or print it in this state, *in other* states from whence we get this material.

A. Well, Mr. Surges, I think you have pointed out that monetarily we have come out ahead on this thing since we started it. And I can almost recall when we first made the approach on this matter, and *there were certainly a great amount of qualms on my mind, I did not have the sincerity of purpose, I probably were a little afraid of you, afraid of the District Attorney and afraid of the people I work for, and also afraid of the publishers which I represented.* Now, I base this on the fact that everything they [the publishers] put out is supposed to be legal. I know my position. I work as a professional man. I did not own any part of the business which I represent. And when we had our meeting, and I know Mr. McCauley *specifically* says we have to do something about it, and I know you had preliminary plans on it and we thought it over quite a bit, and *you came up with this cooperative effort, and I hate to call it "self-censorship," but I think I'd like,* for the lack of another word I don't have, but we—you had a writeup where you would get other people to help us and so forth, which you have. [The "paper" committee once again.] *But in general the whole thing is encompassed around you and I and what you do and other than that, I know that you have been putting in a great amount of work on it where other people have helped you.* I am very, very pleased in the way we have proceeded, and the gist of the whole thing is almost as simple as talking to these gentlemen where I continually spot magazines *and Mr. Surges continually spots magazines* and the complaints that I get *and the complaints he gets and the police department,* and we sit down and talk about it. And I remember one evening when you came up to our place of business, I think we stayed about 7:30, I think *we lopped off about 12 titles in the matter of 30 minutes* . . .

Q. . . . Now, do you think that *this procedure could be facilitated by individual state committees on that subject, statutory committees?*

And in his answer to this Aschmann indicates that he is aware of the illegality of the whole program.

A. Well, I believe the only state that I know specifically that had something similar to this, but I understand it was abolished recently, was the State of Rhode Island, because of some legal problems. And frankly, I think you will find that wholesalers in general want to sit down with people, want to be told or discuss the problem, want to cut off these titles, but there is always some legal effects coming out of New York City and things like that. I don't know what legally could be done on this, Mr. Surges, but I sure want to do something in that vein because I know that we probably can do better and I know *we will do more* in Milwaukee, but I know what we have done here.

Q. And you think it can be done with other distributors in the entire state and in the country?

A. I think the other distributors in our state, which we are predominantly interested in, would welcome such a system. . . . There is only one realm which we cannot—I can't—such as *Playboy*, where they make an outright commitment that they will go, and *it has to be handled on a legal basis.* I'm talking in general all this multiplicity of trash.

What Aschmann means by *Playboy*'s "outright commitment" keeping him from taking a title from his distributing list is made plain a little later in the meeting:

If Mr. Surges sends me a letter tomorrow to take off *Playboy*, I'd be more than glad to do it. I'm confident that two hours later there will be 15 lawyers in here from *Playboy*. I have within—and probably I have violated the law by going as far as I have on this thing—I know when I took off *Tropic of Cancer*, I had quite a problem because I mandatorily took it off, and I don't—I don't attempt to be a censor. My primary purpose here is to attempt to cooperate 100 per cent with a tremendous problem, and *I think we have done something.*

Aschmann speaks always in terms of "trash"—*that* is what he is eliminating. His ideas of trash, however, do not coincide with what other persons believe it to be. As he explains how much "trash" he distributes, this comes out:

First you'd have to go back into my mind, and the only way I can, I go back into trash, what I particularly think is trash. *I have college professors write and call me and absolutely are furious because I cut off some titles;* but in my mind, is all I can explain, and I think I said, what trash is. It is bothering my business, it is bothering my dealers, and I feel, and it is of no basic value in the city. I feel that I distribute, of the over-all trash, 10 per cent.

Surges in an earlier meeting had been asked if he couldn't get permission from the distributors to give out lists which "they" compiled of books not to be distributed. Surges replied to the committee "that the books they were talking about *are such that they cannot get any convictions against them."*

* * *

"SITUATIONS OF RACIAL TENSION" AND
NEWS MEDIA CODES

ALTHOUGH it lacks the force of law, self-regulation at times
certainly has the same effect as prior restraint. In the past,
codes of conduct have been adopted in efforts to head off
threatened legislation. The movie industry, broadcasting, and
advertising have all produced examples of attempts to regulate,
through voluntary codes, certain conduct that sizeable and influential segments of society deemed improper. And the chief
purpose of these codes has been to achieve, through voluntary
compliance, what otherwise might be sought through law.

Codes of conduct among the mass media have usually been
directed at curbing overcommercialism or overexploitation of
sex, and not at restricting information that has been traditionally
considered news. Only during wartime, when the very existence
of the United States has been threatened, have restraints been
placed on form, timing, and content of news reports.

The massive violence that has swept the country since the
Watts riot of 1965 has produced, as a peripheral consequence,
widespread assumptions that media coverage of such disturbances
contributes to their magnitude. In response to these assumptions,
and fearful that the media have, indeed, intensified them by
advertising their existence, media representatives in several cities
collaborated with municipal authorities in drafting codes for
future conduct.

Although none of the codes provide for longer than thirty-
minute news embargoes (some allow the embargoes to be
renewed), it seems undeniable that the codes, along with community attitudes, influence some media to play down all news

involving racial tension. In one of the following articles a radio news director states, in effect, that his station will not broadcast either the voices or the substance of speeches of Negro militants. This kind of self-imposed censorship, tempting though it may be when violence is threatened, seems at other times highly questionable. After all, no society can make rational decisions on its problems if those problems are hidden from it, no matter how well-meaning the media managers who restrict the free dissemination of information may be. At least prior restraint based on law is more or less taken into account by the public; extralegal restraint is invidious to the extent that the public does not know of it.

This section first presents, from *Broadcasting*, a laudatory account of how television covered the Watts riot. The coverage, especially that of the KTLA "telecopter," later was severely criticized for having shown prospective rioters where to go and what to do when they got there. However, there seems ample evidence that other methods, among them word of mouth, were more important than television in summoning participants. In addition, this article points out the little-remembered fact that the helicopter was used only after police banned white newsmen from the riot area.

Next, an actual code—adopted in Indianapolis in 1967—is presented, along with an evaluation of effectiveness compiled by Ben W. Holman of the Community Relations Service of the U.S. Justice Department. Notice the general (though by no means unanimous) favorable response to the code. In addition, there is the remarkable admission by a radio news director that his station does not carry the voices or substance of speeches of H. Rap Brown or Stokely Carmichael, nor does it carry news of peace or civil rights demonstrations.

How Radio-TV Covered
L. A. Riot

When the densely populated Watts district of Los Angeles exploded into a bedlam of shooting and looting the night of Aug. 11-12, the city's broadcasters joined forces to keep Southern California and the nation informed of the internal state of the Negro community and the progress of the law enforcement agencies in bringing the uprising under control. For the next few days the radio and television stations of Los Angeles made riot reports their main order of business. Regular programing was arbitrarily interrupted or pre-empted. Commercials were cancelled. The news came first.

The cost of this news coverage was more than the loss of commercial business. Mobile units were battered by shots and stones; their windows were knocked out; newswagons of ABC-TV and KNXT(TV) were destroyed by fire, with an out-of-pocket loss of $10,000 apiece. Newsmen, who dodged rocks and bullets themselves, mostly came out with no worse than scratches or bruises. A major exception was Ray Fahrenkoph of ABC-TV News who was separated from his companions the night of Aug. 12 and mauled and beaten so badly that he was still in the hospital a week later (BROADCASTING, Aug. 16).

Overtime salaries—the news crews and equipment were all on round-the-clock duty—swelled the cost of reporting the riot.

43

Conservative estimates put the overall cost at well over $100,000 for the city's radio and TV stations.

KGFJ Los Angeles, Negro-oriented radio station, kept radio-equipped mobile units on the streets of the Watts area from early Thursday morning to late Sunday night (Aug. 12-15), the only station with such coverage, as after the first day's destruction of other station units, the police kept cars with white newsmen out of the area. During this period KGFJ broadcast a minimum of three eyewitness reports an hour and also made continuous beeper reports available to some 21 radio stations throughout the nation, as well as to the nationwide radio networks.

Editorials, Too ▪ Tom Hawkins, director of station operations at KGFJ, broadcast hourly editorials for a 48-hour period, appealing to all members of the Negro community to respect the rights of all citizens. Mr. Hawkins also served as co-host with Bob Grant of KABC Los Angeles in a joint KABC-KGFJ four-hour broadcast on Monday evening (Aug. 16, 9 p.m.-1 a.m.), when both stations cancelled regular programing and all commercials to present leaders of the Negro community who discussed the serious situation and what should be done to prevent a recurrence. They also answered questions telephoned by listeners. This special program was also fed to some 50 stations of ABC Radio, West.

With the virtually complete destruction of all food stores within a 40-square-mile area, KGFJ cooperated with the local welfare agencies in arranging to have food made available to those in need and installed an automatic answering system to inform callers about this service and its location.

As at the time of the Bel Air fire and the Baldwin Hills Dam break, KTLA(TV) with its telecopter, flying studio, provided complete TV coverage of the Watts riots. Flying high enough to be out of range of the snipers who continually took pot shots at it, the telecopter's new lens, with a 20-to-1 magnification gave the viewers closeups of the people on the street. Even at night, when such TV coverage is difficult, the fires of burning stores and business buildings gave sufficient light for a clear picture of the action.

More than just a reportorial vehicle, KTLA's telecopter also served as a monitor for the police department. When a policeman on a corner needed help, the copter hovered over his head acting as a guide for supporting police units. It also assisted the fire department by spotting and reporting fires at the outset.

The Price Was Right ■ From the air the KTLA cameras caught looters entering buildings, emerging with their illicit merchandise and proceeding to their cars and driving away. One couple was on camera as they carried a couch from a store, and, tired from trying to hurry with their heavy burden, set it down and stretched out on it for a breather before picking it up again to get it to their auto. As pilot-reporter Larry Scheer commented, "The price is right but it's just too heavy."

KTLA's telemobile studio on wheels was stationed at emergency command headquarters at the central police station, with a color bus unit, two new film units and a two-car unit for field coverage also employed by the station. The KTLA video reporting and the radio coverage of KMPC (both stations are owned by Golden West Broadcasters) were coordinated under the direction of Hugh Brundage, GWB director of news and KTLA's number one on-the-air commentator. His 10-man news team at KTLA worked closely with a similar group from KMPC which also gave birds-eye reports from its "airwatch" helicopter in addition to on-the-ground coverage via mobile units.

During the four days, Aug. 12-15, when the disorder was at its height KTLA devoted 13 hours and 36 minutes of air time to covering the riot, pre-empting 14 programs and 81 commercials.

Far Away Pickups ■ KTLA made the riot coverage available to the TV networks, which monitored the station and distributed selected portions of its picture report to the nation. KERO-TV Bakersfield and KOGO-TV San Diego, both California, also rebroadcast reports picked up live from KTLA and tapes were sent on request to KPIX(TV) San Francisco, KTVU(TV) Oakland-San Francisco, KCRA-TV Sacramento, all California, WGN-TV Chicago, KCTO(TV) Denver and KOOL-TV Phoenix.

KMPC also disseminated its reports of the Negro uprising outside Los Angeles, chiefly in newscasts fed to the 18 radio stations in California, Nevada and Arizona making up the special sports network carrying the play-by-play broadcasts of the Los Angeles Angels. In addition, KMPC news director Val Clenard and helicopter pilot-reporter Captain Max Schumacher sent taped reports totaling 45 minutes to WMCA New York.

Loyd Sigmon, GWB executive vice president and general manager, who authorized KTLA and KMPC news departments to let the riot coverage take precedence over normal operations, estimated that the overall cost was about $25,000 for KTLA, perhaps half that amount for KMPC. A major item at the radio station was more than 58 hours airtime for Captain Schumacher and the helicopter, at $85 an hour.

KFWB Los Angeles also served as riot coverage headquarters for a host of out-of-town stations who were calling in at the rate of over 75 an hour during the peak of trouble, according to Beach Rogers, KFWB newsman. He reported calls from Tennessee, Iowa, Washington, Texas and New York, with some stations calling every hour for the latest information. "WINS New York used us exclusively for their coverage of the riot," Mr. Rogers said.

KNXT(TV), its staff of 48 newsmen alerted when the rioting began, added hourly filmed reports to its regular news schedule on Saturday, stepped them up to every half-hour on Sunday, also provided CBS News with film for network broadcast. The CBS News staff in Los Angeles, in addition to riot reports on the CBS-TV network newscasts, presented a special half-hour report on the network Sunday evening *The Los Angeles Riots—Who's to Blame?*

On the Networks ▪ For the networks, the riot became a continuous hard-news story, the twists and turns of events peppering regular news programing. Radio at times edged TV in getting extra special reports to their affiliates.

ABC-TV did not program specials but covered events in its regular newscasts. It also scheduled an interview with Governor Pat Brown on its *Issues and Answers* Sunday (Aug. 22).

ABC Radio had a special report on Aug. 14 (Saturday, 10-10:25 p.m. EDT) broadcasting interviews with Police Chief William H. Parker and Mayor Samuel W. Yorty and with people involved in the riots. News reports were buttressed by seven special three-minute reports on *ABC Reports* between Aug. 12 and Aug. 16 (*Reports* is broadcast five times daily on a regular basis). The

ABC News team: for TV, Piers Anderton, Bill Edwards and Carlton Cordell, and Bill Sherry as director; for radio, Tom Schell, Jim Harriott and Jim McCulla as the director.

CBS-TV pre-empted *World War I* on Aug. 15 (6:30-7 p.m. EDT) to present a special report on the riots. CBS correspondent Charles Kuralt was anchor man and reports from the riot scene in the Watts section of Los Angeles were provided by correspondent Bill Stout and newsmen Terry Drinkwater and Bruce Morton. CBS-TV also extended the *Sunday News* the same night for special reports.

Aside from regular coverage, CBS Radio added a special, also on Aug. 15, at 5:05-5:30 p.m. EDT with Reed Collins as the commentator.

NBC-TV programed a half-hour special summary report on Aug. 14 (Saturday) at 8:30 p.m. EDT, Tom Petit reporting from Los Angeles and Ed Newman from New York. In addition, NBC's *Today* show concentrated on the Los Angeles story in three of its telecasts (Aug. 12, 13 and 16), giving the coverage a total of 40 minutes.

NBC Radio via its weekend *Monitor* on Aug. 14 and 15 logged 18 news actuality specials pertaining to the riots. These insert reports ranged in length from two to five minutes. Jay Miller, Bill Roddy and Leo McElroy served as correspondents.

MBS moved special reports on its *The World in Review* (Aug. 15, 8:05-8:30 p.m.) and *The World Tonight* in the same time period the next evening. Regular news feeds for the network were provided by KVEN Ventura, Calif., and direct calls from New York to Los Angeles to interview such front-line figures as Mayor Yorty.

Radio Press International sent special on-the-scene interviews to over 150 subscriber radio stations in the United States, Canada, Asia, Africa and Australia.

BROADCASTERS TRIED TO HELP HALT RIOT

Los Angeles broadcasters kept the public informed of the uprising that kept a 40-square-mile area in turmoil for a four-day period. And they did more than just report what was happening. They made an attempt to halt the rioting.

On Friday (Aug. 13) the Southern California Broadcasters Association whose members are some 50 radio stations in the lower part of the state, chiefly in the Los Angeles area, gathered 14 Negro leaders from the strife-torn community at the Ambassador hotel to deliver 45-second messages, appealing to other Negroes to halt the violence and show respect for the human and property rights of others. SCBA also invited all stations in the area, TV as well as radio, to record and broadcast these appeals. A score of radio stations and four TV stations responded and KABC made audio tapes available to stations which were unable to attend the session.

"This piece of public service would not have been possible without SCBA." Ben Hoberman, vice president and general manager of KABC and newly elected chairman of SCBA for 1965-66, said:

"The liaison that this organization has built up over the years, with the whole community as well as the broadcasters, is such that Friday's meeting was set up in a few hours of phone calls from the girls in the SCBA office. The rapport is there and its value in a time of emergency is immediately apparent."

News Code 30 and News Reporting Guideline

INDIANAPOLIS POLICE DEPARTMENT

SPECIAL ORDER
NO. 67-75

NEWS CODE 30 AND NEWS
REPORTING GUIDELINE

DATE ISSUED:
JULY 6, 1967

EFFECTIVE DATE:
JULY 12, 1967

In the event of a Code 1 or Signal 10-15 (Civil Disturbance) where it appears that public knowledge of such situation could create greater problems than exist, the dispatcher handling such radio traffic will inform the officer in charge of Communications at that time and simultaneously with the radio broadcast pertaining to such incident broadcast a "News Code 30", which is a code for all news media to hold information concerning the incident for at least 30 minutes or until cancelled by the authority.

The Desk Lieutenant or officer in charge of Communications will repeat the News Code every 5 minutes thereafter as a countdown.

Example: News Code 30; News Code 25; News Code 20; etc., until the situation clears, then the News Code should be cancelled immediately.

Example: News Code 30 now cancelled.

The liaison officer between the Police Department and the news media in such events shall be the Desk Lieutenant or the officer in charge of Communications at that time. Phone 633-7850 or 633-2811.

The news media has agreed to cooperate fully in the News Code and have agreed to follow the preceding guideline for reporting of racial incidents and disturbances.

Guideline for Reporting of Racial Incidents and Disturbances (Drafted at a meeting of Indianapolis broadcast, newspaper and wire service news personnel, May 24, 1967)

1. Special care should be taken to avoid the use of unverified material. All tips from all sources and all information received over police radios should be thoroughly checked out before broadcast or publication.

2. The purpose of the "News Code 30" agreement is to avoid advertising an impending disturbance or an actual one in its initial stages, which might build it up or perhaps tip the balance between a situation which can be controlled and one which gets out of hand. The embargo period will give police a chance to appraise the situation and set up crowd-control measures, if needed. Where there is a continuing disturbance after the embargo expires, the most considered judgement should be exercised with respect to the probable effects on the situation of what is broadcast or published.

3. In dealing with racial incidents and civil disorders, the interest of news competition may be outweighed by the public interest of maintaining or restoring order.

4. Only experienced news and camera personnel should be sent to the scene. Coverage of this type of story requires seasoned judgement. Cameras, bright lights or microphones should be used with discretion. The danger of acts of violence directed against news personnel can be reduced by making their presence as unobtrusive as possible.

5. Scare headlines, scare bulletins and sensationalism of other kinds should be avoided in broadcast and published reports.

6. In all types of reporting, an individual's race should not be specified unless it is germane to the story.

TO BE READ AT ALL ROLL CALLS THREE (3) CONSECUTIVE
DAYS AND POSTED ON ALL BULLETIN BOARDS THIRTY (30)
DAYS.

(signed)
Daniel T. Veza
Chief of Police

Distribution:
    All Divisional and Branch Commands

Indianapolis: The Code

INDIANAPOLIS, INDIANA

The Code

The Indianapolis News Code 30 is in the form of a special order of the Indianapolis Police Department. It outlines a set of procedures for cooperation between the department and the news media in the event of crisis. The code provides for a voluntary 30-minute moratorium by the media. It includes a set of guidelines on media performance during a crisis situation.

An Overview

There was significant evidence of increased responsibility by the Indianapolis news media in handling situations of racial tension. In interviews with citizens, in and out of the media, the consensus was that during the past summer and fall the media for the most part had refused to publicize rumors and interracial conflict which tended to intensify a volatile situation. It was also generally felt that the code and guidelines were a factor in this heightened responsibility, even though it is difficult to prove this positively.

During the past few months there were instances in which the media tended to adhere to the guidelines, even when the code was not officially put into effect. In the two instances when the code was invoked, the response of the media was overwhelming cooperation. Observation of the moratorium, in fact, was unanimous.

The code appeared to have been influential beyond situations of tension and crisis. A state official said there appeared to have been detectable improvement in coverage of general news stories about race relations in the wake of the series of the meetings that led to adoption of the code. There was concurrence by others of this opinion.

52

Among the weaknesses of the Indianapolis procedures cited were the opinions of several active in human relations activities that they were bypassed by the system. Others doubted the usefulness of the procedures in a prolonged crisis situation. (There was none in Indianapolis this year.)

The Code Tested

During the summer and fall of 1967 the news media were an influential factor in a series of sporadic incidents that did not escalate to crisis proportions. The following type of "baiting" incidents occurred during several weekend nights: On a main downtown street, groups of young white toughs (subteens, teen-agers, and some in their early-20's) stoned any car with a Negro passenger. Without officially using News Code 30, the police moved into the area and quietly dispersed the youngsters. On their own initiative, the news media refrained from sending reporters and cameramen into the areas.

At a predominantly Negro youth center, one Negro youth shot another. The story was handled quietly inside the paper and not treated as front page news. The center was started by OEO until it ran out of funds and is now privately supported.

The United Fund used special funds to conduct traveling dances and parties. After one such affair, in a changing area (whites predominate, and there are several large businesses, but the fringe area has become a Negro community in the last five years), a group of Negroes were throwing stones at white motorists, breaking windshields, and attacking motorists who came into the neighborhood. It took the police an hour to quiet this situation, yet none of the media carried the story.

At an integrated playground, there was an interracial fight involving only a few youngsters. The newspaper coverage of this story was written to play down the confrontation as an unfortunate occurrence and emphasize the majority who were enjoying their sport together in a friendly atmosphere.

There was a period of several days in late July which residents of Indianapolis refer to as the "Week of Tension." While the disorders of Newark, Paterson and Detroit were in progress Indianapolis became engulfed in fear and confusion. There were rumors that rioters were on the scene, being bussed in from Detroit, that Detroiters were in town passing out dope and money, that the circle (heart of the Indianapolis business district) was barricaded, that certain street sections were cordoned by city and/or state police, that National Guard troops were on the way, that some were on the outskirts of town, that large stores were boarding up their windows, that downtown offices were closing early. The media's response to these rumors was as follows:

> A television station broadcast afternoon and evening news stories that there was no foundation of fact for any of the rumors.

> Neither major newspaper printed anything about the rumors until Saturday morning when one reported that the rumors had been investigated and found to have no justification. The substance of the rumors was not published.

> The radio stations evidently exercised sound judgment in avoiding mention of the rumors, but there was an exception. One station reportedly broadcast news with the phrase, "It is reported that . . ." followed by a rumor.

Individual Comment

A radio news manager: The manager and his staff felt that two radio stations that had been particularly unprofessional and irresponsible in the past, had improved somewhat in the wake of adoption of the code and guidelines.

A police official: He felt that the news media had been helpful in keeping racial incidents from spreading into crises. He commented that without news media aid and restraint, the city definitely would have exploded last summer. He also detected improvement of general news coverage of race relations matters by the newspapers since adoption of the code.

A police official: He felt that the news media had been helpful in keeping racial incidents from spreading into crises. He commented that without news media aid and restraint, the city would have definitely exploded last summer. As virtually everyone except the two newspaper representatives observed, the daily editorials were contributing to the prospects for violence. The reporting policy of both papers had been to avoid mention of civil rights stories. Newspaper coverage of Negro events is at a minimum but the factual reporting is done on a straightforward basis and since the adoption of News Code 30 it has been improved to the point where racial news is now reported in a more realistic perspective.

A state official: He said that most incidents do not appear in the press, and when they do, they are handled responsibly.

A city official: He reported that the Ku Klux Klan marches were treated with low-key coverage which he considered as responsible.

A newspaper editorial writer: There has been no real test of News Code 30, but the mere fact that the total news media were brought together at meetings increased each organization's awareness of its delicate position, which could be contributory to the spreading or inception of violence or help curb any such tendency.

A community spokesman: He commented favorably on the improvement of racial news coverage by the media. He cited no specific examples other than the "Week of Tension." He observed that the majority is still complacent about the problems of "poor blacks."

A city official: The absence of radio and television coverage when News Code 30 is in effect works to keep publicity seekers from trying to get into the news. He feels the guidelines are a tremendous help, but it is difficult to separate their influence from other factors. He observed that the horror of this past summer greatly affected news media and heightened their awareness of the necessity for responsible reporting. The Police Department has an Emergency Communications Control Center. In a room adjacent to this center are facilities for the press. There, the media are kept informed and, in the opinion of the spokesman, are a valuable source of consultation.

A city editor: He feels that all the media have been performing responsibly since the establishment of News Code 30. However, he believes that the newspapers were little affected by News Code 30, maintaining that the guidelines fall within the pattern of operation that the papers already have established. He also referred to one radio station that has become more responsible in its news coverage. He feels the station was definitely affected by the meetings that led to adoption of the code and made the observation that it was the first meeting of all media in Indianapolis in at least ten years. Subsequent to the meetings, the Indiana National Guard met with representatives of all media to explain the Guard's planned approach to and conduct in riot situations.

A radio news director: His station checks the veracity of every news lead and does not broadcast stories that might influence situations unfavorably. It is the station's policy not to broadcast the voices nor the substance of speeches of H. Rap Brown or Stokely Carmichael, nor do they broadcast any plans or events pertaining to peace or Civil Rights demonstrations (pro or con). This attitude of withdrawal represents self-imposed censorship.

"CLASSIFICATION" OF THE MOVIES—
A NEW WRINKLE

ALTHOUGH self-regulatory codes are fairly news to the news media (except in wartime), self-regulation has long been a fact of life for other segments of the mass media. Advertising and entertainment, in general, have been subject to industry codes, usually promulgated more in fear of what laws might be in the offing than out of a genuine desire to improve the product. The motion picture industry is particularly reactive to pressures and the threat of legislation, and yet the long history of self-regulatory codes is matched by a history of evasion and disregard of them by movie makers. The following article details the latest effort to deal with movies that have content of dubious value to certain age groups. The new classification system, although it differs from previous attempts, is significant because it is clearly a form of extralegal prior restraint.

The Movies' New Sex-and-Violence Ratings

HOLLIS ALPERT

With movies becoming one of the boldest entertainment forms of our time, the American film industry has at last seen fit to adopt a system of film classification. As explained by the Motion Picture Association of America, the system is "a voluntary film-rating program to guide parents, with special consideration for children." Within and without the film industry, the arguments pro and con had raged for several years over whether classification was necessary. There were those who felt that any kind of restraint on who could see a movie was tantamount to censorship. Less idealistically motivated were some in the film companies who foresaw a financial penalty in limiting the sale of tickets to specified age groups. On the other hand, a great many parents were showing genuine concern over some of the movies their children were seeing.

Classification is certainly one answer. Educators and church groups had called for it. Classification bills had been introduced in several state legislatures. But a recent Supreme Court decision helped to turn the tide in favor of voluntary industry classification. About two years ago, a mother complained when a Long Island candy-store owner sold a magazine containing pictures of nude women to a boy of sixteen. The store owner was fined, and the case went up on appeal all the way to the Supreme Court. The question decided was not that nude pictures in a magazine were necessarily obscene, but that a community had a valid right to protect its children from exposure to lurid materials involving sex and violence. Thus the prosecution was upheld. Even though movies were not mentioned in the decision, film exhibitors suddenly became cautious. Signs limiting attendance to those over eighteen sprouted in theater lobbies when the material on screen was deemed unsuitable for minors.

It will be some time before parents will see the full effect of the new rating system. Films released before November 1, 1968, can continue to play without ratings, and it will be up to the conscience of the distributor or exhibitor whether or not to limit patronage. The distributor of one film, *Therese and Isabelle,* has sensibly demanded that all theaters playing the picture limit patronage to those over eighteen. While it may sound innocuous enough from its title, the picture has several frank and detailed sequences having to do with schoolgirl lesbianism.

But before discussing how well or how badly the system may work, let's take up its four categories. Each category has its own letter symbol. *G,* in which we may expect a large proportion of American films to fall, stands for "Suggested for General Audiences." In the opinion of the Production Code and Rating Administration, *G* movies are "safe" for anyone of any age. The *M* category is described as "Suggested for Mature Audiences– Adults and Mature Young People (parental discretion advised)." Anyone of any age may go, but the very young or immature may find an *M* movie over their heads or, perhaps, dealing rather realistically with human preoccupations. For instance, *The Charge of the Light Brigade* has been rated with an *M*. It contains no nudity, but it does have a couple of extramarital affairs; the war scenes are bitter and realistic; it savagely satirizes the ruling upper classes of nineteenth-century England.

R stands for "Restricted" in the lexicon of the rating administration. "Persons under Sixteen Not Admitted," to this category of film, "unless accompanied by parent or adult guardian." The above-mentioned *Therese and Isabelle* might have fallen into this group if released after November 1, 1968. We may expect a great many foreign films to be rated *R* or *M* since they are often made for audiences with differing tastes and standards.

Movies made outside the purview of the film industry's voluntary Production Code—a set of standards governing taste in movie subject matter—are put in the *X* category. *X* films are those that have not qualified for a Production Code Seal of Approval, usually because of their treatment of "sex, violence, crime, or profanity." Persons under sixteen are strictly not admitted to pictures in this category, and exhibitors can apply a higher age limit if they so desire. In Great Britain, where a similar system of classification has been working for many years, some theater managers have been known to advertise certain films as "the X-iest ever made," thus equating *X* with sex.

Now that children will be protected from movies of "excessive" sex and violence, parents might well want to know just who is doing the assessing of movie content and the pigeonholing of films. A call to the MPAA brought the information that Eugene D. Dougherty, the Production Code Administrator, is the head of the new rating program. Mr. Dougherty has seven assistants, one of whom, I was told, is a woman, a child psychologist with two children of her own. This means that eight people will be rating films for a country with a population of some two hundred million. Their standards will be based, presumably, on tenets of the Production Code which, in general, speak up for "good taste" and restrained treatment of sex, violence and profanity. Yet, only *eight* people?

Suppose a movie gets an *X* from these eight good people? Does the maker or distributor have the right of appeal? He does, says the MPAA. The Association has an appeals board ready and waiting for such emergencies. Who make up the appeals board? People "representative of all essential segments of the industry." And these, we may expect, will be leaders of that industry. In the past, the appeals board ruled against *The Pawnbroker,* when that film was denied a Code seal. *The Pawnbroker* had a modicum of nudity in its strong portrayal of a meaningful story. Mature audiences made their own ruling by turning the picture into a resounding box-office success. These days, of course, *The*

Pawnbroker would probably go into the *R* category, which could also stand for "artistic" as that film definitely was.

In the past, theater exhibitors have tended to disregard denials of a Code seal by the MPAA. We are assured that few among them will do so any longer. Fully 85 percent of them have agreed to play only pictures that have a rating. They won't even show trailers that aren't suitable for audiences viewing the trailer. They have also agreed to publicize all the ratings at the box office and in their lobbies and to feature rating symbols in their advertising. One must certainly compliment Jack J. Valenti, president of the MPAA, for his steering this usually refractory element of the industry into line.

Now, what pictures will go into that largest of categories, *G?* Not too many examples are handy, at the moment, since the system hasn't been operating for long. But it will certainly include the so-called family pictures made by the Walt Disney studio, large-scale musicals such as *Funny Girl* and *Finian's Rainbow,* and also, I am afraid, films like *The Green Berets,* which justify their heavy-handed violence and brutality by waving a flag of "patriotism." I particularly asked a representative of the MPAA about pictures like *The Green Berets* because complaints had come my way from several parents about the way such pictures glorify the nobility of war—so long as Americans are involved in it. What I also didn't like about the picture was the way in which it mocked the viewpoints of a very substantial percentage of the American public opposed to our involvement in the war in Vietnam, according to polls.

"Oh," said the representative, "I'm sure it would have gotten a *G.*"

"But," I said, "it contains violence, much of it sadistic. It shows dozens of human beings being burned to death by American soldiers. It shows gruesome deaths, both American and Vietnamese. Wouldn't you call that excessive violence?"

"But where would *you* put it?" I was asked.

And that certainly is a puzzler. For you could hardly regard that film, with its simplistic, even prejudiced, point of view, as a picture fit for mature audiences. So, along with undeniably entertaining films that will probably give audiences of all ages a good time, the G category will undoubtedly include films in which violence is approved—so long as it's "our side" that does it and wins. What I'm saying is that violence is violence, whoever does it to whom. If we're going to be against violence (as the British and many other European countries are in their films), let's at least be consistent.

The G category will also include the film in which thought is at a minimum, the portrayal of life is saccharine or distorted, and in which Doris Day—or someone like her—will continue to lead an unsullied existence well into advanced age. I rather suspect that G category is really aimed against the portrayal of sex in films. Not that it won't be there. Even Doris Day pictures hint at all sorts of unmentionable situations which at the last moment don't occur, thus allowing audiences to imagine the worst while giving them the cold comfort of knowing it didn't really happen. Again, I am not espousing more sex in films. There's more than enough of it as it is. It's the shilly-shallying about it that strikes me as dishonest, and that G category is probably going to encourage a lot of shilly-shallying from film-makers.

Nevertheless, I do see the MPAA's rating system as having value. By knowing and recognizing the four rating symbols—G, M, R, X—the parent will have a quick guide as to what may be suitable for his or her child to see. Film-makers who are eager to exercise their talents imaginatively and boldly won't have to worry that childish mentalities are setting the boundaries for their creativeness. Those film companies that are not members of the MPAA and are not bound by its code will either have to operate with an X, so long as the theaters cooperate, or apply for a less severe rating. And, those theaters that refuse to abide by the rating system (a not unduly restrictive one) will, by default, be labeled accordingly—for there won't be much left to them but the sleaziest and most sensational junk.

The new rating program also cuts the ground right out from under the advocates of movie censorship. The censorially minded have always tried to justify their aims by crying out against "the immoral influence of movies on the minds of young people." (No evidence exists that this is so, by the way.) One thing the system does is to provide parents with the kind of information and protection for their children that large numbers of them want. Still, there is no substitute—*G, M, R, X* or not—for knowing one's own mind, exercising one's own choice, applying one's own standards of taste. The wise parent will continue to keep informed about movies from reviews and by being with the child in the theater—not depending solely on that admittedly handy symbol at the box office.

Bibliography for Chapter One

BOOKS

Gerald, J. Edward. *The Press and the Constitution, 1931-1947*. Minneapolis: University of Minnesota Press, 1948.

Inglis, Ruth A. *Freedom of the Movies: A Report on Self-Regulation*. Chicago: University of Chicago Press, 1947.

Konvitz, Milton R. *First Amendment Freedoms: Selected Cases on Freedom of Religion, Speech, Press, Assembly*. Ithaca: Cornell University Press, 1963.

Koop, Theodore F. *Weapon of Silence*. Chicago: University of Chicago Press, 1946.

McKeon, Richard, Robert K. Merton, and Walter Gellhorn. *The Freedom to Read: Perspective and Program*. New York: National Book Committee (R. R. Bowker), 1957.

Mock, James R. *Censorship 1917*. Princeton: Princeton University Press, 1941.

Schumach, Murray. *The Face on the Cutting Room Floor: The Story of Movie and Television Censorship*. New York: Morrow, 1964.

ARTICLES

Emerson, Thomas I. "The Doctrine of Prior Restraint," *Law and Contemporary Problems*, XX (Autumn, 1955), 648-671.

Featherer, Esther J. "Advertising Ethics," Freedom of Information Center, Report No. 126. University of Missouri, 1964.

Freston, Edwin. "Prior Restraint of Motion Pictures," *Southern California Law Review*, XXXIV (Spring, 1961), 362-366.

McAnany, P. D. "Motion Picture Censorship and Constitutional Freedom." *Kentucky Law Journal*, L (Summer, 1962), 427-458.

65

Resnick, Edward H. "Prior Restraint—the Constitutional Question," *Boston University Law Review,* XLII (Summer, 1962), 357-732.

CASES

Kingsley International Pictures Corporation v. Regents of the University of the State of New York, 360 U.S. 684 (1959).

Near v. Minnesota, 230 U.S. 697 (1931).

Times Film Corporation v. the City of Chicago, 365 U.S. 43 (1961).

CHAPTER TWO

Right of Access: The Law Giveth and the Law Taketh Away

E NID Campbell, a distinguished Australian law professor and student of access to government records laws in a number of Western countries, has concluded that it is extremely difficult to gauge accurately whether administrative secrecy is increasing, declining, or remaining constant.[1] Professor Campbell, although noting that a tendency toward secrecy is inherent in almost every government, feels that a more convincing explanation of the low visibility of administrative action is simply bureaucratic timidity and inertia. Although Campbell points out that at least one advantage of secrecy in government is that it may delay the speed with which another society is able to make comparable discoveries, the value of this kind of argument, applied at the state and local levels, is questionable. Dallas may not care to have Fort Worth reading about each of its civic advances before the advance has taken place, but the two cities are not enemies. And Campbell also observes the probability that Albert Einstein today would not have access to the information that led him to postulate the equivalence of mass and energy.

The Australian scholar, in the final analysis, concludes that what people learn about the conduct of their government depends heavily "on the use made of the official records by the Press, by radio and television and by writers of public affairs. This use might be great or small depending on how the controllers of the mass media estimate the public interest and the newsworthiness of official doings and misdoings."

Thus the role of the media is crucial. But the records must be open, since the law can make no distinction between a reporter and a housewife: both are citizens, and both have an equal right to know. With our form of representative government, of officials elected by the people, it is imperative that the electorate be fully informed about the United States and the efficiency of the government in fulfilling its responsibilities to the country. How else but through an informed electorate can a democracy function? How else can intelligent decisions be made by citizen-rulers?

[1] Campbell, "Public Access to Government Documents," *The Australian Law Journal*, XLI (July 31, 1967), 73-89.

There is no other way—the citizens must know. They have a right to know.

Generally, the struggle in this country to establish, by law and by the almost universal acknowledgment of public officials, the right to know paralleled the same struggle in England. As James Russell Wiggins has noted in *Freedom or Secrecy*,[2] licensing of the press was abandoned, legislative and Congressional doors were opened, court proceedings were made public, laws of seditious libel were moderated, and defenses against libel were made available. And at local, state, and federal levels, people were granted access to information.

After steadily expanding this right to know into the twentieth century, the people are now faced with a movement toward secrecy that threatens to change our governmental institutions. That movement has been brought about by military crises, changes in the structure of government, expansion in the size and powers of government, and a decline in the belief that people, given a number of possible courses of action, will select the correct one. As a result, doors are shut, and information is denied. In this way, legislative, executive, and judicial establishments of local, state, and federal governments challenge the people's right to scrutinize their representatives' transactions.

Although it is possible to surrender a little freedom without giving up the whole, although it is possible to allow a little secrecy in government without allowing total secrecy, as Wiggins points out, we may be moving to a point "beyond which we cannot go without abandoning free institutions and accepting secret institutions."

Harold L. Cross[3] enumerated in more detail the areas in this century that increasingly have become more secretive—for good or bad: financial dealings between citizens and government, beginning with income tax and then spreading to all manner of

---

[2] Preface to the first edition. The excerpt of Mr. Wiggins' book reprinted in the pages of this chapter is abridged from *Freedom or Secrecy*, Revised Edition. Copyright 1956, 1964 by Oxford University Press, Inc. Reprinted by permission of the author and the publisher.

[3] *The People's Right To Know* (Morningside Heights, N.Y.: Columbia University Press, 1953), pp. 9-10.

government receipts and expenditures, and penalties, settlement of claims, and the like.

Suppression, impoundings, sealings, trials in camera, and other forms of secrecy multiply because of recent statute law and bureau regulations in judicial proceedings and other official action affecting various family relationships such as "divorce actions; proceedings in such courts as 'juvenile,' 'domestic relations,' 'family,' 'youthful offender,' 'wayward minor,' and 'girl's term'; and other matters involving matrimony, support of dependents in the family relationship, and sex."[4]

Although much of this would make unsavory news, still the philosophy that our courts of justice ought to be open so that people can attend and see that justice is rendered is violated. And the records of trials are secret, by and large, although some legislatures have relaxed the definition of "public records" or have expressly created a right of inspection where the common law dawdled, or have removed the requirement that an applicant for inspection must have a "special interest" different from that of his fellow citizens.[5] Under the Public Records Law, many media are now gaining access to these records using "special interest" as a wedge because of their news function.

Full surveillance of the environment not only is made difficult by barriers erected by government and officials but the press itself, in attempting to behave responsibly, sometimes cooperates in withholding news from the public. Decency, respect for the rights of others, and awareness that good may need quiet in order to grow sometimes obtrude, and the reporting of news is sacrificed. Peaceful integration, for example, often can take place if it is done quietly and without hue and cry in the press. Taxpayer's dollars can be saved if speculators are not alerted to new roads programs. On the other hand, public funds occasionally are expended for reports that are withheld for years or forever. This was the case with a study of air pollution in Nashville, made by the U.S. Department of Health, Education and Welfare and a private university. The latter requested, and got, a delay

---

[4] *Ibid.*, p. 2.
[5] *Ibid.*, pp. 2-3.

in releasing the findings that extended into a number of years. In St. Louis a certified public accountant's firm made a report for that city (for $13,000) that was critical of two city hospitals. The report has yet to be released, even though the St. Louis *Globe-Democrat* asked for it in 1964.

Other causes for these reversals in the right of the public to know its own business include the burgeoning right-to-privacy doctrine with concomitant legislation and court decisions, the successful championing in legislative chambers and elsewhere by social and welfare workers and proponents of secrecy, and the tendency of the press, "under pressure of other problems, to let adverse trends go unchallenged."[6]

Thus, citizens of a democracy have a right to know, and yet, with governments self-perpetuating as they tend to be; with politicians eager for reelection as they are; with bureaucrats fearing for their livelihoods as men have a right to fear; and with well-intentioned genuinely concerned persons seeking to protect individual lives, we have erected barriers to the access of public business. Today there are about 850 federal statutes controlling government information. Of these, nearly 200 permit government information to be withheld from the public, while fewer than 100 specifically require dissemination of federal government information. Thus, in terms of numbers alone, the concept of freedom of information can be seen to be in need of real assistance.

This chapter traces the developing concept of the "right to know," shows how that principle is perennially denied at many levels of government, and illustrates various measures used to increase the flow of information from the government to the people.

6 *Ibid.*, p. 7.

The Constitution and the Right to Know

IRVING BRANT

It is an honor to address this conference, devoted to securing the people's right to know the people's business. . . . Observe that I said . . . *securing* the right to know. I did not say *preserving* that right. A right must be secured before it can be preserved. *Secured* has two meanings. It means *obtained*, and it means *made secure*. In neither of these meanings has freedom of information been secured in the United States. It is the long laggard among the great rights that underpin democratic self-government. Freedom of speech, freedom of the press, freedom of assembly—these are solidly established, but the fourth leg is weak and wobbly. Lacking freedom of information, the whole structure is liable to be pushed over or to topple from its own instability.

More than three hundred years ago John Milton wrote: "Give me the liberty to know, and to argue freely, according to the dictates of conscience above all liberties." Milton, by modern standards, was less than a hundred per cent libertarian. . . . But he stated the principle of freedom in universal terms, universal and

Reprinted by permission of the Freedom of Information Center, University of Missouri, Columbia, Mo. This selection comes from the Harold L. Cross Lecture delivered on December 4, 1967, at the Missouri FOI Center.

everlasting. . . . In our own country . . . the full right to know the people's business has been denied, at all levels of government, except as it has been conceded as a matter of grace, or yielded as an unwilling concession to public opinion. The refusal of information has come from heterogeneous sources—from men who regard themselves as champions of liberty but who shiver at imaginary dangers, from others who fear that disclosure will be injurious to individuals, from open or covert distrusters of democracy, from politicians seeking partisan advantage, from statesmen who fear that their righteous policies will be repudiated, from crooks in office who seek to cover up their misdeeds, and most of all, it may be, from bureaucrats who feel the need to hide their blunders, or who act that way just because they are bureaucrats.

Systematic concealment extends from top to bottom of the American political structure. In the federal executive, secrecy enfolds a descending hierarchy:

> The President—any President, not merely the present holder of the office;
> The Central Intelligence Agency;
> The FBI;
> The State Department;
> The Defense Department;
> All the other departments;
> The administrative agencies.

No less secretive are the committees of Congress, especially those dealing with that almost unmentionable subject, congressional ethics. . . .

The instinct for secrecy as a protective device permeates the fifty state governments, and runs down to city councils and school boards. It extends into the judiciary, state and federal, with vast fluctuations that depend on individual judges rather than accepted principles of public law. Among private citizens, the John Birch Society and other hate groups make a loud noise about secrecy in the high echelons of government. But these same groups create a systematic blackout in education by coercing school boards, teachers and textbook publishers. They stifle knowledge in the fields of economics, sociology, politics, civil rights and liberties.

In Tennessee and Arkansas, school children have for years been denied by law the right to learn about the evolutionary history of the Earth we all inhabit. Elsewhere, over enormous rural areas, that same knowledge is denied by religious pressures on public schools. . . .

Diverse indeed are the sources, both public and private, of the pressures for secrecy. . . .

Among the American people at large, the feeling about secrecy in the *federal* government ranges from profound concern among an alert minority to apathy or helpless acquiescence in the majority. Far different is the reaction when city councils or school boards attempt to conduct important business behind closed doors. The President of the United States—any President—can say to the public: "My policies are right, and you would support them if you had the same information that I have." The President can say that and produce barely a ripple of protest. . . . But let a school board say the same thing and what is the reaction? Newspaper editorials thunder, radio crackles, television shudders, and the people say to the school board: "Why, dad blast your souls, if you have better information than we have, give it to us." The school board then caves in, and meetings are open until the next time they have to decide what real estate to purchase for the building program. . . .

Concerning public protest, a law of diminishing returns can be laid down. The intensity of protests against governmental secrecy varies inversely with the size and distance of the government. The difference is reflected in state and federal legislation responsive to such protests. . . .

The great handicap in the fight for freedom of information is the absence of any provision in the Constitution of the United States, spelling out that freedom in unmistakable terms. Only through the combined power of public opinion and judicial authority based on the Constitution can freedom of information be established and national security . . . be safeguarded.

Let us, then, consider constitutional principles. Here we run into a bizarre example of secrecy at the outset. The Philadelphia Convention of 1787, which drafted the Constitution, met for three and one-half months behind closed doors. Its members were pledged to reveal nothing. The pledge was adhered to so faithfully that only the French minister to the United States knew what was going on. . . .

At the close of the convention, the delegates voted that its journal and papers be placed in the hands of the convention president, George Washington. They were to remain in his custody subject to the orders of the new Congress, if that body should come into existence. Delegate James Madison, who took unofficial notes of the entire debate, subjected himself so drastically to the convention's decision that his voluminous and illuminating notes were not published until 1840, four years after his death.

Nobody can say what sort of constitution would have emerged if the convention had been open to the public. Of two things, however, I have no doubt. Had Madison's notes been published before the states held their ratifying conventions, the Constitution never would have been adopted. The dialogue contained far too much that could have been seized upon by demagogues.

But—here is the second certainty: If the convention had been open to the public, the debates would have been very different. The assaults on state sovereignty would have been toned down, the oratorical defenses of it intensified. Popular rights would have been more positively proclaimed. And the Constitution that emerged might conceivably have been the same.

The major evil of secrecy, in relation to the framing of the Constitution, lay in the long concealment of the debates. . . . This long-continued secrecy permitted the growth of a monumental fallacy—the belief that the victory of the small states, in the Philadelphia convention, was a defeat for the advocates of a powerful federal government. . . . The false impression fostered by that secrecy helped to bring on the Civil War. The effect of it lingers even today, in the myth of a constitutional purpose to exalt state sovereignty.

. . . That the great handicap, in the struggle to obtain and

maintain freedom of information, lies in the absence of an express guarantee of it in the Constitution. Does that mean that
no guarantee exists? On the contrary, the entire Constitution is
built on the premise of the people's right to know. Madison,
called "the father of the Constitution," was describing the foundation stone of American government when he . . . [said]:

> Knowledge will forever govern ignorance. And a people who mean
> to be their own governors, must arm themselves with the power *knowl-*
> *edge* gives. A popular government without popular information *or*
> *the means of acquiring it,* is but a prologue to a farce or tragedy, or
> perhaps both.

If that be accepted as true, a constitution devoted to the maintenance of popular government must contain within itself the
means of preventing the suppression of information. In a qualified form, this right is spelled out in Article I, Section 5 of the
Constitution, which reads: "Each house shall keep a journal of
its proceedings, and from time to time publish the same, excepting such parts as may in their judgment require secrecy."

That exception had a narrow purpose. As the clause was first
drafted, it required each house to keep and publish a journal,
but the Senate was exempted when it was not "acting in a legislative capacity." At that stage of the drafting, the entire treaty-
making power was concentrated in the Senate. The main
purpose of the exception, therefore, was to permit secrecy in the
negotiation and consideration of treaties.

When that clause came up for discussion, Madison observed
that it did not require the Senate to *keep* a journal of all proceedings. He offered a substitute providing that each house keep
and publish a journal, but exempting the Senate from *publish-*
ing such part of its proceedings, "when acting not in its legislative capacity . . . as may be judged by that house to require
secrecy."

That is, the Senate could maintain secrecy in the making and
ratification of treaties. This rather clumsy wording was rejected.
Elbridge Gerry of Massachusetts then offered an exception that
applied to the journals of both House and Senate. He moved to

insert, after "publish them," the words "except such as relate to treaties and military operations." This too was rejected. Oliver Ellsworth of Connecticut then remarked: "As the clause is objectionable in so many shapes, it may as well be struck out altogether. The legislature will not fail to publish their proceedings from time to time. The people will call for it if it should be improperly omitted."

This brought a protest from James Wilson of Pennsylvania. "The people," he said, "have a right to know what their agents are doing or have done, and it should not be in the option of the legislature to conceal their proceedings."

Also, Wilson pointed out, there was a clause of this sort in the Articles of Confederation, and its omission would furnish a pretext for opposing the Constitution. The requirement in the Confederation was that Congress should publish its journal each month, "except such parts thereof relating to treaties, alliances or military operations, as in their judgment require secrecy."

The convention then adopted the clause as it appears in the Constitution, requiring each house to keep a journal and to publish it, "excepting such parts as may in their judgment require secrecy." Inclusion of the House of Representatives in this exception was to permit secrecy in military affairs.

The whole debate reveals a strong commitment to freedom of information. . . . The purpose of the constitutional requirement supported those words of Wilson: "The people have a right to know what their agents are doing or have done, and it should not be in the option of the legislature to conceal their proceedings."

It is an established principle of constitutional law that a right of the people which Congress is forbidden to infringe may not be violated by any other branch of government. Consequently the command that Congress shall keep *and publish* a journal of its proceedings extends in principle to the executive branch of government. But this does not give the executive branch unlimited discretion to make exceptions. On that score it is subject to the judgment of Congress, except in matters entrusted solely to the President. But rightly interpreted, the clause per-

mitting exceptions does not give Congress itself unlimited discretion. That clause cannot properly be measured apart from
three other constitutional factors:

First, the limited scope of the permissible secrecy, as indicated
in debate;
Second, the basic principles of republican government;
Third, relevant constitutional amendments.

The Constitution establishes the republican form of government for the United States as a nation. It specifically requires
the United States to guarantee a republican form of government
to every state in this Union. By unavoidable implication, that
binds the United States to maintain the republican form of government for itself, nationally.

The republican form of government is something more than
a technical distinction from monarchy, oligarchy or aristocracy.
Republican government must be popular government. To be
called republican in form, wrote Madison in *The Federalist*, it
must be government "by the great body of the people." The
people must have more than the mere *right* to govern. They
must have the *means* of governing. A guarantee of the republican
form of government amounts to nothing unless it meets the
criterion set forth by Madison: "A popular government without
popular information *or the means of acquiring it*, is but a prologue to a farce or tragedy, or perhaps both." The only means
of acquiring popular information is through freedom of access
to the proceedings of government.

It is with this in mind that we should turn to the command
of the First Amendment: "Congress shall make no law . . .
abridging the freedom of speech or of the press; or the right of
the people peaceably to assemble and to petition the government
for a redress of grievances." That guarantee of freedom includes
the untrammeled right to publish whatever secret information
the press is able to obtain, unless the purpose makes the act an
act of treason in wartime. Beyond that, in my opinion, the role
of a free press in a democratic society creates a presumption of
the right of access to all governmental proceedings affecting pub-

lic policy, combatable only on the most convincing grounds of national security. Without this right of access, the basic function of a free press can be vitiated by Congress and the executive.

During the past forty years the Supreme Court has notably expanded its concept of freedom of speech and press. But no case has come before the Court testing the right to freedom of information, as embraced in the guarantees of the First Amendment. There are, however, signs of flexibility in the closely related right of access to government records for judicial purposes. First, as to Congress

Until 1958, government departments claimed and the courts recognized an almost unlimited privilege of secrecy in the following provision of statute 5 U.S.C.A. 22:

> The head of each department is authorized to prescribe regulations, not inconsistent with law, for the government of this department, and the conduct of its officers and clerks, the distribution and performance of its business, and the custody, use and preservation of the records, papers and property appertaining to it.

As construed both by the executive departments and the courts, that allowed the departments to carry secrecy as far as they pleased, provided they did not violate any particular law. Practically speaking, there was no limit. In 1953 Harold L. Cross published his magnificent study, *The People's Right to Know*. In it he devoted an entire chapter to the iniquities of 5 U.S.C.A. 22 and the judicial construction of it. Largely, I believe, as a result of this exposure, Congress in 1958 passed a one-sentence amendment of this law. It inserted the words: "This section does not authorize withholding information from the public or limiting the availability of records to the public." That declaration had no more actual effect than a pious prayer addressed to empty atmosphere. Negative in form, it gave lip-service to freedom of information but did nothing to enforce it.

Even if this amendment had been effective, it would have done nothing to close another barrier to freedom of information. That lay in the Administrative Procedure Act of 1946. Section 3 of this act, with designed hypocrisy, was entitled "Public Information." Everything it professed to require, in making government business public, was vitiated by the words, "except information held confidential for good cause found." Not content with that, Congress double-locked the door by adding this proviso:

This section applies, according to the provisions thereof, except to the extent that there is involved—
(1) a function of the United States requiring secrecy in the public interest or
(2) a matter relating solely to the internal management of an agency.

The first exception closed the books against investigation of misconduct within a government bureau. The second exception made it possible to conceal internal protests against that misconduct. Taken as a whole, this 1946 statute purporting to establish the right to know merely changed secrecy by executive fiat and judicial acquiescence (under 5 U.S.C.A. 22) into secrecy authorized by statute.

Mounting pressure against concealment . . . led Congress in 1966 to move toward real freedom, even though in the process it took one step back for each two steps forward. The 1966 law laid down meticulous guidelines for access to information and commanded emphatically that all should be open and available, and the right of access should be enforceable in the federal courts —except in nine categories.

Aye, there was the rub. There had to be exceptions, and some of those made were not open to criticism. Others were the product of compromise, necessary in only one respect: to get the bill safely past congressional hurdles. . . .

There has been a significant but so far minority trend in the federal courts toward the assertion of this constitutional right to know. In 1951, the federal circuit court in Philadelphia made a frontal challenge of the right of the Secretary of the Air Force to disregard a court order for production of papers. The document sought was an official report on the cause of the fatal crash of an experimental bomber during a test flight.

The families of three civilian observers killed in the crash sued the United States for damages, alleging negligence. The district judge upheld a motion calling for production of the investigatory report. The Air Force refused on the ground that military secrets were involved. The trial judge then requested that the report be submitted to him in confidence, that he might decide whether the reason for refusal was adequate. Again the Air Force refused. Then, in accordance with rules of procedure established by Congress, the judge instructed the jury that the fact of negligence should be taken as established. The jury awarded damages and the government appealed to the circuit court.

Speaking for the three circuit judges, Judge Maris upheld the lower court's decision. Congress, he said, by subjecting the United States to be sued, "had withdrawn the right of the executive department . . . to determine without judicial review the extent of the privilege against disclosure of government documents."

Judge Maris then presented some striking dicta to support his expressed belief that even if Congress had not made the United States liable in this manner, freedom of information would still be open to judicial protection:

> Moreover, we regard the recognition of such a sweeping privilege against any disclosure of the internal operations of the executive departments of the government as contrary to a sound public policy. . . . It is but a small additional step to assert a privilege against any disclosure of records merely because they might prove embarrassing to government officers. Indeed it requires no great flight of imagination to realize that if the government's contentions in these cases were affirmed the privilege against disclosure might gradually be enlarged by executive determination until, as is the case in some nations today, it embraced the whole range of government activities.

To support his position Judge Maris cited *Wigmore on Evidence,* third edition. . . . After conceding the right of secrecy in conducting foreign relations, Wigmore wrote:

> The question is then reduced to this, Whether there are any matters of fact, in the possession of officials, concerning *solely the internal affairs of public business,* civil or military, which ought to be privileged from disclosure when material to be ascertained upon an issue in a court of justice? [*sic*]

He answered his own question:

> Ordinarily, there are not. . . . Such a secrecy . . . is generally desired for the purposes of partisan politics or personal self-interest or bureau-

cratic routine. The responsibility of officials to explain and justify their acts is the chief safeguard against oppression and corruption.

Wigmore quoted the words of Patrick Henry . . . spoken in debate on ratification of the Constitution: "To cover with the veil of secrecy the common routine of business, is an abomination in the eyes of every intelligent man and every friend to his country." . . .

The circuit court's powerful and persuasive opinion in *United States v. Reynolds* [345 U.S. 1 (1953)] came before the Supreme Court in 1953. By a vote of six to three the decision of the circuit court was reversed. "Judicial control over the evidence in a case," Chief Justice Vinson conceded, "cannot be abdicated to the caprice of executive officers." But, he went on, the claim of privilege should be accepted if it was "possible to satisfy the court, from all the circumstances of the case, that there is a reasonable danger that compulsion of the evidence will expose military matters which, in the interest of national security, should not be divulged." Even the most compelling necessity of the litigant, the Chief Justice concluded, "cannot overcome the claim of privilege if the court is *ultimately satisfied* that military secrets are at stake."

As logic, that falls flat. The district judge was not satisfied that military secrets were at stake. He tried to find out and was not allowed to. The three circuit judges were not satisfied of it. The case came upon a unanimous record of dissatisfaction on that point. How was Mr. Vinson "ultimately satisfied"? Not by weighing evidence, but by the mere word of the Air Force Secretary, who refused to let his word be tested by the facts. The travesty is the greater because, in refusing the original request, the Air Force volunteered to give all the information it safely could about the cause of the crash. Here is the total explanation that it submitted to the judge:

At between 18,500 or 19,000 feet manifold pressure dropped to 23 inches on No. 1 engine.

What would be said if a civilian agency of government put that out as the total explanation of the fatal crash of a commercial airliner, concerning which it had full information?

More significant for the future than the Supreme Court decision in the Reynolds case is the fact that Justices Black, Frankfurter and Jackson dissented, saying that they did so on the grounds given by Judge Maris. . . .

Altogether, seven federal judges said in the Reynolds case that past decisions were wrong—the trial judge in district court, the three circuit judges of appeal, and three dissenting justices of the Supreme Court. . . .

The pendulum that swung one way has since swung back. The landmark opinion of Circuit Judge Maris has not been wiped off the boards forever. The pathway to judicial review of governmental secrecy lies wide open. For many years, the dangerous notion was in circulation, based on exaggeration of some remarks by Chief Justice John Marshall, that the President of the United States is immune to all legal procedures except impeachment. That idea evaporated when the Supreme Court nullified President Truman's seizure of the steel industry.

There is a more pervasive doctrine, sustained to a limited extent by practice, that the President can extend his own immunity from compulsory interrogation to cabinet members and lesser officials. Such a presumption, *in its full reach,* unquestionably can be overcome by statute. In suitable cases it can be overcome by judicial review, whenever the Supreme Court puts together four factors: the implications of the command that Congress shall publish its proceedings, the limited purpose of the exceptions from that command, the mandatory principles of republican government, and the First Amendment of the Constitution.

Since some degree of secrecy is inseparable from national security, and since any law specifically permitting secrecy permits too much, the proper place to locate the discretionary power is in the courts, where I believe it now exists. There it will be decided case by case, with due weight given to the constitutional basis of the right to know, until a body of binding principles is built up. The right to know will then be on an exact parity, in the manner and effectiveness of enforcement, with the guarantee against unreasonable search and seizure, whose force depends on judicial discretion.

The Reynolds case concerned the right to information essential to justice in judicial proceedings. It did not involve the right of newspapers and other media of information to inform the people about the people's business. It may be easier to establish the right of access to information, to prevent miscarriage of justice in the courts, than to establish a general right to know based on national welfare. If that is true, it merely means that the road to the latter freedom lies through the former. But with the right to know fortified by the First Amendment, the advantage may be reversed.

Fundamentally, the two constitutional rights are wrapped up together. Justice in the courts, to individuals, will ever be precarious in a country where the affairs of government are enveloped in secrecy. Equally precarious is the balance between freedom and repression when government is half secret and half open. Where that balance prevails, there will be an automatic, inexorable drift toward tyranny, unless that drift is overcome by a conscious, overpowering drive toward freedom. . . .

Government and the Press

JAMES RUSSELL WIGGINS

The role of the press in a democratic society is seriously threatened by tendencies toward both secrecy and government-press collaboration, stimulated no doubt by the abnormal tensions and anxieties of a cold war period.

In season and out, in Democratic administrations and in Republican administrations, the normal relations between press and government have been distorted by both an impulse to excessive secrecy and a tendency of government officials to try to enlist reporters and editors as their colleagues and their collaborators. The news media have been limited and handicapped in their efforts to report the facts and to comment upon them (their legitimate and proper role), and they have been both coaxed and bullied into a role to which the press has not hitherto aspired and into a responsibility which it has not heretofore wished to assume. Officials of government have tended increasingly to try to give to reporters, and to try to get them to accept, the status of allies and aides of the governmental establishment. With increasing skill and facility the release of information has been used to shape public opinion.

Administrators of the federal establishment, in the midst of a struggle involving the very survival not only of the country but of democratic government itself, have very understandably ac-

Reprinted by permission from *Freedom or Secrecy*, pp. 232-244.

quired an increasing sense of their own rectitude and good intentions. They have felt that in all good conscience they might summon the whole country, and all their countrymen, including the press, to this struggle. Our government has operated in a world climate of such hostility and danger that the normal disclosures and criticisms of a healthy democratic press increasingly, in the minds of public men, have taken on the coloration of disloyalty or at least of irresponsibility.

President Truman demonstrated this state of mind toward the close of his administration when he sternly said to editors critical of military secrecy: "This is your country, too."

During the Eisenhower years, government officials on many occasions exhibited an increasing sense of betrayal when newspaper reporting or criticism tended to discomfit or inconvenience public servants in the midst of official duties undeniably connected with the survival of the republic.

In the end, the experience of the Eisenhower administration with excessive secrecy furnished the nation an object lesson in the danger that is presented to the democratic process by giving unbalanced consideration to the dictates of conventional security. Secrecy, adhered to no doubt for excellent motives, caused a great deal of public confusion in the election campaign of 1960 on two issues that may have had a decisive effect on the outcome of the campaign. President Eisenhower set up the Gaither Committee to make a study of our defenses. This committee made a report to the President but the contents of the report were not disclosed. In spite of the official secrecy, however, the substance of the report did become known through the newspapers. The Gaither Committee, it was reported, had discovered that the United States was threatened by a missile gap. Intelligence opinion at the time had placed an estimate on the missile strength of the Soviet Union based on the capabilities of the Soviet government. The Gaither Committee used this estimate of Soviet missile capability. Later, it was discovered that the Soviet Union had not utilized its full capability, and the real missile gap was between what it could have built and what it did build, and not between Soviet missile power and American missile power. Citizens went to the polls under the impression that the Republican

administration had permitted the United States to fall behind
in missile strength. The Kennedy Administration, once in office,
discovered the truth and quickly acknowledged that the missile
gap did not exist.

During the 1960 campaign, Democrats alleged that, in polls
and surveys conducted by the USIA, the prestige and popularity
of the United States abroad had shown a decline. The surveys
were kept secret by the administration, and this secrecy contributed to another campaign issue that disclosure would have
dissolved.

These two cases illustrate a frequent conflict of purpose that
arises in democratic governments. Maximum military security
sometimes requires secrecy in a situation in which the normal
operation of democracy requires full publicity. The voters needed
to know that there was no missile gap; but security of intelligence
sources in the opinion of the Eisenhower administration officials
required them to maintain secrecy. Those in authority have to
decide which are greater: the claims that democracy makes for
disclosure, or those that security makes for secrecy. The decision
never should be solely a military decision.

President Kennedy began his administration with an address,
to the New York Newspaper Publishers Association, that exhibited the tendency to conceive of the press as a colleague of
the government engaged in a common effort to defend the
nation against external enemies. In his message to the publishers
he said he wished to speak of "our common responsibilities in
the face of a common danger." He appealed for self-discipline
in the reporting by the press. He deplored the publication of
facts about the national defenses that furnished useful information to the enemy. He asked newspapers to examine every story
in the light of the question: "Is it in the interest of the national
security?"

In testimony before the Senate Armed Services Committee on
5 April 1961 Secretary of Defense Robert McNamara exhibited
the same anxiety about disclosure and also indicated that he felt
the press had a responsibility to persuade the world that our
missiles were effective. He criticized publication of remarks by
Pentagon spokesmen that the Nike Zeus was ineffective. He

declared: "What we ought to be saying is that we have the most perfect anti-ICBM system that the human mind will ever devise."

The Secretary said he objected to the disclosure of possible weaknesses in our defenses. He asked, "Why should we tell Russia that the Zeus developments may not be satisfactory?" He objected to the fact the papers were calling attention to missile deficiencies. . . .

One of the hazards of this sort of doctrine, of course, is that government which begins by deceiving the enemy sometimes goes on to deceive its friends and winds up deceiving even itself. The slippery slope between the whole truth and total falsehood is one on which it is hard to come to a stop. . . .

While constituted authority has steadily narrowed the access to information about military matters, the government has increasingly sought to establish a rapport with the press, to enlist it in the causes of the government, to make it, in the words of President Kennedy, a sharer in "common responsibilities." President Kennedy furthered this kind of understanding with the press by many devices, including a succession of luncheons with editors from each state. President Johnson has continued the same sort of cultivation of friendly relations with the press. Reporters who have obtained and published information before official release or who have written stories that seemed to reflect upon the administration or upon the President have been reproached, and editors have been rebuked. Reporters have been made to feel that unkind reports constitute a sort of breach of etiquette or disregard of the rules of hospitality.

These endeavors at both the withholding of information and the management of information disclose a misconception as to the real role of the press in a democratic society. They betray a sense that newspapers ought to be a part of an administration, agents working to the same ends, interpreters of its purposes, a public-relations adjunct of government.

This was not the role of the press as it was understood by the founding fathers. . . .

In a society in which the members of the press are made the guests, the friends, the confidants, the colleagues, and the allies of government, there will be no press to exercise the sort of distant, independent, reserved, and critical function that Jefferson had in mind. The press is only too well aware that its larger interests and those of the country are identical; but its means of serving those identical interests differ from the means appropriate to the agents and officers of government.

Government officials and newspapermen alike have tended to lose sight of the differences in their roles during the long cold war crisis in which everything has been overshadowed by the will to survive, the dictates of security and the hazards of dissent in the face of a common danger. . . .

The personal relations between newspaperman and government may be friendly; but they must be as well those that prevail between auditor and cashier, examiner and accountant, inspector and bureaucrat. They may work for the same ends but they must pursue them by different means, and friendships that subsist between them never will long survive if they are not founded upon the clear understanding that it is the constant duty of the one to scrutinize, criticize, and on occasion oppose the acts of the other. . . .

As long as the cold war lasts, the press itself will be inhibited to a certain degree from behaving with that complete independence and total indifference to the consequences of disclosure that might best serve long-run interests. . . . But the scales need to be weighed far more on the side of disclosure than they have been in the postwar past if public knowledge of government action, taken and intended, is to be sufficient to influence policy and maintain our democracy. The press must not be intimidated into an uncritical silence about government either by fallible rules against disclosure or by the enticements of official cultivation. It must reassert its independence and regain its aloofness. Without diminishing its respect for the sincerity and sacrifices of persons in government, it must restore its respect for its own indispensable role as a critic and censor. It must cheerfully assume its historic irreverence for authority, its disregard of official discretion, and its contempt for many official fears of the consequences of unauthorized disclosure.

The Picture at State Level: "Gains" Reported

A number of gains have been reported at the state level this year in the enactment or improvement of legislation concerning access to public records.

According to the latest information available, including the Sigma Delta Chi Annual Report on Freedom of Information in the States, it would appear that a total of nine states have enacted some form of access legislation this year. New or improved open meeting laws have been reported in Arkansas, California, Connecticut, Florida, Illinois, Iowa, Nebraska, New Hampshire, and Texas. Open records laws have been enacted in Arkansas, Iowa, and New Hampshire.

Nine states, apparently, still have no open records laws on the books: Colorado, Delaware, Massachusetts, Rhode Island, South Carolina, Texas, Virginia, West Virginia, and Wyoming.

Fourteen states are without open meetings legislation: Kentucky, Louisiana, Michigan, Mississippi, Missouri, New York, North Carolina, Oregon, Rhode Island, South Carolina, Tennessee, Virginia, West Virginia, and Wyoming. . . .

New or improved access legislation was introduced in the legislatures of a number of other states. Open meetings legislation was apparently unsuccessful in North Carolina, Ohio, Oregon,

Reprinted by permission of the Freedom of Information Center, University of Missouri, Columbia, Mo. From the *FoI Digest*, IX (September-October, 1967), 4-5.

Washington, Wisconsin, and Wyoming. Open records legislation apparently failed in Alaska, Colorado, New York, and Wyoming.

Although Tennessee did not enact open meetings legislation this year, the Sigma Delta Chi report notes that the Tennessee Senate adopted rules for open sessions at the beginning of the 1967 session. This was the first such action since the state constitution was written in 1840. Under the new rule closed-door committee meetings can be held only when "state or national security is involved." No efforts were made during the year to close Senate committee hearings. Although the Tennessee House did not adopt a similar rule, only one committee attempted to close a session. In the face of almost unanimous criticism, committee members met in open session two days later.

Bibliography for Chapter Two

BOOKS

Bolles, Blair. *Men of Good Intentions*. Garden City, N.Y.: Doubleday & Co., 1960.

Cater, Douglass. *The Fourth Branch of Government*. Boston: Houghton-Mifflin Co., 1959.

The Failing Newspaper Act. Hearings before the Subcommittee on Antitrust and Monopoly of the Committee on the Judiciary, United States Senate, Ninetieth Congress, First Session on S. 1312, Parts I-II.

Lindstrom, Carl E. *The Fading American Newspaper*. Garden City, N.Y.: Doubleday & Co., Inc., 1960.

McClellan, Grant S. *Censorship in the United States*. New York: The H. W. Wilson Company, 1967.

Mollenhoff, Clark R. *Washington Cover-Up*. New York: Doubleday & Co., 1962.

Peterson, Theodore, Jay W. Jensen, and William L. Rivers. *The Mass Media and Society*. New York: Holt, Rinehart and Winston, Inc., 1965.

Rourke, Francis E. *Secrecy and Publicity: Dilemmas of Democracy*. Baltimore: The Johns Hopkins Press, 1961.

Schramm, Wilbur. *Responsibility in Mass Communications*. New York and Evanston: Harper & Row, 1957. Second edition, with William L. Rivers, 1969.

Seldes, Gilbert. *The New Mass Media: Challenge to a Free Society*. Washington, D.C.: Public Affairs Press, 1968. c. 1957.

ARTICLES

Berger, Raoul. "Executive Privilege V. Congressional Inquiry, Parts

I-II," *UCLA Law Review,* XII (April, 1965), 1043-1120; (May, 1965), 1287-1364.

Blanchard, Robert O. "A Watchdog in Decline," *Columbia Journalism Review,* V (Summer, 1966), 17-21.

Freedom of Information Center. "State Access Statutes," Report No. 202. June, 1968. University of Missouri, Columbia, Mo.

Hearings Before a Subcommittee of the House Committee on Governmental Operations on Availability of Information From Federal Departments and Agencies, 85th Cong. 2d Sess. pt. 16 (1958) (Rep. John E. Moss, Chairman).

Kramer and Marcuse. "Executive Privilege—A Study of the Period 1953-1960 (Pts. I-II)," *George Washington Law Review,* XXIX (1961), 623, 827.

Peterson, C. Petrus. "The Legislatures and the Press," *State Government,* XXVII (November, 1954), 223-25.

Williams, Francis. "The Right to Know," *Twentieth Century,* CLXX (Spring, 1962), 6-17.

Wolkinson, Herman. "Demands of Congressional Committees for Executive Papers, Parts I-III," *The Federal Bar Journal,* X (April, 1949), 103-50; (July, 1949), 223-259; (October, 1949), 319-350.

Younger, Irving. "Congressional Investigations and Executive Secrecy: A Study in the Separation of Powers," *University of Pittsburgh Law Review,* XX (June, 1959), 755-784.

Zagel, James. "The State Secrets Privilege," *Minnesota Law Review,* L (1966), 875-910.

CASES

Anderson v. Dunn, 19 U.S. (6 Wheat) 204 (1821).

Baker v. Carr, 369 U.S. 186 (1962).

Barenblatt v. United States, 360 U.S. 109 (1959).

Grosjean v. American Press Co., 297 U.S. 233 (1936).

Jencks v. United States, 353 U.S. 675 (1957).

McGrain v. Daugherty, 273 U.S. 135 (1927).

Myers v. United States, 272 U.S. 52 (1926).

Osborn v. United States, 29 U.S. 323 (1966).

Talley v. California, 362 U.S. 60 (1960).

United States v. Burr, 25 Fed. Cas. No. 14,692 (1807).

United States v. Morton Salt Co., 338 U.S. 632 (1950).

United States v. O'Brien, 232 U.S. 367 (1968).

United States v. Reynolds, 345 U.S. 1 (1953).

Watkins v. United States, 354 U.S. 178 (1957).

Whitney v. California, 274 U.S. 357 (1927).

Youngstown Sheet & Tube Co. v. Sawyer, 343 U.S. 579 (1952).

CHAPTER THREE

The Flow of Ideas—Dams in the Mainstream

W HEN the framers of the Bill of Rights granted the press First Amendment protection, did they envision a situation in which communications corporations might be so powerful that they themselves might restrain freedom of the press? Undoubtedly not. But that situation is rapidly moving from possibility to reality.

At the time the International Telephone and Telegraph Company was negotiating for the merger of the American Broadcasting Company, a *Wall Street Journal* writer, Stanley Penn, put a hypothetical businessman through some not-so-hypothetical business contacts:

> The executive steps into his Avis rent-a-car, drives to his broker's to check on his Hamilton Mutual Fund shares, mails the quarterly premium for his American Universal life insurance policy, checks on financing some capital equipment through the Kellogg Credit Corporation, fires off a cable to Britain and then motors to Camp Kilmer, New Jersey, for a session with the purchasing agent at the Federal Job Corps center there.

What Penn found fascinating was that every item of the man's business had been within the divisions or operations of ITT. Certainly, the power inherent in such diversity gathered under one company is disturbing in its own right. But the threat of the complex having its own nationwide television network (with news and editorial adjuncts), or mass circulation news magazines, or newspapers is alarming.

Although trusts and monopolies are not new developments in American life, the increasing concentration of economic power in a few communications corporations is of recent origin. Metromedia, Inc., a company that had gross revenues in 1967 of nearly $135 million (and retained earnings of more than $34 million), did not exist before 1955, and did not really begin to take off until 1961. Since then, the company has acquired millions of dollars worth of property each year, retaining what it considered the best property and selling off the poorest-producing property. Today Metromedia, through its truly diverse holdings, is engaged in radio and television broadcasting, graphics advertising, production and distribution of films, presentation of touring ice shows (Ice Capades was acquired in 1963 for $5 million), mail marketing, and publishing.

Many other examples exist of companies, certain of whose subsidiaries qualifying for the special protection of the First Amendment, which obviously can do much to restrict free expression if they wish. Time, Inc., founded in 1922, is well known as the publisher of *Time, Life, Fortune,* and *Sports Illustrated,* but not so well known as owner of television and radio stations in Denver, Grand Rapids, Indianapolis, San Diego, and Bakersfield. And not so well known as owner (with Crown Zellerbach) of a $31 million paper mill in St. Francisville, Louisiana, and as owner (with General Electric) of General Learning Corporation, a multimillion-dollar enterprise formed to design, implement, and profit from new developments in education. And as owner of millions of dollars of other investments in this country and abroad which helped to bring the total operating revenues in 1967 of more than $506 million. The list is long and growing: Newhouse Newspapers, Gannett, Times Mirror, Thomson Newspapers, Ltd., and more. And at what point does corporate interest override public interest?

Federal Communications Commissioner, Nicholas Johnson, has asserted that this kind of conglomerate ownership imposes an unnecessary risk on the integrity of the information presented to the American people. Johnson feels that the incentives would be "almost irresistible" for the parent company to use stations, magazines, or newspapers to promote the commercial interests of the corporate family. How can Times Mirror Company, for example, owning 130,000 acres of timberland and five lumber and plywood mills in Oregon, and a $27-million newsprint plant there, afford to let its Los Angeles *Times,* the most important newspaper on the west coast, agitate editorially against lumber interests and in behalf of timber conservation? How can Metromedia, which controls Foster & Kleiser (the largest outdoor advertising firm in the country) and operates a huge direct mail advertising business, afford to let its television stations in New York, Los Angeles, Kansas City, and Washington, D.C., or its radio stations in New York, Philadelphia, Washington, Cleveland,

San Francisco, Baltimore, and Los Angeles editorialize against third-class mail abuses and billboards? How can Time, Inc., with millions invested in Latin American publishing and television, allow its weekly newsmagazine to make disinterested criticism of American foreign policy toward Latin America?

Perhaps these questions cannot be definitely answered until the evidence of experience has accumulated in sufficient quantity. Perhaps it *is* possible for one hand to be completely independent of the other hands. Perhaps, also, we may discover too late that it is not.

Possibly even more important than the threat of immediate suppression of viewpoints through concern for corporate profits is another, much more subtle, form of control: the prevalence of the unquestioned assumption that a certain course of action is the correct one. Unquestioned because the corporation managers, having similar backgrounds, goals, and even personal character-istics, simply do not conceive of alternatives—not through de-liberate efforts to suppress diverse viewpoints, but because real diversity is not represented on corporate boards of direction.

Under efficient management, bigness begets more bigness. The principle of corporate inertia decrees that companies must con-tinue to grow or begin to wither. Stockholders expect continued profits, which then must be reinvested, either in making the parent company larger or in acquiring other money-makers. A major aim of competition has always been the snuffing out of competitors, and things are no different among communications media, which can be as plainly predatory as any robber baron. A smaller newspaper, for example, if it is unlucky enough to be included in the circulation area of a metropolitan daily, will find itself hard pressed for advertising from city merchants, and will probably find that it cannot buy nationally syndicated columnists, features, or even comics because its giant neighbor has snapped up the choice selections under a guarantee of territorial exclusiv-ity. The temptation to sell out becomes increasingly appealing, and one more voice, one more source of opinion, may go silent. Clearly, therefore, although the huge communications corpora-tions obviously can be great forces for good (in developing new technology, in spending money to attract the best talent, in backing the worthwhile though unprofitable endeavor), they may also present threats to the truly free communication of ideas.

Here we deal with two aspects of the problem of dams in the mainstream. Most of the chapter is concerned with delineating the breadth of holdings of many large companies, not just in communications but in other fields, including airlines, defense equipment, motion pictures, churches, real estate, freight lines, oil companies, to name but a few. A second objective is to show how the law thus far works in quite limited ways to attempt to keep the marketplace of ideas genuinely free.

The Media Barons and the Public Interest: An FCC Commissioner's Warning

NICHOLAS JOHNSON

Before I came to the Federal Communications Commission my concerns about the ownership of broadcasting and publishing in America were about like those of any other generally educated person.

Most television programming from the three networks struck me as bland at best. I had taken courses dealing with propaganda and "thought control," bemoaned (while being entertained by) *Time* magazine's "slanted" reporting, understood that Hearst had something to do with the Spanish-American War, and was impressed with President Eisenhower's concern about "the military-industrial complex." The changing ownership of the old-line book publishers and the disappearance of some of our major newspapers made me vaguely uneasy. I was philosophically wedded to the fundamental importance of "the marketplace of ideas" in a free society, and a year as law clerk to my idol, Supreme Court Justice Hugo L. Black, had done nothing to weaken that commitment.

But I didn't take much time to be reflective about the current significance of such matters. It all seemed beyond my ability to influence in any meaningful way. Then, in July, 1966, I became a member of the FCC. Here my interest in the marketplace of ideas could no longer remain a casual article of personal faith. The commitment was an implicit part of the oath I took on assuming the office of commissioner, and, I quickly learned, an everyday responsibility.

Threats to the free exchange of information and opinion in this country can come from various sources, many of them outside the power of the FCC to affect. Publishers and reporters are not alike in their ability, education, tolerance of diversity, and sense of responsibility. The hidden or overt pressures of advertisers have long been with us.

But one aspect of the problem is clearly within the purview of the FCC—the impact of *ownership* upon the content of the mass media. It is also a part of the responsibility of the Antitrust Division of the Justice Department. It has been the subject of recent congressional hearings. There are a number of significant trends in the ownership of the media worth examining—local and regional monopolies, growing concentration of control of the most profitable and powerful television stations in the major markets, broadcasting-publishing combines, and so forth. But let's begin with a look at the significance of media ownership by "conglomerate corporations"—holding companies that own, in addition to publishing and broadcasting enterprises, other major industrial corporations.

During my first month at the FCC I studied the cases and attended the meetings, but purposefully did not participate in voting on any items. One of the agenda items at the July 20 commissioners' meeting proposed two draft letters addressed to the presidents of International Telephone and Telegraph and the American Broadcasting Company, ITT and ABC, Messrs. Harold Geneen and Leonard Goldenson. We were asking them to supply "a statement specifying in further detail the manner in which the financial resources of ITT will enable ABC to improve its program services and thereby better to serve the public interest." This friendly inquiry was my first introduction to the proposed ITT-ABC merger, and the Commission majority's attitudes about it. It was to be a case that would occupy much of my attention over the next few months.

There wasn't much discussion of the letters that morning, but I read carefully the separate statements filed with the letter by my two responsible and experienced colleagues, Commissioners Robert T. Bartley and Kenneth A. Cox, men for whom I was already feeling a respect that was to grow over the following months.

Commissioner Bartley, a former broadcaster with the deep and earthy wisdom one would expect in a Texas-born relative of the late Speaker Sam Rayburn, wrote a long and thoughtful statement. He warned of "the probable far-reaching political, social and economic consequences for the public interest of the increasing control of broadcast facilities and broadcast service by large conglomerate corporations such as the applicants." Commissioner Cox, former lawyer, law professor, counsel to the Senate Commerce Committee, and chief of the FCC's Broadcast Bureau, characterized the proposed merger as "perhaps the most important in the agency's history." He said the issues were "so significant and far-reaching that we should proceed immediately to designate the matter for hearing."

Their concerns were well grounded in broadcasting's history and in the national debate preceding the 1934 Communications Act we were appointed to enforce. Precisely what Congress intended the FCC to do was not specified at the time or since. But no one has ever doubted Congress' great concern lest the ownership of broadcasting properties be permitted to fall into a few hands or to assume monopoly proportions.

The 1934 Act was preceded by the 1927 Radio Act and a series of industry Radio Conferences in the early 1920s. The conferences were called by then Secretary of Commerce Herbert C. Hoover. Hoover expressed concern lest control over broadcasting "come

under the arbitrary power of any person or group of persons."
During the congressional debates on the 1927 Act a leading
congressman, noting that "publicity is the most powerful weapon
that can be wielded in a republic," warned of the domination of
broadcasting by "a single selfish group." Should that happen, he
said, "then woe be to those who dare to differ with them." The
requirement that licenses not be transferred without Commission
approval was intended, according to a sponsoring senator, "to
prevent the concentration of broadcast facilities by a few." Thirty
years later, in 1956, Senate Commerce Committee Chairman
Warren G. Magnuson was still warning the Commission that it
"should be on guard against the intrusion of big business and
absentee ownership."

These concerns of Congress and my colleagues were to take
on fuller meaning as the ITT-ABC case unfolded, a case which
eventually turned into an FCC *cause célèbre*. It also demonstrated
the enormity of the responsibility vested in this relatively small
and little-known Commission, by virtue of its power to grant or
withhold membership in the broadcast industry. On a personal
level, the case shook into me the realization, for the first time in
my life, of the dreadful significance of the ownership structure
of the mass media in America.

THE ITT-ABC MERGER CASE

ITT is a sprawling international conglomerate of 433 separate boards
of directors that derives about 60 percent of its income from its significant holdings in at least forty foreign countries. It is the ninth largest
industrial corporation in the world in size of work force. In addition
to its sale of electronic equipment to foreign governments, and operation
of foreign countries' telephone systems, roughly half of its domestic income comes from U.S. Government defense and space contracts. But it is
also in the business of consumer finance, life insurance, investment
funds, small loan companies, car rentals (ITT Avis, Inc.), and book
publishing.

This description of ITT's anatomy is taken (as is much of this

ITT-ABC discussion) from opinions written by myself and Com-missioners Bartley and Cox. We objected, vigorously, to the four-man majority's decision to approve the merger. So did some senators and congressmen, the Department of Justice, the Com-mission's own staff, the American Civil Liberties Union, a number of independent individuals and witnesses, and a belated but even-tually insistent chorus of newspaper and magazine editorialists.

What did we find so ominous about the take-over of this radio and television network by a highly successful conglomerate orga-nization?

In 1966, ABC owned 399 theaters in 34 states, 5 VHF television stations, 6 AM and 6 FM stations (all in the top 10 broadcasting markets), and, of course, one of the 3 major television networks and one of the 4 major radio networks in the world. Its 137 primary television network affiliates could reach 93 percent of the then 50 million television homes in the United States, and its radio network affiliates could reach 97 percent of the then 55 million homes with radio receivers. ABC had interests in, and affiliations with, stations in 25 other nations, known as the "Worldvision Group." These, together with ABC Films, made the parent corporation perhaps the world's largest distributor of filmed shows for theaters and television stations throughout this country and abroad. ABC was heavily involved in the record production and distribution business, and other subsidiaries pub-lished three farm papers.

The merger would have placed this accumulation of mass media, and one of the largest purveyors of news and opinion in America, under the control of one of the largest conglomerate corporations in the world. What's wrong with that? Potentially a number of things. For now, consider simply that the integrity of the news judgment of ABC might be affected by the economic interests of ITT—that ITT might simply view ABC's program-ming as a part of ITT's public relations, advertising, or political activities. This seemed to us a real threat in 1966, notwithstanding the character of the management of both companies, and their protestations that no possibility of abuse existed. By 1967 the potential threat had become reality.

ITT'S EMPIRE

ITT's continuing concern with political and economic developments in foreign countries as a result of its far-flung economic interests was fully documented in the hearing. It showed, as one
might expect, ITT's recurrent concern with internal affairs in
most major countries of the world, including rate problems, tax
problems, and problems with nationalization and reimbursement,
to say nothing of ordinary commercial dealing. Its involvement
with the United States government, in addition to defense contracts, included the Agency for International Development's insurance of 5.8 percent of all ITT assets.

Testimony was offered on the fascinating story of intrigue surrounding "Operation Deep Freeze" (an underwater cable). It
turned out that ITT officials, using high-level government contracts in England and Canada, had brought off a bit of profitable
international diplomacy unknown to the United States State
Department or the FCC, possibly in violation of law. Further
inquiry revealed that officers and directors of ITT's subsidiaries
included two members of the British House of Lords, one in the
French National Assembly, a former premier of Belgium, and
several ministers of foreign governments and officials of govern-
ment-owned companies.

As it seemed to Commissioners Bartley and Cox and to me
when we dissented from the Commission's approval of the merger
in June, 1967, a company whose daily activities require it to
manipulate governments at the highest levels would face unending temptation to manipulate ABC news. Any public official,
or officer of a large corporation, is necessarily clearly concerned
with the appearance of some news stories, the absence of others,
and the tone and character of all affecting his personal interests.
That's what public relations firms and press secretaries are all
about. We concluded, "We simply cannot find that the public
interest of the American citizenry is served by turning over a
major network to an international enterprise whose fortunes are
tied to its political relations with the foreign officials whose
actions it will be called upon to interpret to the world."

Even the highest degree of subjective integrity on the part of chief ITT officials could not ensure integrity in ABC's operations. To do an honest and impartial job of reporting the news is difficult enough for the most independent and conscientious of newsmen. Eric Sevareid has said of putting on a news program at a network relatively free of conglomerate control: "The ultimate sensation is the feeling of being bitten to death by ducks." And ABC newsmen could not help knowing that ITT had sensitive business relations in various foreign countries and at the highest levels of our government, and that reporting on any number of industries and economic developments would touch the interests of ITT. The mere awareness of these interests would make it impossible for those news officials, no matter how conscientious, to report news and develop documentaries objectively, in the way that they would do if ABC remained unaffiliated with ITT. They would advance within the news organization, or be fired, or become officers of ABC—perhaps even of ITT—or not, and no newsman would be able to erase from his mind the idea that his chances of doing so might be affected by his treatment of issues on which ITT is sensitive.

Only last year CBS was reportedly involved, almost Hearst-like, in a nightmarish planned armed invasion of Haiti. It was an exclusive, and would have made a very dramatic start-to-finish documentary but for the inglorious end: U.S. Customs wouldn't let them leave the United States. Imagine ITT, with its extensive interests in the Caribbean, engaged in such undertakings.

The likelihood of at least some compromising of ABC's integrity seemed inherent in the structure of the proposed new organization. What were the *probabilities* that these potentials for abuse would be exercised? We were soon to see the answer in the bizarre proceedings right before our eyes.

During the April, 1967, hearings, while this very issue was being debated, the *Wall Street Journal* broke the story that ITT was going to extraordinary lengths to obtain favorable press coverage of this hearing. Eventually three reporters were summoned before the examiner to relate for the official record the incidents that were described in the *Journal's* exposé.

An AP and a UPI reporter testified to several phone calls made to their homes by ITT public relations men, variously asking them to change their stories and make inquiries for ITT with regard to stories by other reporters, and to use their influence as members of the press to obtain for ITT confidential information from the Department of Justice regarding its intentions. Even more serious were several encounters between ITT officials and a New York *Times* reporter.

On one of these occasions ITT's senior vice president in charge of public relations went to the reporter's office. After criticizing her dispatches to the *Times* about the case in a tone which she described as "accusatory and certainly nasty," he asked whether she had been following the price of ABC and ITT stock. When she indicated that she had not, he asked if she didn't feel she had a "responsibility to the shareholders who might lose money as a result of what" she wrote. She replied, "My responsibility is to find out the truth and print it."

He then asked if she was aware that I (as an FCC Commissioner) was working with a prominent senator on legislation that would forbid any newspaper from owning any broadcast property. (The New York *Times* owns station WQXR in New York.) In point of fact, the senator and I had never met, let alone collaborated, as was subsequently made clear in public statements. But the ITT senior vice president, according to the *Times* reporter, felt that this false information was something she "ought to pass on to [her] . . . publisher before [she wrote] . . . anything further" about the case. The obvious implication of this remark, she felt, was that since the *Times* owns a radio station, it would want to consider its economic interests in deciding what to publish about broadcasting in its newspaper.

To me, this conduct, in which at least three ITT officials, including a senior vice president, were involved, was a deeply unsettling experience. It demonstrated an abrasive self-righteousness in dealing with the press, insensitivity to its independence and integrity, a willingness to spread false stories in furtherance of self-interest, contempt for government officials as well as the press, and an assumption that even as prestigious a news medium as the New York *Times* would, as a matter of course, want to present the news so as to serve best its own economic interests (as well as the economic interests of other large business corporations).

But for the brazen activities of ITT in this very proceeding, it would never have occurred to the three of us who dissented to suggest that the most probable threat to the integrity of ABC news could come from *overt* actions or written policy statements. After the hearing it was obvious that that was clearly possible. But even then we believed that the most substantial threat came from a far more subtle, almost unconscious, process: that the questionable story idea, or news coverage, would never even be proposed—whether for reasons of fear, insecurity, cynicism, realism, or unconscious avoidance.

CONCENTRATION OF CONTROL OVER THE MEDIA

Since the ITT-ABC case left the Commission I have not ceased to be troubled by the issues it raised—in many ways more serious (and certainly more prevalent) for wholly-domestic corporations. Eventually the merger was aborted by ITT on New Year's Day of this year, while the Justice Department's appeal of the Commission's action was pending before the U.S. Court of Appeals. However, I ponder what the consequences might have been if ITT's apparent cynicism toward journalistic integrity had actually been able to harness the enormous social and propaganda power of a national television network to the service of a politically sensitive corporate conglomerate. More important, I have become concerned about the extent to which such forces *already* play upon important media of mass communication. Perhaps such attitudes are masked by more finesse than that displayed in the ITT-ABC case. Perhaps they are even embedded in the kind of sincere good intentions which caused former Defense Secretary (and former General Motors president) Charles Wilson to equate the interests of his company with those of the country.

I do not believe that most owners and managers of the mass media in the United States lack a sense of responsibility or lack tolerance for a diversity of views. I do not believe there is a small group of men who gather for breakfast every morning and decide what they will make the American people believe that day.

Emotion often outruns the evidence of those who argue a conspiracy theory of propagandists' manipulation of the masses.

On the other hand, one reason evidence is so hard to come by is that the media tend to give less publicity to their own abuses than, say, to those of politicians. The media operate as a check upon other institutional power centers in our country. There is, however, no check upon the media. Just as it is a mistake to overstate the existence and potential for abuse, so, in my judgment, is it a mistake to ignore the evidence that does exist.

In 1959, for example, it was reported that officials of the Trujillo regime in the Dominican Republic had paid $750,000 to officers of the Mutual Radio Network to gain favorable propaganda disguised as news. (Ownership of the Mutual Radio Network changed hands once again last year without any review whatsoever by the FCC of old or new owners. The FCC does not regulate networks, only stations, and Mutual owns none.) RCA was once charged with using an NBC station to serve unfairly its broader corporate interests, including the coverage of RCA activities as "news," when others did not. There was speculation that after RCA acquired Random House, considerable pressure was put on the book publishing house's president, Bennett Cerf, to cease his Sunday evening service as a panelist on CBS's *What's My Line?* The Commission has occasionally found that individual stations have violated the "fairness doctrine" in advocating causes serving the station's economic self-interest, such as pay television.

Virtually every issue of the *Columbia Journalism Review* reports instances of such abuses by the print media. It has described a railroad-owned newspaper that refused to report railroad wrecks, a newspaper in debt to the Teamsters Union which gave exceedingly favorable coverage to Jimmy Hoffa, the repeated influence of the DuPont interests in the editorial functions of the Wilmington papers which it owned, and Anaconda Copper's use of its company-owned newspapers to support political candidates favorable to the company.

Edward P. Morgan left ABC last year to become the commentator on the Ford Foundation-funded Public Broadcasting Laboratory. He has always been straightforward, and he used his final news broadcast to be reflective about broadcasting itself. "Let's face it," he said. "We in this trade use this power more frequently to fix a traffic ticket or get a ticket to a ballgame than to keep the doors of an open society open and swinging. . . . The freest and most profitable press in the world, every major facet of it, not only ducks but pulls its punches to save a supermarket of commercialism or shield an ugly prejudice and is putting the life of the republic in jeopardy thereby."

Economic self-interest *does* influence the content of the media, and as the media tend to fall into the control of corporate conglomerates, the areas of information and opinion affecting those economic interests become dangerously wide-ranging. What *is* happening to the ownership of American media today? What dangers does it pose? Taking a look at the structure of the media in the United States, I am not put at ease by what I see.

Most American communities have far less "dissemination of information from diverse and antagonistic sources" (to quote a famous description by the Supreme Court of the basic aim of the First Amendment) than is available nationally. Of the 1500 cities with daily newspapers, 96 percent are served by single-owner monopolies. Outside the top 50 to 200 markets there is a substantial dropping off in the number of competing radio and television signals. The FCC prohibits a single owner from controlling two AM radio, or two television, stations with overlapping signals. But it has only recently expressed any concern over common ownership of an AM radio station and an FM radio station and a television station in the same market. Indeed, such ownership is the rule rather than the exception and probably exists in your community. Most stations are today acquired by purchase. And the FCC has, in part because of congressional pressure, rarely disapproved a purchase of a station by a newspaper.

There are few statewide or regional "monopolies"—although some situations come close. But in a majority of our states—the least populous—there are few enough newspapers and television stations to begin with, and they are usually under the control of a small group. And most politicians find today, as Congress warned in 1926, "woe be to those who dare to differ with them."

Most of our politics is still state and local in scope. And increasingly, in many states and local communities, congressmen and state and local officials are compelled to regard that handful of media owners (many of whom are out-of-state), rather than the electorate itself, as their effective constituency. Moreover, many mass media owners have a significant impact in more than one state. One case that came before the FCC, for example, involved an owner with AM-FM-TV combinations in Las Vegas and Reno, Nevada, along with four newspapers in that state, seven newspapers in Oklahoma, and two stations and two newspapers in Arkansas. Another involved ownership of ten stations in North Carolina and adjoining southern Virginia. You may never have heard of these owners, but I imagine the elected officials of their states return their phone calls promptly.

NATIONAL POWER

The principal national sources of news are the wire services, AP and UPI, and the broadcast networks. Each of the wire services serves on the order of 1200 newspapers and 3000 radio and television stations. Most local newspapers and radio stations offer little more than wire service copy as far as national and international news is concerned. To that extent one can take little heart for "diversity" from the oft-proffered statistics on proliferating radio stations (now over 6000) and the remaining daily newspapers (1700). The networks, though themselves heavily reliant upon the wire services to find out what's worth filming, are another potent force.

The weekly newsmagazine field is dominated by *Time, Newsweek,* and *U.S. News.* (The first two also control substantial broadcast, newspaper, and book or publishing outlets. *Time* is also in movies (MGM) and is hungry for three or four newspapers.) Thus, even though there are thousands of general and specialized periodicals and program sources with significant national or regional impact, and certainly no "monopoly" exists, it is still possible for a single individual or corporation to have vast national influence.

What we sometimes fail to realize, moreover, is the political significance of the fact that we have become a nation of cities. Nearly half of the American people live in the six largest states: California, New York, Illinois, Pennsylvania, Texas, and Ohio. Those states, in turn, are substantially influenced (if not politically dominated) by their major population-industrial-financial-media centers, such as Los Angeles, New York City, Chicago, and Philadelphia—the nation's four largest metropolitan areas. Thus, to have a major newspaper or television station influence in *one* of these cities is to have significant national power. And the number of interests with influence in *more* than one of these markets is startling.

Most of the top fifty television markets (which serve approximately 75 percent of the nation's television homes) have three competing commercial VHF television stations. There are about 150 such VHF commercial stations in these markets. Less than 10 percent are today owned by entities that do not own other media interests. In 30 of the 50 markets at least one of the stations is owned by a major newspaper published in that market—a total of one third of these 150 stations. (In Dallas-Fort Worth *each* of the network affiliates is owned by a local newspaper, and the fourth, an unaffiliated station, is owned by Oklahoma newspapers.) Moreover, half of the newspaper-owned stations are controlled by seven groups—groups that also publish magazines as popular and diverse as *Time, Newsweek, Look, Parade, Harper's, TV Guide, Family Circle, Vogue, Good Housekeeping,* and *Popular Mechanics.* Twelve parties own more than one third of all the major-market stations.

In addition to the vast national impact of their affiliates the three television networks each *own* VHF stations in all of the top three markets—New York, Los Angeles, and Chicago—and each has two more in other cities in the top ten. RKO and Metromedia each own stations in both New York City and Los Angeles. Metromedia also owns stations in Washington, D.C., and California's other major city, San Francisco—as well as Philadelphia, Baltimore, Cleveland, Kansas City, and Oakland. RKO also owns stations in Boston, San Francisco, Washington, Memphis, Hartford, and Windsor, Ontario—as well as the regional Yankee

Network. Westinghouse owns stations in New York, Chicago, Philadelphia *and* Pittsburgh, Pennsylvania, Boston, San Francisco, Baltimore, and Fort Wayne. These are but a few examples of today's media barons.

There are many implications of their power. Groups of stations are able to bargain with networks, advertisers, and talent in ways that put lesser stations at substantial economic disadvantage. Group ownership means, by definition, that few stations in major markets will be locally owned. (The FCC recently approved the transfer of the last available station in San Francisco to the absentee ownership of Metromedia. The only commercial station locally owned today is controlled by the San Francisco *Chronicle*.) But the basic point is simply that the national political power involved in ownership of a group of major VHF television stations in, say, New York, Los Angeles, Philadelphia, and Washington, D.C., is greater than a democracy should unthinkingly repose in one man or corporation.

CONGLOMERATE CORPORATIONS

For a variety of reasons, an increasing number of communications media are turning up on the organization charts of conglomerate companies. And the incredible profits generated by broadcast stations in the major markets (television broadcasters *average* a 90 to 100 percent return on tangible investment annually) have given FCC licensees, particularly owners of multiple television stations like the networks, Metromedia, Storer Broadcasting, and others, the extra capital with which to buy the New York Yankees (CBS), Random House (RCA), or Northeast Airlines (Storer). Established or up-and-coming conglomerates regard communications acquisitions as prestigious, profitable, and often a useful or even a necessary complement to present operations and projected exploitation of technological change.

The national problem of conglomerate ownership of communications media was well illustrated by the ITT-ABC case. But the conglomerate problem need not involve something as large as ITT-ABC or RCA-NBC. Among the national group owners of television stations are General Tire (RKO), Avco, Westinghouse, Rust Craft, Chris Craft, Kaiser, and Kerr-McGee. The problem of *local* conglomerates was forcefully posed for the FCC in another case earlier this year. Howard Hughes, through Hughes Tool Company, wanted to acquire one of Las Vegas' three major television stations. He had recently acquired $125 million worth of Las Vegas real estate, including hotels, gambling casinos, and an airport. These investments supplemented 27,000 acres previously acquired. The Commission majority blithely approved the television acquisition without a hearing, overlooking FCC precedents which suggested that a closer examination was in order. In each of these instances the potential threat is similar to that in the ITT-ABC case—that personal economic interests may dominate or bias otherwise independent media.

CONCENTRATION AND TECHNOLOGICAL CHANGE

The problem posed by conglomerate acquisitions of communications outlets is given a special but very important twist by the pendency of sweeping technological changes which have already begun to unsettle the structure of the industry.

President Johnson has appointed a distinguished task force to evaluate our national communications policy and chart a course for realization of these technological promises in a manner consistent with the public interest. But private interests have already begun to implement their own plans on how to deal with the revolution in communications technology.

General Sarnoff of RCA has hailed the appearance of "the knowledge industry"—corporate casserole dishes blending radio and television stations, networks, and programming; films, movie houses, and record companies; newspaper, magazine, and book publishing; advertising agencies; sports or other entertainment companies; and teaching machines and other profitable appurtenances of the $50 billion "education biz."

And everybody's in "cable television"—networks, book publishers, newspapers. Cable television is a system for building the best TV antenna in town and then wiring it into everybody's television set—for a fee. It improves signal quality and number of channels, and has proved popular. But the new technology is such that it has broadcasters and newspaper publishers worried. For the same cable that can bring off-the-air television into the home can also bring programming from the cable operator's studio, or an "electronic newspaper" printed in the home by a facsimile process. Books can be delivered (between libraries, or to the home) over "television" by using the station's signal during an invisible pause. So everybody's hedging their bets—including the telephone company. Indeed, about all the vested interests can agree upon is that none of them want us to have direct, satellite-to-home radio and television. But at this point it is not at all clear who will have his hand on the switch that controls what comes to the American people over their "telephone wire" a few years hence.

WHAT IS TO BE DONE?

It would be foolish to expect any extensive restructuring of the media in the United States, even if it were considered desirable. Technological change can bring change in structure, but it is as likely to be change to even greater concentration as to wider diversity. In the short run at least, economics seems to render essentially intractable such problems as local monopolies in daily newspapers, or the small number of outlets for national news through wire services, newsmagazines, and the television networks. Indeed, to a certain extent the very high technical quality of the performance rendered by these news-gathering organizations is aided by their concentration of resources into large units and the financial cushions of oligopoly profits.

Nevertheless, it seems clear to me that the risks of concentration are grave.

Chairman Philip Hart of the Senate Antitrust and Monopoly Subcommittee remarked by way of introduction to his antitrust subcommittee's recent hearings about the newspaper industry, "The products of newspapers, opinion and information, are essential to the kind of society that we undertake to make successful here." If we are serious about the kind of society we have undertaken, it is clear to me that we simply must not tolerate concentration of media ownership—except where concentration creates actual countervailing social benefits. These benefits cannot be merely speculative. They must be identifiable, demonstrable, and genuinely weighty enough to offset the dangers inherent in concentration.

This guideline is a simple prescription. The problem is to design and build machinery to fill it. And to keep the machinery from rusting and rotting. And to replace it when it becomes obsolete.

America does have available governmental machinery which is capable of scotching undue accumulations of power over the mass media, at least in theory and to some extent. The Department of Justice has authority under the antitrust laws to break up combinations which "restrain trade" or which "tend to lessen competition." These laws apply to the media as they do to any other industry.

But the antitrust laws simply do not get to where the problems are. They grant authority to block concentration only when it threatens *economic* competition in a particular economic *market*. Generally, in the case of the media, the relevant market is the market for advertising. Unfortunately, relatively vigorous advertising competition can be maintained in situations where competition in the marketplace of ideas is severely threatened. In such cases, the Justice Department has little inclination to act.

Look at the Chicago *Tribune's* recent purchase of that city's most popular and most successful FM radio station. The *Tribune* already controlled two Chicago newspapers, one (clear channel) AM radio station, and the city's only independent VHF television station. It controls numerous broadcast, CATV, and newspaper interests outside Chicago (in terms of circulation, the nation's largest newspaper chain). But, after an investigation, the Antitrust Division let this combination go through. The new FM may be a needless addition to the *Tribune's* already impressive battery of influential media; it could well produce an unsound level of concentration in the production and supply of what Chicagoans see, read, and hear about affairs in their community, in the nation, and in the world. But it did not threaten the level of competition for advertising money in any identifiable advertising market. So, it was felt, the acquisition was not the business of the Justice Department.

Only the FCC is directly empowered to keep media ownership patterns compatible with a democracy's need for diversified sources of opinion and information.

In earlier times, the Commission took this responsibility very seriously. In 1941, the FCC ordered NBC to divest itself of one of its two radio networks (which then became ABC), barring any single network from affiliating with more than one outlet in a given city. (The Commission has recently waived this prohibition for, ironically, ABC's four new national radio networks.) In 1941 the Commission also established its power to set absolute limits on the total number of broadcast licenses any individual may hold, and to limit the number of stations any individual can operate in a particular service area.

The American people are indebted to the much maligned FCC for establishing these rules. Imagine, for example, what the structure of political power in this country might look like if two or three companies owned substantially all of the broadcast media in our major cities.

But since the New Deal generation left the command posts of the FCC, this agency has lost much of its zeal for combating concentration. Atrophy has reached so advanced a state that the public has of late witnessed the bizarre spectacle of the Justice Department, with its relatively narrow mandate, intervening in FCC proceedings, such as ITT-ABC, to create court cases with names like *The United States vs. The FCC*.

This history is an unhappy one on the whole. It forces one to question whether government can ever realistically be expected to sustain a vigilant posture over an industry which controls the very access of government officials themselves to the electorate.

I fear that we have already reached the point in this country where the media, our greatest check on other accumulations of power, may themselves be beyond the reach of any other institution: the Congress, the President, or the Federal Communications Commission, not to mention governors, mayors, state legislators, and city councilmen. Congressional hearings are begun and then quietly dropped. Whenever the FCC stirs fitfully as if in wakefulness, the broadcasting industry scurries up the Hill for a congressional bludgeon. And the fact that roughly 60 percent of all campaign expenses go to radio and television time gives but a glimmer of the power of broadcasting in the lives of senators and congressmen.

However, the picture at this moment has its more hopeful aspect. There does seem to be an exceptional flurry of official concern. Even the FCC has its proposed rulemaking outstanding. The Department of Justice, having broken into the communications field via its dramatic intervention before the FCC in the ITT-ABC merger case, has also been pressing a campaign to force the dissolution of joint operating agreements between separately owned newspapers in individual cities, and opposed a recent application for broadcasting properties by newspaper interests in Beaumont, Texas. It has been scrutinizing cross-media combinations linking broadcasting, newspaper, and cable television outlets. On Capitol Hill, Senator Phil Hart's Antitrust and Monopoly Subcommittee and Chairman Harley Staggers' House Interstate and Foreign Commerce Committee have both summoned the Federal Communications Commission to appear before them in recent months, to acquaint the Commission with the committees' concern about FCC-approved increases in broadcast holdings by single individuals and companies, and about cross-ownership of newspapers, CATV systems, and broadcast stations. Representatives John Dingell, John Moss, and Richard Ottinger have introduced legislation which would proscribe network ownership of any nonbroadcast interests. And as I previously mentioned, President Johnson has appointed a task force to undertake a comprehensive review of national communications policy.

Twenty years ago Robert M. Hutchins, then chancellor of the University of Chicago, was named chairman of the "Commission on Freedom of the Press." It produced a thoughtful report, full of recommendations largely applicable today—including "the establishment of a new and independent [nongovernmental] agency to appraise and report annually upon the performance of the press," and urged "that the members of the press engage in vigorous mutual criticism." Its proposals are once again being dusted off and reread.

What is needed now, more than anything else, is to keep this flurry of interest alive, and to channel it toward constructive reforms. What this means, in practical fact, is that concern for media concentration must find an institutional home.

The Department of Justice has already illustrated the value of participation by an external institution in FCC decision-making. The developing concept of a special consumers' representative offers a potentially broader base for similar action.

But the proper place to lodge continuing responsibility for promoting diversity in the mass media is neither the FCC nor the Justice Department nor a congressional committee. The initiative must come from private sources. Plucky Nader-like crusaders such as John Banzhaf (who single-handedly induced the FCC to apply the "fairness" doctrine to cigarette commercials) have shown how responsive government can be to the skillful and vigorous efforts of even a lone individual. But there are more adequately staffed and funded private organizations which could play a more effective role in policy formation than a single individual. Even the FCC, where the public interest gets entirely too little representation from private sources, has felt the impact of the United Church of Christ, with its interest in the influence of broadcasting on race relations and in the programming responsibility of licensees, and of the American Civil Liberties Union, which submitted a brief in the ITT-ABC case.

Ideally, however, the resources for a sustained attack on concentration might be centered in a single institution, equipped to look after this cause with the kind of determination and intelligence that the Ford Foundation and the Carnegie Corporation, for example, have brought to bear in behalf of the cause of public broadcasting and domestic satellites. The law schools and their law reviews, as an institution, have performed well in this way for the courts, but have virtually abdicated responsibility for the agencies.

Such an organization could devote itself to research as well as representation. For at present any public body like the FCC, which has to make determinations about acceptable levels of media concentration, has to do so largely on the basis of hunch. In addition, private interest in problems of concentration would encourage the Justice Department to sustain its present vigilance in this area. It could stimulate renewed vigilance on the part of the FCC, through participation in Commission proceedings. And it could consider whether new legislation might be appropriate to reach the problem of newspaper-magazine-book publishing combinations.

If changes are to be made (or now dormant standards are to be enforced) the most pressing political question is whether to apply the standards prospectively only, or to require divestiture. It is highly unlikely, to say the least, that legislation requiring massive divestiture of multiple station ownership, or newspaper ownership of stations, would ever pass through Congress. Given the number of station sales every year, however, even prospective standards could have some impact over ten years or so.

In general, I would urge the minimal standard that no accumulation of media should be permitted without a specific and convincing showing of a continuing countervailing social benefit. For no one has a higher calling in an increasingly complex free society bent on self-government than he who informs and moves the people. Personal prejudice, ignorance, social pressure, and advertiser pressure are in large measure inevitable. But a nation that has, in Learned Hand's phrase, "staked its all" upon the rational dialogue of an informed electorate simply cannot take any unnecessary risk of polluting the stream of information and opinion that sustains it. At the very least, the burden of proving the social utility of doing otherwise should be upon him who seeks the power and profit which will result.

Whatever may be the outcome, the wave of renewed interest in the impact of ownership on the role of the media in our society is healthy. All will gain from intelligent inquiry by Congress, the Executive, the regulatory commissions—and especially the academic community, the American people generally, and the media themselves. For, as the Supreme Court has noted, nothing is more important in a free society than "the widest possible dissemination of information from diverse and antagonistic sources." And if we are unwilling to discuss *this* issue fully today we may find ourselves discussing none that matter very much tomorrow.

PROBLEMS CREATED BY BIGNESS—
MORE SPECIFICS

THE average newspaper reader, finding that his local paper does not carry a column or other feature that he thinks it should, will probably conclude that the publisher is both too stingy and too lacking in a sense of public responsibility. This may not be the case, especially if a metropolitan paper is nearby.

The following testimony by the editor of the Riverside, California, Press-Enterprise, before a Senate subcommittee, illustrates the kind of difficulty a smaller competitor faces.

125

Statement of Norman Cherniss, Editor, Riverside, Calif., Press-Enterprise

MR. CHERNISS. This statement is confined to the problem of territorial exclusivity of syndicated features, a problem bearing directly upon the ability of newspapers, especially certain smaller ones, to compete and, therefore, to survive.

I shall use my own newspaper's experience as an example because, of course, I am most familiar with it and because in most respects I believe it is not untypical of the experience of many small- and medium-sized newspapers within or near the shadow of a giant metropolitan newspaper.

A brief description of my newspapers and their operation is necessary.

The Press is an afternoon newspaper serving the city of Riverside and suburbs. Riverside is 60 miles southeast of Los Angeles. There are two editions. Paid circulation for the first quarter of 1967 was put at 35,365.

The Daily Enterprise is a morning newspaper serving the whole of Riverside County, a geographic entity almost as large as the State of New Jersey. The variations and extent of the county are

Taken from *The Failing Newspaper Act. Hearings Before the Subcommittee on Antitrust and Monopoly of the Committee on the Judiciary of the U.S. Senate, 90th Congress, 1st Session, pursuant to Senate Resolution 26 on S. 1312.* 1967. Part I, pp. 297-301. See Editors' Note at the end of chapter.

such as to require four zone editions. The Enterprise is trucked each day for home delivery as far away from Riverside, at the western end of the county, as the Colorado River-Arizona line, a distance of more than 200 miles. Enterprise paid circulation for the first quarter of 1967 was put at 39,907.

The combined daily circulation for the first quarter of 1967 was 75,238. The Sunday Press-Enterprise circulation for the same period was 76,962.

The two newspapers have been jointly published since 1932. There is no fiction of competition between the two; in many respects they are morning and evening editions of the same newspaper—the morning edition designed principally for Riverside County, the evening edition for Riverside city and environs. Most syndicated features appear in both newspapers; stories appearing in one paper very often appear unchanged in the other. The same editorial page serves both. Duplication of circulation between the two newspapers is virtually nil.

I would emphasize that the Press and Daily Enterprise are not "suburban" newspapers or "community" newspapers as those descriptions are ordinarily used. The Press is a medium-sized newspaper serving a medium-sized city; the Enterprise is a medium-sized newspaper serving a vast county.

They are meant to be complete newspapers, not supplementary to any metropolitan newspaper. While they have primary responsibility for coverage of local news, heavy emphasis is laid on State, National, and international news coverage. The Press-Enterprise utilizes the leased wires of the Associated Press, United Press International, and the New York Times News Service.

Like all but a very few other newspapers, large or small, the Press-Enterprise depends heavily on syndicated features of various kinds to supplement its straight news coverage and its own features. We purchase and present a substantial number of what we consider to be good and popular ones—comics, cartoons, columnists, serializations, and so on.

But we have had over the years a problem in securing good and popular syndicated features. The problem, one of increasing magnitude in recent years, is caused by the territorial exclusivity insisted upon by, and ordinarily granted, one large newspaper in our general area.

That newspaper is the Los Angeles Times.

The problem has become more acute since 1962 when the afternoon Mirror and the morning Examiner were closed down, leaving the Times and the Herald Examiner as the two newspapers in Los Angeles.

When there were both the Times and the Mirror—under the same ownership—the Times bought feature rights for a territory which included Riverside County, but the Mirror did not. Now, anything purchased by the Times-Mirror Co. is purchased for much of southern California, including Riverside County.

During the trial of the Justice Department's antitrust suit against the Times—the *United States v. The Times-Mirror Company*—it was stipulated and acknowledged by Mr. Norman Chandler, the chairman of the board and chief executive officer of that company—

That the Times customarily seeks an exclusive territory for syndicated features which it purchases which runs from Santa Barbara to San Diego and east to the Colorado River. (pp. 2273-2274 of the transcript.)

Mr. Chandler explained that—

We do not like to have all of the smaller papers scattered all through southern California acquiring the features and the comics that we use. That is normal procedure in any newspaper throughout the country. (p. 2275 of the transcript.)

Mr. Chandler was asked by the Government attorney:

For those [syndicates] who give you exclusive territory, is it not the Times' policy to refuse to grant permission to other daily newspapers in that area to publish features for which the Times has an exclusive?

His answer was:

That is correct. And we will pay more to get an exclusive feature and territorial rights than we will otherwise. That, too, is normal newspaper procedure (p. 2276 of the transcript).

The syndicate with a new feature or service has a choice of offering it first to a single metropolitan Los Angeles paper or first to the several papers in the hinterland. In former years salesmen often approached the smaller papers first, garnered what sales they could from them and then went on to Los Angeles. More recently the pattern has been to offer the feature first in Los Angeles and only to the newspapers of the hinterland if there is no Los Angeles customer.

Prior to the consolidation in Los Angeles, if an offer of a feature there resulted in a sale to the Mirror or to the Herald Express or to the Examiner, the feature continued to be available to newspapers outside the metropolis. Now there is only one major Los Angeles market for most syndicated features and any sale means the end of the opportunity of other area newspapers to buy.

Selling exclusively to one newspaper is obviously to the advantage of the syndicate. It usually means more money and greater convenience, both in selling and in distribution. Exclusivity is obviously to the advantage also of the one larger newspaper permitted to buy.

It is to the absolute disadvantage of the smaller newspapers of the same area, which are not permitted to buy, which are not always even informed of a new feature before the larger customer is first advised and solicited.

The system operates to the benefit of the few—as syndicate and one newspaper of a given area—and to the detriment of the many, the other newspapers of the same area.

I have given the nature of the problem. May I cite some manifestations, some selected examples of the problem?

We have, of course, a long list of rejections from various syndicates. Usually, these are simple routine notices that the feature inquired about is not available in our area. That means only one thing: It has been sold in Los Angeles.

More often, in recent years, we have received no written response to inquiries concerning the availability of features. Rather, we are informed by telephone or by personal visit of a salesman. So, there is often no written record beyond our inquiry. Where that has become the practice, it seems to date back to the time the Justice Department began taking an announced interest in this general matter of syndication.

However, there are some samples. Some are out of the ordinary. This is from a 1963 letter from William Woestendiek, then editorial director of Newsday:

Thank you for your letter about [the late] Marguerite Higgins. We are planning to syndicate her but we have offered her to the Los Angeles papers and we shall have to wait for their answers because I imagine they might object to your running the column.

What distinguishes that from other, somewhat similar instances is that at least there was the good grace and candor to inform us of what was going on. More often we simply do not receive a reply until the decision has been made in Los Angeles.

When Max Freedman some years ago left the Manchester Guardian to write a three-times-weekly column, we both phoned and wired the syndicate involved not only to express our interest, but to order. We thought we bought the column on the telephone. Subsequently we were informed this was an unfortunate mistake. The Freedman column had to go to the Los Angeles Times because the Times was a subscriber to the Chicago Daily News Foreign Service. The Freedman column was not part of that service but was being distributed by an allied syndicate. We lost out, despite the oral confirmation of our actual order.

I have mentioned the Chicago Daily News Wire Service. It is, because the Daily News itself is an afternoon service, primarily for afternoon newspapers. We have an afternoon newspaper; we cannot buy the Daily News Wire Service. The Los Angeles Times, a morning newspaper, subscribes. The Daily News Wire Service is the only strictly afternoon wire there is with which to supplement the basic services, the AP and UPI.

May I quote from an October 1963 letter of mine to Mr. Bernard Hollander, of the Department of Justice:

We were visited last week by Frank Perley of Publishers' Syndicate [very recently merged with the Hall Syndicate]. In mid-October Mr. Perley arrived to give me an answer to my July and August inquiries as to the availability of the Joseph Kraft column. He advised me, of course, that it is not available because exclusivity has been granted the

Los Angeles Times. I asked him why it took from July to October to get this information, and he told me the syndicate did not want to put anything in writing. He also advised us it would be futile for us to inquire about the Carl Rowan column when it starts because the Los Angeles Times has already sewed it up, too.

Mr. Perley also volunteered the information that his comic strip, "The Wizard of Id," had been offered to the Los Angeles Times, but that the Times had said no. However, according to Mr. Perley, the syndicate is of the opinion that the Times will change its mind, and, therefore, is not offering it for sale in the Southern California territory. That is, to our experience, a whole new facet of this problem—the feature which might be sold and, therefore, cannot be made available.

In the altogether likely event—I emphasize likely—that my newspaper would have been interested in purchasing serialization rights to such major books as "Journey of the Soul," Pope John's story, or Theodore White's "Making of a President, 1964," it could not have done so. In the unlikely event my newspaper had even wanted to bid against the Los Angeles Times for the southern California area rights to these particular syndicated features, it could not have done so. For we simply did not know that they had been serialized and syndicated until announcement of their impending publication was made in the Times.

This is an old story—syndicates or their salesmen, with or without public announcement of a new feature, go first to Los Angeles. If their luck is good, they go only to Los Angeles.

I come to the case of Orphan Annie, the comic strip, still well-known, whether for purposes of entertainment or, I understand, political enlightenment.

In its letters-to-the-editor column of April 1, 1966, the Los Angeles Times advised an inquiring reader that "after many years in the Times, Orphan Annie has been retired, at least for the time being, in favor of a new comic strip . . . ."

We immediately inquired of the Chicago Tribune-New York News Syndicate whether the strip was now available to us, since it was not appearing in the Times. The syndicate's April 3, 1966, letter acknowledged our "interest in the welfare of our gal Annie . . . although she is not available for your readers at this point."

On May 4, 1966, we inquired again and received a letter dated May 10 from the Chicago Tribune-New York News Syndicate:

Thank you for your inquiry of May 4th concerning the availability of On Stage [which had also been removed from the Times' comic page] and Orphan Annie. Both these features are still under contract to the Los Angeles Times and we are unable to offer them to other newspapers in the area.

Should the situation change, we would be most happy to reconsider your inquiry.

In a letter dated December 28, 1966, signed Henry Raduta, Mr. Raduta once again in response to an inquiry, wrote as follows:

Thank you for your thoughtful inquiry of December 19th concerning the availability of Little Orphan Annie.

A recent report from our western representative reveals that in all probability this feature will be restored in the Los Angeles Times in the near future. As you know, they have it under contract and indications are that they plan to continue it in their next renewal contract.

We certainly appreciate your interest in this feature and will keep your thoughtful inquiry in mind.

Well, the situation is not changed, our thoughtful inquiry is still in mind, we have not heard further from the syndicate about this particular feature, and the Orphan Annie strip has not been restored to the Los Angeles Times.

Fourteen months after it was removed "temporarily" from the Times' comic page, it is still purchased; it is unpublished by the purchaser, the Times, and it is unavailable to any other interested newspaper in the area for which the Times has territorial rights.

Now, I am not prepared to argue that Little Orphan Annie is the weightiest syndicated newspaper feature offered or that having it or not having it is essential to the success of my newspaper or any other. I do not know whether it would mean even one new subscriber. I can easily think of other, also unavailable features, which I consider more significant.

But I do suggest that there is a principle involved. I do suggest that to buy and withhold from publication for 14 months in a sizable area—whatever the feature and whatever the reason —is serious business. If it can be done for one sizable geographic area, much of southern California, what is the limit?

If suppression is not the proper word to describe this practice, the proper word is something very like suppression.

I do not for an instant suggest anything so ulterior or so base in this particular episode of Little Orphan Annie as a deliberate attempt to stifle opinion. But the present system with which I have been dealing would seem to permit just that. And, as I said, I think there is a principle involved. . . .

Editors' Note. Note long after Mr. Cherniss gave this testimony, and largely as a result of his agitation and that of similarly affected publishers, the Justice Department was able to prevail upon news syndicates to end their practice of granting "territorial exclusivity." The philosophy that implemented the practice undoubtedly lives on, however.

Big Frogs in a Little Pond: A Local Picture

Frightening as the picture is of concentration among the national communications giants, in some localities media ownership patterns are the same. In a study published in the summer of 1968, two commissioners of the Federal Communications Commission, Kenneth A. Cox and Nicholas Johnson, detailed the picture in Oklahoma.[1] Similar trends are apparent in virtually every state and community. In a $19 million stock deal not long ago, Fuqua acquired television stations in Columbus, Georgia, and Chattanooga, Tennessee, along with 140 owned or leased movie houses in the Southeast. Fuqua has interests in power lawn mowers, land clearing and tillage implements, mobile homes, boat building, motor freight, and community antenna television systems in Georgia. Avco, in addition to its legal limit of five television stations, is thoroughly locked into what is usually called the military-industrial complex, manufacturing missile and space products, electronic components, and aircraft parts. The list is long indeed. But thanks to the efforts of these two FCC commissioners, we have good evidence of the ties which exist between the mass media of communication in Oklahoma and various business endeavors.

Johnson and Cox found that although there are 83 commercial radio and 10 commercial television stations in Oklahoma (as of

[1] *Broadcasting in America and the FCC's License Renewal Process: An Oklahoma Case Study.*

135

1966), there are not 93 separate ownerships in the state. There are only 73. And of the 73, the top four accounted for 56% of the revenue and 88% of the income of the totals earned by all 73 firms in 1966. The leader among these four top firms is part of what Cox and Johnson call a "galaxy of interests" owned by the E. K. Gaylord family. Among the holdings of this family is the Oklahoma Publishing Company, which publishes the Oklahoma City *Oklahoman* (circulation 170,709) and the Oklahoma City *Times* (circulation 116,379). The company owns WKY-AM-TV in Oklahoma City, and also publishes three state editions of the monthly Farmer-Stockman, with a circulation of nearly half a million in Oklahoma, Kansas and Texas. The company owns Mistletoe Express, which provides trucking service to 400 Oklahoma cities. The company owns television stations in Dallas-Fort Worth, Houston, Tampa, and Milwaukee. Publishers Petroleum Division of Oklahoma Publishing Company, Commissioners Cox and Johnson found, is involved in oil exploration and production.

The FCC commissioners took a close look at the other business interests of the officers, directors, and stockholders of the corporation that owns KOCO-TV in Oklahoma City and has interests in KVOO-TV in Tulsa and KBMT-TV in Beaumont, Texas. They found investments in 30 different companies, among them banks; real estate firms; oil, drilling and pipeline businesses; insurance; ranching; and agriculture. "It is obvious," Cox and Johnson conclude drily, "that a few firms and a few stations enjoy a dominant position in the state. Political candidates for statewide office will have to be cognizant of the influence of these few firms and stations."

There never has been an anti-trust case based upon monopoly of ideas or of access to the marketplace of ideas. The law comes into play only when economic monopoly seems present. But economic monopoly usually results in monopoly of expression in the mass media. An example of this is the case of *U.S. v. Times Mirror Company*.[2] In 1964, Times Mirror, whose annual operating revenues are more than $250 million, bought the San Ber-

2 *U.S. v. Times Mirror Company*, 274 F. Supp. 606.

nardino *Morning Sun* and *Evening Telegram*. The effect of this transaction, contended the Justice Department, was to raise a nearly total barrier to the entry of other daily newspapers in the San Bernardino County market area. Not only should Times Mirror divest itself of the Sun Co., argued government attorneys, but the huge firm should be barred from further acquisitions in Southern California.

After a 26-day trial, Judge Warren J. Ferguson of the Ninth U.S. Judicial District ordered divestiture. He refused, however, to enjoin Times Mirror from possible future acquisition of newspapers in Southern California, that area which Los Angeles *Times* editor Nick Williams has said will someday be solid metropolis from Santa Barbara to the Mexican border. "The court cannot prejudge the newspaper business with sufficient certainty to grant the injunction," Judge Ferguson declared.

It now seems possible to predict with a little more certainty the future of the daily newspaper business in San Bernardino County, at least. Within a year after the court ordered divestiture, Times Mirror reached an agreement with the Gannett Co. to sell the Sun Co. to Gannett. The agreement means, in effect, absentee ownership of the Sun Co. by another large communications firm. Gannett publishes 30 dailies and 13 weeklies in New York, Connecticut, New Jersey, Illinois and Florida. It operates three television stations and six radio stations, and is involved in community antenna television. It is part owner of a paper mill. The Gannett Co. had gross operating revenues in 1967 of $110 million.

Given the Sun Co.'s net worth (purchase price to Times Mirror was $15 million), it is difficult to see how any but a very large company could have entered the bidding. Perhaps the outcome indeed was preordained. Perhaps we have already gone too far down the road of economic concentration for true diversity to survive. In 1945, ruling on another restraint of trade case involving news media, the Supreme Court in its majority opinion asserted that "the widest possible dissemination of information from diverse and antagonistic sources is essential to the welfare of the public. . . ."[3] As we have observed, it is sometimes difficult

3 *Associated Press v. U.S.*, 326 U.S. 1, 20.

to enforce this concept in law, though such sentiment would seem to be a basic postulate of a democratic society. Recently, however, the Department of Justice and the Federal Communications Commission, to name two governmental bodies charged with protecting the public interest, have moved to exert what legal resources there are to maintain and create diversity.

The FCC, for example, has announced its intention of forbidding licensees of one type of broadcasting station to acquire another kind of radio or television station in the same market. This one and one, or one to a customer, rule would prevent future development of companies owning a television station, an AM broadcasting station, and an FM radio station all in one city. The FCC would not, however, require licensees already holding multiple broadcast outlets in one market to divest themselves of their holdings. The Justice Department, meanwhile, has successfully brought suit seeking to outlaw joint printing arrangements of two newspapers in Tucson, Arizona. Forty-four newspapers in 22 cities have been operating under similar plans which combine advertising and printing departments of otherwise competing newspapers, thus presenting a unified economic fortress against which it is difficult if not impossible for a new paper in town to compete. Whether or not all 44 newspapers will be forced to end their joint agreements will probably not be made clear for some years. What is clear, however, is that the Supreme Court in this case, *Citizen Publishing Co. et al. v. U.S.* (37 LW 4208), has given new meaning to the words it uttered a quarter century ago: "Freedom to publish is guaranteed by the Constitution, but freedom to combine to keep others from publishing is not. Freedom of the press from governmental interference under the First Amendment does not sanction repression of that freedom by private interests."[4]

4 *Ibid.*

Bibliography for Chapter Three

BOOKS

Braddon, Russell. *Roy Thomson of Fleet Street*. New York: Walker, 1965.

Brucker, Herbert. *Freedom of Information*. New York: Macmillan, 1949.

Ernst, Morris L. *The First Freedom*. New York: Macmillan, 1946.

Field, Marshall. *Freedom Is More Than a Word*. Chicago: University of Chicago Press, 1945.

Gerald, J. Edward. *The Press and the Constitution, 1931-1947*. Minneapolis: University of Minnesota Press, 1948.

————. *The Social Responsibility of the Press*. Minneapolis: University of Minnesota Press, 1963.

Lent, John A. *Newhouse, Newspapers, Nuisances*. New York: Exposition Press, 1966.

Levin, Harvey J. *Broadcast Regulation and Joint Ownership of Media*. New York: New York University Press, 1960.

Rucker, Bryce W. *The First Freedom*. Carbondale: Southern Illinois University Press, 1968.

Stelzer, Irwin M., ed. *Selected Antitrust Cases*. Homewood, Ill.: Richard O. Irwin, Inc., 1966.

Weybright, Victor. *The Making of a Publisher*. New York: Reynal & Co., 1967.

ARTICLES

Arthur, Robert A. "TV: The 21″ Bore," *Nation*, CCI (September, 1965), 227-231.

Brady, Robert A. "The Problem of Monopoly in Motion Pictures," *Annals of the American Academy of Political and Social Science*, CCLIV (November, 1947), 125-136.

Flackett, J. M. "Newspaper Mergers: Recent Developments in Britain and the United States," *Antitrust Bulletin,* XII (Winter, 1967), 1033-1055.

Goodman, Paul. "Censorship and Mass Media," *Yale Political,* III (Autumn, 1963), 23-40.

Turner, Donald F. "Conglomerate Mergers and Section 7 of the Clayton Act," *Harvard Law Review,* LXXVIII (May, 1965), 1313-1395.

Whitney, John Hay. "How a Newspaper Can Be Suppressed," *U.S. News and World Report,* LX, No. 18 (May 2, 1966), 37.

CASES

Associated Press v. United States, 326 U.S. 1 (1945).

Lorain Journal Co. v. United States, 342 U.S. 143 (1951).

Times-Picayune v. United States, 345 U.S. 594 (1953).

United States v. Citizen Publishing Co., 394 U.S. 131 (1969).

United States v. Kansas City Star, 240 F.2d 643 (1957).

United States v. Times-Mirror Corp., 274 F. Supp. 606 (1967).

CHAPTER FOUR

Conflict with the Courts: First versus Sixth Amendment

THE press and those two legal institutions—the bar and the courts—have long been wary of one another. Their most recent dispute—the so-called free press-fair trial controversy—has been characterized in its latest outcroppings more by the increased intensity of the debate than by newness of either side's arguments. More than a century ago, for example, legal periodicals were expressing worry about how to get an opinion-free jury in "the greatest newspaper-reading country in the world," and prominent editors were thundering their resolve to print accounts of the judicial process, no matter what.

On balance, this basic distrust between two powerful institutions is probably healthy, since each plays a watchdog role toward the other. Each side approaches the issue from different directions, and each side appears to have certain basic (sometimes undeclared) assumptions that lead to conflict. The press assumes that the Sixth Amendment's words "speedy and public trial" were intended to protect society's right to see that justice is done, while the bar maintains that the right to a fair trial is for the individual's welfare and, through his welfare, society's welfare. Another assumption of the legal profession is that the structure of the court system assures a fair trial in most cases, and that exceptions may be rectified at some time during the process. The press observes that examples of corruption in the past indicate that this assumption is not necessarily valid, and that close public scrutiny by the press is therefore essential. The assumption of the law is that government is trustworthy, or at least trustworthy enough to remedy its ills. The press assumes that often it is not. The bar, in calling for restraints on the publicity accorded prosecutors and other officials of the courts, assume that not only is government trusted but it is believed when it or its agent claims an air-tight case. The press is more skeptical. The bar's skepticism activates when it examines the assertion by the press that crime news is primarily for the public interest and benefit, that such news deters crime. And sells papers, the bar adds.

These assumptions, and many others, mean that the dispute will not soon be settled. A start has been made after much discussion. Most participants have stated their case, in law journals, journalism publications, in resolutions adopted by professional

143

organizations, and in books and popular press articles. These latest attempts, which differ from certain previous efforts in this area that used contempt-of-court power to seek restraint of the press, have as their central effort the control of the officers of the court. By following this "clean up our own house" theory, the legal profession seeks to close down prejudicial news at its source and thereby to avoid a direct clash with the press on Sixth Amendment issues.

Leading off with a brief comment from a law journal of 1872, which shows that the problem of fair trials and a free press is indeed an old one, this chapter presents a well-articulated appeal for understanding of mutual problems of bar and press. Next we present an example of the kinds of standards that the courts are being asked to enforce. In this case, the Federal Judicial Conference rules are probably going to be the standards adopted in most of the states, since all appeals eventually find themselves, if they go far enough, in the federal system. Finally, we present a candid article by the famous trial attorney, Elmer Gertz, in which he describes the kinds of uses to which the bar puts the press.

The Problem Endures

At no period have the relations between that old and venerate institution, the judiciary, and that young and vigorous institution, journalism, attained such an importance, or excited so much anxiety as at present. Modern civilization possesses no greater intelligent force than that which resides in the press; nor can modern civilization be preserved without the regulating, pacifying, conservative influence of the bench. . . . But there is an occasional civil or criminal matter, properly belonging to the courts, but, at the same time, by its public and popular bearings, belonging also to journalistic criticism, from which the emergency of the press and the bench arises. . . .

Albany Law Journal, November 30, 1872.

An Appeal For Cooperation On Fair Trial–Free Press Issue

JUDGE EDWARD J. DEVITT

Something must be done about prejudicial news publicity contaminating the fair conduct of criminal trials in the United States, and I appeal to you radio and television newsmen to join the legal profession in solving the problem.

Six times in recent years the United States Supreme Court has reversed criminal convictions because of prejudicial news publicity. The cases of Dr. Sam Sheppard and Billie Sol Estes are two well-known examples. Other appellate federal and state courts have taken similar action in numerous cases. Effective law enforcement suffers when appellate courts must reverse convictions because improper publicity has tainted trials.

We of the legal profession must admit fault in neglecting our own responsibility for so long. Prejudicial publicity in criminal cases is caused in most instances, not directly by the press, but by lawyers, court attaches, witnesses, parties and police investigative officers associated with the case, and sometimes, by the judge himself. They talk too much. They are wont to make out-of-court

Chief Judge, U.S. District Court, District of Minnesota, and chairman of the Fair Trial-Free Press Legal Advisory Committee of the American Bar Association. This address was delivered before the Eastern Regional Conference of the Radio-Television News Directors Association, in Rockefeller Plaza, New York, on June 29, 1968. Reprinted by permission.

comments about the guilt or innocence of a defendant; to recite the defendant's past criminal record; to report about a confession the defendant allegedly has made: to prognosticate the possibility of a guilty plea; or to tell of the refusal of a defendant to take a lie detector test or to be fingerprinted. All of this information well may be wrong, misleading, or inadmissible at trial, and when transmitted to the public through the news media, especially in a celebrated case, forms the basis of an extrajudicial prejudgment of guilt of an accused person by the very members of the public from whom jurors have been, or are, summoned to decide the case.

How would any of us like to be judged by a juror who heard on a television newscast the expressed opinion of the chief of police who apprehended us, that he was "absolutely positive" of our guilt! The Chief of Police of Chicago said that in a recent highly publicized case. This *ex cathedra* summary judgment by such an important public official carries with it in the public mind a de-facto conviction even before trial. Or, how would you like to be Dr. Sam Sheppard and, during your trial in Cleveland, Ohio in 1954, learn that your trial judge had expressed the opinion that you are "guilty as hell."

The Warren Commission, in its investigation of President Kennedy's assassination, recommended that the Bar and news media establish ethical standards to prevent prejudicial publicity. The Supreme Court, in the Dr. Sam Sheppard case, said that the Bar must take action. And now we have.

I was privileged to serve as a member of a Committee of the American Bar Association which prepared recommended standards of conduct in connection with the trial of criminal cases to meet the evil of prejudicial publicity. That report was adopted overwhelmingly in February of this year [1968], by the ABA House of Delegates meeting in Chicago. The recommendations have been strongly endorsed by many judicial and legal organizations, including the National Conference of State Trial Court Judges. Similar recommendations have been proposed for use by federal judges.

Some courts have already adopted, and are enforcing, such ethical standards. Three weeks ago the Supreme Court of New Jersey upheld the revocation of permission for a noted defense lawyer to represent an accused murderer in the courts of that state because of the lawyer's dissemination of prejudicial pretrial publicity. It is already apparent that these suggested standards of fair play have been effective in curbing the release of prejudicial publicity in connection with newsworthy criminal investigations. Compare, for instance, the release of information anent the assassination of Rev. Martin Luther King and of Senator Robert Kennedy with the Roman-circus atmosphere surrounding the apprehension and custody of Lee Harvey Oswald. The Chief of Police of Los Angeles and the newspaper and broadcasting media have acted responsibly and with good judgment in connection with the custody of Sirhan Bishara Sirhan, the alleged assassin of Senator Kennedy, and are deserving of commendation for the restraint and wise discretion exercised in their handling of the matter, especially at a time of such high tension and fast-moving events.

But a substantial segment of the press continues to believe that our recommendations do violence to the First Amendment right of a free press. We are accused of "keeping the public in the dark," of seeking to conduct star chamber courts, of hiding the possibility of graft and corruption, and depriving the public of its "right to know." Is that so? Is there any challenge to a free press? And what exactly are the ABA recommendations?

Here, in simple layman's language, is what our American Bar Association report recommends:

It prohibits out-of-court talking about the case by court attaches, lawyers, and the police, from the time of arrest to the end of the trial, but not after that. During that period these persons would be permitted to give newsmen the defendant's name, the hour and place of his arrest, information about whether the defendant resisted arrest or was armed at the time, a description of any physical evidence seized, and the nature of the charge against him. But these same persons would be barred from referring to any previous criminal record, the results of fingerprint and lie detector tests, whether the accused has confessed, as well as stating the identity of witnesses or expressing an opinion as to the guilt or innocence of the accused. These restrictions are recommended to be promulgated by court rule in so far as they pertain to lawyers and court officials, and by statute or rule in the executive branch of the government as they pertain to police departments. This is the heart of the Committee recommendations.

In essence, therefore, these recommendations embody an attempt to establish reasonable guides for professional conduct well within the rights of the Bench and Bar with no interference with the constitutional guarantees of press freedom.

So we ask our friends of the Press, wherein do these recommendations impinge upon the First Amendment guarantee of a free press? Does a newsman have a constitutional right to exposure to, and response from, a talkative policeman or a voluble prosecuting attorney? The answer, obviously, is no. But, it should be emphasized, the newsman is not prohibited by these standards from acting on his own initiative to get his information from any other proper available source. We express the hope, though, that his subscription to the ethics of his profession and to principles of fair play will prompt him to refrain from publishing prejudicial information likely to prevent a fair trial.

Time magazine, in its issue of March 1, 1968, fairly appraised the effect of the ABA suggested standards when it said:

What the new rules really mean is that reporters will have to stop relying on bull sessions in the station house or the district attorney's office and do more legwork.

And then the Time magazine article concluded:

. . . If the press and officials respond as they should, the idle gossip pieces that slur a defendant should be eliminated without real impairment of the public's right to know.

Indeed, what we of the Bench and Bar in this country are seeking to do through the suggestions contained in the ABA Report, and through similar recommendations of a New York Bar Association Committee under the Chairmanship of the highly respected Senior Circuit Judge Harold Medina of New York, is to put our own house in order and to stop prejudicial publicity at the source.

That, indeed, is what the press has been urging us to do for many years. The New York Times has said editorially:

The press cannot be expected to refrain from printing statements issued by public officials, as for example the United States Attorney, even though such statements may be prejudicial to a fair trial. The only way to stop this abuse is to stop it at the source. New York Times, September 5, 1956, p. 26.

This is exactly what we seek to do. It is the proper way and the only way to solve the problem.

The mission of the Committee of which I am Chairman is to assist in bringing about a full understanding of, and an implementation of, the ABA standards. The Committee believes the best way to accomplish this is, not through quarreling about whether your First Amendment right to a free press or our Sixth Amendment right to a fair trial is superior, but rather through cooperation of the bar and the media in the several states and localities. Substantial progress has been made in that direction. . . .

. . . We have been pleased that in most localities leaders of the media have demonstrated a readiness to join in discussions of meaningful voluntary codes. Such codes already exist in a half dozen states, and in recent weeks Oklahoma has joined the list with an agreement to which the state bar association has subscribed. Concurrence in the code now is under consideration by the state organizations of the press and broadcasting.

Two points about the voluntary codes ought to be clearly understood. If they are to be effective they need to be specific in their terms, so everyone will understand what they mean. They also should have the substantial acceptance of all the media and not just a few.

Wherever the bar and the media join in such agreements I don't think there will be any serious trouble in securing the cooperation also of the law enforcement agencies. In many cases representatives of those agencies have been included in the membership of the committees working on voluntary codes. I believe most police officials will want to cooperate when they see that the bar and media are serious in wanting to correct a situation which has allowed too many convicted criminals to go free on appeals.

There is another point on which I would like to be very clear. It is *not* the purpose of the American Bar Association standards to impede the reporting of crime news to the public. We are as interested as you are in preventing abuse or misuse of the standards as an excuse for withholding news of crime, including investigations in progress and arrests. Our committee has asked the state and local bar associations all over the country to be alert to such abuses and to use their good offices to help correct them. That is one of the important functions which can, and we believe will, be performed by the joint bar-media committees that are being formed in many places.

It is unfortunate, I think, that the formulation of the ABA standards by the Reardon committee and their adoption by the House of Delegates has been construed by many in the media as an "attack" on the press and broadcasting or as criticism of them. It isn't that at all.

Actually, the criticism is more directed to members of the legal profession as being the main source of prejudicial pretrial information that has found its way into the pattern of crime news coverage all of these years. The main objective was to stop lawyers and judges from talking too much about pending cases. The Reardon report freely acknowledged that it was from lawyers, judges, court attaches, and law enforcement officers that most of the prejudicial statements came.

But you all must recognize that you *can* eliminate these prejudicial statements without hampering crime news coverage or compromising the precepts of free press. The handling of the arrest of the suspect in the Senator Kennedy assassination is a good example. The Los Angeles police and prosecuting authorities followed the Reardon guidelines fully, and yet I don't think anyone can say honestly that the public was denied the essential information it was entitled to have about that heinous crime.

I believe that we are going to see in the months and years ahead a steadily mounting voluntary movement—by the media, by law enforcement, and by the bar—in this direction. The Reardon committee has brought the facts about this problem to the attention of all concerned more vividly than it ever has been done before. I believe we all have come to realize the reality of the problem. We are beginning to see the standards applied and we are beginning to see that they do work without injury to anyone, but with the promise that criminal trials in the future will be as fair as it is humanly possible to make them, and less vulnerable to attack in the appellate courts.

That is important progress. All of us can take satisfaction in it, and in what can be achieved to strengthen our processes of criminal law administration if we will end the disputatious exchanges and focus on a positive approach.

May I close by telling you of the success already enjoyed by a joint media-bar committee in my native state of Minnesota.

The Fair Trial-Free Press issue has been a hot one there, particularly in the Twin Cities area where the CBS television outlet, WCCO, and the St. Paul newspapers have expressed vigorous and sustained editorial opposition to the recommendations contained in the Reardon report.

About a year ago the leaders of the broadcasters association, the press, the police and the bar got together and formed a Fair Trial-Free Press Council with the stated purpose of working toward the solution of this and other common problems through discussion and through mutual persuasion of men of good will. There have been, and still are, substantial disagreements between the constituency in this Council which functions under the able leadership of the Honorable Walter Rogosheske, a Justice of the Minnesota Supreme Court. But, after many meetings and much frank discussion, the Council was able to agree upon the joint issuance of recommended guidelines for the bar, police officers, and the press which substantially embody the principal recommendations contained in the Reardon report. I hold in my hand a small card the like of which has been issued widely to police officers, prosecuting attorneys, newsmen and others in Minnesota which contains on one side the type of information which generally should be made public, and on the other side the type of information which should not be made public in connection with the apprehension of a person charged with the commission of a crime. As I have stated, these recommended guidelines substantially follow the suggestions contained in the ABA Report.

One of the principal objections to the Reardon recommendations by the newsmen of Minnesota was that police and investigative officers and prosecuting attorneys were over-reacting to the Supreme Court decision in the *Sheppard* case and to the recommendations of the Reardon committee with the result that information which could properly be released to the news media without prejudice to a fair trial was being withheld because of misinterpretation of the extent of the recommended standards. The problem is well on its way to solution in Minnesota, largely because of the cooperation of the news media on the one hand and the lawyers and police investigative officers on the other.

As Chairman of the ABA Legal Advisory Committee on Fair Trial-Free Press, I appeal to you representatives of the radio and television newsmen to join with us in effecting, through positive mutual action, a solution to this difficult problem. Can we not agree that there is some merit in what each of us says about our respective views, but even greater merit in what we can do together to insure both a free press and a fair trial each under the protection of the United States Constitution?

United States Judicial Conference Recommendations

EDITORS' COMMENT

The United States Judicial Conference, composed of the chief judges of the eleven United States Courts of Appeals, the chief judge of every Federal District Court, the chief judges of the Court of Claims and the Court of Customs and Patents, and headed by the Chief Justice of the United States, adopted the following recommendations in September 1968. Adoption meant virtually that the federal judiciary was directed to follow these rules, which means that many if not most state courts will follow suit.

Unlike the Reardon Report to the House of Delegates of the American Bar Association, which proposed that judges use the contempt power to control publication of news about criminal cases, the Judicial Conference Recommendations do not attempt to regulate the press. They seek to regulate the speech of various officers of the court. Whether or not the recommendations will thereby avoid clashing with the First Amendment remains to be seen.

SPECIFIC RECOMMENDATIONS

A

Recommendation Relating to the Release of Information by Attorneys in Criminal Cases

It is recommended that each United States District Court adopt a rule of court regulating public discussion by attorneys of pending or imminent criminal litigation, and that this rule contain substantially the following:

"It is the duty of the lawyer not to release or authorize the release of information or opinion for dissemination by any means of public communication, in connection with pending or imminent criminal litigation with which he is associated, if there is a reasonable likelihood that such dissemination will interfere with a fair trial or otherwise prejudice the due administration of justice.

"With respect to a grand jury or other pending investigation of any criminal matter, a lawyer participating in the investigation shall refrain from making any extrajudicial statement, for dissemination by any means of public communication, that goes beyond the public record or that is not necessary to inform the public that the investigation is under way, to describe the general scope of the investigation, to obtain assistance in the apprehension of a suspect, to warn the public of any dangers, or otherwise to aid in the investigation.

"From the time of arrest, issuance of an arrest warrant or the filing of a complaint, information, or indictment in any criminal matter until the commencement of trial or disposition without trial, a lawyer associated with the prosecution or defense shall not release or authorize the release of any extrajudicial statement, for dissemination by any means of public communication, relating to that matter and concerning:

"(1) The prior criminal record (including arrests, indictments, or other charges of crime), or the character or reputation of the accused, except that the lawyer may make a factual statement of the accused's name, age, residence, occupation, and family status, and if the accused has not been apprehended, a lawyer associated with the prosecution may release any information necessary to aid in his apprehension or to warn the public of any dangers he may present;

"(2) The existence of contents of any confession, admission, or statement given by the accused, or the refusal or failure of the accused to make any statement;

"(3) The performance of any examinations or tests or the accused's refusal or failure to submit to an examination or test;

"(4) The identity, testimony, or credibility of prospective witnesses, except that the lawyer may announce the identity of the victim if the announcement is not otherwise prohibited by law;

"(5) The possibility of a plea of guilty to the offense charged or a lesser offense;

"(6) Any opinion as to the accused's guilt or innocence or as to the merits of the case or the evidence in the case.

"The foregoing shall not be construed to preclude the lawyer during this period, in the proper discharge of his official or professional obligations, from announcing the fact and circumstances of arrest (including time and place of arrest, resistance, pursuit, and use of weapons), the identity of the investigating and arresting officer or agency, and the length of the investigation; from making an announcement, at the time of seizure of any physical evidence other than a confession, admission or statement, which is limited to a description of the evidence seized; from disclosing the nature, substance, or text of the charge, including a brief description of the offense charged; from quoting or referring without comment to public records of the court in the case; from announcing the scheduling or result of any stage in the judicial process; from requesting assistance in obtaining evidence; or from announcing without further comment that the accused denies the charges made against him.

During the trial of any criminal matter, including the period of selection of the jury, no lawyer associated with the prosecution or defense shall give or authorize any extrajudicial statement or interview, relating to the trial or the parties or issues in the trial, for dissemination by any means of public communication, except that the lawyer may quote from or refer without comment to public records of the court in the case.

"After the completion of a trial or disposition without trial of any criminal matter, and prior to the imposition of sentence, a lawyer associated with the prosecution or defense shall refrain from making or authorizing any extrajudicial statement for dissemination by any means of public communication if there is a reasonable likelihood that such dissemination will affect the imposition of sentence.

"Nothing in this Rule is intended to preclude the formulation or application of more restrictive rules relating to the release of information about juvenile or other offenders, to preclude the holding of hearings or the lawful issuance of reports by legislative, administrative, or investigative bodies, or to preclude any lawyer from replying to charges of misconduct that are publicly made against him."

B

Recommendation Relating to the Release of Information by Courthouse Personnel in Criminal Cases

It is recommended that each United States District Court adopt a rule of court prohibiting all courthouse personnel, including among others, marshals, deputy marshals, court clerks, bailiffs and court reporters, from disclosing to any person, without authorization by the court, information relating to a pending criminal case that is not part of the public records of the court. Such a rule should specifically forbid the divulgence of information concerning arguments and hearings held in chambers or otherwise outside the presence of the public.

C

Recommendations Relating to the Conduct of Judicial Proceedings in Criminal Cases

1. Provisions for Special Orders in Widely Publicized and Sensational Cases

It is recommended that each United States District Court adopt a rule of court providing in substance as follows:

In a widely publicized or sensational case, the Court, on motion of either party or on its own motion, may issue a special order governing such matters as extrajudicial statements by parties and witnesses likely to interfere with the rights of the accused to a fair trial by an impartial jury, the seating and conduct in the court-

*room of spectators and news media representatives, the management
and sequestration of jurors and witnesses, and any other matters
which the Court may deem appropriate for inclusion in such an
order.*

2. More Liberal Use of Traditional Techniques for Insuring an
Impartial Jury (Continuance, Change of Venue, Sequestration of
Jurors and Witnesses, Voir Dire, Cautionary Instructions to
Jurors)

---

*It is recommended that in criminal cases likely to attract substantial
public interest the United States District Courts make more extensive
use of existing techniques designed to ensure an impartial jury.*

D

Recommendation Relating to the Use of Photography, Radio, and Television Equipment in the Courtroom and its Environs

---

*It is recommended that each United States District Court adopt a rule
of court providing in substance as follows:*

*The taking of photographs in the courtroom or its environs or
radio or television broadcasting from the courtroom or its environs,
during the progress of or in connection with judicial proceedings,
including proceedings before a United States Commissioner,
whether or not court is actually in session, is prohibited.*

*Such a rule should define the area included as environs at each place
where judicial proceedings are held.*

WILL RULES SOLVE THE PROBLEM?

H OW EFFECTIVE are such rules as the foregoing in assuring that
justice has a better chance? The question remains open,
since little hard evidence exists on the extent to which jurors in
real trial situations are influenced by statements by principals in
the press.

Well, then, how effective are such rules in restricting dissemination of statements and claims in sensational cases? Again the
evidence is scarce, although there is some suggestion that rules do
reduce somewhat the level of publicity. But Judge W. Preston
Battle's rules in the James Earl Ray case did not, of course, prevent Ray himself from selling his story to author and journalist
William Bradford Huie, who then serialized Ray's account in
Look, with a circulation of several million.

The following article by the noted Chicago attorney, Elmer
Gertz, illustrates some rather subtle ways in which lawyers use,
and are used by, the press. Gertz, who is the author of *A Handful
of Clients* and many law journal and popular press articles, writes
with many years' first-hand experience with sensational murder
and obscenity cases, as well as with wide acquaintance with the
workings of the mass media.

A Lawyer "Uses" The Press

ELMER GERTZ

With increasing fervor, the judiciary and the legal profession generally have been calling for some firm measure of control over the parties, the attorneys, the court personnel including the judges, and, not least of all, the communications media, so that the "supreme good" of justice will be assured in criminal cases. As the Supreme Court and the lesser courts have reversed conviction after conviction because of community prejudice engendered by the press, as in the instances of Estes, Sheppard and Ruby, the American Bar Association, judicial conferences and others have sought to formulate codes of conduct for all participants and reporters, with heavy sanctions for violations. The aim has been to create the sort of cloistered atmosphere that is supposed to exist in England where the reporting of certain legal proceedings, such as criminal cases and divorces, is highly limited, and such limitations strictly enforced. It is not enough to proclaim this or that rule or guideline, we have learned from the situation in New Orleans, where, in connection with the notorious Clay Shaw case, the presiding judge solemnly set forth certain guidelines and then said that he would enforce them only after the trial was over and the mischief done.

The outcry is not alone on the part of those who want strict rules, so as to prevent miscarriages of justice. The communications media, with allies within the legal profession and the halls of justice, have warned of the dire consequences, the constitutional dangers, of any inhibition of the freedom of the press. Such protestations on the part of the press often simply result from the desire to carry on in accustomed ways, regardless of consequences. I know, at first hand, the mischief resulting from rampant reporting—I did not live through the Jack Ruby case in vain. But I know another side to the story as well, and it should be told before opinions harden.

If press excesses have created, at times, the atmosphere making a fair trial and due process of law difficult, if not impossible, then press silence has on many occasions resulted in unjust results. It does no good to pardon an Evans in England, posthumously, after he has been hanged for a murder he did not commit. It would have been much better for there to have been the vigilance and outcry that might have prevented the grossly wrong result.

One must distinguish between publicity-seeking for its own sake (a rather heady dish for most human beings in and out of the legal profession) and the use of publicity for special and limited purposes. There are people who are unhappy unless their activities are fully chronicled by all of the communications media. When the press does not come to them, they go to it, regardless of the effect upon a particular case or cause. They leak information, sometimes indiscreetly. They play to those who play them up, regardless of the consequences. Of course, if one is involved in a sensational case, such as the Leopold or Ruby proceedings, one cannot avoid publicity, even if one is as shy and unseeking as a maiden aunt. The task there is to relax, if necessary, while one is being raped. In such a situation, one can sometimes choose what one will tolerate or permit; but one may be confronted, as I frequently was, with the problem of how to use those who would use us—for legitimate purposes, towards a necessary and proper goal. There may be partially formed rules and practices, but there is nothing scientific about it. There is art, intuition, a gift for such things, and sheer luck.

The press people are shrewd and cynical and they know when they are being used. They resent pushers. They use the would-be users. They reject what is useless, despite the importunities and devices of the publicity-seekers. If they sense that one is essentially in good faith, and that what one seeks from them is legitimate and newsworthy, they are often cooperative. United in a good cause, a lawyer and his cohorts of the press can accomplish a good deal in the quest for justice or in undoing an improper result. They must be a team; neither must be taken advantage of; confidences must be exchanged mutually, and not doled out in a one-sided fashion, begrudgingly or selectively. On very few occasions has my confidence been betrayed by any good reporter; on no occasion have I knowingly harmed any one of the press with whom I have worked.

Now, those who believe that a case is to be tried only in court will protest that what I have said and done are wrong, in violation of the Reardon report, contrary to the canons of my profession. I hope, and at the same time I regret, that they are wrong in fact; no matter how right they may be in theory. It would be wonderful, indeed, if, in all contests between individuals and the state, one could rely totally, to the exclusion of all else, upon the judicial processes, so eloquently and nobly buttressed by the Bill of Rights. As long as men err, as long as there are imperfections, inertia, bureaucracy, corruption, prejudice, uncertainties, and imponderables of all kinds, those of us who are sworn to defend the disadvantaged, the unpopular, the falsely accused or wrongly convicted must use all means that are at our command, not least of all the press. And the press, recognizing that at its best it can be a great crusading instrumentality, must, willingly or unwillingly, accept the responsibility of determining when it will work with or reject the defenders and advocates of those who are in trouble with society.

Let me now give a few personal experiences out of a professional career that approaches its fortieth year. The story could be amplified by me or any other lawyer whose cases have attracted attention.

In 1924, in Chicago, Nathan F. Leopold, Jr. and Richard Loeb, two teenagers, the brilliant sons of wealthy German-Jewish parents, kidnapped and slew young Bobby Franks, crimes so irrationally motivated and unexpected as to shock the entire world. There was an immediate clamor, intensified by the politically ambitious State's Attorney, that the two young men be hanged. Newspapers and magazines everywhere, not excluding relatively staid ones like the *New York Times,* devoted their front pages and a vast amount of space to the sordid story, from the moment the crimes were committed, through the course of their solution, the obtaining of the scarcely believable confessions, the preparation for the trial, the trial (which was really a hearing in aggravation and mitigation, since pleas of guilt were entered), the awaiting of sentence, and beyond that climactic moment. Indeed, during the ensuing generation, the case was the subject of a flood of publicity, intensified on such special occasions as when Loeb was slain in prison in ambiguous circumstances. Students of such matters have declared that, at least as of that date, no criminal case in history received more attention in the press. The atmosphere in the Chicago area was so charged that it is doubtful if any jury could have been uninfluenced by it, especially a jury inflamed by the State's Attorney and his staff, one of whom, named Savage, epitomized the rabid nature of the handling of the case. Clarence Darrow exerted his usual shrewdness and all of his skill as an advocate of understanding and compassion merely to save the lives of the boys. He circumvented the mob clamor and the press frenzy only in that his clients were not hanged, but the judge sentenced the defendants to life plus ninety-nine years and urged that they never be released from prison on parole, although the law of Illinois provided for such ultimate disposition of the most hardened criminals. The State's Attorney filed his solemn certificate that it was a miscarriage of justice not to have hanged the culprits, and he implored posterity to keep them locked up forever.

Thereafter Loeb and Leopold, particularly Leopold, led exemplary lives in prison. Leopold's work in establishing and maintaining a correspondence school that taught inmates more than one hundred subjects has become a classic story; also his sociological research, the eye bank he nurtured, his wartime experimentation in malaria, his personal achievement in mastering many languages. But whatever he did to redeem himself, the shadow of the press hung over him, making his release from prison highly unlikely. Others might be paroled without clamor, but a public, made sensitive by the press, would not tolerate mercy being shown to Leopold.

This was illustrated at the time of the malaria experimentation at Stateville Penitentiary. It was announced that the prisoners who played a role in that dangerous work would receive consideration by the Illinois Parole and Pardon Board and the Governor. Leopold probably did more than anyone else in this venture which led to great medical discoveries; but Governor Green failed to act in his case and, I believe, in his case alone, and his successor, Governor Stevenson, made little more than a token concession. He reduced one of Leopold's sentences, so that he became eligible for parole consideration in 1953, rather than 1958. When the matter came up before the Board at that time, the Board, reflecting the press-engendered public antipathy, not only rejected parole but gave Leopold a savage set, or continuance, of twelve years, making him ineligible for consideration until 1965!

That was the situation when I entered the case formally in the spring of 1957. (Earlier I had been a sort of personal adviser.) Our task was to get Leopold out of prison at that time, rather than in 1965, or in view of his bad health, never. This meant the speedy creation of a different and more favorable climate of public opinion and making Governor Stratton and the Parole Board aware of it and willing to chance criticism. I tell the story with full particularity in my book, *A Handful of Clients*. Here I summarize the story in the light of further reflection since the publication of my book.

Where earlier the press had been Leopold's enemy, he and I had to turn the media and the individual writers and editors into friends. The press had reported his 1924 crimes on each anniversary of the grisly events and on other appropriate and inappropriate occasions as well in virtually the same spirit as in the beginning. We could not ask them not to do so, because they would have resented this as an interference with their freedom. But we could give them opportunities to publish more friendly reports. Leopold had turned down all requests for interviews for a considerable period of time, since he and his family felt that this publicity simply acerbated an already bad situation. Now we decided that carefully selected persons would be given the opportunity to tell the truth about his three decades of remorse and rehabilitation. These new genre stories, we felt, would affect public opinion favorably, sooner or later. Thus Gladys Erickson, one of the star crime and human interest reporters for *Chicago's American,* once part of the Hearst empire and now an autonomous part of the *Chicago Tribune* group, was given the chance to talk with Leopold about his many prison activities and accomplishments and she wrote warm friendly accounts of him from 1952 to the time of his ultimate release and beyond. Her viewpoint undoubtedly affected Leopold's jailer, Warden Joseph E. Ragen, about whom she wrote a book prior to Leopold's release. Increasingly, Ragen was in Leopold's corner, letting it be known that he regarded Leopold as fit for the free world. Either alone or in the company of others, like Ralph G. Newman, I often conferred with the Warden and received from him sage advice on what to do (or not do) to effectuate Leopold's release.

Leopold and his family cooperated fully with John Bartlow Martin, one of the best informed of the popular writers on crime. Martin was given access to Leopold's prison "jacket" (the official record of his imprisonment, commencing with the dire statements of the judge and State's Attorney and on through each day thereafter). He wrote a series of factfilled articles for the *Saturday Evening Post* that had a terrific impact everywhere because no one could accuse the author of being anyone's partisan, least of all Leopold's. In due course, Martin got up from a sick bed to testify in Leopold's behalf at the 1958 parole hearing.

Life was permitted to send photographers and reporters to Stateville, and this led to a highly sympathetic picture story of the too-long–imprisoned man.

Marcia Winn, a perceptive and somewhat unsentimental feature writer for the *Chicago Tribune,* was allowed to tape-record an interview with Leopold. Although skeptical at first, she became convinced of his genuine rehabilitation and said so in an impressive article in the *Chicago Tribune,* a newspaper long known for its hard line on crime and criminals. Miss Winn went beyond her article; she gave us letters for the Governor and the Board, emphasizing her high opinion of Leopold. Her husband, George

Morganstern, a *Tribune* editorial writer, gave us an equally strong letter, as did Walter Trohan, long the head of the Washington Bureau of the *Tribune*. Trohan's letter was due, at least in part, to a special circumstance—his affection for Leopold's oldest brother and his friendship for Ralph Newman. There were others motivated in the same fashion, among them the great poet and folk figure, Carl Sandburg, who ultimately appeared as a witness at the parole hearing.

Leo Lerner, the highly articulate and sensitive editor of a powerful chain of neighborhood newspapers in the Chicago area, was won over. His papers frequently published articles in support of Leopold's release and then, when I became persuaded that public opinion was now in favor of setting aside the 1924 dictum of Judge Caverly and releasing Leopold, I got him to conduct an impartial poll over a period of weeks and it confirmed my judgment of the situation. There were other polls as well, all indicating that the public was ready to accept Leopold, if those charged with the authority would sanction it.

Gradually, what was at first a trickle became a vast flood of favorable publicity. Governor Stratton was quoted as being disturbed by "the Leopold propaganda machine." Others, like the influential radio and television commentator, Len O'Connor, sneered publicly at what he regarded as an artificial fervor created by Newman and Gertz.

It is difficult now to realize how wide the coverage of the parole hearing was. As at the time of the original crime and trial, there were front-page stories everywhere in the world. Some newspapers had as many as six pages in one day devoted to the matter, including prize-winning photographs.

When Governor Stratton turned down our application for executive clemency in 1957, he stated in an address over television and radio that parole was the time-tried and successful procedure for "terminal rehabilitation" in Illinois, and he urged that Leopold was always eligible for parole. In making these statements, the Governor ignored the fact that when the board had denied parole to him in 1953 it had continued further consideration of the matter for twelve years, that is, until 1965. This meant that, contrary to what the Governor stated, Leopold was not eligible for consideration unless, somehow, we could persuade the board to reconsider its ruling. There were provisions in the law for applications for rehearing, but it was expressly required that these applications could be considered only on the basis of new evidence. What new evidence was there? We could argue that the continuing rehabilitation of Leopold and the unjustness of keeping him in prision while others were released was such "new evidence." But would this argument be entertained?

At this time I had unusually close relationship with some people connected with the *Chicago Tribune,* despite my history of opposition to the *Tribune,* climaxed by my pamphlet, *The People vs. The Chicago Tribune,* which the *Tribune* had described as the most scurrilous pamphlet ever written. Could I use that relationship to dramatize the application for rehearing, to impress the public and board with respect to it? The surviving members of Leopold's family winced at the slightest reference to him in the press. They were unable even to think clearly on such matters, and I could not discuss the situation frankly. Indeed, I had to inhibit, conceal, and sometimes misstate my intentions in order to prevent the kicking over of the traces by misguided persons. I discussed the matter with Leopold himself, and he left the decision up to me. There was a further problem—we could not appear to favor one newspaper over another. Anyone who deals with the press knows that what belongs to everyone sometimes is used by no one. The communications media want scoops, exclusive stories. I bore that in mind throughout this case and others. One day I might give a particular reporter or commentator something that I did not give to the others, but I was careful to pass around similar favors to the ones who might be skipped. This is Machiavellian, but effective.

Leopold and I labored over the petition for rehearing. His tendency always has been to be as succinct as possible. Although I generally approve of brevity, I know that there are circumstances in which an eloquent and persuasive plea uses up a lot of words. This was one such occasion. I convinced Leopold of this, and what was drafted was an essay that ran into many pages and thousands of words. It was duly filed with the board and simultaneously I let a star reporter of the *Tribune* know that the document was being filed. The *Tribune* has great persuasive powers. It obtained access to the full document, and the following Sunday, in all editions of that widely circulated newspaper, the main headline and several columns were devoted to giving the gist of our petition and the most telling passages in full. It was clear from the context that the *Tribune* approved. Whether this was the determining factor in the result I will never know, but I still believe that it did no harm and probably did a world of good. In any event, by a divided vote, the board granted a rehearing, despite its prior continuance of twelve years, and at last we were in the position to present our case for parole. The family never forgave me for this apparent playing with the press, but I still feel that I was fully justified, that without it Leopold might have languished forever in prison.

More than ten years later, Leopold told me:

> The "leaking" of our petition for rehearing, in August 1957, to the Tribune I still think was a master-stroke, with consequences that there just is no way to assess. The additions and emendations you made to the text of that petition; especially the additions and emendations you made to my carefully rehearsed speech to the Board—without any given one of these, the result might well have been different.

Two books were complicating factors in connection with our efforts to get Leopold released from prison—the one his own book, *Life Plus Ninety-Nine Years,* and the other Meyer Levin's book, *Compulsion.* Before it was ever known that Leopold would be released, he wrote a narrative about his years in prison. In the original manuscript, he avoided all references to the commission of the crime and minimized the account of the trial. He tried to confine the book to the process of remorse and rehabilitation which began after he was sentenced in September 1924. Those who read the manuscript in its original form, other than myself, were not unduly impressed by it. I felt that it had substance, both qualitatively and from a literary viewpoint. A publisher saw the manuscript and liked it; he agreed, in fact, to pay a very substantial advance. The editor urged Leopold to add some material about the trial. Reluctantly, he agreed. Dealing with the trial meant, in effect, dealing with the crime, reviving old wounds, at the very time it was essential that Leopold's "image" be a good one. I went through the manuscript and then the printer's proofs with great care. I blue-pencilled several passages which I thought quite dangerous; I added a few sentences and even a paragraph or two. But, essentially, it was Leopold's book as he had written it. Read as a whole, with the changes imposed by me, I was sure that it would do him much good. The book was to be serialized in several newspapers, including the *Chicago Daily News*. Of course, the editor chose the most sensational passages for serial publication and, by chance, such publication occurred at the very time the board was to consider our application for parole. This almost precipitated a disaster. It took much explaining on the part of Leopold and myself to persuade the board not to count the serialization against him. Carl Sandburg helped smooth over matters at the parole hearing when he called the book a masterpiece of its kind. The managing editor of the *Chicago Daily News* wrote to the board, at my request, pointing out that Leopold was not responsible for the time, place, and contents of the serialization. I was told by the editor that it was fortunate that he had intervened. Thus we were learning again that publicity still could be a very dangerous thing, that it did not necessarily work in our favor. For example, there were episodes in the newspaper excerpts about Loeb and Leopold stopping to eat, with an unnaturally good appetite, after the slaying of Bobby Franks, and of the glorious time Leopold had on a date with his favorite girl thereafter. There were statements to indicate that the memory of Loeb was still cherished by Leopold. These things took much and intricate explaining. We worked feverishly before and during the hearing to create exactly the right impression, so as to overcome the initial antipathy. It would have been much better if the book had not appeared until after Leopold's release.

The Levin book, *Compulsion*, was a different story. We had had nothing to do with its publication; Leopold had sought to discourage the writing of it, even offering, by way of consolation, to let Levin work with him on another project. Leopold, while in prison, urged his attorney to take steps to prevent publication of Levin's book and, after it was out, to prevent a movie and play based on it. The novel had first appeared a year prior to our efforts to secure executive clemency. It was a best-seller and still going strong when the parole was under consideration. At that juncture, the play was announced as coming to Chicago. I blustered, threatened to enjoin the play, and it was not shown in Chicago at the time or, indeed, at any time. The moving picture was a different matter; projected before the parole, it was not actually released until later. The whole *Compulsion* mess is involved in litigation that has gone on for a decade. My task in the winter of 1957-1958 was to do what I could to minimize its effect on the public and the officials who would have to determine whether or not to release Leopold. I have given an extended account of the matter in *A Handful of Clients* and in the files of the courts in Chicago. The story is likely to become a classic; but, alas, I cannot say more of it at this time, except to reaffirm that it troubled us sorely while the fate of Leopold was being decided.

Soon I was involved with the Paul Crump case.

Paul Crump had been convicted of slaying a guard at a Chicago stock yards plant in particularly brutal circumstances, and sentenced to death. Protesting his innocence, he had appealed to the Illinois Supreme Court and the conviction was set aside because it was not revealed that the chief witness against him was a drug addict. Tried again, he was once more convicted and sentenced to death. This time, no court disturbed the verdict and it seemed only a matter of time until he would pay with his life. In his first days at the Cook County jail, Crump was a savage creature, determined, it seemed, to die with a snarl on his lips. The warden, Jack Johnson, then rightly regarded as a compassionate and wise penologist, worked on the virile, handsome, and antagonistic young man until he won his respect. Others, too—principally the Episcopalian priest Father James Jones and the Assistant Warden, Hans Mattick—helped to transform Crump into a warmhearted, thoughtful, and creative human being. His good works at the jail became known to those within the confines of the institution, but it was unlikely that they would result in the saving of his life. He began to read a good deal and then to write, at first poetry and then a novel, which was ultimately published as *Burn, Killer, Burn!* It was a remarkable achievement for a Negro with little education, who had lived a sordid life. Bit by bit, outsiders began to learn of this remarkable candidate for the electric chair; among them were Miriam Rumwell of the Chicago office of *Time* magazine, Bill Friedkin, the brilliant young radio and television director, and Lois Solomon, editor of a four-page periodical called *The Paper*. I was nominally the publisher and, in truth, the author of many of the leading articles that appeared in *The Paper*. We devoted an entire issue to Paul Crump—his story as we thought we knew it, specimens of his poetry, and photographs of him by Ted Williams that managed to capture the quality that persuaded many people that his life ought to be spared. It was the first favorable publicity about Crump that appeared anywhere. Some people took notice of it. He became more than a name to them.

There was a Negro newspaper at that time in Chicago known as the *Courier,* an offspring of the Pittsburgh periodical of the same name. It was edited by Paul Hunter, a white man. He saw in Paul Crump the subject of a crusade. Encouraged by those of us who were striving to save Crump's life, he managed to publish a continuous series of exciting front-page articles on Crump.

John Johnson, publisher of *Ebony,* was encouraged to undertake the publication of Crump's novel. His magazines told of the remarkable story of the young man whose life was about to be snuffed out.

Before long, it became more than a local story. *Life,* prodded by Miriam Rumwell, devoted some pages to the case in a sympathetic spirit.

One could sense the growing support for the once unknown convict. His name became familiar to an increasingly large number of persons, even to the man in the street.

In his book, *The Jury Returns,* Louis Nizer has a long opening section dealing with the Paul Crump case. It tells of the crime, the trials, the appellate reviews, Crump's experiences in prison, and then gives a detailed account of the hearing, in which Nizer and Donald Page Moore appear publicly as Crump's lawyers. The account of the commutation hearing is accurate as far as it goes, but it does not go far enough. Nizer did not enter the case until its last two or three days. When he got into it he did a very brilliant job and deserves much of the credit for the result. The difficulty, however, is that he did not know what had preceded his entrance into the case, or, if he knew, he chose not to deal with it. The truth of the matter is that there was a long campaign preceding the commutation hearing. In it many persons were involved, including myself. With excessive generosity, Crump has overstated my role and, privately but not publicly, Donald Page Moore has expressed very great gratitude. I mention the fact not for the purpose of self-praise, but as a necessary prelude to an account of the manipulation of the communications media and the public in the successful effort to save Crump's life. If this work had not been done, the hearing would have been of no avail—Nizer or no Nizer. My own feeling is that the appearance of Crump on a television program of Irving Kupcinet, the widely influential newspaper columnist and television and radio personality, meant perhaps as much as the hearing. It was unprecedented that a condemned man should be permitted to participate in such a program, even if it was taped at the place of confinement. The program was fortuitous. That brilliant and compassionate young woman, then known as Lois Solomon, was the sister-in-law of Irving Kupcinet. She was, as I have pointed out, one of the very earliest advocates of Crump and interested Donald Page Moore and myself in his cause. She interested Kup in it and when she felt that his proposed program would lack the most persuasive participants, she unloosed me upon her brother-in-law. I persuaded him to add Hans Mattick, the former Assistant Warden at the County Jail, and Mattick made up for some of the deficiencies of the others. It was necessary that he be on the program, in view of the fact that the prosecutor was also on the program. The prosecutor, either through embarrassment at confronting his victim, or because of some change of heart, was easier on Crump than might have been expected. The public could well form the conclusion that he no longer believed in the devastating penalty that he had brought about. Far and away the most effective member of the panel was Crump himself. Anyone observing him, no matter how critically, would have concluded that it would be tragic to execute such a person. There can be no doubt that, if not the Governor and members of the Parole Board, then persons close to them viewed and were affected by the program. This was a high point, but it did not stand alone. There were many other radio and television programs, in none of which Crump himself participated, but his spirit pervaded all of these programs. Moore, I, and a few others participated in a long session moderated by the highly influential Studs Terkel. This program was played and replayed on several occasions prior to the commutation hearing. It is in the permanent archives of prize-winning FM radio station WFMT and has been replayed several times during the ensuing years. It was reprinted in the station's magazine.

If I may sum up my own role in the case, it was to act more as a public relations consultant than as a lawyer. I influenced every journalist I knew in Crump's behalf. The result was editorials and columns and news articles in periodicals in and out of Illinois. I persuaded the *St. Louis Post Dispatch* to run a leading editorial, the various newspapers of the Paul Simon downstate chain and others to do likewise. I wrote articles myself and I was interviewed by John Justin Smith and others.

Smith played an extremely important role. Very early he was persuaded of the rehabilitation of Crump and he filled his column with accounts of it, including front page interviews with me when he wanted enlightenment on various legal and quasi-legal points. Smith persisted even in the face of opposition by some of his colleagues. He helped create the image of Crump as a completely rehabilitated person. By the time of the commutation hearing he was so emotionally involved that he had to flee to a retreat in Wisconsin. He had a bad case of nerves and reached the conclusion that all of the efforts were to be unsuccessful, as did my own secretary.

In any such campaign it is sometimes as important not to say things as to say them. We deeply hurt one of our strongest adherents, the brilliant young Bill Friedkin, when we decided that it was too dangerous to release the program that he had prepared for the ABC network. Viewed after the events, it was a powerful program and it won several national and even international awards, but at the time it seemed to us that its hostility towards the police would cause every law enforcement officer in Chicago to hasten forth to attack Crump. I remember spending some time with

Sterling Quinlan, who then headed the ABC office in Chicago. Quinlan is as vibrant a personality as his nickname, "Red," would suggest. He was committed enough to Crump's cause to listen attentively as I talked with him, and at some great sacrifice he agreed that the program would not be aired until after the result was announced by the Governor. I know that I was not alone in persuading "Red." Donald Moore was especially vehement. There was a private viewing of the tape. Many thought it a very effective show; others, like myself, were fearful. As I learned from Nathan Leopold, when you are in doubt in such matters, the safest counsel to follow is the most conservative. If there is a chance that something may hurt, then don't do it.

The press played a decisive role, as we have seen, in the effort to save Paul Crump's life. Having accomplished this laudable result, it thereupon lost its touch with the realities of the situation. Within a matter of months, the communications media began to persuade the public, on the flimsiest of evidence, that Crump was not, after all, rehabilitated, that perhaps the commutation of his death sentence was a mistake. Perhaps, we were somewhat to blame for this through our very desire to do the right thing. We decided that having been so widely publicized, Crump ought to retreat from the limelight, serve a period of time in prison, then make an effort to be released. Theoretically, this was perfect; everyone applauded our decision. But one day a *Chicago Tribune* reporter, not known for tenderness toward criminals (he had been one of the few *Tribune* men hostile to Leopold), visited Pontiac Penitentiary in order to interview Crump. He had the Warden's blessing; indeed, he had been shown, improperly I believe, the prisoner's "jacket" or confidential file. Crump refused to talk with him unless he had my approval. A call was placed to me from the Warden's office by the reporter. I explained our viewpoint. Having received a turndown from me, he called Donald Page Moore, my predecessor in the case, the lawyer who had done so much for Crump, but was no longer connected with the case by his own choice. Moore was not told that I had turned down the reporter. He, on his own, reached the same conclusion. It was not until years later, when a national magazine began making inquiry, that we exchanged recollections and learned of the shenanigans of which the press is sometimes capable. In any event, the *Tribune* published a story telling of Crump's reprehensible conduct—he had loitered near a drinking fountain one hot July day; someone regarded his writing (acclaimed elsewhere) as obscene; he had not sufficiently humbled himself before a certain corrupt guard. An official of the state's penal system was quoted as saying that the trouble was that Crump (who had closed the door on publicity) craved publicity! The other newspapers and the radio and television people immediately swallowed the line of no-rehabilitation. There were editorials and news articles to that effect. A mischievous myth was born. It still prevails. It has done incalculable harm to Crump and to the penal system. It makes it difficult to press Crump's claim for release and hardens arguments for executive clemency in other cases.

How was I, Crump's attorney and friend, to respond to this unfair reporting and its repercussions? When CBS broadcast an editorial attacking Crump, they gave me equal time to reply. I appeared on various radio and television programs. When the *Chicago Daily News* editorialized against Crump, I acquainted one of its star columnists with the facts and he verified them. He again devoted columns to the defense of Crump. Still matters went from bad to worse, affecting Crump's emotional well-being.

While Louis Nizer was preparing his long essay on Paul Crump, he talked and wrote to me about his intentions. He was assured by his publisher that this was the most powerful writing that he had ever done, and the excerpts I read pleased me very much. Nizer thought that when his book came out it would be widely circulated, an eventuality he could justly anticipate, in view of the very great success enjoyed by *My Days in Court*. The Crump section would be the leadoff of the book. It would receive the widest possible attention. It would set in motion an irresistible effort to get Crump out of prison. In theory this was sound, but, in fact, Nizer's hopes did not materialize. The book sold well, but not as well as his earlier work. It was reviewed well, but not as well as his earlier work. The pages on Crump received some attention, chiefly in the review that I myself wrote for the *Chicago Daily News*, but there was scarcely a ripple of interest engendered by it for a campaign to free Crump. By the perverse logic of some people, it may even have forestalled such a campaign. In the course of my own efforts in behalf of Crump, I talked with many people about him and was amazed at how few referred to him in the context of what Nizer had written. Indeed, I can not recall even one instance. The book has now gone into a paperback edition and will, undoubtedly, sell widely. Perhaps there will be a delayed response. If such is the case, there is as yet no indication of it.

From the very beginning there were press complications with respect to the Jack Ruby case and they never really were solved. The Dallas community had been subjected to an experience that was excessively traumatic—the assassination of the President compounded by the assassination of his assassin. Immediately there was created an atmosphere, throughout the world, in which the Dallas Establishment was suspect. There were not alone suspicions, but charges of all kinds, whispered, shouted and in print. If anything, the situation is being worsened, rather than improved, as the demonologists like Mark Lane, Harold Weisberg and their ilk are being given credence and support by the irrepressible District Attorney of New Orleans, Jim Garrison. Before and during the Ruby trial, the Dallas community was outraged by the presence of "foreigners," outsiders who had no sympathy for their institutions, such as the chief counsel for the defense, Melvin Belli, and the learned psychiatrists he had brought with him to the embattled city. It was little wonder that there was a death verdict by the jury, and the hysterical outcry by Belli thereafter. When, after a period in which everything seemed to be tossed up in the air for grabs, my associates and I came into the case, there was still an atmosphere that was un-Texan insofar as the Dallas community was concerned. True, Phil Burleson, who was of and for Dallas, was still on the case, as he had been with Belli, but now somewhat higher in authority and esteem; and Sam Houston Clinton, Jr., another Texan, was on the defense team, but he was from Austin, not Dallas, and he was connected with such outlandish agencies as the Texas Civil Liberties Union and the trade unions. The others of us gave the defense its leadership and tone, and it was not Texan. There were Sol A. Dann from Detroit, William M. Kunstler from New York, and I from Chicago, all three of us Jews, active liberals, articulate and uninhibited. Dann was in the midst of his battle with the Chrysler empire; Kunstler was contending against the House Un-American Activities Committee (headed by a Dallas man) and racists everywhere; I was showing my usual devotion to unpopular causes. It was little wonder that it took gigantic effort on our part even to get into the case; the Texas courts wondered why "foreign" attorneys were required by an indigent defendant. Then when we finally got in, we were told that we should hire Texas psychiatrists, rather than "foreigners," in connection with sanity hearings and the new trial, if one were granted. It was little short of miraculous that we finally prevailed, getting the death sentence set aside. We were confident that we would win in the new round, since the higher court removed the case from Dallas. But who knows? It cannot be said that we ever won over the Dallas press. True, they were less hostile than earlier, but it was never clear that they were reconciled to our presence. This was evinced by such things as misquoting Kunstler, publishing the more rabid statements of Dann, and reporting the proceedings at times as if Burleson, the Dallas lawyer, were in command, whereas he was really part of a team of equals. We had to change the atmosphere in the courts unassisted by the kind of communications cooperation I had known in the Leopold and Crump cases.

Sometimes it is a big thing, sometimes a little thing, sometimes you just do not know how bad or small it looms. Big, little, or medium, you desperately want to correct it. In the Ruby case there were several examples of this sort of dilemma; one growing out of the other. I wanted to persuade the public in my native Chicago and ultimately a jury of twelve men and women in Wichita Falls, Texas, that Ruby had killed Oswald by the merest chance; that there was no premeditation or malice in it; that there was not the slightest suggestion of conspiracy. The problem was complicated by one of the curiosities of Texas law—while murder "with malice," of which Ruby had been convicted, might carry a death penalty, the same act of murder "without malice" could be punished by no more than a five-year sentence, and with the additional bonus of time subtracted for any period already spent in jail. One day my friend of the *Chicago Daily News,* John Justin Smith, called me. I regarded him as a friend, not alone because he had been helpful in the Leopold, Crump and Ruby cases, three of the highlights of my professional career, but even more because of his generally compassionate nature. "Elmer," he began, "it is time that I wrote something about you in connection with the Ruby case. What is new?" This was not long after the Texas Court of Criminal Appeals had reversed the death sentence and we were awaiting the re-trial of the case. Thereupon, I ventilated my thoughts about Ruby's being guilty only of murder "without malice" and that he should receive no more than a five-year sentence. "Does this mean that he can get out of jail in as short a time as ninety-days?" he inquired. The mathematics of the situation made this possible, and I said so. The next day there was spread across the entire front page of the *Daily News* my prophecy that my client might be released in ninety days! Len O'Connor, the most skeptical of Chicago's television commentators, devoted his entire program to tearing apart my thesis that Ruby had acted "without malice." "Why was he carrying a gun!" O'Connor demanded to know. This pointed up what my wife had long insisted upon—that in my numerous speeches, interviews and conversations I did not demonstrate sufficiently the innocent nature of Ruby's gun toting. I had thought that everyone knew that in Texas there was a different attitude towards guns than in Chicago, despite our city's unfounded reputation for violence. I called Smith, rather than O'Connor, to explain the matter to him and he in turn fed my information to Virginia Kay, a *Daily News* columnist, who duly printed it. Thereafter I was always careful to indicate the reasons for Ruby's having a gun on his person, unconnected with any desire to shoot Oswald. Whether or not I influenced public thinking on the matter I do not know, but certainly I tried hard enough. This, I am convinced, is a legitimate use of the press.

The Kennedy assassination and its bizarre aftermath have taxed my ingenuity to the utmost. Until the day I die, I suspect, I will have to answer publicly all of the wild and woolly charges with respect to Ruby, some of them touching me personally, as when the taped interview of him was released after his death.

I am persuaded that no matter what is proposed about press limitations, lawyers and the press will always enjoy an intimate relationship. Such, at least, has been my experience. The examples could be multipled.

Bibliography For Chapter Four

BOOKS

American Bar Association. Project on Minimum Standards for Criminal Justice. *Standards Relating to Fair Trial and Free Press.* Chicago: American Bar Association, 1966.

American Newspaper Publishers Association. *Free Press and Fair Trial.* New York: ANPA, 1967.

Friendly, Alfred, and Ronald Goldfarb. *Crime and Publicity: The Impact of News on the Administration of Justice.* Washington: Twentieth Century Fund, 1967.

Gillmor, Donald M. *Free Press and Fair Trial.* Washington: Public Affairs Press, 1966.

Inbau, Fred, ed. *Free Press—Fair Trial: A Report of the Proceedings of a Conference on Prejudicial News Reporting in Criminal Cases.* Chicago: Northwestern University School of Law and Medill School of Journalism, 1964.

Lofton, John. *Justice and the Press.* Boston: Beacon Press, 1966.

Special Committee on Radio and Television of the Association of the Bar of the City of New York. *Radio, Television, and the Administration of Justice.* New York: Columbia University Press, 1965.

ARTICLES

Goggin, Terrence P., and George M. Hanover. "Fair Trial v. Free Press: The Psychological Effect of Pre-Trial Publicity on the Juror's Ability To Be Impartial; A Plea for Reform," *Southern California Law Review,* XXXVIII (1965), 672-688.

Ross, Irwin. "Trial by Newspaper," *The Atlantic,* September, 1965.

CASES

Bridges v. California, 314 U.S. 252 (1941).

181

Craig v. Harney, 331 U.S. 367 (1947).

Estes v. Texas, 381 U.S. 532 (1965).

Irvin v. Dowd, 366 U.S. 717 (1961).

Pennekamp v. Florida, 328 U.S. 331 (1946).

Shepherd v. Florida, 341 U.S. 50 (1951).

Sheppard v. Maxwell, 384 U.S. 333 (1966).

CHAPTER FIVE

A Mass Media By-Product— Invasion of Privacy

As the mass media thrived in an American society becoming more closely governed, more urban, and more of a huge familial complex, an insidious and, more often than not, blatant force crossed the threshold bringing disquiet, discomfort, and distress. This force—the invasion of privacy—steadily grew into a Frankenstein that today is one of the major concerns of both its victims and the thoughtful members of the American family.

There are many reasons for this monstrous growth. Man himself is to blame, for media are the extensions of man and he has always relished the knowledge of the intimate details of the lives and doings of others. Man, too, has always sought order and security in his life and protection from predators. The government, computer-stored statistics, and advanced crime-prevention techniques promise him these prized possessions. In the mass society created by the media many have lost their identity. With this loss of identity, of individuality, many suffer unknowingly or uncomplainingly the indignities of the human spirit accompanying this intrusion upon their private matters. They answer questions from researchers, from organization men, and government officials, fully and freely. They submit readily, almost eagerly, to media invasion. In this mass media society, man tends to become "other-directed." If this were not true, if from pioneer American stock there had evolved that peculiar and admirable "true American," then long before now this intruder on privacy would have been destroyed by a rising mass of angry men.

The judges, who have been confronted in the courtroom more than three hundred times in this century with this illegitimate member of the American family, have reacted in a variety of ways. Some have allowed him to continue his wild growth. Others have erected minor obstacles in his paths. A few have roped off areas from him and have posted signs—signs that he studiously ignores as he snips ropes and wanders into forbidden fields.

In view of the actions of President Kennedy and President Johnson in this area to curtail federal wiretapping (strongly stated in Attorney General Ramsey Clark's Memorandum on Wiretaps, a sweeping regulation of 1967 forbidding all wiretapping and virtually all eavesdropping by Federal agents except in national security cases—the product of a two-year study ordered by President Johnson), one would expect President Nixon to hesitate before reversing this protective trend. This was not the case. Within one month after taking office, he issued a directive allowing wiretapping in the fight against crime.

To forestall a descent by the public into a dangerous pessimism and an overwhelming feeling that control of supersurveillance technology is impossible and that court rulings protecting them from this invasion will not be in the offing in this decade, Congress and the state legislatures should now enact, as Alan Westin advocates, a general statutory system for the control of physical surveillance by new devices. The present dangers are eloquently described by Justice William O. Douglas in the first article in this chapter. The law of privacy is revealed through interpretive law-journal articles. Although Dean Prosser's influential analysis of the tort of privacy has been omitted, his ideas appear in summary form in Edward J. Bloustein's "Privacy as an Aspect of Human Dignity: An Answer to Dean Prosser." Bloustein's thesis —that the tort cases involving privacy are of one piece and involve a single tort (a dignitary tort) and that the "injury is to our individuality, to our dignity as individuals"—is more what we believe the invasion of privacy is all about.

The Present: Inroads on the Right to Privacy

WILLIAM O. DOUGLAS

These cases present important questions of federal law concerning the privacy of our citizens and the breach of that privacy by government agents. *Lewis v. United States* involves the breach of the privacy of the home by a government agent posing in a different role for the purpose of obtaining evidence from the homeowner to convict him of a crime. *Hoffa v. United States* raises the question whether the Government in that case induced a friend of Hoffa's to insinuate himself into Hoffa's entourage, there to serve as the Government's eyes and ears for the purpose of obtaining incriminating evidence. *Osborn v. United States* presents the question whether the Government may compound the invasion of privacy by using hidden recording devices to record incriminating statements made by the unwary suspect to a secret federal agent.

Thus these federal cases present various aspects of the constitutional right of privacy. Privacy, though not expressly mentioned in the Constitution, is essential to the exercise of other rights guaranteed by it. . . .

No one is more eloquent in the defense of the right of privacy than Justice William O. Douglas. This is Mr. Justice Douglas, dissenting in *Osborn v. United States* and *Lewis v. United States,* and concurring with Mr. Justice Clark in *Hoffa v. United States. (Editors.)*

We are rapidly entering the age of no privacy, where everyone is open to surveillance at all times; where there are no secrets from government. The aggressive breaches of privacy by the Government increase by geometric proportions. Wiretapping and "bugging" run rampant, without effective judicial or legislative control.

Secret observation booths in government offices and closed television circuits in industry, extending even to rest rooms, are common.[1] Offices, conference rooms, hotel rooms, and even bedrooms (see *Irvine v. California*, 347 U.S. 128) are "bugged" for the convenience of government. Peepholes in men's rooms are there to catch homosexuals. See *Smayda v. United States*, 352 F. 2d 251. Personality tests seek to ferret out a man's innermost thoughts on family life, religion, racial attitudes, national origin, politics, atheism, ideology, sex, and the like.[2] Federal agents are often "wired" so that their conversations are either recorded on their persons (*Lopez v. United States*, 373 U.S. 427) or transmitted to tape recorders some blocks away.[3] The Food and Drug Administration recently put a spy in a church organization.[4] Revenue agents have gone in the guise of Coast Guard officers.[5] They have broken and entered homes to obtain evidence.[6]

Polygraph tests of government employees and of employees in industry are rampant.[7] The dossiers on all citizens mount in

[1] See generally Hearings before the Subcommittee on Administrative Practice and Procedure of the Senate Committee on the Judiciary, Invasions of Privacy, 89th Cong., 1st Sess. (1965).

[2] See generally Hearings before a Subcommittee of the House Committee on Government Operations, Special Inquiry on Invasion of Privacy, 89th Cong., 1st Sess. (1965); Hearings before the Subcommittee on Constitutional Rights of the Senate Committee on the Judiciary, Psychological Tests and Constitutional Rights, 89th Cong., 1st Sess. (1965).

[3] See, *e.g.*, Hearings before the Subcommittee on Administrative Practice and Procedure, *supra*, n. 1, pt. 2, at 389.

[4] *Id.*, at 783.

[5] *Id.*, pt. 3, at 1356.

[6] *Id.*, at 1379, 1415.

[7] See generally Hearings before a Subcommittee of the House Committee on Government Operations, Use of Polygraphs As "Lie Detectors" By the Federal Government, 88th Cong., 2d Sess. (1964).

number and increase in size. Now they are being put on computers so that by pressing one button all the miserable, the sick, the suspect, the unpopular, the offbeat people of the Nation can be instantly identified.[8]

These examples and many others demonstrate an alarming trend whereby the privacy and dignity of our citizens are being whittled away by sometimes imperceptible steps. Taken individually, each step may be of little consequence. But when viewed as a whole, there begins to emerge a society quite unlike any we have seen—a society in which government may intrude into the secret regions of man's life at will.

We have here in the District of Columbia squads of officers who work the men's rooms in public buildings trying to get homosexuals to solicit them. See *Beard v. Stahr,* 200 F. Supp. 766, 768, judgment vacated, 370 U.S. 41. Undercover agents or "special employees" of narcotics divisions of city, state, and federal police actively solicit sales of narcotics. See generally 31 U. Chi. L. Rev. 137, 74 Yale L. J. 942. Police are instructed to pander to the weaknesses and craven motives of friends and acquaintances of suspects, in order to induce them to inform. See generally Harney & Cross, The Informer in Law Enforcement 33–34 (1960). In many cases the crime has not yet been committed. The undercover agent may enter a suspect's home and make a search upon mere suspicion that a crime will be committed. He is indeed often the instigator of, and active participant in, the crime—an *agent provocateur.* Of course, when the solicitation by the concealed government agent goes so far as to amount to entrapment, the prosecution fails. *Sorrells v. United States,* 287 U.S. 435; *Sherman v. United States,* 356 U.S. 369. But the "dirty business" *(Olmstead v. United States,* 277 U.S. 438, 470 (Mr. Justice Holmes dissenting)) does not begin or end with entrapment. Entrapment is merely a facet of a much broader problem. Together with illegal searches and seizures, coerced confessions, wiretapping, and

---

[8] See generally Hearings before a Subcommittee of the House Committee on Government Operations, The Computer and Invasion of Privacy, 89th Cong., 2d Sess., July 26, 27, and 28, 1966.

bugging, it represents lawless invasion of privacy. It is indicative of a philosophy that the ends justify the means.[9]

We are here concerned with the manner in which government agents enter private homes. In *Lewis* the undercover agent appeared as a prospective customer. Tomorrow he may be a policeman disguised as the grocery deliveryman or telephone repairman, or even a health inspector. . . .[10]

Entering another's home in disguise to obtain evidence is a "search" that should bring into play all the protective features of the Fourth Amendment. When the agent in *Lewis* had reason for believing that petitioner possessed narcotics, a search warrant should have been obtained.[11]

Almost every home is at times used for purposes other than eating, sleeping, and social activities. Are the sanctity of the home and its privacy stripped away whenever it is used for business? If so, what about the "mom and pop" grocery store with

[9] We know from the Hearings before Senate and House Committees that the Government is using such tactics on a gargantuan scale and has become callous of the rights of the citizens.

Hearings before the Subcommittee on Administrative Practice and Procedure of the Senate Committee on the Judiciary, Invasions of Privacy, *supra,* n. 1. pt. 3, at 1477 (1965).

[10] We are told that raids by welfare inspectors to see if recipients of welfare have violated eligibility requirements flout the Fourth Amendment. See Reich, Midnight Welfare Searches and the Social Security Act, 72 Yale L. J. 1347 (1963).

[11] In *Lewis,* a federal narcotics agent, posing as an operator of a bar and grill, went to petitioner's home for the purpose of obtaining narcotics from him. He had no search warrant, though there were grounds for obtaining one. Agent Cass testified that he had been assigned to investigate narcotics activities in the Boston area in June 1963. He became acquainted with one Gold, a friend of petitioner, from whom he learned that one might obtain marihuana from the petitioner. It was then that Agent Cass, representing himself as "Jimmy the Pollack," telephoned the petitioner stating "a friend of ours told me you have some pretty good grass [marihuana]." Petitioner replied, "Yes, he told me about you, Pollack . . . I believe, Jimmy, I can take care of you." When Cass told him that he needed five bags, petitioner gave him his address and directions, and told him to come right over. On the basis of our prior decisions this information would certainly have made a sufficient showing of probable cause to justify the issuance of a warrant. Yet none was sought or obtained. . . .

living quarters in the rear? . . . What about the insurance man who works out of his home? Is the privacy of his home shattered because he sells insurance there? And the candidate who holds political conferences in his home? . . . Are their homes transformed into public places which the Government may enter at will merely because they are occasionally used for business? I think not. A home is still a sanctuary, however the owner may use it. There is no reason why an owner's Fourth Amendment rights cannot include the right to open up his house to limited classes of people. And, when a homeowner invites a friend or business acquaintance into his home, he opens his house to a friend or acquaintance, not a government spy.

This does not mean he can make his sanctuary invasion-proof against government agents. The Constitution has provided a way whereby the home can lawfully be invaded, and that is with a search warrant. Where, as here, there is enough evidence to get a warrant to make a search I would not allow the Fourth Amendment to be short-circuited. . . .

The formula approved today by the Court in *Hoffa v. United States, ante,* p. 293, makes it possible for the Government to use willy-nilly, son against father, nephew against uncle, friend against friend to undermine the sanctity of the most private and confidential of all conversations. The Court takes the position that whether or not the Government "placed" Partin in Hoffa's councils is immaterial. The question of whether the Government planted Partin or whether Hoffa was merely the victim of misplaced confidence is dismissed as a "verbal controversy . . . unnecessary to a decision of the constitutional issues." *Hoffa v. United States, ante,* at 295. But, very real differences underlie the "verbal controversy." As I have said, a person may take the risk that a friend will turn on him and report to the police. But that is far different from the Government's "planting" a friend in a person's entourage so that he can secure incriminating evidence. In the one case, the Government has merely been the willing recipient of information supplied by a fickle friend. In the other, the Government has actively encouraged and participated in a breach of privacy by sending in an undercover agent. If *Gouled* [v. *United States,* 255 U.S. 298] is to be followed, then the Government unlawfully enters a man's home when its agent crawls through a window, breaks down a door, enters surreptitiously, or, as alleged here, gets in by trickery and fraud. I therefore do not join in the *Hoffa* opinion. . . .

Once electronic surveillance, approved in *Lopez v. United States*, 373 U.S. 427, is added to the techniques of snooping which this sophisticated age has developed, we face the stark reality that the walls of privacy have broken down and all the tools of the police state are handed over to our bureaucracy on a constitutional platter. The Court today pays lip service to this danger in *Osborn v. United States*, but goes on to approve what was done in the case for another reason. In *Osborn*, use of the electronic device to record the fateful conversation was approved by the two judges of the District Court in advance of its use.[12] But what the Court overlooks is that the Fourth Amendment does not

[12] The recent regulation of the Federal Communications Commission that bans the use of monitoring devices "unless such use is authorized by all of the parties engaging in the conversation" (31 Fed. Reg. 3400) is of course applicable only when air waves are used; and it does not apply to "operations of any law enforcement officers conducted under lawful authority." *Ibid.* If *Silverman* v. *United States*, 365 U.S. 505, is read in the context of our prior decisions, then the majority view is that the use of an electronic device to record a conversation in the home is not a "search" within the meaning of the Fourth Amendment, unless the device itself penetrates the wall of the home. Section 605 of the Federal Communications Act, 48 Stat. 1103, 47 U.S.C. § 605, that governs the interception of communications made "by wire or radio" reaches only the problem of the persons to whom the message may be disclosed by federal agents as well as others (*Nardone* v. *United States*, 302 U.S. 379, 308 U.S. 338), not the practice itself.

Though § 605 protects communications "by wire or radio," the Court in *On Lee* v. *United States*, 343 U.S. 747, 754, held that § 605 was not violated when a narcotics agent wearing an electronic device entered the combination home and office of a suspect and engaged him in conversation which was broadcast to another agent stationed outside. "Petitioner [the suspect] had no wires and no wireless. There was no interference with any communications facility which he possessed or was entitled to use. He was not sending messages to anybody or using a system of communication within the Act."

If that decision stands, then § 605 extends no protection to messages intercepted by the use of electronic devices banned by the new 1966 Federal Communications Commission rule.

authorize warrants to issue for *any* search even on a showing of probable cause. The first clause of the Fourth Amendment reads:

The right of the people to be secure in their persons, houses, papers, and effects, against unreasonable searches and seizures, shall not be violated. . . .

As held in *Boyd v. United States,* 116 U.S. 616, a validly executed warrant does not necessarily make legal the ensuing search and seizure.

It is not the breaking of his doors, and the rummaging of his drawers, that constitutes the essence of the offence; but it is the invasion of his indefeasible right of personal security, personal liberty and private property, where that right has never been forfeited by his conviction of some public offence—it is the invasion of this sacred right which underlies and constitutes the essence of Lord Camden's judgment. [*Entick v. Carrington,* 19 How. St. Tr. 1029.] Breaking into a house and opening boxes and drawers are circumstances of aggravation; but any forcible and compulsory extortion of a man's own testimony or of his private papers to be used as evidence to convict him of crime or to forfeit his goods, is within the condemnation of that judgment. In this regard the Fourth and Fifth Amendments run almost into each other. *Id.,* at 630.

It was accordingly held in *Gouled* v. *United States, supra,* at 309, that a search warrant "may not be used as a means of gaining access to a man's house or office and papers solely for the purpose of making search to secure evidence to be used against him in a criminal or penal proceeding" but only to obtain contraband articles or the tools with which a crime had been committed. That decision was by a unanimous Court in 1921, the opinion being written by Mr. Justice Clarke. That view has been followed (*United States* v. *Lefkowitz,* 285 U.S. 452, 465; *Harris* v. *United States,* 331 U.S. 145, 154; *United States* v. *Rabinowitz,* 339 U.S. 56, 64) with the result that today a "search" that respects all the procedural proprieties of the Fourth Amendment is nonetheless unconstitutional if it is a "search" for testimonial evidence.

As already indicated, *Boyd* v. *United States, supra,* made clear that if the barriers erected by the Fourth Amendment were not strictly honored, serious invasions of the Fifth Amendment might result. Encouraging a person to talk into a concealed "bug" may not be compulsion within the meaning of the Fifth Amendment. But allowing the transcript to be used as evidence against the accused is using the force and power of the law to make a man talk against his will, just as is the use of a warrant to obtain a letter from the accused's home and allowing it as evidence. "[I]llegitimate and unconstitutional practices get their first footing . . . by silent approaches and slight deviations from legal modes of procedure." 116 U.S., at 635. The fact that the officer could have testified to his talk with Osborn is no answer. Then an issue of credibility between two witnesses would be raised. But the tape recording carrying the two voices is testimony introduced by compulsion and, subject to the defense that the tape was "rigged," is well nigh conclusive proof.

I would adhere to *Gouled* and bar the use of all testimonial evidence obtained by wiretapping or by an electronic device. The dangers posed by wiretapping and electronic surveillance strike at the very heart of the democratic philosophy. A free society is based on the premise that there are large zones of privacy into which the Government may not intrude except in unusual circumstances. As we noted in *Griswold* v. *Connecticut, supra,* various provisions of the Bill of Rights contain this aura of privacy, including the First, Third, Fourth, Fifth, and the Ninth Amendments. As respects the Fourth, this premise is expressed in the provision that the Government can intrude upon a citizen's privacy only pursuant to a search warrant, based upon probable cause, and specifically describing the objects sought. And, the "objects" of the search must be either instrumentalities or proceeds of a crime. But wiretapping and electronic "bugging" invariably involve a search for mere evidence. The objects to be "seized" cannot be particularly described; all the suspect's conversations are intercepted. The search is not confined to a particular time, but may go on for weeks or months. The citizen is completely unaware of the invasion of his privacy. The invasion of privacy is not limited to him, but extends to his friends and acquaintances— to anyone who happens to talk on the telephone with the suspect or who happens to come within range of the electronic device. Their words are also intercepted; their privacy is also shattered. Such devices lay down a dragnet which indiscriminately sweeps in all conversations within its scope, without regard to the nature of the conversations, or the participants. A warrant authorizing such devices is no different from the general warrants the Fourth Amendment was intended to prohibit.

Such practices can only have a damaging effect on our society. Once sanctioned, there is every indication that their use will indiscriminately spread. The time may come when no one can be sure whether his words are being recorded for use at some future time; when everyone will fear that his most secret thoughts are no longer his own, but belong to the Government; when the most confidential and intimate conversations are always open to eager, prying ears. When that time comes, privacy, and with it liberty, will be gone. If a man's privacy can be invaded at will, who can say he is free? If his every word is taken down and evaluated, or if he is afraid every word may be, who can say he enjoys freedom of speech? If his every association is known and recorded, if the conversations with his associates are purloined, who can say he enjoys freedom of association? When such conditions obtain, our citizens will be afraid to utter any but the safest and most orthodox thoughts; afraid to associate with any but the most acceptable people. Freedom as the Constitution envisages it will have vanished.

I would reverse *Lewis* and *Osborn* and dismiss *Hoffa*.

Privacy As An Aspect of Human Dignity: An Answer to Dean Prosser

EDWARD J. BLOUSTEIN

INTRODUCTION

Three-quarters of a century have passed since Warren and Brandeis published their germinal article, "The Right of Pri-

Edward J. Bloustein, formerly a professor of law at New York University School of Law, is now President of Bennington College. Reprinted by permission of President Bloustein and the *New York University Law Review*, from the article of the same title appearing in the *New York University Law Review*, XXXIX (December, 1964), 962-1007.

This article was prepared for the Special Committee on Science and Law of the Association of the Bar of the City of New York and an early version of the paper was delivered at the Committee's Conference on the Impact of Technological Advances on the Law of Privacy held at Sterling Forest, New York, in May 1964. Although the author is indebted to the members of the Committee, especially its Chairman, Oscar Ruebhausen, its Secretary, Bevis Longstreth, and its Research Director, Alan Westin, for many valuable suggestions, the views expressed are the author's and not those of the Committee on Science and Law.

vacy."[1] In this period many hundreds of cases, ostensibly founded upon the right to privacy, have been decided,[2] a number of statutes expressly embodying it have been enacted,[3] and a sizeable scholarly literature has been devoted to it.[4] Remarkably enough, however, there remains to this day considerable confusion concerning the nature of the interest which the right to privacy is designed to protect. The confusion is such that in 1956 a distinguished federal judge characterized the state of the law of privacy by likening it to a "haystack in a hurricane."[5] And, in 1960, the dean of tort scholars wrote a comprehensive article on the subject which, in effect, repudiates Warren and Brandeis by suggesting that privacy is not an independent value at all but rather a composite of the interests in reputation, emotional tranquility and intangible property.[6]

My purpose in this article is to propose a general theory of individual privacy which will reconcile the divergent strands of legal development—which will put the straws back into the haystack. The need for such a theory is pressing. In the first place, the disorder in the cases and commentary offends the primary canon of all science that a single general principle of explanation is to be preferred over a congeries of discrete rules. Secondly, the conceptual disarray has had untoward effects on the courts; lacking a clear sense of what interest or interests are involved

[1] Warren & Brandeis, The Right of Privacy, 4 Harv. L. Rev. 193 (1890) [hereinafter cited as Warren & Brandeis].

[2] See, *e.g.*, Annot., 138 A.L.R. 22 (1942); Annot., 168 A.L.R. 446 (1947); Annot., 14 A.L.R.2d 750 (1950).

[3] N.Y. Civ. Rights Law §§ 50-51; Okla. Stat. Ann. tit. 30, §§ 839-40 (1951); Utah Code Ann. §§ 76-4-7, 76-4-9 (1953); Va. Code Ann. § 8-650 (1950).

[4] E.g., Feinberg, Recent Developments in the Law of Privacy, 48 Colum. L. Rev. 713 (1948); Green, Right of Privacy, 27 Ill. L. Rev. 237 (1932); Lisle, Right of Privacy (A Contra View), 19 Ky. L.J. 137 (1931); Nizer, Right of Privacy: A Half Century's Developments, 39 Mich. L. Rev. 526 (1941); O'Brien, The Right of Privacy, 2 Colum. L. Rev. 437 (1902); Winfield, Privacy, 47 L.Q. Rev. 23 (1931); Yankwich, Right of Privacy: Its Development, Scope, and Limitations, 27 Notre Dame Law. 499 (1952).

[5] Ettore v. Philco Television Broadcasting Co., 229 F.2d 481 (3d Cir. 1956) (Biggs, C.J.).

[6] Prosser, Privacy, 48 Calif. L. Rev. 383 (1960) [hereinafter cited as Prosser, Privacy].

in privacy cases has made it difficult to arrive at a judicial consensus concerning the elements of the wrong or the nature of the defenses to it. Thirdly, analysis of the interest involved in the privacy cases is of utmost significance because in our own day scientific and technological advances have raised the spectre of new and frightening invasions of privacy.[7] Our capacity as a society to deal with the impact of this new technology depends, in part, on the degree to which we can assimilate the threat it poses to the settled ways our legal institutions have developed for dealing with similar threats in the past.

The concept of privacy has, of course, psychological, social and political dimensions which reach far beyond its analysis in the legal context;[8] I will not deal with these, however, except incidentally. Nor do I pretend to give anything like a detailed exposition of the requirements for relief and the character of the available defenses in the law of privacy. Nor will my analysis touch on privacy problems of organizations and groups. My aim is rather the more limited one of discovering in the welter of cases and statutes the interest or social value which is sought to be vindicated in the name of individual privacy.

I propose to accomplish this by examining in some detail Dean Prosser's analysis of the tort of privacy and by then suggesting the conceptual link between the tort and the other legal contexts in which privacy finds protection. My reasons for taking this route rather than another, for concentrating initially on the tort cases and Dean Prosser's analysis of them, are that privacy began its modern history as a tort and that Dean Prosser is by far the most influential contemporary exponent of the tort. Warren and Brandeis who are credited with "discovering" privacy thought

[7] See, e.g., Brenton, The Privacy Invaders (1964); Dash, Knowlton & Schwartz, The Eavesdroppers (1959); Gross, The Brain Watchers (1962); Packard, The Naked Society (1964); Big Brother 7074 is Watching You, Popular Science, March 1963; 1410 Is Watching You, Time, Aug. 1963; Hearings Before the Subcommittee on the Use of Polygraphs as "Lie Detectors" By the Federal Government of the House Committee on Government Operations, 88th Cong., 2d Sess., pt. 3 (1964).

[8] See, e.g., Arendt, The Human Condition (1958); Hoffer, The True Believer: Thoughts on the Nature of Mass Movements (1951); Orwell, 1984 (1949).

of it almost exclusively as a tort remedy. However limited and inadequate we may ultimately consider such a remedy, the historical development in the courts of the concept of privacy stems from and is almost exclusively devoted to the quest for such a civil remedy. We neglect it, therefore, only at the expense of forsaking the valuable insights which seventy-five years of piecemeal common law adjudication can provide.

The justification for turning my own search for the meaning of privacy around a detailed examination of Dean Prosser's views on the subject is simply that his influence on the development of the law of privacy begins to rival in our day that of Warren and Brandeis.[9] His concept of privacy is alluded to in almost every decided privacy case in the last ten years or so,[10] and it is reflected in the current draft of the Restatement of Torts.[11] Under these

[9] Dean Wade, writing in the Virginia Law Weekly Dicta, Oct. 8, 1964, p. 1, col. 1, described the influence of Dean Prosser in this fashion:

> Another event took place some four years ago which may quickly bring the state of the law to maturity, and may also modify the habit of referring to the Warren-Brandeis article as both the origin and the true description of the nature of the right [to privacy]. This was the publication by William L. Prosser of an article entitled very simply *Privacy*, in 48 California Law Review 383, in August 1960.

[10] See, e.g., Norris v. Moskin Stores, Inc., 272 Ala. 174, 176, 132 So. 2d 321, 323 (1961); Gill v. Curtis Publishing Co., 38 Cal. 2d 273, 239 P.2d 630 (1952); Carlisle v. Fawcett Publishing, Inc., 201 Cal. App. 2d 733, 734, 20 Cal. Rptr. 405, 411 (Dist. Ct. App. 1962); Werner v. Times-Mirror Co., 193 Cal. App. 2d 111, 118, 14 Cal. Rptr. 208, 214 (Dist. Ct. App. 1961); Felly v. Johnson Publishing Co., 160 Cal. App. 2d 718, 720, 325 P.2d 659, 661 (Dist. Ct. App. 1959); Barbieri v. News Journal Publishing Co., 189 A.2d 773, 774 (Del. 1963); McAndrews v. Roy, 131 So. 2d 256, 261 (Fla. 1961); Harms v. Miami Daily News, Inc., 127 So. 2d 715, 717 (Fla. 1961); Ford Motor Co. v. Williams, 108 Ga. App. 21, 29-30 nn.6 & 7, 132 S.E.2d 206, 211 nn.6 & 7 (1964); Peterson v. Idaho First Nat'l Bank, 83 Idaho 578, 583, 367 P.2d 284, 287 (1961); Yoder v. Smith, 253 Iowa 506, 507, 112 N.W.2d 862 (1962); Bremmer v. Journal-Tribune Publishing Co., 247 Iowa 817, 821, 76 N.W.2d 762, 764 (1956); Carr v. Watkins, 227 Md. 578, 583, 585-86, 177 A.2d 841, 843, 845-46 (1962); Hawley v. Professional Credit Bureau, 245 Mich. 500, 514, 325 P.2d 659, 671 (1956); Hubbard v. Journal Publishing Co., 67 N.M. 473, 475, 368 P.2d 147, 148-49 (1961); Spahn v. Messner, Inc., 43 Misc. 2d 219, 221, 250 N.Y.S.2d 529, 532 (Sup. Ct. 1964).

[11] "[T]here is every reason to expect that when the second edition of the

circumstances, if he is mistaken, as I believe he is, it is obviously important to attempt to demonstrate his error and to attempt to provide an alternative theory.

DEAN PROSSER'S ANALYSIS
OF THE PRIVACY CASES

Although it is not written in the style of an academic exposé of a legal myth, Dean Prosser's 1960 article on privacy has that effect; although he does not say it in so many words, the clear consequence of his view is that Warren and Brandeis were wrong, and their analysis of the tort of privacy a mistake. For, after examining the "over three hundred cases in the books,"[12] in which a remedy has ostensibly been sought for the same wrongful invasion of privacy, he concludes that, in reality, what is involved "is not one tort, but a complex of four."[13] A still more surprising conclusion is that these four torts involve violations of "four different interests,"[14] none of which, it turns out, is a distinctive interest in privacy.[15]

The "four distinct torts" which are discovered in the cases are described by Dean Prosser as follows:

1. Intrusion upon the plaintiff's seclusion or solitude, or into his private affairs.
2. Public disclosure of embarrassing facts about the plaintiff.
3. Publicity which places the plaintiff in a "false light" in the public eye.

Restatement on Torts is completed and adopted by the American Law Institute, [Dean Prosser's] analysis will be substituted for the very generalized treatment now to be found in section 867." Wade, supra note 9. Dean Prosser, it should be noted, is the Reporter for the Restatement of the Law Second, Torts, and Dean Wade is one of his advisers.

12 Prosser, Privacy 388.

13 Id. at 389.

14 Ibid. Actually, Dean Prosser subsequently identifies only three distinct interests since, in his view, both the public disclosure and the "false light" cases involve the same interest in reputation. See note 18 infra and accompanying text.

15 Prosser, Privacy 389-407, 422-23.

4. Appropriation, for the defendant's advantage, of the plaintiff's name or likeness.[16]

The interest protected by each of these torts is: in the intrusion cases, the interest in freedom from mental distress,[17] in the public disclosure and "false light" cases, the interest in reputation,[18] and in the appropriation cases, the proprietary interest in name and likeness.[19]

Thus, under Dean Prosser's analysis, the much vaunted and discussed right to privacy is reduced to a mere shell of what it has pretended to be. Instead of a relatively new, basic and independent legal right protecting a unique, fundamental and relatively neglected interest, we find a mere application in novel circumstances of traditional legal rights designed to protect well-identified and established social values. Assaults on privacy are transmuted into a species of defamation, infliction of mental distress and misappropriation. If Dean Prosser is correct, there is no "new tort" of invasion of privacy, there are rather only new ways of committing "old torts." And, if he is right, the social value or interest we call privacy is not an independent one, but is only a composite of the value our society places on protecting mental tranquility, reputation and intangible forms of property.

* * *

Dean Prosser has described the privacy cases in tort as involving "not one tort, but a complex of four,"[20] as "four disparate torts under . . . [a] common name."[21] And he believes that the reason the state of the law of privacy is "still that of a haystack in a hurricane," as Chief Judge Biggs said in *Ettore v. Philco Television Broadcasting Co.,* [22] is that we have failed to "separate and distinguish" these four torts.[23]

16 Id. at 389.
17 Id. at 392, 422.
18 Id. at 398, 401, 422-23; see note 14 supra.
19 Id. at 406, 423.
20 Prosser, Privacy 389.
21 Id. at 408.
22 229 F.2d 481 (3d Cir. 1956).
23 Prosser, Privacy 407. See also notes 181 & 188 supra.

I believe to the contrary that the tort cases involving privacy are of one piece and involve a single tort. Furthermore, I believe that a common thread of principle runs through the tort cases, the criminal cases involving the rule of exclusion under the fourth amendment, criminal statutes prohibiting peeping toms, wiretapping, eavesdropping, the possession of wiretapping and eavesdropping equipment, and criminal statutes or administrative regulations prohibiting the disclosure of confidential information obtained by government agencies.

The words we use to identify and describe basic human values are necessarily vague and ill-defined. Compounded of profound human hopes and longings on the one side and elusive aspects of human psychology and experience on the other, our social goals are more fit to be pronounced by prophets and poets than by professors. We are fortunate, then, that some of our judges enjoy a touch of the prophet's vision and the poet's tongue.

Before he ascended to the bench, Justice Brandeis had written that the principle which underlies the right to privacy was "that of an inviolate personality."[24] Some forty years later, in the *Olmstead* case,[25] alarmed by the appearance of new instruments of intrusion upon "inviolate personality," he defined the threatened interest more fully.

The makers of our Constitution undertook to secure conditions favorable to the pursuit of happiness. They recognized the significance of man's spiritual nature, of his feeling and of his intellect. . . . They sought to protect Americans in their beliefs, their thoughts, their emotions and their sensations. They conferred as against the government, the right to be let alone—the most comprehensive of rights and the right most valued by civilized men.[26]

Other Justices of our Supreme Court have since repeated, elucidated and expanded upon this attempt to define privacy as an aspect of the pursuit of happiness.[27]

---

24 Warren & Brandeis 205.
25 Olmstead v. United States, 277 U.S. 438 (1928).
26 Id. at 478.
27 See, e.g., Poe v. Ullman, 367 U.S. 497, 522 (1961) (dissenting opinion of Harlan, J.); Public Util. Comm'n v. Pollak, 343 U.S. 451, 467 (1952) (dissenting

More obscure judges, writing in the more mundane context of tort law, have witnessed this same connection. In two of the leading cases in the field, *Melvin v. Reid*[28] and *Pavesich v. New England Life Ins. Co.*[29]—one a so-called public disclosure case, the other a so-called appropriation or "false light" case—the right to recovery was founded upon the state constitution provision insuring the pursuit of happiness.[30] Judge Cobb, writing in *Pavesich,* declared:

> An individual has a right to enjoy life in any way that may be most agreeable and pleasant to him, according to his temperament and nature, provided that in such enjoyment he does not invade the rights of his neighbor or violate public law or policy. The right of personal security is not fully accorded by allowing an individual to go through his life in possession of all his members and his body unmarred; nor is his right to personal liberty fully accorded by merely allowing him to remain out of jail or free from other physical restraints. . . .
>
> Liberty includes the right to live as one will, so long as that will does not interfere with the rights of another or of the public. One may desire to live a life of seclusion; another may desire to live a life of publicity; still another may wish to live a life of privacy as to certain matters and of publicity as to others. . . . Each is entitled to a liberty of choice as to his manner of life, and neither an individual nor the public has a right to arbitrarily take away from him his liberty.[31]

Some may find these judicial visions of the social goal embodied in the right to privacy vague and unconvincing. I find them most illuminating. Unfortunately, the law's vocabulary of mind is exceedingly limited. Our case law too often speaks of distress, anguish, humiliation, despair, anxiety, mental illness, indignity, mental suffering, and psychosis without sufficient discrimination of the differences between them. Justice Brandeis and Judge Cobb help us see, however, that the interest served in the

opinion of Douglas, J.); Goldman v. United States, 316 U.S. 129, 136 (1942) (dissenting opinion of Murphy, J.).

[28] 112 Cal. App. 285, 297 Pac. 91 (Dist. Ct. App. 1931).

[29] 122 Ga. 190, 50 S.E. 68 (1905).

[30] 112 Cal App. 285, 297 Pac. 91 (Dist. Ct. App. 1931); 122 Ga. 190, 50 S.E. 68 (1905).

[31] 122 Ga. 190, 195-96, 50 S.E. 68, 70 (1905).

privacy cases is in some sense a spiritual interest rather than an interest in property or reputation. Moreover, they also help us understand that the spiritual characteristic which is at issue is not a form of trauma, mental illness or distress, but rather individuality or freedom.

An intrusion on our privacy threatens our liberty as individuals to do as we will, just as an assault, a battery or imprisonment to our person does. And just as we may regard these latter torts as offenses "to the reasonable sense of personal dignity,"[32] as offensive to our concept of individualism and the liberty it entails, so too should we regard privacy as a dignitary tort.[33] Unlike many other torts, the harm caused is not one which may be repaired and the loss suffered is not one which may be made good by an award of damages. The injury is to our individuality, to our dignity as individuals, and the legal remedy represents a social vindication of the human spirit thus threatened rather than a recompense for the loss suffered.

What distinguishes the invasion of privacy as a tort from the other torts which involve insults to human dignity and individuality is merely the means used to perpetrate the wrong. The woman who is indecently petted[34] suffers the same indignity as the woman whose birth pangs are overseen.[35] The woman whose photograph is exhibited for advertising purposes[36] is degraded and demeaned as surely as the woman who is kept aboard a pleasure yacht against her will.[37] In all of these cases there is an interference with individuality, an interference with the right of the individual to do what he will. The difference is in the character of the interference. Whereas the affront to dignity in the one category of cases is affected by physical interference with the

---

[32] The phrase is used in the Restatement of Torts to describe an "offensive battery," i.e., one not involving bodily harm. Restatement, Torts § 18 (1934).

[33] Gregory and Kalven describe privacy as a dignitary tort in the index to their casebook, but seem to treat it as within the mental distress category in the text. See Gregory & Kalven, Cases on Torts 883-99, 1307 (1959).

[34] Hatchett v. Blacketer, 162 Ky. 266, 172 S.W. 533 (1915).

[35] DeMay v. Roberts, 46 Mich. 160, 9 N.W. 146 (1881).

[36] Flake v. Greensboro News Co., 212 N.C. 780, 195 S.E. 55 (1938).

[37] Whittaker v. Sanford, 110 Me. 77, 85 Atl. 399 (1912).

person, the affront in the other category of cases is affected, among other means, by physically intruding on personal intimacy and by using techniques of publicity to make a public spectacle of an otherwise private life.

The man who is compelled to live every minute of his life among others and whose every need, thought, desire, fancy or gratification is subject to public scrutiny, has been deprived of his individuality and human dignity. Such an individual merges with the mass. His opinions, being public, tend never to be different; his aspirations, being known, tend always to be conventionally accepted ones; his feelings, being openly exhibited, tend to lose their quality of unique personal warmth and to become the feelings of every man. Such a being, although sentient, is fungible; he is not an individual.

The conception of man embodied in our tradition and incorporated in our Constitution stands at odds to such human fungibility. And our law of privacy attempts to preserve individuality by placing sanctions upon outrageous or unreasonable violations of the conditions of its sustenance. This, then, is the social value served by the law of privacy, and it is served not only in the law of tort, but in numerous other areas of the law as well.

To be sure, this identification of the interest served by the law of privacy does not of itself "solve" any privacy problems; it does not furnish a ready-made solution to any particular case of a claimed invasion of privacy. In the first place, not every threat to privacy is of sufficient moment to warrant the imposition of civil liability or to evoke any other form of legal redress. We all are, and of necessity must be, subject to some minimum scrutiny of our neighbors as a very condition of life in a civilized community. Thus, even having identified the interest invaded, we are left with the problem whether, in the particular instance, the intrusion was of such outrageous and unreasonable character as to be made actionable.

Secondly, even where a clear violation of privacy is made out, one must still face the question whether it is not privileged or excused by some countervailing public policy or social interest. The most obvious such conflicting value is the public interest in news and information which, of necessity, must sometimes run counter to the individual's interest in privacy.[38] Again, identification of the nature of the privacy interest does not resolve the conflict of values, except insofar as it makes clear at least one of the elements which is to be weighed in the balance.

One may well ask, then, what difference it makes whether privacy is regarded as involving a single interest, a single tort, or four? What difference whether the tort of invasion of privacy is taken to protect the dignity of man and whether this same interest is protected in non-tort privacy contexts?

The study and understanding of law, like any other study, proceeds by way of generalization and simplification. To the degree that relief in the law courts under two different sets of circumstances can be explained by a common rule or principle, to that degree the law has achieved greater unity and has become a more satisfying and useful tool of understanding. Conceptual unity is not only fulfilling in itself, however; it is also an instrument of legal development.

Dean Prosser complains of "the extent to which defenses, limitations and safeguards established for the protection of the defendant in other tort fields have been jettisoned, disregarded, or ignored" in the privacy cases.[39] Because he regards intrusion as a form of the infliction of mental distress, it comes as a surprise and cause for concern that the courts, in the intrusion cases, have not insisted upon "genuine and serious mental harm," the normal requirement in the mental distress cases.[40] Because he believes the public disclosure cases and the "false light" cases involve injury to reputation, he is alarmed that the courts in these cases have jettisoned numerous safeguards—the defense of truth and the requirement, in certain cases, of special damages, for instance—which were erected in the law of defamation to preserve a proper balance between the interest in reputation and

---

[38] See, e.g., Sidis v. F-R Publishing Corp., 113 F.2d 806, 809 (2d Cir. 1940); Hubbard v. Journal Publishing Co., 69 N.M. 473, 475, 368 P.2d 147, 148 (1962); Franklin, A Constitutional Problem in Privacy Protection: Legal Inhibitions on Reporting of Fact, 16 Stan. L. Rev. 107 (1963).

[39] Prosser, Privacy 422.

[40] Ibid.

the interest in a free press.[41] And because he conceives of the use of name and likeness cases as involving a proprietary interest in name or likeness comparable to a common law trade name or trademark, he is puzzled that there has been "no hint" in these cases "of any of the limitations which have been considered necessary and desirable in the ordinary law of trade-marks and trade names."[42]

The reason for Dean Prosser's concern and puzzlement in each instance is based on his prior identification of the interest the tort remedy serves. If the intrusion cases serve the purpose of protecting emotional tranquility, certain legal consequences concerning necessary allegations and defenses appropriate to the protection of that interest seem to follow. The same is true for the other categories of cases as well. If he is mistaken in his identification of the interest involved in the privacy cases, however, the development of the tort will take—actually, as I have shown above, it has already taken—an entirely different turn, and will have entirely different dimensions.

The interest served by the remedy determines the nature of the cause of action and the available defenses because it enters into the complex process of weighing and balancing of conflicting social values which courts undertake in affording remedies. Therefore, my suggestion that all of the tort privacy cases involve the same interest in preserving human dignity and individuality has important consequences for the development of the tort. If this, rather than emotional tranquility, reputation or the monetary value of a name or likeness is involved, courts will be faced by the need to compromise and adjust an entirely different set of values, values more similar to those involved in battery, assault and false imprisonment cases than in mental distress, defamation and misappropriation cases.

The identification of the social value which underlies the privacy cases will also help to determine the character of the development of new legal remedies for threats posed by some of the

[41] Id. at 422-23.
[42] Id. at 423.

aspects of modern technology. Criminal statutes which are intended to curb the contemporary sophisticated electronic forms of eavesdropping and evidentiary rules which forbid the disclosure of the fruits of such eavesdropping can only be assimilated to the common law forms of protection against intrusion upon privacy if the social interest served by the common law is conceived of as the preservation of individual dignity. These statutes are obviously not designed to protect against forms of mental illness or distress and to so identify the interest involved in the common law intrusion cases is to rob the argument for eavesdropping statutes of a valuable source of traditional common law analysis.

A similar argument may be made concerning other contemporary tendencies in the direction of stripping the individual naked of his human dignity by exposing his personal life to public scrutiny. The personnel practices of government and large-scale corporate enterprise increasingly involve novel forms of investigation of personal lives. Extensive personal questionnaires, psychological testing and, in some instances, the polygraph have been used to delve deeper and deeper into layers of personality heretofore inaccessible to all but a lover, an intimate friend or a physician. And the information so gathered is very often stored, correlated and retrieved by electronic machine techniques. The combined force of the new techniques for uncovering personal intimacies and the new techniques of electronic use of this personal data threatens to uncover inmost thoughts and feelings never even "whispered in the closet" and to make them all too easily available "to be proclaimed from the housetops."[43]

The character of the problems posed by psychological testing, the polygraph and electronic storage of personal data can better be grasped if seen in the perspective of the common law intrusion and disclosure cases. The interest threatened by these new instruments is the same as that which underlies the tort cases. The feeling of being naked before the world can be produced by having to respond to a questionnaire or psychological test as well as by having your bedroom open to prying eyes and ears.

[43] For a description of the threat, see the authorities cited in note 7 supra.

And the fear that a private life may be turned into a public spectacle is greatly enhanced when the lurid facts have been reduced to key punches or blips on a magnetic tape accessible, perhaps, to any clerk who can throw the appropriate switch.

This is not to say, of course, that the same adjustments of conflicting values which have been made in the tort privacy cases can be assumed to apply without modification to resolve the questions of public policy raised by the use of sophisticated electronic eavesdropping equipment, psychological techniques of probing the individual psyche or the electronic data processing equipment. Nor is it to say that the expansion of the tort remedy will provide a satisfactory legal or social response to these new problems. It is rather only to say that, in both instances, community concern for the preservation of the individual's dignity is at issue and that the legal tradition associated with resolving the one set of problems is available for use in resolving the other.

Privacy in Broadcasting

EUGENE N. ALEINIKOFF

It takes but little consideration of the words "privacy" and "broadcasting" to recognize their inherently antithetical meanings. Privacy, of necessity, implies the shutting out of the outside world; broadcasting connotes public exposure to the widest extent possible. The issue of privacy in particular and the press in general has been commonly identified as a conflict between the competing interests of a democratic society in the right of the individual to be let alone and the right of the public to be fully informed. Though both are valued and deep-felt liberties, accommodation has often been difficult since long before the intrusion of television into the American way of life.

With the communications revolution in which we are now well engulfed, the legitimate bounds of private confidence and public knowledge increasingly require re-definition. There no longer appears to be any practical way of isolating oneself from continuous and direct outside view—and not just in the reportorial sense. . . .

Similar electronic marvels are occurring every day in broadcasting science, almost too frequently to be noticed. The television wrist watch is no longer far removed from the transistor radio; foreseeable are popular television records selling at prices not much higher than our present phonograph long-playing records.

Reprinted by permission of the *Indiana Law Journal* from the article, "Privacy in Broadcasting," *Indiana Law Journal*, XLII (Spring, 1967), 373-384.

Color television has become commonplace after many years of development; three-dimensional television may well arrive much sooner. Communications satellites are fast enveloping the world, permitting simultaneous and far-flung international broadcasting; home videotape recorders will soon permit retention of missed television programs for later viewing. In short, all broadcasts are rapidly becoming universally and permanently available for the viewing and listening audience.

As privacy has become less private and broadcasting more broad, it is not surprising that privacy suits have finally begun to rival defamation suits against broadcasters in the state and federal courts across the country. Their frequency would probably be even greater were it not for the unbelievable attraction which television appearance seems to hold for most average citizens, and the painstaking care exercised by broadcasters in requiring their production staffs to insist upon personal releases in all but the most clear-cut cases of communications privilege. Despite these efforts, the kind of privacy litigation that may arise is exemplified by the well-publicized proceedings in the New York *Youssoupoff* case.[1]

Rasputin Re-Interred: Youssoupoff v. CBS. The Youssoupoff case involved two Chicago housewives who had been inspired to write an amateur television script on the Rasputin legend for a local contest. Conceiving of a half-hour vignette of the slaying of Rasputin, the authors did most of their research at the public library. Their script corresponded closely with their reference sources with few embellishments, as they intended to present an authentic historical episode rather than merely a heightened dramatic adaptation for television. Whether the authors believed all of the actual participants to be dead or were unfamiliar with the possible legal risks, Prince Youssoupoff among others was featured by name.

"If I should Die," as the television program was entitled, was produced and broadcast in Chicago over CBS station WBBM in December, 1962, on a partly sponsored basis. It was re-broadcast

<hr />

[1] Youssoupoff v. Columbia Broadcasting System Inc., 41 Misc. 2d 42, N.Y.S.2d 701 (Sup. Ct.), *aff'd mem.*, 19 App. Div. 2d 865, 244 N.Y.S.2d 1 (1963).

the following month over the CBS station in New York City—this time without commercial sponsorship. But in New York, the program apparently attracted more notice than in Chicago; for early in 1963, Prince Youssoupoff instituted an action against CBS under the New York statute making use of a person's name, portrait or picture for "advertising purposes or for purposes of trade" actionable if without written consent.[2]

CBS's defense was initially two-fold: foremost, that the program fell within the well-established news and information exceptions to the right of privacy; secondarily, that the program was not produced for commercial purposes. . . .

The court found the program not dissimilar in content to the Prince's own accounts, and held that use of the dramatic form on the program could not, as a matter of law, convert the information privilege into privacy liability. Hence the plaintiff was not entitled to judgment on the pleadings alone. Nevertheless, the plaintiff might be able on trial to prove that the dramatization tended to "outrage public opinion or decency in respects other than those produced by admitted historical facts" or tended to establish commercial exploitation of the Prince's personal life. Accordingly, the defendant's motion for summary judgment was also denied.

The trial court's opinion was upheld on appeal, and the case went to trial in the fall of 1965. A long three weeks of testimony ensued—most of which was the Prince's examination and cross-examination on what actually happened on that fateful day some fifty years earlier 5000 miles away. Taking their lead from the court's earlier opinions, his lawyers attempted to concentrate on two particulars in which the program had allegedly been both misleading and embarrassing: first, that the Prince lured Rasputin to his palace by promising that his wife would also be present; and second, that the Prince's motivation in killing Rasputin was

2 N.Y. CIV. RIGHTS LAW §§ 50, 51. It is interesting to speculate to what extent the privacy suit against the CBS program was inspired by an earlier successful libel suit by the Prince's wife in England against a feature motion picture on the same subject. Youssoupoff v. Metro-Goldwyn-Mayer Pictures, Ltd., [1934] 50 T.L.R. 581.

personal revulsion rather than patriotic fervor. CBS endeavored to refute both contentions from, among other sources, the published writings and public statements of the Prince himself. And these two rather narrow points gradually became the focal issues in what had begun as a much broader proceeding.

The jury returned a verdict for CBS—principally, it can be presumed, on the basis of the program's historical accuracy, although perhaps also from a belief that the Prince had suffered no compensable embarrassment from his prominent depiction on the CBS program.

Fact—Fiction: Spahn v. Messner. The rationale of the *Youssoupoff* opinions before trial was clearly an adaptation for television of the "fact-fiction" test previously developed in the New York courts with respect to print media. The theory seems fairly simple and straightforward. Factual reports of current or historical events have been considered to be informational and educational, and therefore to override the privacy right of any individual involved. Fictional accounts have been assumed to be aimed at entertainment alone and to be inspired by those commercial motives against which the right of privacy is intended to be a protection. On these assumptions, the judicial inquiry can be limited to determining whether a given publication is factual or fictional in character in order to assess liability.[3]

The fact-fiction formula was consistently applied throughout the proceedings in another recent New York case, *Spahn v. Messner.*[4] Warren Spahn, a pitcher for the then Milwaukee Braves, brought suit against the New York publisher of a juvenile book entitled, appropriately enough, "The Warren Spahn Story." Spahn's argument was that although the book was generally complimentary, it was published without his consent—and al-

[3] Origin of the New York fact-fiction distinction has been attributed as far back as Binns v. Vitagraph Co., 210 N.Y. 51, 103 N.E. 1108 (1913). For perceptive analysis and persuasive criticism, see Note, *Right of Privacy v. Free Press: Suggested Resolution of Conflicting Values,* 23 IND. L.J. 179 (1953).
[4] Spahn v. Julian Messner, Inc., 43 Misc. 2d 219, 250 N.Y.S.2d 529 (Sup. Ct. 1964), aff'd, 23 App. Div. 2d 216, 260 N.Y.S.2d 451 (1965), aff'd, 18 N.Y.2d 324, 221 N.E.2d 543 (1966), *vacated and remanded,* 87 S. Ct. 1706 (1967).

though it generally reflected his biography, it contained specific incidents that were either highly sensationalized or substantially untrue.

In the *Spahn* case, the New York courts uniformly held on trial and appeal that, compared with the actual circumstances, there were enough discrepancies to hold the book fictional rather than factual. Consequently, despite the fact that Spahn was admittedly a very public figure whose name and biography might not have been entitled to privacy if accurately publicized, the publisher was held not to be entitled to exemption from the New York right of privacy act. Spahn was therefore awarded an injunction and $10,000 in damages.

But what was inherently involved in the *Spahn* case was not so much the right of "privacy" as the right of "publicity"—that is to say, the right of a celebrity to control the commercial exploitation of his personality.[5] The New York courts have been reluctant to recognize any such property right standing on its own, but have been willing at times to find ways to include this type of commercialization within the "purposes of trade" language of the New York Civil Rights Law, so long as true educational and informational publications are not affected. As was said at one stage of the appeals in the *Spahn* case:

> It is true, as it ought to be, that a public figure is subject to being exposed in a factual biography, even one which contains inadvertent or superficial inaccuracies. But surely, he should not be exposed, without his control, to biographies not limited substantially to the truth.[6]

Unfortunately, this "fact-fiction" analysis is not always easy to match up in the earlier New York decisions, even when closely contemporaneous. For example, in 1950 a "true" comic book was held to be privileged,[7] although in 1951 an allegedly accurate article in a "true" detective magazine was held subject to possible

[5] *Cf.* Gordon, *Right of Property in Name, Likeness, Personality and History,* 55 Nw. U.L. Rev. 553 (1960).
[6] 23 App. Div. 2d at 221, 260 N.Y.S.2d at 456.
[7] Molony v. Boy Comics Publishers, Inc., 277 App. Div. 166, 98 N.Y.S.2d 119 (1950).

liability.[8] At about the same time, an admittedly enriched and possibly embarrassing biography of Maestro Koussevitsky was held exempt from injunction,[9] while what was probably a less contrived magazine article on a World War II pilot was held actionable.[10] And in the California courts, it is interesting to contrast two motion-picture cases: *Stryker v. Republic Pictures*,[11] where an ex-marine hero could not prevail against use of his characterization in a movie entitled "The Sands of Iwo Jima," and *Melvin v. Reid*,[12] where a reformed prostitute successfully had sued over use of her notorious past as the plot for a feature film.

Nevertheless, the "fact-fiction" test was readily embraced once again by the highest New York court when it ruled on the final appeal of *Spahn v. Messner* last October. In its opinion, moreover, the New York Court of Appeals pointed to another New York case, *Hill v. Hayes,* then pending for some time on appeal in the U.S. Supreme Court.[13]

Constitutional Considerations: Hill v. Hayes. Early in January of this year, the Supreme Court finally handed down its decision reversing *Hill v. Hayes,* in *Time Inc. v. Hill.*[14] With one fell swoop, Justice Brennan's opinion for the majority undercut the entire "fact-fiction" hypothesis on first and fourteenth amendment grounds, leaving the New York Civil Rights Law with markedly diminished application.

The *Hill* case involved a 1955 *Life Magazine* feature that compared an admittedly fictional novel, play, and movie—all by Jo-

[8] Garner v. Triangle Publications, 97 F. Supp. 546 (S.D.N.Y. 1951).

[9] Koussevitzky v. Allen, Towne & Heath, Inc., 188 Misc. 479, 68 N.Y.S.2d 779 (Sup. Ct.), *aff'd,* 272 App. Div. 759, 69 N.Y.S.2d 432 (1947).

[10] Sutton v. Hearst Corp., 277 App. Div. 155, 98 N.Y.S.2d 233 (1950).

[11] Stryker v. Republic Pictures Co., 108 Cal. App. 2d 196, 238 P.2d 670 (1951).

[12] Melvin v. Reid, 112 Cal. App. 285, 297 Pac. 91 (1931).

[13] Hill v. Hayes, 27 Misc. 2d 863, 207 N.Y.S.2d 901 (Sup. Ct. 1960), *aff'd,* 18 App. Div. 2d 485, 240 N.Y.S.2d 286 (1963), *aff'd,* 15 N.Y.2d 986, 207 N.E.2d 604 (1965), *prob. juris. noted,* 382 U.S. 936 (1965), *reargument ordered,* 384 U.S. 995 (1966). For an early evaluation of the New York decisions and thoughtful presentation of the possible constitutional issues involved, see Silver, *Privacy and the First Amendment,* 24 FORDHAM L. REV. 553 (1966).

[14] Time, Inc. v. Hill, 385 U.S. 374 (1967).

seph Hayes and called "The Desperate Hours"—with a celebrated incident three years earlier in which escaped convicts held the Hill family captive in their Pennsylvania home for some twenty hours. In reporting on the opening of the play, *Life* went so far as to photograph scenes reenacted by the cast in the actual Hill house (from which the Hill family had in the meantime moved to Connecticut in what may be presumed to have been a search for anonymity); it also described "The Desperate Hours" as reflecting the Hills' unpleasant experience, when in fact there were essential differences (including the family's treatment at the hands of the convicts).[15]

With these adverse aspects of artificiality, commerciality and misrepresentation present, it was easy for the New York courts to uphold the Hills' claim and award substantial damages to the family. *Life's* sensationalized approach was found to be aimed primarily at increased sales of the magazine and advertising for the play, and so was viewed as not serving any bona fide news or public interest purpose legitimately exempt from privacy actions.

Bringing to bear the same principles that guided its decision in *New York Times v. Sullivan*,[16] however, the Supreme Court reversed. Expressly disagreeing with the New York Court of Appeals in *Spahn v. Messner*,[17] the majority opinion is direct and forthright:

We hold that the constitutional protections for speech and press pre-

15 The Hill family incident occurred in the fall of 1952; the Hayes' novel was published in the spring of 1953; the *Life* picture article appeared early in 1955 just before the Broadway opening of the play; the motion picture was released in 1956 after the beginning of the Hill law suit.

16 New York Times Co. v. Sullivan, 376 U.S. 254 (1964).

17 Although the first amendment issue had been pointedly raised on final appeal in *Spahn v. Messner,* the New York Court of Appeals distinguished *New York Times v. Sullivan* on the basis that it was applicable only to suits against public officials for official conduct. Judge Keating, for the unanimous court said: "The free speech which is encouraged and essential to the operation of a healthy government is something quite different from an individual's attempt to enjoin the publication of a fictitious biography of him. No public interest is served by protecting the disseminator of the latter. We perceive no constitutional infirmities in this respect." 18 N.Y.2d at 329, 221 N.E.2d at 546.

clude the application of the New York statute to redress false reports of matters of public interest in the absence of proof that the defendant published the report with knowledge of its falsity or in reckless disregard of the truth.[18]

Fictional or factual, false or true, commercially or altruistically inspired, therefore, a right of privacy action against a published story, report, article or other account is henceforth constitutionally barred not only if substantially accurate or inadvertently inexact, but even if materially and injuriously incorrect through indisputable lack of research care. Anything more than liability limited to calculated falsehood, the Supreme Court has held, would illegally impair the exercise of the freedoms of speech and press.

II

In reversing the *Hill* case, the Supreme Court has undoubtedly cleared a wider swath of journalistic freedom for television as well as the rest of the American press. No longer need broadcasters be excessively apprehensive about being able to prove historical or reportorial accuracy to the last detail in order to avoid the appearance of fictionalization or sensationalism. In effect, television has been relieved of the fact-fiction strait-jacket sought to be imposed in the *Youssoupoff* case—always an especially uncomfortable fit for the broadcaster for a variety of obvious reasons.

First, accuracy of character and situation portrayal has never been a reliable standard for distinguishing between entertainment and information. Television fiction usually involves dramatization, but dramatization is not necessarily inconsistent with fact. Television non-fiction is most often presented in a documentary format, but all documentary producers must select between differing interpretations by historians and other experts in presenting what is hopefully an objective program. The *Youssoupoff* case itself indicates the pitfalls that lie in the path of the most conscientious researcher of historical material for television production.

[18] 385 U.S. at 387-88. On appeal, the Supreme Court specifically vacated the judgment and remanded the case to the New York Court of Appeals "for further consideration in the light of Time, Inc. v. Hill."

Second, commercial sponsorship is an equally unreliable index upon which to judge program content or purpose. Television advertising is not limited to amusement programs, and not all unsponsored programs are informational in character. A factual biography of a popular hero may be motivated by greater commercial reasons than a fictional sketch of a lesser figure; a fully sponsored documentary film may be more profitable than a partially sponsored dramatic episode. Besides, even when broadcast on a purely public service basis, almost all programs are surrounded (and perhaps interrupted) by so-called "spot" advertisements not very different from sponsor messages. Commercial television invariably involves considerations of profit; educational television is always nonprofit by definition—but certainly neither should be considered susceptible to or immune from privacy claims on that basis alone.

Third, fact and fiction are too often indistinguishable by the television public. The immediate and intimate impact of the television picture, the widely varied nature and format of television programs in adjacent time periods, the ever-expanding range of television production and broadcast techniques, the immense and multifarious television audience, the domestic interruptions and channel-switching that usually attend home-viewing—all these make it difficult for the viewer to determine what programs are "live" or recorded, actual or reenacted, impromptu or scripted, news or history, drama or documentary. The characteristic misimpressions of television viewers about what they see are as notorious as their unending capacity to sit before the television tube.[19]

Last, the fact-fiction line is frequently blurry in television production. Documentary film producers have for some time been exploring new dramatic techniques to re-create historic events and report on current happenings. Dramatic programs have often proved most successful when using documented dialogue ver-

[19] Television lawyers are still haunted by the Orson Welles "Martian invasion" radio broadcast and the spate of lawsuits that followed almost thirty years ago. Hence the usual network practice, through subtitles and superimpositions, introductions and explanations, to explain the nature of programs, segments or sequences which might possibly be subject to misunderstanding.

batim. The combined dramatic-actuality techniques of the latest "cinema-verité" films and "non-fiction" novels are indicative of the way in which television programs too are increasingly becoming intermixtures of fact and fiction, of information and entertainment.

In short, the way taken in the *Youssoupoff* case—searching into the murky past for minute details surrounding myth-like events—seems at best to have been a slippery road through swampy land. Far firmer footing has now been provided by the Supreme Court in the *Hill* case: Legal liability has been constitutionally limited to intentional or reckless falsification of fact.

Even the dissenters in the *Hill* case did not disagree with the interposition of a constitutional barrier around inaccurate reports so long as reasonable journalistic efforts are made, irrespective of possible harm to private individuals. Going further than the majority opinion, moreover, Justices Douglas and Black in their concurring opinions saw the interests of a free press precluding any privacy suit irrespective of purposeful falsification, intentional injury, or outright malice. Justice Black viewed the privacy right as judge-made and certainly not in a class with basic constitutional freedoms; Justice Douglas . . . simply saw no individual privacy in connection with a public event.

For none of the nine Supreme Court Justices, then, has the emphasis on the fact-fiction test in the *Youssoupoff* and *Spahn* cases been justifiable. Whatever the right of "privacy" or "publicity" may be, it cannot lead to legal recovery for the use of an individual's name, picture, or biography in print or through the air waves in the absence of proven malicious intent or undoubted "recklessness" in the false publication of damaging material of public interest. In a communications media such as television, which is subject to such intense public scrutiny and close federal regulation, a finding of intentional or reckless mendacious harm should be rare indeed.[20]

[20] O'Neil, *Television, Tort Law and Federalism*, 53 CALIF. L. REV. 421, 464 (1965): "Under the general rubric of 'public interest,' the FCC undoubtedly has power to consider flagrant violations of state tort law in appraising the performance of a licensee."

The *Hill* case need not, however, be construed to have banished all considerations of privacy from broadcasting. In refusing to invalidate the New York statute altogether, for example, the Supreme Court has permitted its continued application to the unauthorized use of an individual's name or picture for product endorsement or other advertising use.[21] Since no public informational purpose is served and private profit alone is concerned, commercial endorsements can properly be statutorily required to be dependent on personal permission. Even for Justices Douglas and Black, there would appear to be no constitutional inhibition on as much absolute liability for trade advertising as absolute freedom for press content is required by constitutional mandate. The omnipresent television commercial, therefore, continues to be a potential source of privacy suits.

The Supreme Court's footnotes have also explicitly left the door open to further consideration of two other regions of the privacy area: (1) the extent of permissible protection of "intimate personal details of an embarrassing nature,"[22] and (2) the unlicensed publication of recorded material surreptitiously obtained.[23] While both are somewhat related in their emphasis on personal integrity, differences in immediacy and import might well lead to different approaches by state courts without fear of constitutional transgression.[24]

The appropriate extent of the private life of a public figure in our society is almost as ill-defined as the appropriate limits on public exposure of a private individual. The Kennedy-Manchester dispute earlier this year points up how innately subjective is the judgment of what is personal and what is historical about a

[21] Sections 50 and 51 of the New York Civil Rights Law were, of course, specifically aimed at unauthorized advertising use when enacted in 1903. In Roberson v. Rochester Folding Box Co., 171 N.Y. 538, 64 N.E. 444 (1902), the New York Court of Appeals had refused protection against use of the plaintiff's picture in defendant's advertisement on the ground that no privacy right existed absent state legislative enactment.

[22] 385 U.S. at 383 n.7.

[23] *Id.* at 384 n.9.

[24] Emphasizing the importance of similar footnote reservations by the Supreme Court in *New York Times Co. v. Sullivan* is Pauling v. Globe-Democrat Publishing Co., 362 F.2d 188 (8th Cir. 1966).

public official; scandal-sheet exploitation of crime victims and others involuntarily in the news is not easy to distinguish from standard stories in our daily newspapers and weekly magazines. As pointed out in the *Hill* opinion, most law suits in which the issue has been raised give lip-service to the principle of personal privacy, but then hold for the defendant on the ground of public privilege.[25]

Outside of the *Hill* case's perimeters encompassing "newsworthy people and events," however, it would not be unreasonable to insist upon responsible reporting in this connection. For so long as responsible reporting includes the twin requirements of professional research of content and reasonable relationship of subject-matter, there should be neither undue restriction on publication nor too broad an invasion of privacy.[26] Such a standard would also exclude liability for the coincidental use of a private name and address in a broadcast or an article, or for the incidental inclusion of a bystander in a film or photograph,[27]

---

[25] The best known example is Sidis v. F-R Publishing Corp., 113 F.2d 806 (2d Cir.), *cert. denied,* 311 U.S. 711 (1940), dismissing a privacy action against a *New Yorker* magazine profile about the disappointing adulthood of a child genius.

Some courts have tended to be more sympathetic towards subjects of reprinted photographs rather than merely of written text—either where originally unauthorized or taken without consent for news purposes valid at the time. Leverton v. Curtis, 192 F.2d 974 (3d Cir. 1951); Reed v. Real Detective Publishing Co., 63 Ariz. 294, 162 P.2d 133 (1945); Barber v. Time, Inc., 348 Mo. 1199, 159 S.W.2d 291 (1942); see Note, *The Right of Privacy in News Photographs,* 144 VA. L. REV. 1303 (1958).

[26] *Cf.* Emerson, *Toward a General Theory of the First Amendment,* 72 YALE L.J. 877, 927 (1963); see also Franklin, *A Constitutional Problem in Privacy Protection: Legal Inhibitions on Reporting of Fact,* 16 STAN. L. REV. 107, 146 (1963). Note that the requirement of "reasonable relationship and relevancy," even where the report is concededly factual, has already been suggested by commentators and courts. Silver, *Privacy and the First Amendment,* 24 FORDHAM L. REV. 553 (1966); Lahiri v. Daily Mirror, Inc., 162 Misc. 776, 295 N.Y. Supp. 382 (Sup. Ct. 1937). As to the standard of professional research required to avoid liability, Justice Harlan's opinion in Curtis Publishing Co. v. Butts and Associated Press v. Walker, 87 S. Ct. 1975 (1967), is indicative of the probable judicial approach.

[27] With respect to name coincidences, *compare* Krieger v. Popular Publications, Inc., 167 Misc. 5, 3 N.Y.S.2d 480 (Sup. Ct. 1937), *with* Swacker v.

without in any way inhibiting recourse by a truly injured individual to the remedies for defamation, unfair competition, or copyright infringement.[28]

Secret surveillance—aural or visual—is in a rather different category. To subject a private individual in person, without his knowledge or consent, to an almost limitless television or radio audience, "live" or by recording, is surely an unjustifiable violation of privacy unless an indisputable and unequivocal "news" item is involved. The Federal Communications Commission last year promulgated regulations against the use of radio and television devices for eavesdropping purposes,[29] the unauthorized interception and divulgence of wired or wireless communications had long previously been prohibited by federal statute.[30] Local action against electronic eavesdropping has been taken by both state courts and state legislatures.[31] It seems essential to the democratic process that any identifiable results of such invidious activity should be kept off the broadcast air as well.

The *Hill* decision . . . does not mean that the right of privacy no longer prohibits the undesirable use of radio and television tapes, films, or other recordings without consent in all but the clearest newscasting circumstances. True, where outright commercial use is not involved, the concept of consent might be rather flexible: in most cases, it should be implied from awareness without objection or exposure without reservation;[32] once given,

Wright, 154 Misc. 822, 277 N.Y. Supp. 296 (Sup. Ct. 1935). With respect to picture inclusions, *compare* Blumenthal v. Picture Classics, Inc., 235 App. Div. 570, 257 N.Y. Supp. 800 (1932), *aff'd,* 261 N.Y. 504, 185 N.E. 713 (1933), *with* Buzinski v. DoAll Co., 31 Ill. App. 2d 191, 175 N.E.2d 577 (1961), *and* Jacova v. Southern Radio & Television Co., 83 So. 2d 34 (Fla. 1955).

28 That those types of actions also are subject to constitutional standards has been indicated with respect to defamation in *New York Times Co. v. Sullivan,* and with respect to unfair competition in the twin cases Sears, Roebuck & Co. v. Stiffel Co., 376 U.S. 225 (1964), and Compco Corp. v. Day-Brite Lighting, Inc., 376 U.S. 234 (1964).

29 FCC RULES, Part 2, Subpart H, § 2.701, and Part 15, Subpart A, § 15.11, and Subpart E, § 15.220, 31 Fed. Reg. 3400 (1966) (effective April 8, 1966).

30 Federal Communications Act of 1934, ch. 652, § 605, 48 Stat. 1103 (1934), 47 U.S.C. § 605 (1964).

31 FCC Report and Order, Docket No. 15262, at 3 (Feb. 25, 1966).

32 Johnson v. Boeing Airplane Co., 175 Kan. 275, 262 P.2d 808 (1953); *cf.* Cohen

it should be considered irrevocable and subject only to restrictions expressed at the time;[33] and it should normally be assumed to be a condition of appearance at public gatherings or places so long as no undue emphasis is made or confidentiality breached.[34] But the personal option to refuse to be the subject of scrutiny or recording must always be carefully safeguarded if the right of privacy is to be meaningful in our society in the future. Here the privacy right more closely reflects the considerations of *Griswold v. Connecticut* than those of *New York Times v. Sullivan,* and it is to be hoped that the distinction will be appropriately marked by the Supreme Court when the earliest opportunity arises.

v. Marx, 211 P.2d 320 (Cal. App. 1950); see Sweenek v. Pathe News, 16 F. Supp. 746 (E.D.N.Y. 1936); Continental Optical Co. v. Reed, 25 Ind. App. 643, 86 N.E.2d 306 (1949). *But see* Durgom v. Columbia Broadcasting System, Inc., 29 Misc. 2d 394, 214 N.Y.S.2d 752 (Sup. Ct. 1961) (citing explicit New York statute requiring written consent).

[33] Jenkins v. Dell Publishing Co., 143 F. Supp. 952 (W.D. Pa. 1956), *aff'd,* 251 F.2d 447 (3d Cir. 1958), *cert. denied,* 357 U.S. 921 (1958); *cf.* Sinclair v. Postal Tel. & Cable Co., 72 N.Y.S.2d 841 (Sup. Ct. 1935); Dahl v. Columbia Pictures Corp., 12 Misc. 2d 573, 166 N.Y.S.2d 708 (Sup. Ct. 1957), *aff'd mem.,* 183 N.Y.S.2d 992 (App. Div. 1959). But see Garden v. Parfumerie Rigaud, Inc., 151 Misc. 692, 271 N.Y. Supp. 187 (Sup. Ct. 1933).

[34] Peterson v. KMTR Radio Corp., 18 U.S.L. WEEK 2044 (Cal. Super. Ct., July 26, 1949); *cf.* Gautier v. Pro-Football, Inc., 304 N.Y. 354, 107 N.E.2d 485 (1951); Gill v. Hearst Publishing Co., 40 Cal. 2d 224, 253 P.2d 441 (1953).

Bibliography For Chapter Five

BOOKS

Brenton, Myron. *The Privacy Invaders*. New York: Coward-McCann, Inc., 1964.

Brown, Robert M. *The Electronic Invasion*. New York: John F. Rider Publisher, Inc., 1967.

Dash, Samuel, Richard F. Schwartz, and Robert E. Knowlton. *The Eavesdroppers*. New Jersey: Rutgers University Press, 1959.

Engberg, Edward. *Spy in the Corporate Structure and the Right to Privacy*. New York: World Publishing Co., 1967.

Gross, M. L. *The Brain Watchers*. New York: New American Library, 1963.

Hofstader, Samuel H. and George Horowitz. *The Right of Privacy*. New York: Central Book Company, 1964.

Long, Edward V. *The Intruders*. New York: Frederick A. Praeger, 1967.

Ottenberg, Miriam. *The Federal Investigators*. Englewood Cliffs, New Jersey: Prentice-Hall, Inc., 1962.

Packard, Vance. *The Naked Society*. New York: David McKay Company, Inc., 1964.

Shils, Edward A. *The Torment of Secrecy*. Glencoe, Ill.: Free Press, 1956.

Westin, Alan F. *Privacy and Freedom*. New York: Atheneum, 1967. (An excellent bibliography.)

Zelermeyer, William. *Invasion of Privacy*. Syracuse, New York: Syracuse University Press, 1959.

ARTICLES

Davis, Gary L. "Electronic Surveillance and the Right of Privacy," *Montana Law Review*, XXVII (Spring, 1966), 173-192.

"Recent Developments in the Right of Privacy," *Chicago Law Review,* XV (Summer, 1948), 926-939.

Franklin, Marc A. "A Constitutional Problem in Privacy Protection: Legal Inhibitions On Reporting of Fact," *Stanford Law Review,* XVI (December, 1963), 107-147.

Johnson, Gerald W. "The Invasion of Privacy: Laus Contemptionis," *American Scholar,* XXVIII (Autumn, 1959), 447-457.

"Privacy," *Law and Contemporary Problems,* XXXI (Spring, 1966), 251-435. Entire issued devoted to privacy.

"Privacy and Behavioral Research," Executive Office of the President, Office of Science and Technology, Government Printing Office, 1967. February, 1967. Pamphlet.

Prosser, William L. "Privacy," *California Law Review,* XLVIII (August, 1960), 383-423.

The Right of Privacy, Virginia Law Weekly, Dicta Comp, XVI (1965).

Strunksy, Robert. "The Invasion of Privacy: The Modern Case of Mistaken Identity," *American Scholar,* XXIX (Spring, 1960), 219-226.

W. T. R., III. "The Fourth Amendment Right of Privacy: Mapping the Future," *Virginia Law Review,* LIII (October, 1967), 1314-1359.

CASES

Goldman v. U.S., 316 U.S. 129 (1942).

Griswold v. Connecticut, 381 U.S. 479 (1965).

Irvine v. State of California, 347 U.S. 128 (1954).

Jenkins v. Dell Publishing Co., 143 F. Supp. 953 (W. D. Pa. 1956), *aff'd* 251 F. 2d 447 (3d Cir. 1958), *cert. denied,* 357 U.S. 921 (1958).

Lopez v. U.S., 373 U.S. 427 (1963).

Mapp v. Ohio, 367 U.S. 643 (1961).

Melvin v. Reid, 112 Cal. App. 285, 297 Pac. 91 (Dist. Ct. App. 1931).

NAACP v. Alabama, 357 U.S. 449 (1958).

Olmstead v. U.S., 277 U.S. 438 (1928).

Pavesich v. New England Life Ins. Co., 122 Ga. 190, 50 S. E. 68 (1905).

Public Utilities Commission v. Pollak, 343 U.S. 451 (1952).

Roberson v. Rochester Folding Box Co., 171 N. Y. 538, 64 N. E. 444 (1902).

Sweezy v. New Hampshire, 354 U.S. 234 (1957).

Talley v. California, 362 U.S. 60 (1960).
Time Inc. v. Hill, 385 U.S. 374 (1967).
Watkins v. U.S., 354 U.S. 178 (1957).

CHAPTER SIX

Libel: When the Search for Truth Goes Astray

ONE of the tenets of the Libertarian philosophy is that everyone who enters the marketplace of ideas does so from a sincere desire to learn Truth. Yet, like so many philosophies that seem on the whole worthwhile, Libertarianism quite obviously has flaws. One of the greatest flaws is the assumption that all men are equally committed to the search for Truth. The law, dealing with practicalities and not abstractions, historically has taken a long and skeptical look at this assumption. (The result is another philosophical modification of Libertarianism—that everyone has the right of free speech, but he is responsible for abuses of that right.)

(The rationale behind libel law, like the rationale in many other complex subjects, is superficially simple. A person has a right to his good name. If another person falsely blemishes that name, the injured person has a right to seek redress. And this is about the only simple aspect of the whole subject of libel.)

The media—long before they became "mass" media—had to contend with legal risks accompanying the publishing of libelous statements. Recent years have seen two divergent trends in the law of libel: public figures are more difficult to libel, and private citizens are collecting larger damages.)

This might well be called the era of the "supersuits." Nothing illustrates this more aptly than the following accounts of three sensational cases brought by former Senator Barry Goldwater, former Major General Edwin A. Walker, and former Coach Wallace Butts. Goldwater sued for $2 million and was awarded $75,000 in damages, but the decision is being appealed. Walker, in a series of suits, asked for damages totaling $33,250,000, and collected nothing. Butts was awarded initially $3,060,000, a judgment that later was sliced to $460,000.

Goldwater sued *Fact* magazine, publisher Ralph Ginzburg, and managing editor Warren Boroson for the story entitled "1,189 Psychiatrists Say Goldwater Unfit to be President" which appeared in the September-October 1964 edition of the magazine.

Walker had charged that the Associated Press in a news story had falsely reported him to be a leader of rioting students who were protesting integration at the University of Mississippi.

In the case of Butts, the football coach obtained judgment against the *Saturday Evening Post* for publishing an article stating that he collaborated with another coach to fix a Georgia-Alabama football game.

Recently, five libel suits, for $5 million each, have been filed by the mother of accused Presidential assassin Lee Harvey Oswald against a congressman and several writers and publishers. Marguerite Oswald claims the defendants made false and misleading statements about her and her son and that some of the publications exposed her "to hatred, contempt, and ridicule." Named in the libel suits are these persons and groups associated with books or magazine articles about the assassination: Representative Gerald Ford and John R. Stiles and Simon & Schuster, Inc.; Jim Bishop and Funk and Wagnall Company; Stephen White, the Macmillan Publishing Company and CBS; Jimmy Breslin and the New York Magazine Company; and William Manchester, Harper & Row Publishers, Inc., and Cowles Communications, Inc. These suits are costly to defend and, with their exorbitant damages, they constitute real threats to the publishing world. No publication, of course, can afford to be without libel insurance.

Again the law, as we shall see in the following pages, is both defender and restrainer of freedom. By permitting the individual to defend his good name, the law at times prevents full and complete discussion. Yet notable exceptions are allowed, chiefly in the area of public affairs, because of the need for close public scrutiny of officials' qualifications and private as well as public actions.

What *Is* Libelous?

HEATHCOTE W. WALES

(At common law, two discrete elements are necessary to a cause of action for libel: the writings must be false[1] and defamatory of the plaintiff. The defendant has the burden of proving the truth of any defamatory remarks as legal justification for their publication.[2] Since the harm against which libel law guards is injury to plaintiff's reputation[3]—his character as others view him—mere

Reprinted by permission of *The University of Chicago Law Review,* from Heathcote W. Wales, "Dirty Words and Dirty Politics: Cognitive Dissonance in the First Amendment," *The University of Chicago Law Review,* XXXIV (Winter, 1967), 367-386.

[1] This element originally applied to civil libel only. The English rule that truth is no defense in criminal libel was first adopted in this country in People v. Croswell, 3 Johns. Cas. 337 (N.Y. 1804). Statutes in nearly every state since have changed the rule.

[2] The defense of truth must extend to all defamatory imputations drawn from the publication. "Substantial," not literal, truth is required. See, *e.g.,* Bell Publishing Co. v. Garrett Engineering Co., 154 S.W.2d 885 (Tex. Civ. App. 1941).

[3] In describing the harm function of defamation, Professor Emerson, who distinguishes between words and actions in determining what the government may constitutionally regulate, says: "[T]he injury, at least in substantial part, does not flow from action resulting from the communication—action which can be intercepted by regulation addressed specifically to it—but directly from the communication itself. In this sense, therefore, true private defamation tends toward the category of 'action,' and hence is subject to reasonable regulation." Emerson, *supra* note 1, at 922.

falsity is not sufficient to make out a case.[4] The plaintiff must also show that the statements taken as a whole[5] defame him in the eyes of others, that they tend to hold him up to hatred, ridicule, or contempt.[6]

The two elements of falsity and defamatory harm satisfied, plaintiff's case is complete.[7] Libel law in a majority of jurisdictions does not require proof of an element of intent or negligence;[8] absolute liability is the standard.[9] However, in raising a

[4] Examples of the principle that even lies must be defamatory include Kimmerle v. New York Evening Journal, 262 N.Y. 99, 186 N.E. 217 (1933) (woman "courted by a murderer"); Cohen v. New York Times Co., 153 App. Div. 242, 138 N.Y.S. 206 (1912) (man is dead); Pogany v. Chambers, 206 Misc. 933, 134 N.Y.S.2d 691 (Sup. Ct. 1954) (brother of a Communist).

In addition, words used in anger are often not actionable. See, *e.g.*, Hansen v. Dethridge, 67 N.Y.S.2d 168 (N.Y. City Ct. 1946) (accusation of libel); Tomakian v. Fritz, 75 R.I. 496, 67 A.2d 834 (1949) ("drunken driver"); Morrissette v. Beatte, 66 R.I. 73, 17 A.2d 464 (1941) (accusation of sodomy).

[5] Statements that are clearly meant to be humorous and are so taken by readers would not be actionable, while a seemingly innocent statement may be devastating to the plaintiff, as in Braun v. Armour & Co., 254 N.Y. 514, 173 N.E. 845 (1930), where plaintiff was said to have sold bacon in his store. Plaintiff was a kosher meat dealer.

[6] See generally GREGORY & KALVEN, CASES ON TORTS 947, 968-73 (1959); PROSSER, TORTS § 106 (3d ed. 1964); *Developments in the Law of Defamation*, 69 HARV. L. REV. 875, 892-901 (1956). The statements need not be regarded as defamatory by a majority of the recipients, but only by "a considerable and respectable class in the community." Peck v. Tribune Co., 214 U.S. 185 (1909).

[7] At common law, the jury is allowed to infer general damages from the defamatory nature of the remarks. However, in jurisdictions employing the distinction between libel per se (writings defamatory on their face) and libel per quod (writings defamatory in the light of extrinsic facts), special damages (pecuniary loss) must be proved for the latter. See, *e.g.*, Rose v. Indianapolis Newspapers, Inc., 213 F.2d 227 (7th Cir. 1954); O'Connell v. Press Publishing Co., 214 N.Y. 352, 108 N.E. 556 (1915); Ellsworth v. Martindale-Hubbell Law Directory, Inc., 66 N.D. 578, 268 N.W. 400 (1936). See generally GREGORY & KALVEN, *supra* note 5, at 912-82; *Developments, supra* note 5, at 889-91.

[8] A minority exception in cases concerning the defamation of public figures, including candidates for public office, was established in Coleman v. MacLennan, 78 Kan. 711, 98 Pac. 281 (1908). The *Times* case turned this into a constitutionally required exception.

[9] The early common law required an element of malice, but in Bromage v. Prosser, 4 B. & C. 247, 107 Eng. Rep. 1051 (1825), the fiction of "malice in law" was created, with no proof of ill will or lack of honest belief required.

defense of privilege, the defendant may open up the question of his intent. Two categories of privilege may be pleaded by a defendant, defeasible and absolute,[10] but only for the former is intent relevant.

Defeasible privilege is most important in the freedom it gives journalists and other critics in their discussions of public figures and public issues.[11] The "fair comment" rule grants a qualified privilege to discussion not only of politicians and public officials,[12] but also of writers,[13] sports figures,[14] entertainers,[15] and others

[10] Absolute privilege exists in four areas:

(1) For legislators. U.S. CONST. art. I, § 6: "[F]or any Speech or Debate in either House, they shall not be questioned in any other Place." Many state constitutions have similar provisions for state legislators.

(2) For persons involved in judicial proceedings. See, *e.g.*, Hayslip v. Wellford, 195 Tenn. 621, 263 S.W.2d 136 (1933), *cert. denied*, 346 U.S. 911 (1954) (grand juror); Dunham v. Powers, 42 Vt. 1 (1868) (petit juror); Massey v. Jones, 182 Va. 200, 28 S.E.2d 623 (1944) (witness); Scott v. Stansfield, L.R. 3 Ex. 220 (1868) (judge).

(3) For persons in executive government offices. See, *e.g.*, Barr v. Matteo, 360 U.S. 564 (1959) (lower federal officers and employees making authorized communications in the performance of their duties); Spalding v. Vilas, 161 U.S. 483 (1896) (Postmaster General).

(4) When plaintiff explicitly consents to the libel. See, *e.g.*, Shinglemeyer v. Wright, 124 Mich. 230, 82 N.W. 887 (1900).

[11] Newspapers may report records of public proceedings, even though defamatory, provided their report is accurate. See, *e.g.*, Cresson v. Louisville Courier-Journal, 299 Fed. 487 (6th Cir. 1924) (report of majority of congressional committee).

In the private arena, an individual has the right to verbal self-defense. Israel v. Portland News Publishing Co., 152 Ore. 225, 53 P.2d 529 (1936). Statements furthering the interests of a third party where some duty to make the communication exists will be privileged. Toogood v. Spyring, 1 C.M. & R. 181, 149 Eng. Rep. 1044 (Ex. 1834). Discussion by a group of mutual interests is privileged. See, *e.g.*, Slocinski v. Radwan, 83 N.H. 501, 144 Atl. 787 (1929) (congregation members discussing morals of their minister).

[12] See, *e.g.*, Bailey v. Charleston Mail Ass'n, 126 W. Va. 292, 27 S.E.2d 837 (1943).

[13] See, *e.g.*, Potts v. Dies, 132 F.2d 734 (D.C. Cir. 1942) (magazine article writer).

[14] See, *e.g.*, Cohen v. Cowles Publishing Co., 45 Wash. 2d 262, 273 P.2d 893 (1954) (jockey's handling of horse).

[15] See, *e.g.*, Cherry v. Des Moines Leader, 114 Iowa 298, 86 N.W. 323 (1901) (singer-dancer).

234 WHAT "IS" LIBELOUS

whose activities or beliefs make them public figures.[16] Under this rule, error as to opinion is privileged, but, in a majority of jurisdictions, error as to fact is not.[17] The obvious policy of the rule is to encourage open discussion and criticism of issues and people in the public eye, albeit with factual accuracy rigorously required. Further justification lies in the notion that most people who might be defamed under the rule have voluntarily exposed their works or themselves in certain capacities to the public. Their reputations are, to some extent, public property.

The most significant limitation on this and other defeasible privileges is the intent with which the defamer publishes his remarks. A showing of malice, that the defendant published his remarks out of ill will for the plaintiff, will generally defeat the privilege. Similarly, defendant's disbelief in his own opinions, excessive vehemence in his defamation, or unnecessary communication of the remarks to persons having no legitimate interest in them, all work to defeat the privilege. The plaintiff must show that defendant abused the policy behind the privilege, that is, that the defendant was not attempting to obtain truth for his readers by open discussion of public issues and public figures.[18]

---

[16] See, *e.g.*, Brewer v. Hearst Publishing Co., 185 F.2d 846 (7th Cir. 1950) (alternative holding) (proponent of vivisection).

[17] The minority rule of nine states established in Coleman v. MacLennan, 78 Kan. 711, 98 Pac. 281 (1908), permits good faith error as to fact. See note 8 *supra*.

[18] In a more general statement of the rule: "One who upon a conditionally privileged occasion publishes false and defamatory matter of another abuses the occasion if he does not act for the purpose of protecting the particular interest for the protection of which the privilege is given." RESTATEMENT, TORTS § 603 (1938).

Truth—the Complete Defense

ROBERT H. PHELPS
E. DOUGLAS HAMILTON

Now . . . truth is a complete defense everywhere, both in civil suits and in criminal prosecutions. The newsman who can establish it can avoid paying damages in civil action and stay out of jail in criminal cases. Moreover, in civil suits in most states truth is an absolute defense, that is, good even if the publisher spoke the words from malice. In criminal prosecutions in most states and in civil suits in a few states, truth is a qualified defense, good unless the other side shows that actual malice lay behind the libel.

The states where the law says that malice negates the defense of truth in civil cases are Delaware, Florida, Illinois, Maine, Massachusetts, Nebraska, New Hampshire, Pennsylvania, Rhode Island, West Virginia and Wyoming. But the problem is not as serious as it sounds. Even though the law in these states holds that the truth must be spoken for good purposes or justifiable ends, the writer or editor need have no fear if what is printed is true. Nor need they fear criminal prosecution if what they printed is true and there was no personal ill will behind it.

From Robert H. Phelps and E. Douglas Hamilton's *Libel: Rights, Risks, Responsibilities* (New York and London: The Macmillan Company, Collier-Macmillan Ltd., 1966), p. 107. Reprinted by permission of the publishers.

The Defamation of a Public Official—*After Times v. Sullivan*

JOHN ALKAZIN

Freedom of expression on matters of public concern is a principle that is well established in American constitutional law and in the decisions of the United States Supreme Court. The right of an individual citizen to speak his mind on political issues is one which the founders of our country sought to protect by enacting the first amendment to the Constitution which ordains: "Congress shall make no law . . . abridging the freedom of speech, or of the press. . . ."[1] In speaking of this liberty in *Stromberg v. California,* the United States Supreme Court stated that the "opportunity for free political discussion to the end that government may be responsive to the will of the people and that changes may be obtained by lawful means . . . is a fundamental principle of our constitutional system."[2] And in *New York Times*

Reprinted by permission of the *University of San Francisco Law Review.* From John Alkazin, "The Defamation of a Public Official," *University of San Francisco Law Review,* I (April, 1967), 356-368.

[1] U.S. CONST. amend. I.

[2] Stromberg v. California, 283 U.S. 359, 369 (1931). The freedom of speech and of the press guaranteed by the first amendment has been extended to the states through the due process clause of the fourteenth amendment. Bridges v. California, 314 U.S. 252, 270 (1941); Whitney v. California, 274 U.S. 357, 375-376 (1927) (concurring opinion).

236

Company v. Sullivan, Mr. Justice Brennan expressed the basic rationale of the decision in the following words:

> We consider this case against the background of a profound national commitment to the principle that debate on public issues should be uninhibited, robust, and wide-open, and that it may well include vehement, caustic, and sometimes unpleasantly sharp attacks on government and public officials.[3]

Problems arise when the constitutional safeguards guaranteeing free speech come into direct opposition with the established rules of the law of defamation. Either one or the other must prevail. Recent decisions of the United States Supreme Court have, in the interests of free speech, brought about some rather drastic changes in the law of libel insofar as it directly concerns public officials. It is the purpose of this comment to examine how these decisions have affected the law of defamation, to indicate the inadequacy of the rule enunciated in the *New York Times* and subsequent cases, and to discuss the effect of the decision on California law.

THE NEW YORK TIMES DECISION

Prior to 1964, the rule concerning defamation of public officials held by the majority of jurisdictions was that misstatements of fact were not privileged, and thus provided grounds for an action in libel. The majority of state courts felt that the value to the community of information to the public was outweighed by the harm which could be caused to the reputations of men in public positions. Furthermore, it was feared that good men would be deterred from seeking office if misstatements of fact were considered privileged.[4]

---

[3] New York Times Co. v. Sullivan, 376 U.S. 254, 270 (1964). See Note, 18 VAND. L. REV. 1429, 1433 (1965); Kalven, *The New York Times Case: A Note on the Central Meaning of the First Amendment,* 1964 SUP. CT. REV. 191; Pedrick, *Freedom of the Press and the Law of Libel: The Modern Revised Translation,* 49 CORNELL L. Q. 581 (1964).

[4] Post Publishing Co. v. Hallam, 59 Fed. 530 (6th Cir. 1893), was the leading case followed by the majority of courts. See Noel, *Defamation of Public*

However, in 1964, this majority position was completely overthrown by the landmark case of *New York Times Company v. Sullivan* in which the Supreme Court held that under the first and fourteenth amendments to the Constitution a state could not award damages to a public official for defamatory falsehood relating to his official conduct unless the official proved actual malice—that the falsehood was published with knowledge of its falsity or with reckless disregard of whether it was true or false.[5]

But who is a "public official"? The *Times* court expressly declined to answer this question.[6] The extent of the privilege was not indicated, and no guidelines were laid down to aid other courts in interpreting the rule.

Four months after the *Times* decision, the defamation of a public official was again before the Supreme Court in *Garrison v. Louisiana*.[7] Relying on the *Times* rule, the Court held that the constitutional guarantees of free expression apply in cases involving criminal as well as civil libel, and that therefore the nonmalicious comments made by the defendant disparaging judicial conduct of eight judges in New Orleans were privileged. The Court reiterated the proposition established in *Times* that "where the criticism is of public officials and their conduct of public business, the interest in private reputation is overborne by the larger public interest secured by the Constitution, in the dissemination of truth."[8] A few comments were made on what "official conduct" might be the subject of criticism,[9] but the Court again refrained from defining a "public official."

Officers and Candidates, 49 COLUM. L. REV. 875, 891 (1949) for a list of states following the majority viewpoint.

5 New York Times Co. v. Sullivan, *supra* note 3.

6 "We have no occasion here to determine how far down into the lower ranks of government employees the 'public official' designation would extend . . . , or otherwise to specify the categories of persons who would or would not be included." New York Times Co. v. Sullivan, 376 U.S. at 283 n. 23.

7 Garrison v. Louisiana, 379 U.S. 64, 74, 79 (1964).

8 *Id.* at 72, 73.

9 "(A)nything which might touch on an official's fitness for office is relevant. Few personal attributes are more germane to fitness for office than dishonesty, malfeasance, or improper motivation, even though these characteristics may also affect the official's private character." *Id.* at 77.

In *Rosenblatt v. Baer*[10] the Supreme Court again affirmed the rule enunciated in *New York Times* and finally attempted to provide guidelines, albeit minimal, for defining the general classification of a "public official." In *Rosenblatt* the plaintiff, who was formerly employed by a county as supervisor of its recreation area, brought suit alleging that a column written by the defendant and published in the Laconia *Evening Citizen* contained defamatory falsehoods. The column was written during the first ski season after plaintiff's discharge from his position as supervisor of the area. The column made no express reference to plaintiff but did state that the recreation area was doing "hundreds of percent" better than the previous year and asked what happened to the income from the operation of the resort in previous years.[11] The jury awarded damages to plaintiff but before an appeal was heard in the New Hampshire Supreme Court the United States Supreme Court decided *New York Times Co. v. Sullivan*. In affirming the judgment for plaintiff[12] the New Hampshire Supreme Court held that the award was not barred by the *New York Times* decision and that it was not necessary for plaintiff to show actual malice in order to recover.

On certiorari the United States Supreme Court reversed the New Hampshire judgment and remanded for further proceedings. Mr. Justice Brennan delivering the opinion of the Court stated that the trial judge erred in his instruction authorizing the jury to award plaintiff damages without regard to evidence that the asserted implication of the column was made of and concerning him.[13] Under the instructions given in the state court

---

[10] Rosenblatt v. Baer, 383 U.S. 75 (1966).

[11] "This year, a year without snow till very late, a year with actually few very major changes in procedure; the difference in cash income simply fantastic, almost unbelievable." *Id.* at 78.

[12] Baer v. Rosenblatt, 106 N.H. 26, 203 A.2d 773 (1965).

[13] "(N)o explicit charge of speculation was made; no assault on the previous management appears. The jury was permitted to award damages upon a finding merely that respondent was one of a small group acting for an organ of government, only some of whom were implicated, but all of whom were tinged with suspicion. In effect, this permitted the jury to find liability merely on the basis of his relationship to the government agency, the operations of which were the subject of discussion." Rosenblatt v. Baer, 383 U.S. 75, 82 (1966).

the jury was permitted to find that *negligent* misstatement of fact would defeat any privilege to discuss the conduct of government operations. Justice Brennan remarked that this was contrary to the test in *Times* and *Garrison* where it was stated that recovery by public officials for misstatements of fact could be allowed only when the statement was made with knowledge of its falsity or with reckless disregard of whether the statement was true or false.

The *Rosenblatt* decision again applies the good-faith privilege when the individual bringing suit is a "public official," but, like *Times* and *Garrison*, the Court does not precisely determine who is included in the classification of "public officials." *Rosenblatt* left open the possibility that plaintiff could have adduced proof that he was not a "public official" and that his claim would therefore have been outside the *New York Times* rule. Justice Brennan's instructions to the trial court suggest that if plaintiff was not a "public official" the statements would not be privileged regardless of their public nature.[14] While *Rosenblatt*, like *Times*, does not expressly define the term "public official," the *Rosenblatt* decision does set out the underlying basis for the *Times* rule:

Criticism of government is at the very center of the constitutionally protected area of free discussion. Criticism of those responsible for government operations must be free, lest criticism of government itself be penalized. It is clear, therefore, that the public official designation applies at the very least to those among the hierarchy of government employees who have, or appear to the public to have, substantial responsibility for or control over the conduct of governmental affairs. . . . Where a position in government has such apparent importance that the public has an independent interest in the qualifications and performance of the person who holds it, beyond the general public interest in the qualifications and performance of all government employees, . . . the *New York Times* malice standards apply.[15]

---

14 *Id.* at 87-88.

15 *Id.* at 85-86. See Noel, *Defamation of Public Officers and Candidates*, 49 COLUM. L. REV. 875, 896-897, 901-902; Annot., 95 A.L.R.2d 1412, 1453 (1964); PROSSER, TORTS § 110 (3rd ed. 1964); 1 HARPER & JAMES, TORTS § 5.26 (1956); New York Times Co. v. Sullivan, 376 U.S. 254, 280 n.20 (1964) (list of states

Thus, in the decision of *Rosenblatt v. Baer* the Supreme Court reiterated the proposition established in *New York Times Company v. Sullivan* that misstatements of fact concerning public officials must be made with malice to be actionable. The federal constitutional rule thus established by these two cases supersedes what was formerly the rule in the majority of jurisdictions which had been that both negligent and malicious misstatements of fact gave rise to a cause of action.[16]

WHO IS A "PUBLIC OFFICIAL"?

Even after the decisions in the *Times* and *Rosenblatt* cases the problem still remains: Who is a "public official"? Should the rule extend only to candidates for public office and elected or appointed public officials, or should it include any public figure? In short, should the rule established be confined to the political arena or should it extend to include matters of public concern?

As indicated above, the *New York Times* case expressly refrained from making any determination whatsoever on the extent of the rule.[17] And although an exact definition of a "public official" does not appear in the *Rosenblatt* decision, minimum guidelines were set down and the possibility of future expansion of the rule was recognized. As Justice Brennan stated:

> It is clear, therefore, that the "public official" designation applies *at the very least* to those among the hierarchy of government employees who have, or appear to the public to have, substantial responsibility for or control over the conduct of government affairs.[18] (Emphasis added.)

The privilege to make good-faith misstatements of fact concerning official conduct is therefore limited to matters involving governmental conduct. The whole tone of the *Rosenblatt* decision

and commentators following the minority view); Note, 113 U. PA. L. REV. 284, 288 (1964); Note, 18 VAND. L. REV. 1429, 1445 (1965).
[16] See note 4, *supra;* Annot., 110 A.L.R. 393, 412 (1937); Annot., 150 A.L.R. 348, 358 (1944).
[17] See note 6 *supra.*
[18] Rosenblatt v. Baer, 383 U.S. 75, 85 (1966).

suggests that if the plaintiff is not a public official negligent misstatements of fact concerning him will provide grounds for a cause of action for defamatory falsehood, regardless of public concern.[19] If the defendant fails to establish that the plaintiff was a "public official" he will be liable even though the good-faith comments he made concerned a matter in which a majority of the public may have an interest. It is here submitted that the privileges should not be limited to a "public official" situation but should be expanded to include cases where the subject of comment is a matter of public concern.

Many courts and commentators have attempted to establish when a privilege should be accorded to misstatements of fact concerning public men.[20] The "absolutist" position has been frequently advocated by Mr. Justice Black who concurred in separate opinions in both the *New York Times* and *Rosenblatt* cases. Justice Black would extend an absolute privilege to anyone who chose to attack a public official on the ground that all libel and slander laws violate the constitutional protections of the first amendment. Speaking of the publication in the *Rosenblatt* case, Justice Black stated that it was this very kind of publication that the *New York Times* rule was adopted primarily to protect.

> Unconditional freedom to criticize the way such public functions are performed is . . . necessarily included in the guarantees of the First Amendment. And the right to criticize a public agent engaged in public activities cannot safely . . . depend upon whether or not that agent is arbitrarily labeled a "public official" . . . An unconditional right to say what one pleases about public affairs is . . . the minimum guarantee of the First Amendment.[21]

Justice Black thus solves the problem of who is a public official in a very simple manner: he believes that all libel laws infringe

---

[19] See Note, 75 YALE L. J. 642, 651 (1966).

[20] For some examples where the "public official" designation has, and has not, been applied, see Note, 18 VAND. L. REV. 1429, 1443-1444 (1965); Bertlesman, *Libel and Public Men,* 52 A.B.A.J. 657 (1966); Note, 15 DE PAUL L. REV. 376 (1965); Note, 30 ALBANY L. REV. 316 (1966); Note, 34 FORDHAM L. REV. 761 (1966).

[21] Rosenblatt v. Baer, 383 U.S. 75, 94-95 (1966).

upon the constitutional liberties of free speech and press and that therefore they should be barred in both federal and state courts.[22] The absolute privilege doctrine advocated by Justice Black has met with strong criticism, and as one commentator has put it, to adopt his view is tantamount to holding that " a completely open season on public officials would best serve the public interest. Fabricated charges of embezzlement of public funds, of bribery, of espionage for a foreign power, could be made freely and without legal accountability under this view."[23] Few courts or commentators would carry the guarantees of the first amendment as far as this, nor would the majority in *Rosenblatt v. Baer*.[24] While the Supreme Court has only applied the privilege to make good-faith misstatements of fact to cases involving those responsible for the conduct of governmental affairs the door has been left open to expand the privilege in future decisions and it is here submitted that the dictates of public interest demand such an expansion.

What direction should this expansion take? While it does not appear that our highest court is going to abolish the laws of libel, the privilege should be extended beyond the narrow class of public officials so that it includes matters of public concern as well. What appears to be an intelligent analysis of the whole problem is contained in the majority opinion written by Justice Burch for the Kansas Supreme Court in *Coleman v. MacLennan,* the leading case expressing what was heretofore the minority view.[25] It was this case which Mr. Justice Brennan relied upon in formulating the *New York Times* rule, though Justice Brennan did not adopt all of its tenets. The Kansas court felt that

22 *Id.* at 95.

23 Pedrick, *Freedom of the Press and the Law of Libel: The Modern Revised Translation,* 49 CORNELL L. Q. 581, 596 (1964). For reference to others following somewhat varied "absolutist" positions, and for a criticism of Justice Black's stand, see Pedrick, *supra* at 595 n.50.

24 "This conclusion does not ignore the important social values which underlie the law of defamation. Society has a pervasive and strong interest in preventing and redressing attacks upon reputation." Rosenblatt v. Baer, 383 U.S. 75, 86 (1966).

25 Coleman v. MacLennan, 78 Kan. 711, 98 Pac. 281 (1908).

. . . the correct rule, whatever it is, must govern in cases other than those involving candidates for office. It must apply to all officers and agents of government, municipal, state and national; to the management of all public institutions—educational, charitable and penal; to the conduct of all corporate enterprises affected with a public interest . . . and to innumerable other subjects involving the public welfare.[26]

Thus the Kansas court would consider privileged any communication made in good faith upon any subject in which the party communicating had an interest or duty—public or private, legal, moral or social. The constitutional privilege, therefore, should not be limited to cases involving "public officials" but should include matters of public concern as well.

Federal and state decisions since 1964 indicate the difficulty encountered because of the indefiniteness of the rule expounded in *Times* and *Rosenblatt* and the need for the establishment of uniform guidelines to govern the application of this privilege. Some courts have rigidly followed *Times* and do not apply the privilege unless the plaintiff may in some way be designated a "public official." Other courts, adopting the reasoning of Judge Burch in the *Coleman* decision, have expanded the *Times* rule to include matters of public interest and public figures, and it is submitted that these latter cases represent the best solution to the extent of the *Times* rule.

RECENT DECISIONS

A brief analysis of defamation cases decided since *New York Times Company v. Sullivan* could be instrumental in formulating the extent of the privilege accorded by that decision. For purposes of discussion, these cases may be classified into three general groups: (1) those which have refused to recognize the privilege where the plaintiff is merely a public figure and not a public official; (2) those which have applied the *Times* rule where the plaintiff, though not a public official, is closely associated with a public official; and (3) those cases in which the

[26] *Id.* at 735-736.

plaintiff has voluntarily pressed his views upon the public concerning a matter of public concern.

Of the first group of cases, *Associated Press v. Walker*[27] and *Curtis Publishing Co. v. Butts*[28] are representative. In the *Associated Press* case a well-known former general brought suit for libel against a newspaper association for reporting that he had led a charge of students against federal marshals and had assumed command of a crowd in riot at the University of Mississippi campus. The Texas Court of Civil Appeals affirmed a judgment for plaintiff, adopting as its rationale the pre-*Times* majority view (as espoused in *Post v. Hallam*[29]) that only statements of opinion, and not of fact, were privileged. The Texas court apparently considered the *New York Times* rule inapplicable because the plaintiff was not a "public official." And in the *Curtis Publishing Co.* case a football coach secured a libel judgment in the United States Court of Appeals for the Fifth Circuit against a national magazine which published an article stating that he collaborated with another coach to fix a football game. The case never reached the *Times* rule because it was held that defendant waived any defense on constitutional issues (thereby waiving the *Times* defense) by failing to raise objections at the trial level. However, the court pointed out that it did not regard the plaintiff, an employee of a state university, as a public official within the meaning of the *New York Times* decision.[30]

In the second group of cases mentioned above the courts have extended the *Times* rule to situations where the plaintiff, though

27 393 S.W.2d 671 (Tex. Civ. App. 1965).

28 351 F.2d 702 (5th Cir. 1965).

29 Post Publishing Company v. Hallam, 59 Fed. 530 (6th Cir. 1893).

30 Curtis Publishing Co. v. Butts, *supra* note 28, at 712-713 n.23. One judge dissented, believing that defendant could not have waived a constitutional right which had not been enunciated at the time; see 351 F.2d 702, 723-724 (dissenting opinion). For cases which have not invoked the *Times* rule, see: Youssoupoff v. C.B.S., Inc., 48 Misc.2d 700, 265 N.Y.S.2d 754 (Sup. Ct. 1965) (assassination of Rasputin); Spahn v. Julian Messner, Inc., 43 Misc.2d 219, 250 N.Y.S.2d 233 (1964), *aff'd* 260 N.Y.S.2d 451 (1965) (fictional biography of a baseball player); Dempsey v. Time, Inc., 43 Misc.2d 754, 252 N.Y.S.2d 186 (1964), *aff'd* 254 N.Y.S.2d 80 (1964) (alleging that a former professional boxer cheated to win his title).

not a public official, is so closely associated with a public official that the rule can be said to apply to him. *Pearson v. Fairbanks Publishing Company*[31] and *Gilberg v. Goffi*[32] are examples of this limited extension of the *Times* rule. The *Pearson* case held that a newspaper columnist who advocated the cause of a senatorial candidate could not sue for libel under the *Times* rule unless actual malice was shown. The reason given was that plaintiff occupied the same standing in law as the senatorial candidate whose cause he was publicly supporting. Similarly, in *Gilbert v. Goffi* the defendant made charges of conflict of interest against a candidate for mayor on the ground that the candidate was a member of a law firm that practiced in the municipal courts of the city. Plaintiff, the candidate's law partner, sued for libel alleging that the editorial derogated his professional integrity. The court invoked the *Times* rule and held that plaintiff's action was "so closely related to criticism of a public official that the *Times* case is determinative."[33]

In the above cases, whether or not plaintiff was a "public official" or closely associated with such official was a determinative factor in the ultimate decision. However, two recent cases have abandoned the "public official" test and instead have applied a "public figure" or "public concern" test. In so doing, these cases have stated excellent guidelines for future application of the *New York Times* rule.

In the first of these cases, *Pauling v. National Review, Inc.*,[34] plaintiff, winner of the Nobel Prize for chemistry and the Nobel Peace Prize, brought a libel action against the corporate owner, the individual publisher and the editor of a national periodical for an article to the effect that plaintiff was un-American and a Communist sympathizer. The complaint was dismissed directly on the doctrine of *New York Times Co. v. Sullivan* which had been decided after suit was initiated but before this decision was rendered. The New York Supreme Court expressly pointed out

31 33 U.S.L. Week 2307 (Alaska Super. Ct. 1964).
32 251 N.Y.S.2d 823 (1964), *aff'd* 15 N.Y.2d 1023, 260 N.Y.S.2d 29 (1965).
33 *Id.* at 825.
34 269 N.Y.S.2d 11 (1966).

that neither *Times*[35] nor *Rosenblatt*[36] limited the privilege to make good-faith misstatements of fact to just those cases which involved "public officials" and that therefore the court was justified in expanding the rule to include those who have voluntarily placed their opinions and actions before the public. The court held, therefore, that when a "private citizen has, by his conduct, made himself a public figure engaged voluntarily in public discussion of matters of grave public concern and controversy . . ."[37] then such citizen cannot recover for defamatory falsehood unless it is proven that the statement was made with knowledge of its falsity or with a reckless disregard of whether it was false or not.

A similar conclusion was reached in *Walker v. Courier-Journal and Louisville Times Company, Inc.*[38] The plaintiff, again General Walker,[39] sought judgment for libel against a newspaper and a radio and television station for comments made by those media in reliance on reports released by the Associated Press. In dismissing the complaint the District Court held that by virtue of the *Times* decision the freedom of expression had superseded the law of libel in matters of "grave national interest." The court recognized that Walker was not a "public official" within the meaning of the *Times* decision. However, the language of the Kansas Supreme Court in *Coleman v. MacLennan*[40] was quoted with approval in arriving at the conclusion that if the matter were one of public concern the privilege should be recognized. In a concise summary the District Court held:

. . . [T]he Supreme Court of the United States has served clear notice that the broad Constitutional protections afforded by the first and fourteenth amendments will not be limited to "public officials" only, for to have any meaning the protections must be extended to other categories

---

[35] 376 U.S. 254, 283 (1964).
[36] Rosenblatt v. Baer, 383 U.S. 75, 85 (1966).
[37] Pauling v. National Review, Inc., 269 N.Y.S.2d 11, 18 (1966).
[38] 246 F. Supp. 231 (W.D. Ky. 1965).
[39] See discussion of Associated Press v. Walker, *supra,* note 27.
[40] "This privilege extends to a great variety of subjects and includes matters of public concern, public men, and candidates for office." Coleman v. MacLennan, 78 Kan. 711, 714, 98 Pac. 281, 285 (1908).

of individuals or persons involved in the area of public debate or who become involved in matters of public concern.[41]

One of the functions of the first amendment is to protect freedom of speech and of press on all matters in which there is some element of public participation.[42] In January of 1967, the United States Supreme Court, perhaps recognizing the conceptual difficulties in the "public official" limitation,[43] moved in the direction of expanding the constitutional privilege. In *Time, Inc. v. Hill*,[44] Mr. Justice Brennan stated:

> We hold that the constitutional protections for speech and press preclude the application of the New York statute to redress false reports of matters of public interest in the absence of proof that the defendant published the report with the knowledge of its falsity or in reckless disregard of the truth.

The Supreme Court, then, has apparently recognized that the privilege to make good faith misstatements of fact applies whenever the matter involved is of grave public concern and legitimate public interest. The reasoning of the Kansas Supreme Court in *Coleman v. MacLennan*, in holding that the privilege exists where the subject involves important matters of public concern, should therefore be explicitly adopted as establishing the extent and limits of the constitutional privilege.

41 Walker v. Courier-Journal, 246 F. Supp. 231, 233 (W.D. Ky. 1965).
42 Pedrick, *Freedom of the Press and the Law of Libel: The Modern Revised Translation,* 49 CORNELL L. Q. 581, 592 (1964).
43 Note, 18 VAND. L. REV. 1429, 1443-1445 (1965).
44 385 U.S. 374, 87 S. Ct. 534, 542 (1967).

Defamation by Broadcast: A Lively Dispute

GEORGE J. VAN OS

I. INTRODUCTION

The popularity ratings of the television program continued to decline. The sponsors were insistent. They demanded a program capable of attracting the public interest and capturing the nationwide television audience. The emcee of the program made one last effort. He began his program by joking about a well-known personality. Then, warming to the subject, he began to tell derogatory stories about this individual. Were they true? The emcee did not know nor did he care. But he did know that he had everything to gain and nothing to lose. If the maltreated person desired to rectify the situation, it would involve a lengthy courtroom procedure and the ambiguous and unpredictable rules of defamation were on the defendant's side. Let him try to prove it!

Before the problems arising from the above situation can be fully appreciated, it is necessary to understand the development of the law of defamation and the distinctions that have evolved. If they should appear artificial, and in many cases impractical,

Reprinted by permission of Dennis & Co., Inc., from *Houston Law Review*, II (Fall, 1964), 238-250.

consider that the law changes slowly with due regard for the past while a dynamic, technological society changes abruptly and without looking back.

II. IN RETROSPECT

Defamation is defined as the taking from one's reputation.[1] The early authorities, when confronted with a situation involving defamation treated one in writing as libel while the spoken word, if defamatory, was slander.[2] The courts have continued to adhere to this distinction.[3] From these basic principles, libel has become defamation which is received through the sense of sight, or perhaps also by touch or smell,[4] while slander is received by the sense of hearing.[5]

The most important difference between libel and slander lies in the amount of evidence necessary to prove the plaintiff's claim. Libel is actionable without proof of actual damages;[6] it is only necessary to prove a statement libelous,[7] that the defendant made

---

[1] BLACK LAW DICTIONARY (4th ed. 1951); see, *e.g.*, Fey v. King, 194 Iowa 835, 190 N.W. 519, 521 (1922), Sheridan v. Davies, 139 Kan. 256, 31 P.2d 51, 54 (1934); Deiner v. Star-Chronicle Publishing Co., 232 Mo. 232 Mo. 416, 135 S.W. 6, 11 (1911).

[2] Ratcliffe v. Evans, [1892] 2 Q.B. 524; Thorley v. Lord Kerry, 4 Taunt. 355, 128 Eng. Rep. 367 (1812); Villers v. Monsley, 2 Wils. K.B. 403, 95 Eng. Rep. 886 (1769); Harman v. Delany, 2 Strange 898, 93 Eng. Rep. 925 (1731); Iveson v. Moore, 1 Ld. Raym. 486, 91 Eng. Rep. 1224 (1700); Austin v. Culpepper, 2 Show. K.B. 313, 89 Eng. Rep. 960 (1683); King v. Lake, Hardres 470, 145 Eng. Rep. 552 (1670).

[3] Dyer v. MacDougall, 93 F. Supp. 484 (E.D.N.Y. 1950); Ajouelo v. Auto-Soler Co., 61 Ga. App. 216, 6 S.E.2d 415 (1930); Harrison v. Pool, 24 Ga. App. 587, 101 S.E. 765 (1920); Coper v. Vannier, 20 Ill. App.2d 761, 156 N.E.2d 761 (1959); Lily v. Belks Dept. Store, 178 S.C. 278, 182 S.E. 889 (1935).

[4] PROSSER, TORTS § 93, at 586 (2d ed. 1955).

[5] *Ibid.*

[6] Keller v. Safeway Stores, 15 F. Supp. 716 (Mont. 1936); Clark v. McClurg, 215 Cal. 279, 9 P.2d 505 (1932); State *ex rel.* Lopez v. Killigrew, 202 Ind. 397, 174 N.E. 808 (1931); Natchez Times Publishing Co. v. Dunigan, 221 Miss. 320, 72 So.2d 681 (1954), 46 A.L.R.2d 1280 (1954); Sydney v. McFadden Newspaper Publishing Corp., 242 N.Y. 808, 151 N.E. 209 (Ct. App. 1926).

[7] For purposes of discussion the words will be considered defamatory unless otherwise stated.

the statement, and that the statement was published.[8] It was assumed that damage would occur if the libel was published.[9] Slander, however, requires that actual damages be proven before the plaintiff will prevail.[10] The courts did not consider it likely that a spoken word would ordinarily cause enough harm to the plaintiff to warrant a presumption that damages did occur.[11] At a time when newspapers and other means of communication were scarce and distances between towns were great, it seems they reached a just result. These distinctions and assumptions arose before the modern methods of communication had come into existence, yet they persist despite being rendered obsolete by modern technology.

Gradually, four types of slander have become actionable without proof of actual damage. These were of such a serious nature that judges thought those words would normally cause damage and did not require the proof ordinarily necessary in slander. The four types of slander per se are:[12] (1) an imputation of a serious crime;[13] (2) an imputation of a loathsome disease;[14] (3)

---

[8] Harum, *Remolding of Common Law Defamation,* 49 A.B.A.J. 149, 150 (1963).

[9] PROSSER, *op. cit. supra* note 4, at 587.

[10] Pollard v. Lyon, 91 U.S. (23 Wall.) 308 (1876); Kirk v. Ebenhoch, 354 Mo. 762, 191 S.W.2d 643 (1946); Sleight v. Woods, 145 Misc. 824, 260 N.Y.S. 825 (Sup. Ct. 1932); Sawyer v. United States Cigar Stores, 180 S.C. 70, 185 S.E. 38 (1936); Montgomery Ward & Co. v. Peaster, 178 S.W.2d 302 (Tex. Civ. App.—Eastland 1944).

[11] PROSSER, *op. cit. supra* note 9.

[12] "Words slanderous per se are words which intrinsically, without innuendo, import injury and are words from which damage, by consent of men generally, flows as a natural consequence." Koerner v. Lawler, 180 Kan. 318, 304 P.2d 926, 929 (1956); see, *e.g.,* Hudson v. Schmid, 132 Neb. 583, 272 N.W. 406 (1937); Hewitt v. Wasek, 35 Misc.2d 946, 231 N.Y.S.2d 884 (Sup. Ct. 1962); Maas v. Sefcit, 138 S.W.2d 897 (Tex. Civ. App.—Austin 1948).

[13] LeMoine v. Spicer, 146 Fla. 758, 1 So.2d 730 (1941) (plaintiff accused of being drunk at fraternal meeting, an indictable offense); Davis v. Carey, 141 Pa. 314, 2 Atl. 633 (1891) (plaintiff accused of arson to defraud insurance company); Tabet v. Kaufman, 67 S.W.2d 1072 (Tex. Civ. App.—San Antonio 1934) (plaintiff accused of being a thief); Heming v. Power, 10 M. & W. 564, 152 Eng. Rep. 595 (1842) (plaintiff accused of incest).

[14] McDonald v. Nugent, 122 Iowa 651, 98 N.W. 506 (1904) (venereal disease); Sally v. Brown, 220 Ky. 576, 295 S.W. 890 (1927) (venereal disease); Simpson v. Press Pub. Co., 33 Misc. 228, 67 N.Y.S. 401 (Sup. Ct. 1900) (leprosy); Taylor v. Hall, 2 Strange 1189, 93 Eng. Rep. 1118 (1743) (pox).

an imputation causing harm to a person in his trade or occupation,[15] and (4) in some jurisdictions, an imputation of unchastity to a woman.[16] It would seem from these exceptions to the law of slander that the courts were not entirely satisfied with the basic elements of defamation and viewed the law as it existed with some misgivings.

While the courts have continued to direct these rules to libel and slander, they have begun to apply different reasoning. Cardozo stated, "what gives the sting to the writing is its permanence of form,"[17] and agreed with the easier manner provided for proving a case of libel.[18] It must be remembered, however, that Cardozo was not speaking in reference to radio and television when he made that statement.[19]

The first awareness of the impending problem arose in *Youssepoff v. Metro-Goldwyn-Mayer Pictures, Ltd.*,[20] which dealt with a defamation suit against a motion picture studio for false representations made in a motion picture.[21] In *Youssepoff* it was stated that the projection on the screen "is a permanent matter

---

[15] Meyerson v. Hurburt, 98 F.2d 232 (D.C. Cir. 1938) (businessman's credit called bad); Louisville Taxicab & Transfer Co. v. Ingle, 229 Ky. 518, 17 S.W.2d 709 (1929) (chauffeur called a drinker); Rush v. Cavanaugh, 2 Pa. 187 (1845) (attorney called a shyster); Harman v. Delaney, 2 Strange 898, 93 Eng. Rep. 925 (1731) (gunsmith accused of shoddy practice).

[16] Biggerstaff v. Zimmerman, 108 Colo. 194, 114 P.2d 1098 (1941); Simons v. Harris, 215 Iowa 479, 245 N.W. 875 (1932) (plaintiff called a g-d-damn dirty whore); Cushings v. Helderman, 117 Iowa 637, 91 N.W. 940 (1902) (unmarried woman accused of sexual intercourse); Matthew v. Crass, Cro. Jac. 323, 79 Eng. Rep. 276 (1614) (plaintiff accused of intercourse). Several courts have accomplished the same result by holding that an imputation of unchastity is equivalent to charge of crime of adultery or fornication. See, *e.g.*, Davis v. Sladden, 17 Ore. 259, 21 Pac. 140 (1889); Zeliff v. Jennings, 61 Tex. 458 (1884).

[17] Ostrowe v. Lee, 256 N.Y. 36, 175 N.E. 505, 506 (Ct. App. 1931).

[18] *Ibid.*

[19] Ostrowe v. Lee, *supra* note 17 (involved defamation by letter and similar defamation by telephone).

[20] 50 T.L.R. 581, 99 A.L.R. 864 (1934).

[21] The motion picture was entitled *Rasputin, the Mad Monk,* and represented the plaintiff as Princess Natasha who the picture alleged had been seduced by Rasputin.

to be seen by the eye and is the proper subject of an action for *libel*, if defamatory."[22] (Emphasis added.) The fact that the spoken word accompanied the presentation was regarded as an ancillary matter merely explaining to the viewer what was to be seen.[23] *Brown v. Paramount-Publix Corp.*[24] dealt with a similar situation[25] and stated, "In the hands of a wrongdoer these devices have untold possibilities toward producing an effective *libel.*"[26] (Emphasis added.)

The problem of defamation by radio and television is not so easily solved. The courts have been slow to realize the peculiar problems connected to these media of communication and have attempted to categorize defamation by broadcast into the antiquated libel and slander pigeonholes. This failure to take cognizance of great changes in mass communication has resulted in much confusion and harsh results.

III. CONFUSION

The most settled idea is that defamatory material read from a script and broadcast is libel.[27] This rationale follows the "permanence of form"[28] doctrine in determining whether the rules of libel or slander are to be applied. All that can be said of this

[22] Youssepoff v. Metro-Goldwyn-Mayer Pictures, Ltd., 50 T.L.R. 581, 99 A.L.R. 864, 875 (1934).

[23] *Ibid.*

[24] 240 App. Div. 520, 270 N.Y.S. 544 (Sup. Ct. 1934), *accord,* Kelly v. Loew's, 76 F. Supp. 473 (D. Mass. 1948).

[25] Plaintiff sued for representation by motion picture, *An American Tragedy*, that she was an immoral, slovenly person.

[26] Brown v. Paramount-Publix Corp., *supra* note 24, at 547.

[27] Sorensen v. Wood, 123 Neb. 348, 243 N.W. 82, *appeal dismissed,* 290 U.S. 599 (1932); Landau v. Columbia Broadcasting System, 205 Misc. 357, 128 N.Y.S.2d 254 (Sup. Ct. 1954); Hartmann v. Winchell, 296 N.Y. 296, 73 N.E. 2d 30 (Ct. App. 1947); Gibler v. Houston Post Co., 310 S.W. 2d 377 (Tex. Civ. App.—Houston 1958, error ref'd n.r.e.). *Contra,* Meldrun v. Australian Broadcasting System, [1932] Vict. L.R. 425 (all defamation by broadcast slander whether read from script or spoken extemporaneously); *see also* Bohlen, *Fifty Years of Torts,* 50 HARV. L. REV. 725, 729-31 (1937).

[28] Ostrowe v. Lee, *supra* note 17.

criterion is that it is artificial and impractical. Does the listener know that the defamatory material is being read or does he care? Is the capacity for harm any greater because it is read rather than spoken extemporaneously?

The necessary corollary to the libel-if-script theory is the principle of slander-if extemporaneous. *Locke v. Gibbons*[29] held that extemporaneous remarks on radio must be considered slander. *Remington v. Bentley*[30] applied the rules of slander to defamation resulting from an extemporaneous remark on a television broadcast. This extention of libel and slander distinctions to television seems especially strained in view of the past opinions holding defamation by motion picture to be libel.[31] An argument might have been made that a television program does not possess the permanence of form of a motion picture, which seems to be so important in determining libel. But this is becoming less persuasive as taping methods have become perfected.[32] The countless number of repeated programs further weakens this argument.

The decisions involving defamation by broadcast have not been accepted without much dispute. *Hartmann v. Winchell*[33] regarded a defamation by script as libel but attached no significance to the visibility of the script. Justice Fuld in *Hartmann* asked for a re-examination of the law of libel. In dicta, *Summit Hotel Co. v. National Broadcasting Co.*[34] stated that defamation by radio possesses attributes of libel and slander and should be regarded as a new form of action. *Shor v. Billingsley*[35] held a

29 164 Misc. 877, 299 N.Y.S. 188 (Sup. Ct. 1937), *aff'd*, 253 App. Div. 887, 2 N.Y.S.2d 1015 (1938).

30 88 F. Supp. 166 (S.D.N.Y. 1949).

31 Brown v. Paramount-Publix Corp., *supra* note 24; Youssepoff v. Metro-Goldwyn-Mayer Pictures, Ltd., *supra* note 20. *But see* Young v. New Mexico Broadcasting Co., 60 N.M. 475, 291 P.2d 776 (1956).

32 Comment, 33 Miss. L.J. 115, 122 (1961). See also Haley, *The Law on Radio Programs*, 5 Geo. Wash. L. Rev. 157, 171 (1937) (discusses taping of radio programs).

33 296 N.Y. 296, 73 N.E.2d 30 (Ct. App. 1947).

34 336 Pa. 182, 8 A.2d 302 (1939). See also Kelly v. Hoffman, 137 N.J.L. 695, 61 A.2d 14 (1948).

35 4 Misc. 2d 857, 158 N.Y.S. 476 (Sup. Ct. 1957).

defamatory remark on television to be libel even if extemporaneous and rejected the contention that the application of libel rules to radio and television must be made by the legislature. Other courts have simply avoided any determination of libel or slander and based their decision on other grounds.[36]

The Georgia court made the most significant step forward in 1962, when following the advice of the court in *Summit Hotel*; the court created a new tort. The Georgia Appellate Court in *American Broadcasting-Paramount Theatres, Inc. v. Simpson*[37] held that defamation by broadcast is not governed by traditional libel and slander law and created the tort "defamacast," which is actionable per se. This is the first decision that has taken some positive steps to remove the artificiality and confusion.

IV. ENTER THE SCHOLAR

While the courts were creating this confusion with vague opinions and artificial distinctions, legal writers became more aware of the problem and began to advance various theories as to how a defamation by broadcast should be treated. Before examining these theories and discussing their pros and cons, it is necessary to determine the ultimate objective that is sought.

It would be a simple task to begin by categorizing the various possibilities of defamation by broadcast and applying certain rules to each category. A defamation by script might be treated in one manner and an extemporaneous defamation in another. We might further divide radio and television into separate categories. A division of television, radio, script, and extemporaneous remarks into separate classifications would only lead to the pitfalls already occasioned by the early common law distinctions of libel and slander. The capacity for harm will remain constant regardless of any classification. What is needed is a treatment that will encompass all areas of defamation by broadcast.

---

[36] Lynch v. Lyons, 303 Mass. 116, 20 N.E.2d 953 (1939) (required proof of actual damages in slander action); Miles v. Louis Wasmer, Inc., 172 Wash. 466, 20 P.2d 847 (1933) (held slanderous per se and unnecessary to distinguish between libel or slander).
[37] 106 Ga. App. 230, 126 S.E.2d 873 (1962).

Any treatment that is adopted must take cognizance of the right of free speech guaranteed to the individual. The fact that the individual is a broadcaster does not in any way lessen this guarantee. At the same time, a remedy must be available for any abuse of this freedom. In view of the recent Supreme Court decision of *New York Times v. Sullivan*,[38] any decision that tends to abridge the right of free speech would be quickly reversed or rendered unconstitutional. True, *Sullivan* does not involve defamation by broadcast,[39] but the increased emphasis on the individual's right of free speech could easily reach the area of defamation by broadcast.

There is no reason why a court should be handcuffed by obsolete rules. The damage that may be accomplished by the widespread coverage of radio and television must be appraised in a realistic manner. Any idea that is finally accepted must be viewed with an eye toward the future. It is entirely possible that if this is not done, the same problems may arise with another revolutionary type of communication. The practical problems of proof must be viewed so as not to exclude the individual who has neither the technological knowledge nor the funds to maintain an exhaustive investigation of the broadcasting facilities. Primarily, a bold new concept is needed. Three distinct interests are involved. Any decision must balance the interests of the individual, the interests of the broadcasting media, and the public benefit from the communication facilities.

(A) Strict Liability

One solution advanced is the consideration of defamation by broadcast as libelous in nature, and imposing liability without fault.[40] Those favoring this theory argue that the active partic-

---

[38] 376 U.S. 254 (1964).

[39] *Sullivan* involved a newspaper editorial advertisement and a privileged defamation. The Supreme Court held that state action in restricting free speech in connection with a factually incorrect statement would not be allowed when regarding the official conduct of a public official.

[40] Donnelly, *Defamation by Radio: A Reconsideration*, 34 IOWA L. REV. 12 (1948); Keller, *Federal Control of Defamation by Radio*, 12 NOTRE DAME LAW. 134 (1937); Leflar, *Radio and TV Defamation: "Fault" or "Strict Liabil-*

ipation of the broadcasting station is necessary before the defamation can be published.[41] The law of defamation imposes the risk of publication of a libel on the publisher, and not on the victim.[42] A newspaper is subject to this burden and a broadcaster should not be exempt.[43] This view would impose joint liability on the broadcasting facilities and the speaker in their capacity as publishers[44] and would abolish any distinction between defamation from a script and defamation by an extemporaneous remark. The proposition that extemporaneous remarks are beyond the control of the station is disputed. Many believe that the station would take the proper corrective measures if a harsher burden were placed on the station.[45] These corrective measures include the transferring of responsibility for payment of damages[46] to the speaker and increased charges for time spots to aid in payment of defamation insurance premiums.[47]

Another factor to be considered is the financial advantage that

---

ity", 15 OHIO ST. L.J. 252 (1954); Remmers, *Recent Trends in Defamation by Radio*, 64 HARV. L. REV. 727 (1951); Vold, *Extemporaneous Defamation: A Rejoinder*, 25 MARQ. L. REV. 57 (1941); Vold, *Defamatory Interpolations in Radio Broadcasts*, 88 U. PA. L. REV. 249 (1940); Vold, *The Basis for Liability for Defamation by Radio*, 19 MINN. L. REV. 611 (1935); Vold, *Defamation by Radio*, 2 J. RADIO L. 673 (1932); Comment, 17 MARQ. L. REV. 138 (1933); Note, 11 NEB. L. REV. 325 (1937); 11 WIS. L. REV. 115 (1935).

41 Keller, *supra* note 40; Remmers, *supra* note 40; Vold, *Extemporaneous Defamations: A Rejoinder*, 25 MARQ. L. REV. 57 (1941); Vold, *Defamatory Interpolations in Radio Broadcasts*, 88 U. PA. L. REV. 249 (1940); Vold, *The Basis for Liability for Defamation by Radio*, 19 MINN. L. REV. 611 (1935); Note, 11 NEB. L. REV. 325 (1935).

42 Peck v. Tribune Co., 214 U.S. 185 (1909); Taylor v. Hearst, 107 Cal. 262, 40 Pac. 392 (1895); Sweet v. Post Publishing Co., 215 Mass. 450, 102 N.E. 660 (1913); Walker v. Bee-News Publishing Co., 122 Neb. 511, 240 N.W. 570 (1932).

43 *Ibid.*

44 Keller, *supra* note 40; Remmers, *supra* note 40; Vold, *Defamatory Interpolations in Radio Broadcasts*, 88 U. PA. L. REV. 249 (1940); Vold, *The Basis for Liability for Defamation by Radio*, 19 MINN. L. REV. 611 (1935).

45 Keller, *supra* note 40; Vold, *The Basis for Liability for Defamation by Radio*, 19 MINN. L. REV. 611 (1935).

46 *Ibid.*

47 Donnelly, *supra* note 40; Keller, *supra* note 40; Vold, *The Basis for Liability for Defamation by Radio*, 19 MINN. L. REV. 611 (1935); Vold, *Extemporaneous Defamation: A Rejoinder*, 25 MARQ. L. REV. 56 (1941).

is derived from operating a radio or television station. Those favoring this liability argue that the owners of radio and television stations enter such a business for the economic advantages presented, and that these owners should be prepared to assume risks ordinarily present in such a situation which he knows or should know may arise.[48]

A possible objection to this proposition is the "floodgates of litigation" problem. It has been said that given such an opportunity, "victims" of harmless remarks will descend upon the courts seeking a remedy, and waste the time of a court already congested with an overload of law suits.[49] This apprehension, when discarded, seldom materializes.

The most pronounced objection to this theory is the stringent controls that radio and television stations will be required to impose upon their broadcasters. This will cause much of the individuality of the broadcaster to be lost. The broadcaster of news would become a news reporter rather than a news commentator. It should not be forgotten that radio and television stations perform a service to the public in providing information, analysis, political viewpoints, and entertainment. If a broadcaster were required to be too careful in his discussion of any controversial matter, the importance of the matter and its effect might be lost to the vast majority of the public. To stereotype each broadcaster in the same mold cannot help but disserve the public interest. True, an exception might be made for particular types of broadcasts, but this exception would only serve to further illustrate that absolute liability is not the complete answer to the problem.

(B) Negligence

Many have disputed the imposition of absolute liability and favor the application of the rules of negligence to any defamation by broadcast.[50] Negligence would provide the courts with

---

[48] Keller, *supra* note 40; Vold, *The Basis for Liability for Defamation by Radio*, 19 MINN. L. REV. 611 (1935); Vold, *Defamatory Interpolations in Radio Broadcasts*, 88 U. PA. L. REV. 249 (1940); Note, 11 NEB. L. REV. 325 (1941).
[49] Harum, *supra* note 8.
[50] Bohlen, *Fifty Years of Torts*, 50 HARV. L. REV. 725, at 731 (1937); Farnum, *Radio Defamation and the American Law Institute*, 16 B.U.L. REV. 1 (1936);

a familiar standard. By treating the case as an ordinary negligence action, the standard of conduct of the defendant and the failure to conform to that standard would become prime factors in the plaintiff's recovery.[51] The plaintiff would also be required to prove actual damages flowing from the defendant's negligence.[52] The burden of proof would be placed on the plaintiff and the defendant could avail himself of any defenses that might exist.[53]

The similarity between a disseminator of information and the broadcaster lends support to this theory.[54] The most common forms of disseminators are newsstand operators and book dealers. Despite their obvious participation in the publication of any defamation, the courts have held that a disseminator is not liable for statements contained in materials sold or published by him unless he has been guilty of some fault approximating negligence by failing to discover the defamation before publishing it.[55] An analogy would seem to exist between the radio and television broadcaster and the newsstand operator, in that both supply the facilities through which the defamation is published. Those favoring this theory argue that the same rule should be applied to defamation by broadcast.[56]

Graham, *Defamation and Radio*, 12 WASH. L. REV. 282 (1937); Guider, *Liability for Defamation in Political Broadcasts*, 2 J. RADIO L. 708 (1932); Haley, *supra* note 32; Seitz, *Responsibility of Radio Stations for Extemporaneous Defamation*, 24 MARQ. L. REV. 117 (1940); Sprague, *More Freedom of the Air*, 11 AIR L. REV. 17 (1940); Sprague, *Freedom of the Air*, 8 AIR L. REV. 30 (1937); Comment, 12 ORE. L. REV. 149 (1932); Note, 46 HARV. L. REV. 132 (1932).

[51] See, *e.g.*, Cowles v. City of Minneapolis, 128 Minn. 452, 151 N.W. 184 (1915); Jackson v. Central Torpedo Co., 117 Okla. 245, 246 Pac. 426 (1926); Yerkes v. Northern Pac. Ry. Co., 112 Wis. 184, 88 N.W. 33 (1901).

[52] Sprague, *Freedom of the Air*, 8 AIR L. REV. 30 (1937).

[53] See, *e.g.*, Lane v. Cardwell, 306 S.W.2d 290 (Ky. 1957); Memphis St. Ry. Co. v. Cavell, 135 Tenn. 462, 187 S.W. 179 (1916); Clark v. Lang, 124 Va. 544, 98 S.E. 673 (1919).

[54] Bohlen, *supra* note 50; Farnum, *supra* note 50; Graham, *supra* note 50; Comment, *supra* note 50.

[55] Bowerman v. Detroit Free Press, 287 Mich. 443, 283 N.W. 642 (1939); Balabanoff v. Fossani, 192 Misc. 615, 81 N.Y.S.2d 732 (Sup. Ct. 1948); Vizetelly v. Mudie's Select Library, [1907] 2 Q.B. 170.

[56] See authorities cited note 54 *supra*.

Many feel that the broadcaster should not bear the same burden as the newspaper which is held strictly liable.[57] They distinguish the two by arguing that a newspaper has a greater amount of control over the publication.[58] Through the use of proofreaders and editorial staffs, the chance of an undetected libel is effectively eliminated. On the other hand, extemporaneous remarks of a broadcast are subject to very little control, and to avoid an unjust result the laws of negligence should be imposed in this situation.

Whatever might be said for this approach, it fails to take into account the possibility of a situation arising where the plaintiff would suffer unwarranted hardship. It is entirely possible that a defamation be broadcast without any negligence attaching to the operators or broadcasters, and the defamatory statement, benefit the station through increased audience appeal or product appeal. The plaintiff would suffer injury to his reputation but would be unable to be remunerated due to the broadcaster's lack of negligence. To allow this result presents a fallacy in the theory of common law liability attached to defamation by broadcast. This situation may occur more often than we at first realize. Such programs as "man on the street" could become breeding grounds for defamatory remarks and, if this idea is applied without certain exceptions, the program would be almost immune to liability.

(C) State Statutory Control

The advancement of these theories, their discussion and attendant confusion has resulted in an attempt at statutory control by the state legislatures. The National Association of Broadcasters has also urged legislation covering defamation by broadcast. The Association has formulated a model statute[59] which provides for liability if, and only if, the failure to exercise due care has been

---

[57] Bohlen, *supra* note 50; Graham, *supra* note 50; Haley, *supra* note 32; Seitz, *supra* note 50; Note, 46 HARV. L. REV. 133 (1932); 18 IOWA L. REV. 98 (1932).

[58] *Ibid.*

[59] An Act Relating to Defamation by Radio and Television, prepared by the Legal Department, National Association of Broadcasters (1954). For pertinent text see Remmers, *supra* note 40, at 741 n.71.

alleged and proved.[60] The statute further provides that only those actual damages which have been alleged and proved will be allowed.[61]

Statutes establishing the lack of due care as a necessary element of defamation by broadcast have been adopted in twenty-two states.[62] Sixteen of these states[63] place the burden of proof on the plaintiff while the other six[64] require the defendant to show that due care was exercised.

The provision regarding the proof of actual damages has been adopted directly from the model statute in the broadcast defamation statutes of Arizona,[65] Nebraska,[66] and Wyoming.[67] Georgia[68] and Louisiana[69] have followed the model statute with only minor changes in wording. Oregon's statute provides for recovery of general and special damages that the plaintiff can prove by competent evidence but extends the application of the statute to publication in newspapers, motion pictures, and radio and television.[70]

The effectiveness of any state legislative control to solve the

[60] "[No liability shall attach] unless it shall be alleged and proved by the complaining party, that such owner, licensee, operator, or such agent or employer, has failed to exercise due care to prevent the publication or utterance of such statement in such broadcast." See authorities cited note 59 *supra*.

[61] "[I]n any action for damages for any defamatory statement published or uttered in or as a part of visual or sound radio broadcast, the complaining party shall be allowed only such actual damages as he has alleged and proved." See authorities cited note 59 *supra*.

[62] Arizona, California, Colorado, Florida, Georgia, Iowa, Kansas, Kentucky, Louisiana, Michigan, Minnesota, Nebraska, Nevada, New Mexico, North Carolina, Ohio, South Dakota, Tennessee, Texas, Virginia, West Virginia, Wyoming.

[63] Arizona, Florida, Georgia, Kansas, Kentucky, Louisiana, Michigan, Nebraska, New Mexico, North Carolina, South Dakota, Tennessee, Texas, Virginia, West Virginia, and Wyoming.

[64] California, Colorado, Iowa, Minnesota, Nevada, and Ohio.

[65] ARIZ. REV. STAT. ANN. § 652 (1956).

[66] NEB. REV. STAT. § 86.603 (1943).

[67] WYO. STAT. ANN. § 1-872 (1957).

[68] GA. CODE ANN. § 105-714 (1949).

[69] LA. REV. STAT. ANN. § 1353 (1951).

[70] ORE. REV. STAT. § 30.155 (1955).

problem is doubtful. Any statute is always subject to interpretation by the court. What interpretation will be given is often unpredictable. A case in point is *American Broadcasting-Paramount Theatres, Inc. v. Simpson.*[71] Georgia's statute provides for defamation by broadcast and states that the complaining party should be allowed only such "actual, consequential, or punitive damages" as have been alleged and proved.[72] The Georgia Appellate Court paid little attention to the statute and stated that the traditional rules of libel and slander are no longer applicable. The court then established the new tort of "defamacast" and held that defamation by broadcast "falls into a new category. . . . In this category defamation by broadcast or 'defamacast' is actionable per se."[73] Thus it was not necessary to determine whether the defamation was libel or slander.

A major problem involved in any state statutory regulation in this area is the lack of uniformity among the states. The fact that a neighboring state may involve a different procedure and theory, poses a knotty conflict of laws problem. The victim's right to compensation should not fluctuate according to the boundaries of each state. The widespread coverage of a broadcast by today's nationwide networks demands a uniform method of approaching the problem.

(D) Federal Control

Federal control over defamation by broadcast has been advanced because of the lack of uniformity of state statutory control.[74] The incredibly vast potential for harm is another reason given for the advancement of this theory. The victim's right to recover should not fluctuate arbitrarily according to the position which the state has taken on the scope and extent of the broadcaster's liability. The uniform body of federal law would provide the certainty of a single statutory scheme.

---

[71] 106 Ga. App. 320, 126 S.E.2d 873 (1962); Note, 1 Hous. L. Rev. 58 (1963).

[72] See statute *supra* note 68.

[73] American Broadcasting-Paramount Theatres, Inc. v. Simpson, *supra* note 71 at 879.

[74] Keller, *supra* note 40; Korbel, *Defamation by Broadcast: The Need for Federal Control*, 49 A.B.A.J. 771 (1963).

It is submitted by those favoring federal control that the inter-state commerce clause affords ample authority for the legislative exercise of federal control over radio and television broadcasting.[75] An administrative body could be established to decide any disputes or the Federal Communications Commission could be granted jurisdiction over defamation by broadcast.[76]

The problem of what theory to follow and what purpose to accomplish still remains, however. The reasoning ultimately adopted would be the result of the pressures imposed by outside interests and it is doubtful that the interests of the individual would be fully served. It is also dubious that any individual would be able to withstand the economic burden of pursuing the administrative remedies and then resorting to the court structure. This system would seem to be too slanted in favor of the operators of radio and television and impose an unjust burden on the individual.

If federal control should become imperative, a far more reasonable method is available. The passage of a federal statute describing the treatment of defamation by broadcast would place the problem within the jurisdiction of the federal courts. The law would provide the required certainty and the use of the federal court system would make it unnecessary to establish an additional administrative agency.

V. LOOKING FORWARD

These various theories, like all innovations, have their disadvantages. The fundamental proposition is that all interests must be balanced. This proposition would preclude the application of absolute liability to defamation by broadcast. Absolute liability seems quite reasonable when considering who can best bear the risk of a defamation, but certainly cannot be said to balance any interests.

The application of the rules of negligence to defamation by broadcast would seem to balance the interests of both the

[75] *Ibid.*
[76] Korbel, *supra* note 74.

broadcaster and the individual, but overlooks the almost impossible task imposed on the plaintiff of proving negligence. The fact that the defamation resulted from a script rather than extemporaneously, or from a lack of proper control, would be extremely difficult to prove. The situation involving a lack of negligence, a benefit to defendant, and a loss of reputation to the plaintiff is not taken into account.

State statutory control lacks the uniformity needed and subjects the plaintiff to the different procedures and underlying purposes behind each legislative enactment. Any method of federal control would require the plaintiff to resort to the endless procedure of administrative bodies, and would aid the defendant operator in that he would be able to afford the time and legal expense attendant to such proceedings.

What is needed is a new tort that will abolish the old distinctions and establish a practical and expedient method of deciding defamation by broadcast cases. This is not as radical a move as one might first think. The Georgia court has established the tort of "defamacast", and many writers have been asking for a completely new approach for many years.

The problem of what elements the new tort should contain still remains. The negligence theory imposes an unjust burden on the plaintiff. This burden can be lessened by the application of the doctrine of res ipsa loquitur, in that there will then be an inference of negligence cast upon the defendant. The conditions necessary for the application of res ipsa loquitur would appear to be present in a defamation by broadcast. These conditions, simply stated, are: (1) the damage must be of a kind that does not ordinarily occur in the absence of negligence; (2) it must be caused by an instrumentality within the exclusive control of the defendant, and (3) it must not be due to any voluntary action on the part of the plaintiff.[77] The plaintiff, to establish the inference of negligence, must prove that the three conditions are present. The defendant would have the opportunity to rebut

77 Jesconowski v. Boston & Me. R.R., 329 U.S. 452 (1947); Gray v. McLaughlin, 207 Ark. 191, 179 S.W.2d 686 (1944); Gebhart v. McQuillen, 230 Iowa 181, 297 N.W. 301 (1941); Roberts v. Texas & Pac. Ry. Co., 142 Tex. 550, 180 S.W.2d 330 (1944); 9 WIGMORE, EVIDENCE § 2509 (3d ed. 1940).

the inference of negligence. The plaintiff would have difficulty in proving the actual operations of a radio or television station, whereas this would not present a problem to the defendant. Each party would be required to prove up certain elements, but neither party would be hindered by an unjust burden of proof.

The plaintiff would of course be required to prove the defamatory nature of the statement, but should not be required to prove the actual damages. The law of libel and negligence would then become interwoven.

In a situation where the defendant proves a lack of negligence the plaintiff could offer proof that the defendant has received a benefit. The jury would then have the alternative of awarding the plaintiff the amount of the benefit received by the defendant. The possibility of proving any benefit received might seem unrealistic, but rating systems and popularity indexes used by the broadcasting media would provide the plaintiff with the necessary proof.

A legitimate, uniform basis for decision has not been reached as of this writing. Courts continue to cling to time-worn distinctions and attempt to justify their decisions by strained and oftentimes vague reasoning. The courts that refuse to be influenced by the ancient categories of libel and slander will have accomplished a great service.

Bibliography for Chapter Six

BOOKS

Angoff, Charles. *Handbook of Libel.* New York: Essential Books, Duell, Sloan, and Pearce, 1946.

Ashley, Paul Pritchard. *Say It Safely: Legal Limits in Journalism and Broadcasting.* 3d ed. Seattle: University of Washington Press, 1966.

Davis, Jerome. *Character Assassination.* New York: Philosophical Library, 1950.

Gavin, Clark. *Foul, False, and Infamous: Famous Libel and Slander Cases of History.* New York: Abelard Press, 1950.

Harper, Fowler, and Fleming James, Jr. "Defamation." *The Law of Torts,* Vol. 1. Boston and Toronto: Little, Brown & Company, 1956. Pp. 349-473.

Hill, Mavis Millicent. *Auschwitz in England: A Record of Libel Action.* New York: Stein & Day, 1965.

McEwen, Robert L., and P. S. C. Lewis. *Gatley on Libel and Slander.* 5th ed. London: Sweet & Maxwell, 1967.

Nelson, Harold L. *Libel in News of Congressional Investigating Committees.* Minneapolis, Minn.: University of Minnesota Press, 1967.

Rose, A. *Libel and Academic Freedom on Trial.* Minneapolis, Minn.: University of Minnesota Press, 1967.

Thomas, Ella Cooper. *Libel and Slander and Related Actions.* Dobbs Ferry, New York: Oceana Publications, 1963.

ARTICLES

Becht, Arno C. "The Absolute Privilege of the Executive in Defamation," *Vanderbilt Law Review,* XV (October, 1962), 1127-1171.

Bertlesman, William O. "Libel and Public Man," *American Bar Association Journal,* LII (July, 1966), 657-662.

266

Bliss, Robert M. "Development of Fair Comment as a Defense to Libel," *Journalism Quarterly*, XLIV (Winter, 1967), 627-637.

Broadfoot, John W. "Defamation in Radio and Television—Past and Present," *Mercer Law Review*, XV (Spring, 1964), 450-466.

Donnelly, Richard C. "Right of Reply: An Alternative to an Action for Libel," *Virginia Law Review*, XXXIV (December, 1948), 867-900.

Franklin, Marc A. "The Origins and Constitutionality of Limitations on Truth as a Defense in Tort Law," *Stanford Law Review*, XVI (July, 1964), 789-848.

Fridman, G. H. L. "Compensation of the Innocent," *The Modern Law Review*, XXVI (September, 1963), 481-498.

Harnett, Bertram and John V. Thornton. "The Truth Hurts: A Critique of a Defense to Defamation," *Virginia Law Review*, XXXV (May, 1949), 425-445.

Nelson, Harold L. "Newsmen and the *Times* Doctrine," *Villanova Law Review*, XII, No. 4 (Summer, 1967), 738-750.

Pedrick, Willard H. "Freedom of the Press and the Law of Libel: The Modern Revised Translation," *Cornell Law Quarterly*, XLIX (Summer, 1964), 581-608.

Pound, Roscoe. "Equitable Relief Against Defamation and Injuries to Personality," *Harvard Law Review*, XXIX (April, 1916), 640-682.

Wade, John W. "Defamation and the Right of Privacy," *Vanderbilt Law Review*, XV (October, 1962), 1093-1125.

CASES

Associated Press v. Walker, 389 U.S. 702 (1968).

Beauharnais v. Illinois, 343 U.S. 250 (1952).

Coleman v. MacLennan, 78 Kan. 711, 98 Pac. 281 (1908).

Curtis Publishing Co. v. Butts, 389 U.S. 702 (1968).

Garrison v. Louisiana, 379 U.S. 64 (1964).

Near v. Minnesota, 283 U.S. 697 (1931).

New York Times Co. v. Connor, 365 F.2d 567 (5th Cir. 1966).

New York Times Company v. Sullivan, 376 U.S. 254 (1964).

People v. Croswell, 3 Johns. Cas. (N.Y.) 337 (1804).

Post Publishing Co. v. Hallam, 59 Fed. 530 (6th Cir. 1893).

Remington v. Bentley, 88 F. Supp. 166 (S.D.N.Y. 1949).

Rosenblatt v. Baer, 383 U.S. 75 (1966).

Stromberg v. California, 283 U.S. 359 (1931).

CHAPTER SEVEN

The Control of Ideas—About Sex, Religion, Politics, and Commerce

LOS ANGELES, for one month running, arrests the actors performing in *The Beard*. A high school principal near Binghamton, N.Y., orders the senior class to halt rehearsals of *Inherit the Wind* because five Baptist ministers protest presentation of the play based on the Scopes trial. The chairman of the speech and drama department at Middle Tennessee State University stands in the doorway and turns away about 100 students and other patrons of a student production of *Dylan* because it is too "suggestive." Governor Lester Maddox of Georgia demands the dismissal of a young tenth-grade teacher who placed *Be Ready With Bells and Drums* on an optional reading list. (The prize-winning film, *A Patch of Blue*, was made from the book.) Salesmen protest a CBS-TV production of *Death of a Salesman* and suggest a prologue that would warn that Willy Loman would have been a failure "in anything else he tackled." An Oklahoma Literature Commission bans 14 books presented to it by a Citizens for Decent Literature group headed by a paving contractor. The contractor hopes eventually to get banned a total of 232 books—among them Ian Fleming's *Thunderball* and Salinger's *Catcher in the Rye*.

From these few examples, it is obvious that there is wide general agreement that ideas are dangerous and that whoever controls ideas controls the minds of men (or at least children). Historians, legal scholars, and philosophers have observed that each generation must win its right to freedom of expression anew. And although the area of obscenity is by no means the only field where this generation's battle is being fought, our society does seem tied in knots over this issue. Yet, as the excerpt from anthropologist West La Barre points out, there is no universal agreement on what is obscene. The only general tendency seems to be a capacity toward repression. Usually (as the bulk of readings in this chapter illustrate) the urges to repress surface from somewhere in the depths of the psyche and have little, if any, logic on their side. A good example is that of a Wisconsin judge, on the way to declaring Henry Miller's *Tropic of Cancer* legally obscene. In support of his decision, the judge listed all the scatological words he could find in the book. The list was long, but he spelled out all the words uncompromisingly until he reached

271

the word "ass." This three-letter word was too much, and he spelled it "a___." There it stands today in the official decision, a monument to the kinks in his own subconscious.

Occasionally, however, people are motivated by reasons that, if no less complex than the urge to suppress discussion of sexual matters, are at least simpler to recognize: dishonesty and greed. Downtown merchants complain of a newspaper's weather stories forecasting rain or snow on sale days. Great consumer boycotts are organized to force businessmen to conform to political views that are not their own. The media must air the conflicts engendered by such forces, since in doing so society is informed of its imperfections. Perhaps more important, when the conflicts are communicated, they are raised to the plane of discussion. And, we hope, good sense.

Obscenity: An Anthropological Appraisal

WESTON LA BARRE

. . . A Haida Indian woman is embarrassed to be caught by
a strange man without her labret or lower lip plug. Among many
Negro groups in Africa, propriety requires the buttocks to be
covered, not the genitals. Philippine Islanders and Samoans think
it indecent for the navel to be exposed, though every other part
may go uncovered. In China, it is an obscenity for a woman to
expose her artificially deformed feet to a strange man. Foot modesty is probably a very ancient Asiatic pattern, for it is found
also among the Siberian Koryak, and an Eskimo woman in her
igloo may be stripped down to a tiny Bikini skin garment before
strange men if only she keeps her boots on, since removal of the
boots has a sexual connotation. Among the Canary Islanders, a
people isolated perhaps from Neolithic to early modern times,
it was immodest for a woman to expose her breasts or feet. The
Koryak regard it as deeply sinful to look upon the face of a dead
person. Ainu women cover the mouth when speaking to a man.
Some of the body parts involved with modesty seem strange indeed. Rameses III (1198-1167 B.C.) boasted in one of his inscrip-

Reprinted with permission from a symposium, "Obscenity and the Arts,"
appearing in *Law and Contemporary Problems*, XX (Autumn, 1955), published by the Duke University School of Law, Durham, North Carolina.
Copyright, 1955, by Duke University.

tions that his rule was so successful that he had made it possible for an Egyptian woman to go anywhere she liked *with her ears exposed,* and no stranger would molest her. The Japanese have erotized the nape of a woman's neck.[1]

With respect to obscene or publicly prohibited *acts,* there is the same lack of universality in what we happen to regard as obscenity. We have already seen that public coitus, repeatedly attested to in firsthand accounts,[2] is by no means unknown in Oceania, though normative ethicists would make this perhaps the very first of obscenities "universally" abhorred by all peoples of the world. Nor among physiological acts is it only coitus that is obscene in public contexts. In some cases, *eating* is an obscene act when performed in the presence of other people or in public. . . . All that we can postulate of the social animal, man, is that he has the *capacity* for repression through socialization or enculturation, and hence can have very intense *reactions* to the prohibited or the obscene as defined by his society—but so far as any "universality" of descriptive *content* of these categories is concerned, this is wholly the prescription, cultural or legal, of his own social group or subgroup.

[1] See authorities cited in La Barre, *The Cultural Basis of Emotions and Gestures,* 16 J. PERSONALITY 49 (1947), reprinted in SELECTED READINGS IN SOCIAL PSYCHOLOGY 49 (S. H. Britt ed. 1949), also reprinted in PERSONAL CHARACTER AND CULTURAL MILIEU 487 (D. G. Haring ed. 1949). See also L. HOPF, THE HUMAN SPECIES 307-08 (1909); Cook, *The Aborigines of the Canary Islands,* 2 AM. ANTHROPOLOGIST N.S. 451, 470 (1900); WALDEMAR JOCHELSON, THE KORYAK 104 (Jesup North Pacific Expedition Pub. No. 6, 1908); J. BATCHELOR, THE AINU OF JAPAN 35 (n.d.); J. H. BREASTED, A HISTORY OF EGYPT 484-85 (2d ed. 1919).

[2] *E.g.,* 1 C.P.C. FLEURIEU, VOYAGE AUTOUR DU MONDE PAR MARCHAND 172 (1787). For the Marquesas, see also the early voyages cited by LA BARRE, *op. cit. supra* note 1, at 344. The practice appears to be established especially for Tahiti (where it was reported by Captain Cook and numerous others), but it was also found in the Margonne and Caroline Islands and perhaps elsewhere.

Nudity in American Film

After a rather prim beginning, American films began experimenting with bare breasts in the '20s, only to have these disrobings result in formation of the Hays Office in 1922 and establishment of the industry's self-imposed Production Code in 1934. With few exceptions, the American public saw little screen flesh until the late '50s. Despite the obvious problems in attempting a complete survey of nudity in major American and European pix, a brief rundown of changing attitudes should help underscore the nature and extent of the problem currently confronting censors and filmmakers.

Indirection and teasing became the rule once the Production Code was instituted. Sexual intercourse (and any concomitant nudity) was frankly taboo until the early '50s. Even then, it could only be shown by such symbolism as fireworks ("To Catch a Thief"), lashing waves ("From Here to Eternity"), rearing stallions ("Not As a Stranger"), and slow pans up to the heavens ("Island in the Sun").

Lacking sex as a raison d'etre for nudity, filmmakers had only two devices at their disposal for showing skin—bathing and exotic dancing. The latter was carefully circumscribed by the Code regulation forbidding exposed navels, while the former consisted of bosoms carefully guarded by a mountain of bubbles. The public could speculate as erotically as it wanted, but what was actually seen on American screens could handily be viewed on any public beach.

Reprinted by permission of Variety, Inc., from "Nudity: Past, Present, and Future," *Variety*, CCXLVIII (August 23, 1967), 7, 20.

European films, at least as exhibited in the U.S., were no more revelatory. Standing brazenly as an exception was the 1933 Czechoslovakian pic "Ecstasy," with a bare-breasted Hedy Lamarr romping through the woods to a fate American censors felt worse than death. The film quickly earned a "C" rating from the (then-named) Legion of Decency and generally played in sexploitation or other peripheral houses. (See separate article in this issue on sexploiters and nudies.)

"Ecstasy" remained an isolated case, however, for 20 years. Female nudity at its most daring meant Maureen O'Hara wearing a skin-colored bathing suit with long, draped hair as "Lady Godiva" (1955). Male nudity meant waist-high shower sequences in "East of Eden" and "Picnic" (both 1955). Two mid-'50s Swedish films, "One Summer of Happiness" and Ingmar Bergman's "Monika," featured relatively innocuous bare-breast footage, but both got a limited number of playdates. ("Monika" was so uncirculated that it didn't even merit the Catholic's "C" of disapproval.)

And then God created Brigitte Bardot. In a series of successful imports, the French sexkitten made the bathtowel a potent sexual symbol and revealed a considerable amount of anatomy in the process. Her decolletage plunged far lower than Jane Russell's in "The Outlaw" (the most censor-hounded film of the '40s), while her reputation grew among members of the derriere-garde.

These pix—"The Light Across the Street," "Please! Mr. Balzac," "And God Created Woman," "The Night Heaven Fell," "Love Is My Profession," "Come Dance with Me," "Love on a Pillow," and "Contempt"—made her the most seen and "C"-ed French actress in the world. Her first widely distributed film, "And God Created Woman," became the biggest grossing foreign-lingo pic in U.S. screen history, with rentals of $3,000,000. (Several European films have since surpassed it.)

Taking its cue from this example, Hollywood began showing more skin. Janet Leigh's shower in "Psycho" (1960), Natalie Wood's bath in "Splendor in the Grass" (1961), and the nudist camp sequences in "The Prize" (1963) and "A Shot in the Dark" (1964) went considerably further than previous U.S.-made pix.

Dual versions of American films—"hot" footage for Europe, more restrained views for the U.S.—also became a more common practice. "Cry Tough" (Linda Cristal), "The Victors" (Elke Sommer), "The Carpetbaggers" (Carroll Baker), "The Americanization of Emily," "Genghis Khan," "Casino Royale," and "Gunn" (Sherry Jackson) all were shot via this double standard.

American-made bare-bottom footage was introduced to U.S. screens in "Cleopatra" (1963). The celebrated epic, with one sequence featuring Elizabeth Taylor sprawled face down on a massage table, drew fire from the Legion of Decency for "its continual emphasis upon immodest costuming throughout." This reproach, and the veiled hint that only 20th-Fox's financial crisis on the film's behalf saved the pic from a "C" rating, sufficiently curbed the trend toward nudity in American films for a few years. Until 1966's religiously sanctioned "Bible" with its rear views of both Adam and Eve and the bare-breasted native girls in "Hawaii," Hollywood films relied exclusively on suggested nudity via bare backs and protectively clutched sheets.

SEALED VERDICT

Indie filmmaker Sidney Lumet earned the distinction of making first major American (albeit non-Hollywood) film with bare-breast footage in "The Pawnbroker" (1965). Furthermore, the pic got a Production Code Seal after producer Ely Landau argued that the scene was necessary to make a "vital, valid, vivid dramatic point." Thus Code administrator Geoffrey Shurlock conceded the possibility that nudity, previously taboo except in "intrinsically" unobjectionable scenes of "native life," might be acceptable under certain aesthetic conditions. This relaxed view apparently prevailed when the Code Seal was recently granted to "Beach Red."

The Legion of Decency, then headed by Msgr. Thomas F. Little, had little truck with this argument, however. The film was condemned, with Msgr. Little's regretful explanation that "they could have had the same scene and shot it from the back."

The (now-titled) National Catholic Office for Motion Pictures recently reversed this decision when the film's new distrib, American International, excised the offending footage.

Bare-breast sequences in U.S. prints of European films have continued to proliferate, with little pretense at "artistic necessity." Within the last few years, Americans have seen fully exposed bosoms in "Seven Capital Sins," "The Young World," "Le Bonheur," "Night Games," and "The Game Is Over." The last-named French import is particularly notable because the breasts belong to Yank actress Jane Fonda, who a year earlier had lent her callipygian attractions to her soon-to-be hubby and director, Roger Vadim, for "Circle of Love." A Times Square furor resulted when a poster showing same had to be covered on the billboard over the DeMille Theatre.

BOTTOMS UP

Not that other femmes aren't after her laurels. Shirley MacLaine is protected only by flowing tresses in a segment of "Woman Times Seven," while Hayley Mills' post-adolescent bottom is on view in "The Family Way." . . . The aforementioned Miss Taylor, who has supported her "Cleopatra" footage with some notably plunging necklines in other recent pix, is ostensibly seen in a fully nude back shot in the upcoming "Reflections in a Golden Eye." Advance reports indicate, however, that a stand-in was used for this footage to spare the star any unseemly embarrassment.

"Reflections," which threatens to be the sexual trendsetter of American film history for its depiction of homosexuality and sado-masochism, is also supposedly graced with bare-bottom footage of Marlon Brando. Peter Fonda joins the ole-swimming-hole ranks in the current "The Trip." Other recent examples include Jean-Paul Belmondo ("Leda" and "Tender Scoundrel"), Alan Bates ("Georgy Girl" and "King of Hearts"), Richard Harris ("This Sporting Life"), Anthony Quinn ("Zorba the Greek") and Maurice Roeves ("Ulysses"). None of these films has drawn any complaints from the NCOMP, which feels there is nothing essentially prurient in shots of men's buttocks.

QUO VADIS?

Obviously there is little left. The 1962 "Les Liaisons Dangereuses" and 1966 "Blow-Up" both contained glimpses of female parts so fleeting that aficionados still argue the point. Beyond dispute is the slow, all-revealing pan up a hefty prosty's body in the Swedish "My Sister, My Love." Needless to say, all three films earned "C" ratings, but their very presence on commercial screens throughout the country is seen by some as a portent of things to come.

As for the boys, recently and "maturely," Andy Warhol's "The Chelsea Girls" and "My Hustler" have appeared. If and when other underground pix surface, their b.o. success (?) may encourage commercial filmmakers to try their luck in this area as well.

Obscenity, the Censors, and Their Foes

E. R. HUTCHISON

The censors feel that the moral fiber of America is being rotted away by obscenity or pornography (they make no distinction between the two words), and that [Henry] Miller's books are prime examples of obscenity. Quoting such persons as Clarence Keating of the Citizens for Decent Literature and J. Edgar Hoover of the FBI, the censors hold that there is a correlation between the rise in both juvenile delinquency and adult crime and the ready availability in recent years of obscene materials. Censors ignore the attraction that taboos have for the public, and press for illegal and legal bans against readers of any age having access to what the censors themselves regard as obscene. Though they have gnawing fears for others who read such material, most suppressors of vice claim personal immunity to any such ill effects. In an American society and world situation which breed anxiety, it is no doubt a truthful observation that more often than not the censors' fears are founded upon their own compulsions and frustrations. But that does not lessen their effectiveness as censors—it merely adds a shrillness to their voice

Selection reprinted by permission of Grove Press, Inc., from E. R. Hutchison's *Tropic of Cancer On Trial: A Case History of Censorship* (New York: Grove Press, Inc., 1968), pp. 28-31.

that make it, many times, more appealing to the part of the American public that wants to be told what it should read.

Censors come in all sizes and shapes. Many are members of church committees, parent-teacher associations, Daughters of the American Revolution, American Legion, etc. Many are law enforcement officers. Whatever their backgrounds and associations, they are all censors—they are sure of what should be read or seen or heard, and through some channel of authority or influence they are able to enforce their views.

Facing these haunted foes of questionable literature are libertarians, most artists, and some newspaper and book publishers. Most would uphold the stand taken by the great defender of freedom of expression in America, the Civil Liberties Union. This stand is that the hallmark of American civilization is freedom of expression. What we have achieved, what we are, and what we represent to the world, we owe to freedom of expression. When this is appreciated, and when the dangers of an opposing policy are understood, then there can be no hesitation in taking the stand—No Censorship. Miller's faithful followers and allies, eyeing distastefully an American society teetering on a seesaw of sexual suppression and sexual exploitation, would support Karl Shapiro's observation that Miller is one of the few healthy Americans alive today, and that "the circulation of his books would do more to wipe out the obscenities of Broadway, Hollywood, and Madison Avenue than a full-scale social revolution."

If one of the two clear stands on censorship (censorship or no censorship) were taken by each of the groups involved in this battle, the obscenity problem in America would be complex enough. But within the groups themselves are people and organizations who favor halfway or quarter-way measures. *Some* control, they believe, is necessary, if only to "protect" minors. And in some instances their belief in the necessity for some control stems primarily from their concern for children. (Trying to thrust from the mind, no doubt, that parents, ideally, should have sole responsibility for their children's reading.) No definition of obscenity, legal or otherwise, is acceptable to all persons in this battle. Add to this confusion of aims the various levels of control of questionable literature in our pluralistic society—from extralegal pressures by private groups through official actions by city, county, state, and federal officers—and the truly demoralizing and chaotic state of affairs begins to be seen. Mix in then what is known to happen all too often—when the word obscenity drifts in the door, unchaperoned, reason tends to fly out the window—and you have a Molotov cocktail capable of setting fires in most American communities. And it has.

Shielding the libertarians and their right to read, especially from 1945 onward, is the United States Supreme Court. Before the Civil War there was little obscenity censorship. After the war, in the 1870's, Anthony Comstock, using the Hicklin rule, started a forty-year reign of terror that had even H. L. Mencken submitting manuscripts to censors for approval. The Hicklin rule came from an 1868 English court case, *Queen v. Hicklin*. Under its definition of obscenity—anything of possible harm to a child—censors have ever since flailed poor writers and great writers, purveyors of pornography and purveyors of great books. In 1873, Comstock engineered congressional passage of a comprehensive law (the Comstock Act) that barred obscene literature from the mails. (He then became a special agent of the Postal Inspection Service to help enforce it.)

Censorship activities by the Postmaster General and his forty thousand post offices were not drastically curtailed until *Hannegan v. Esquire, Inc.* (1945) and the *Lady Chatterley* case in the Federal Second Circuit Court of Appeals, *Grove Press, Inc. v. Christenberry* (1960).

The Customs Bureau's role in obscenity censorship was upstaged when the Tariff Act was amended in 1930 to allow the Secretary of the Treasury to admit classics and books of recognized value. When Judge Woolsey decided in favor of Joyce's *Ulysses* in 1933, books on the whole (but not *Lady Chatterley* or the *Tropics,* for example) were emancipated from Customs censorship.

The issue of constitutional protection for those charged with publishing or selling obscene literature reached the United States Supreme Court for the first time in *Doubleday & Co. v. New York* (1948). The book up for burning was Edmund Wilson's

Memoirs of Hecate County. Doubleday argued that fiction and nonfiction treating sex problems could be suppressed only when the publication created a "clear and present danger" to some substantial interest of the state. This basic constitutional issue remained unresolved when the Court divided equally and the ban on *Hecate County* was sustained. But starting in 1957 a series of Supreme Court decisions established that court as one of the bulwarks against censorship in America. In *Butler v. Michigan* (1957) the Court ruled a Michigan statute based on the Hicklin rule unconstitutional, stating that the statute reduced the Michigan adult population to reading only what is fit for children.

Obscenity and the Supreme Court: Nine Years of Confusion

RAYMOND F. SEBASTIAN

* * *

I. THE EVOLUTION OF A STANDARD: PRE-1966

In 1957 the Supreme Court for the first time was "squarely presented" with the problem of the relation of obscenity to the first amendment. This problem necessitated the formulation of a definition of obscenity—a definition which, although later supplemented, has given rise to confusion and misunderstanding in the lower courts. The 1957 decisions of *Roth v. United States* and *Alberts v. California*[1] involve the question whether publications admitted to be obscene are entitled to constitutional protection. In *Roth* the defendant had been convicted pursuant to a federal statute prohibiting the mailing of obscene matter.[2] In *Alberts* the defendant had been convicted in a California court of selling obscene books, a statutory misdemeanor. In both cases

---

Copyright 1966 by the Board of Trustees of the Leland Stanford Junior University. This reprint (by permission) is from a Note first published in the November 1966 issue of Volume 19 of the *Stanford Law Review*, pp. 167-189.

[1] 354 U.S. 476 (1957).

[2] 18 U.S.C. § 1461 (1964).

the Supreme Court in a single opinion by Mr. Justice Brennan affirmed the convictions, holding that obscenity was not "within the area of constitutionally protected speech or press" because it was "utterly without redeeming social importance."[3] The test approved by the majority for identifying obscenity was "whether to the average person, applying contemporary community standards, the dominant theme of the material taken as a whole appeals to prurient interest."[4] The Court further held that the use of the word "obscene" without a further definition in the two antiobscenity statutes under consideration did not make the statutes void for failing to give adequate notice of what was prohibited.[5]

According to the Chief Justice, concurring, the defendants' conduct subjected them to both federal and state sanctions. They had openly advertised their erotic wares and had "plainly engaged in the commercial exploitation of the morbid and shameful craving for materials with prurient effect";[6] therefore, they could constitutionally be punished. . . . Justices Black and Douglas, dissenting, favored a test which emphasized overt acts and antisocial conduct rather than thoughts. In their view obscenity should present a clear and present danger to society in order to justify prohibition, a test consistent with other free speech decisions.[7]

The second major review by the Supreme Court of obscenity regulation, *Manual Enterprises v. Day*,[8] yielded a new addition to the original *Roth* standard: the element of "patent offensiveness."[9] The question was whether certain magazines[10] declared nonmailable under federal law were in fact obscene. Mr. Justice

---

[3] 354 U.S. at 484-85.
[4] *Id*. at 489. The Court concluded that "a tendency to arouse lustful thoughts" was synonymous with appeal to prurient interests. *Id*. at 487 n.20.
[5] *Id*. at 491-92.
[6] *Id*. at 496.
[7] *Id*. at 509. For an example of a free speech decision applying the test of clear and present danger, see Dennis v. United States, 341 U.S. 494 (1951).
[8] 370 U.S. 478 (1962).
[9] *Id*. at 482.
[10] The magazines were *MANual, Trim,* and *Grecian Guild Pictorial*.

Harlan wrote for the Court, joined only by Mr. Justice Stewart. Although the magazines were obviously aimed at a reading audience of homosexuals, Harlan found that, since patent offensiveness was lacking, the Court did not need to consider the question of the audience by which prurient appeal was to be judged. He felt that, in most cases involving obscenity, patently offensive material would also appeal to prurient interests. "It is only in the unusual instance where, as here, the prurient interest appeal of the material is found limited to a particular class of persons that occasion arises for a truly independent inquiry into the question whether or not the material is patently offensive."[11]

The third and more recent attempt at articulation of the standard was *Jacobellis v. Ohio*,[12] involving the French film *Les Amants*. Mr. Justice Brennan, writing for the Court but joined only by Mr. Justice Goldberg, emphasized his *Roth* reference to social importance, holding that no work "that has literary or scientific or artistic value or any other form of social importance, may . . . be branded as obscenity and denied the constitutional protection."[13] Moreover, Mr. Justice Brennan's interpretation of the standard set out in *Roth* required "in the first instance a finding that the material 'goes substantially beyond customary limits of candor in description or representation of such matters.' "[14]

Mr. Justice Stewart concurred on the ground that the film was not in the category of hard core pornography, a term which he did not define.[15] Justices Black and Douglas concurred on the basis of their previously stated belief that absent any showing of clear and present danger obscenity could not be censored.[16]

Mr. Chief Justice Warren, joined by Mr. Justice Clark, dissented because consideration of the "use to which various materials are put," the test he suggested in *Roth*, rather than the

[11] 370 U.S. at 486.
[12] 378 U.S. 184 (1964).
[13] *Id.* at 191.
[14] *Ibid.*, quoting Roth v. United States, 354 U.S. 476, 487 n.20 (1957).
[15] "I know it when I see it . . . ." *Id.* at 197.
[16] *Id.* at 196-97.

nature of the materials themselves, would have led to affirmance of the defendant's conviction instead of reversal.[17]

Two decisions, involving questions somewhat tangential to the definition of obscenity, shed some light on the developing standard. In *Kingsley Int'l Pictures Corp. v. Regents of Univ. of N.Y.*[18] the Court, in an opinion by Mr. Justice Stewart, held that advocacy of improper sexual ethics was not a proper basis for censorship. Subsequently, in *Smith v. California,*[19] the Court determined that *scienter* (knowledge that disseminated material was obscene) would be required to sustain a conviction for distributing obscene matter.

At this point in the development of obscenity standards, many serious questions remained unresolved. Grappling with these questions was the task which fell to state courts and lower federal courts.

II. APPLYING THE STANDARDS: POST-*JACOBELLIS* PROBLEMS OF THE LOWER COURTS

One of the most common features of lower court opinions subsequent to *Jacobellis* was the complaint that the Supreme Court had enunciated no intelligible standards to apply in obscenity cases. Typical were comments that "if a firm and clear guideline had been established, we would certainly follow it,"[20] and that "[i]n cases involving obscenity there are many words and terms which, like globules of quicksilver, elude any firm grasp of

17 *Id.* at 201. This emphasis on conduct would later gain the support of a majority of the Supreme Court. *See* text accompanying notes 66-77 *infra.*
18 360 U.S. 684 (1959).
19 361 U.S. 147 (1959).
20 Gent v. State, 239 Ark. 474, 393 S.W.2d 219, 226 (1965), *prob. juris. noted sub nom.* Gent v. Arkansas, 384 U.S. 937 (1966) (No. 874, 1965 Term; renumbered No. 50, 1966 Term). The Supreme Court limited its notation of probable jurisdiction to issues of vagueness and prior restraint. Justices Black, Douglas, and Stewart would have noted probable jurisdiction without limitation.

them."[21] The validity of the complaints is demonstrated by an examination of some of the problems encountered by lower courts attempting to interpret the standards for identifying obscenity.

Perhaps the most striking example of the confused state of affairs in some lower courts is the opinion of a New Jersey superior court judge.[22] The judge mistakenly combined the elements of social importance and appeal to the prurient interests of the average man, asking if the average man could find the material socially important.

> It is inconceivable to this court that "the average person" could read *Fanny Hill* and receive the slightest social, literary or historical value from it. The fact that a selected group of literary experts do find such values does not, in my opinion, mean that the "average person" would, should or could find the same. In short, the book is utterly without redeeming social value.[23]

The quoted passage also illustrates the propensity of state lower court judges to be extremely parochial in their outlook and to disregard completely the testimony of literary experts in obscenity cases.[24]

(A) The Relevant-Audience Confusion

Lower courts have been unable to give a consistent answer to the question: what if material appeals to the prurient interests of some groups, but not others? In *United States v. Klaw*[25] the court rejected the average man as the focus for applying the obscenity standard. The court indicated that there might be "good reason for proscribing material that is more likely to reach and be

---

[21] United States v. One Carton Positive Motion Picture Film Entitled "491," 247 F. Supp. 450, 463-64 (S.D.N.Y. 1965).
[22] *See* G. P. Putnam's Sons v. Calissi, 86 N.J. Super. 82, 205 A.2d 913 (Super. Ct. 1964).
[23] *Id.* at 96, 205 A.2d at 922.
[24] *See* A Book Named "John Cleland's Memoirs of a Woman of Pleasure" v. Attorney Gen., 383 U.S. 413, 415 n.2 (1966). *But see* Trans-Lux Distrib. Corp. v. Maryland Bd. of Censors, —— Md. ——, 213 A.2d 235, 238-44 (1965) (uncontradicted evidence of the film's importance and serious purpose).
[25] 350 F.2d 155 (2d Cir. 1965).

responded to in a prurient way by a deviant segment of the community . . . ."[26]

In contrast, in *United States v. One Carton Positive Motion Picture Film Entitled "491"*[27] the Government introduced evidence of appeal to adolescents and homosexuals. The court rejected as irrelevant the evidence of prurient appeal to special groups because of the focus of the obscenity standard on the average man. The court then, however, turned around 180 degrees to find that the relevant audience *was* important in determining the social importance of the allegedly obscene work.[28]

A third court ignored the problem altogether. In *Haldeman v. United States*[29] the court did not consider the question of appeal to a particular audience and held simply that a pamphlet available through the mails which described "various forms of sex deviations . . . with no evident attempt to embellish a sordid subject"[30] was not obscene. Moreover, this court apparently accepted the hard core pornography definition of obscenity suggested by Mr. Justice Stewart in *Jacobellis*.[31]

(B) Prurient Appeal

What effect is obscenity supposed to have in order to satisfy the prurient appeal element? If appeal to prurient interests is synonymous with a tendency to arouse lustful thoughts, material which repels rather than attracts the average person should not be considered as appealing to prurient interests. Nevertheless, the Supreme Court of Missouri has recently held that several nudist magazines aroused prurient interests, apparently on the dubious

---

26 *Id.* at 164 n.10.

27 247 F. Supp. 450 (S.D.N.Y. 1965).

28 *Id.* at 467.

29 340 F.2d 59 (10th Cir. 1965).

30 *Id.* at 60.

31 *Id.* at 62. The term "hard core pornography" is, of course, subject to a variety of definitions; of all the definitions, however, the following is perhaps the most generally accepted: "Pornography is daydream material, divorced from reality, whose main function is to nourish erotic fantasies of the sexually immature, or as the psychiatrists say, to nourish auto-eroticism." Lockhart & McClure, *Obscenity Censorship: The Constitutional Issue—What Is Obscene?*, 7 UTAH L. REV. 289, 297 (1961).

theory that "it is unquestioned that . . . the average normal American . . . regards complete nudity . . . as shocking, vulgar, and indecent."[32] Moreover, the equally dubious assertion was made that since the photographs were in color the nudes would "appear more natural and would likely increase the prurient appeal."[33]

(C) A Part Versus the Whole

In *People v. Bruce*[34] the Illinois Supreme Court agreed to reargument in light of the *Jacobellis* decision. The original decision had affirmed the defendant's conviction for giving an obscene performance, but after reargument the court reversed. "[W]e must concede that some of the topics commented on by defendant are of social importance. Under Jacobellis the entire performance is thereby immunized."[35]

The court felt constrained to reverse even though it was of the opinion that the presentation subjected society "to the gradual deterioration of its moral fabric . . ." and went beyond customary limits of candor.[36] The concurring judge refused to concede that fragments of social importance immunized the whole performance, resting reversal instead upon the fact that the setting was a nightclub, where the audience was adult and could leave at will.[37] The concurring position appears to be an application of the relevant-audience concept but can also be explained by the distinction sometimes drawn between voluntary and involuntary exposure to obscene material. Some commentators argue that only in the latter case should the disseminator be subject to prosecution.[38]

---

[32] State v. Vollmar, 389 S.W.2d 20, 28-29 (Mo. 1965).

[33] *Id.* at 28. This decision squarely conflicts with Mr. Justice Harlan's admonition that "[o]f course not every portrayal of male or female nudity is obscene." Manual Enterprises v. Day, 370 U.S. 478, 490 (1962).

[34] 31 Ill. 2d 459, 202 N.E.2d 497 (1964).

[35] *Id.* at 461, 202 N.E.2d at 498.

[36] *Ibid.*

[37] *Id.* at 462, 202 N.E.2d at 498.

[38] *See* W. GELLHORN, INDIVIDUAL FREEDOM AND GOVERNMENTAL RESTRAINTS 102 (1956). *See also* text accompanying note 110 *infra.*

(D) Commercial Exploitation

In *Film Entitled "491"* the court held that the exploitation of the film by "grind" movie houses, including sexually oriented advertising, was not determinative of the question of obscenity.[39] Such a holding squarely conflicts with the Warren emphasis in *Jacobellis* and *Roth* on the use to which the materials in question were put.

III. THE ATTEMPT TO CLARIFY THE STANDARD

(A) Reconsideration of the Utility of Censorship

(1) Justification for Censorship. The question of why society should in any manner censor obscene publications would seem basic to any inquiry into the standards for identifying obscenity, yet the question is seldom considered in depth by the courts. Rather decisions are often based on one or more of the following assumed evils of obscenity: "(1) the incitement to antisocial sexual conduct; (2) psychological excitement resulting from sexual imagery; (3) the arousing of feelings of disgust and revulsion; and (4) the advocacy of improper sexual values."[40]

These supposed evils are immaterial or unproven. The advocacy of improper sexual values is clearly within the sphere of protected speech.[41] Psychological excitement resulting from sexual imagery is much too broad a criterion because it encompasses a great deal of advertising, entertainment, and even everyday experience.[42]

---

[39] United States v. One Carton Positive Motion Picture Film Entitled "491," 247 F. Supp. 450 (S.D.N.Y. 1965) at 467.

[40] Kalven, *The Metaphysics of the Law of Obscenity*, 1960 SUPREME COURT REV. 1, 3-4.

[41] *See* Kingsley Int'l Pictures Corp. v. Regents of Univ. of N.Y., 360 U.S. 684 (1959).

[42] "[T]he Court may take judicial notice of the fact that our advertising, our motion pictures, our television and our journalism are in large measure calculated to produce sexual thoughts and reactions. We live in a sea of sexual

Arousal of feelings of disgust is a social problem only if the person repelled is involuntarily exposed to the obscene material. An example of involuntary exposure is the display of obscene material on a signboard. Passersby who casually glanced at the signboard might be confronted with something offensive to them. The originator of the signboard might be prosecuted for exposing the public involuntarily to obscene material; whereas, if the the same person were to show the same kind of material in private to those who wished to see it, he should not be subject to prosecution on the theory that his audience was revolted or disgusted. In the former case a kind of nuisance was involved, while in the latter case there was no nuisance because exposure was sought voluntarily. Those who seek out obscenity should have no standing to assert that they are repelled by it. Thus, a nightclub audience which went to hear the late Lenny Bruce should not have expected him to be prosecuted for shocking them.[43]

Courts and commentators favoring censorship justify obscenity regulation primarily "because [obscenity] . . . is thought to incite antisocial sexual behavior and crime."[44] The quoted passage clearly illustrates a major reason for the controversy over obscenity censorship: it is *thought* that obscenity incites antisocial behavior and crime, but a causal relationship has never been *proven*. In fact, present empirical evidence indicates that obscenity does not lead to antisocial conduct.

[U]ntil the phenomenon is reliably demonstrated, we can hardly assume that the observation of illicit sex practices will lead to *criminal* sexual behavior. Indeed, common experience contradicts this hypothesis for most people. . . . And, with the empirical evidence we do have, a quite different thesis is also possible: obscene materials provide a way of releasing strong sexual urges without doing harm to others.[45]

provocation." Brief for Appellant 12, A Book Named "John Cleland's Memoirs of a Woman of Pleasure" v. Attorney Gen., 383 U.S. 413 (1966).

43 *See* People v. Bruce, 31 Ill. 2d 459, 462, 202 N.E.2d 497, 498 (1965) (concurring opinion).

44 United States v. Klaw, 350 F.2d 155, 163 (2d Cir. 1965).

45 Cairns, Paul & Wishner, *Sex Censorship: The Assumptions of Anti-Obscenity Laws and the Empirical Evidence,* 46 MINN. L. REV. 1009, 1035-36

Although seldom articulated in the cases, "[i]t is possible to assert a fifth evil: the impact of obscenity on character and hence, slowly and remotely, on conduct."[46] Mr. Justice Harlan expressed such a concern in *Alberts v. California,* stating further that it is reasonable to believe that over a long period of time indiscriminate distribution of materials which degrade sex "will have an eroding effect on moral standards."[47] Proponents of this view see in obscenity a threat to the personal and social structure.[48] Such assertions, however, are easy to make, difficult to prove, and have historically been relied upon to justify all kinds and degrees of censorship.[49]

Assumptions that obscenity is in some way socially harmful, or that its cathartic effect is in some way helpful, or even that there is no effect are at this point equally credible. Given this equality and considering the interests which merit the protection of the first amendment, should not those who allege that obscenity leads to antisocial sexual conduct have to carry the burden of proof or be defeated? Absent convincing proof of the effect of allegedly obscene material, the Supreme Court has two alternatives. It may choose to protect society from obscenity on the assumption that this is the greatest good and that to wait for conclusive proof might lead to societal injury, or it may choose to protect the freedom of individual choice on the ground that interference with personal liberties must rest on a more substantial base than unproven assumptions.

It is possible to argue that when in doubt the Court should defer to any reasonable judgment of the legislature. The Supreme Court generally has deferred to legislative judgment in cases of *economic* regulation.[50] In the area of individual liberties, how-

---

(1962); *accord,* B. KARPMAN, THE SEXUAL OFFENDER AND HIS OFFENSES 485 (1964).

[46] Kalven, *supra* note 40, at 4 n.19.

[47] 354 U.S. 476, 502 (1957) (concurring opinion).

[48] Slough & McAnany, *Obscenity and Constitutional Freedom—Part II,* 8 ST. LOUIS U.L.J. 449, 457 (1964).

[49] "The advocates of censorship, in other words, regard it as a means by which to prevent debasement of the individual virtues, the cultural standards, and the common security . . . ." GELLHORN, *op. cit. supra* note 38, at 52.

[50] Since 1937 no economic regulation has been invalidated by the United

ever, the Court has taken a very different approach. A good exposition of this difference is that

[t]he right of a State to regulate, for example, a public utility may well include, so far as the due process test is concerned, power to impose all of the restrictions which a legislature may have a "rational basis" for adopting. But freedoms of speech and of press, of assembly, and of worship may not be infringed on such slender grounds. They are susceptible of restriction only to prevent grave and immediate danger to interests which the State may lawfully protect.[51]

Surprisingly, the Court's obscenity decisions reflect a deference to legislative judgment normally reserved only for economic regulation. Moreover, in the obscenity area the Court has departed from the general civil liberties approach that has characterized its Bill of Rights decisions during recent years. For instance, by extending protection against self-incrimination and unreasonable searches[52] the Court has in effect said it will act to protect the freedom of the individual unless and until the claims that such protection is harmful to society are proven true. The Court has also taken extensive measures to insure individual liberty in the right-to-counsel cases[53] over objections that the result would be injurious to society. Thus, the protections of the fourth, fifth, and sixth amendments have been vigorously defended and extended by the Court in the face of strong opposing argument.

Not only has the Court in obscenity cases departed from the general approach that protects individual liberty, it has also departed from the first amendment's clear and present danger test.[54] Consideration of the scope of protection afforded by the first amendment may provide at least a partial explanation for these departures.

States Supreme Court on substantive due process grounds. N. DOWLING & G. GUNTHER, CASES ON CONSTITUTIONAL LAW 899 (7th ed. 1965).

[51] West Virginia Bd. of Educ. v. Barnette, 319 U.S. 624, 639 (1943).

[52] See, e.g., Malloy v. Hogan, 378 U.S. 1 (1964) (fifth amendment privilege against self-incrimination applied to the states); Mapp v. Ohio, 367 U.S. 643 (1961) (fourth amendment applied to the states).

[53] See, e.g., Miranda v. Arizona, 384 U.S. 436 (1966); Escobedo v. Illinois, 378 U.S. 478 (1964).

[54] See, e.g., Dennis v. United States, 341 U.S. 494 (1951).

One position on the scope of the first amendment, that taken by Alexander Meiklejohn, is that the "prize of victory which our forefathers won when the First Amendment was adopted was not the unlimited right of the people to 'speak.' It was the unlimited right of 'Religious and Political Freedom' . . . ."[55]

To us, in this view, speech unrelated to religious or political freedom, such as obscene speech, occupies a less favored position with regard to first amendment protection. Such speech may be subjected to more regulation than may speech associated with religious or political matters.

Whatever the historical merit of this theory, the Supreme Court has declared that all speech must be measured by the same standards.[56] Notwithstanding this declaration, however, the Court may have drifted toward the Meiklejohn theory.[57] While adhering to the clear and present danger test for political speech, the Court may have actually meant that obscenity is unworthy of protection.

Justices Douglas and Black do not accept this reading of the first amendment. In their view the obscenity standard as set out in *Roth* conflicts with the protection afforded speech by the first amendment: "Certainly that standard would not be an acceptable one if religion, economics, politics or philosophy were involved.

---

[55] Meiklejohn, *What Does the First Amendment Mean?*, 20 U. CHI. L. REV. 461, 464 (1953).

[56] "Like insurrection, contempt, advocacy of unlawful acts, breach of the peace, *obscenity*, solicitation of legal business, and the various other formulae for the repression of expression that have been challenged in this Court, libel can claim *no talismanic immunity from constitutional limitations*. It must be measured by standards that satisfy the First Amendment." New York Times Co. v. Sullivan, 376 U.S. 254, 269 (1964) (emphasis added). If labels for different kinds of speech are meaningless and confer no immunity from constitutional limitations, how can obscenity, listed above, be constitutionally unworthy of protection? In fact, the *Times* case prompted Professor Kalven to conclude that "[n]o category of speech is any longer beneath the protection of the First Amendment. . . . Obscenity, too, it would seem, 'can claim no talismanic immunity . . . .'" Kalven, *The New York Times Case: A Note on "the Central Meaning of the First Amendment,"* 1964 SUPREME COURT REV. 191, 217-18.

[57] *See* Brennan, *The Supreme Court and the Meiklejohn Interpretation of the First Amendment,* 79 HARV. L. REV. 1 (1965).

How does it become a constitutional standard when literature treating with sex is concerned?"[58]

Some expression unrelated to politics or religion can be as valuable to society as speech which is related. At the very least the first amendment should protect speech of ideational content and importance equal to that of political speech generally, regardless of subject matter. Ideally the first amendment should protect all expression of any arguable value. If the clear and present danger test is thought to do this in the political area, that test should be applied to all speech. Only in this way will important minority expression be protected.

Even if obscenity were proven to have a long-term effect on morals, could it on this basis alone be prohibited? Is not long-term change of attitudes upon confrontation with new ideas the usual pattern in our society? Furthermore, other types of speech are permitted to exert a deleterious influence in the long run. For example, if political speech presented a *long-range* threat to society, it could not be proscribed without reading the "present" out of the clear and *present* danger test.

(2) Limitations on Regulation. The validity of the commonly asserted justifications for obscenity regulation, discussed above, involves issues of the constitutional limitations on the power of federal and state governments to censor obscenity. Two further questions, the first also of constitutional dimensions, remain.

Does regulation of obscenity have a deterrent effect on non-obscene expression? This question has never been squarely considered by the Supreme Court when formulating the substantive standards for identifying obscenity, but it has been the subject of concern in many of the cases involving acceptable procedures for regulating obscenity.

State regulation of obscenity must "conform to procedures that will insure against the curtailment of constitutionally protected expression, which is often separated from obscenity only by a dim and uncertain line."[59] Fear of deterring nonobscene expression has led to the requirement that the issue of obscenity be

[58] Roth v. United States, 354 U.S. 476, 512 (1957) (dissenting opinion).
[59] Bantam Books, Inc. v. Sullivan, 372 U.S. 58, 66 (1963).

determined in an adversary proceeding *prior* to any seizure of the material in question. "[I]f seizure of books precedes an adversary determination of their obscenity, there is danger of abridgment of the right of the public in a free society to unobstructed circulation of nonobscene books."[60]

The Court gave tangential consideration to this question in *Butler v. Michigan*.[61] The state attempted to justify absolute prohibition of allegedly obscene materials on the ground that adolescents had to be protected from exposure to the material. The Supreme Court rejected this argument, concluding that it would reduce expression concerning sex to the adolescent level. Thus, although a statute prohibiting distribution of some material to adolescents might be constitutional, an all-encompassing statute that restricted adult reading in the process was not.

If prohibition of obscenity were shown to have a deterrent effect on nonobscene expression, could such prohibition be successfully attacked by analogizing to *Butler* and the procedural cases? It could be argued that a substantive definition of obscenity which impedes the distribution of nonobscene material is as open to constitutional attack as a procedural device which has the same effect.

Moreover, it is probable that censorship is in fact more restrictive than would appear prima facie.

> The ends of censorship are stated as limited objectives, but they have tended in operation to throw suspicion on reason, the arts, and freedom. The means of censorship are devices used in the interest of individual morality and common security, but they have tended in operation to advance uniformity at the expense of discrimination and conformity at the expense of freedom.[62]

If this is true, one solution is to declare all obscenity censorship unconstitutional. This, however, is not politically feasible and, further, is open to the objection that the baby is being thrown out with the bath water. Perhaps the only acceptable solution is

---

[60] A Quantity of Copies of Books v. Kansas, 378 U.S. 205, 213 (1964).
[61] 352 U.S. 380 (1957).
[62] R. McKeon, R. Merton & W. Gellhorn, The Freedom To Read 19 (1957).

to strive for a substantive definition of obscenity which will minimally inhibit nonobscene expression. . . .

What is the utility of governmental attempts to regulate the morals of adults? One major objection to censorship of morals-related literature is that it encourages evasion and hypocrisy.[63] Prohibition of obscene literature may drive distribution underground, thus failing in its purpose and encouraging evasion of the law. Prohibition of liquor is probably the classic example of the possible evils of governmental interference with private morals. . . . In short, censorship is self-defeating because it perpetuates the evil it is designed to destroy.

The validity of such objections cannot, of course, be verified; they remain in the realm of the conjectural. Arguably, however, censorship of obscenity has had its day and the results are unimpressive. . . .

(B) A Restatement of the Original Standard: The New Decisions

In *A Book Named "John Cleland's Memoirs of a Woman of Pleasure" v. Attorney Gen.*[64] the only question before the Court was whether the book *Fanny Hill* was obscene under the *Roth* standard of prurient appeal and social importance. Massachusetts, in a proceeding directed against the book itself, had found it obscene. . . .[65]

Mr. Justice Brennan, joined by Mr. Justice Fortas and the Chief Justice, held that the Massachusetts Supreme Judicial Council had erred: "in holding that a book need not be 'unqualifiedly worthless before it can be deemed obscene.' A book cannot be proscribed unless it is found to be *utterly* without redeeming social value." Thus, social importance was declared independent of the other elements of the obscenity test; it could not be balanced against offensiveness or prurient appeal. But Justice Brennan left the door open for a new trial by declaring that a book with only a "minimum of social value" might constitu-

---

[63] M. Ernst & A. Schwartz, Censorship: The Search for the Obscene 250 (1964).

[64] 383 U.S. 413 (1966).

[65] *See* Attorney Gen. v. A Book Named "John Cleland's Memoirs of a Woman of Pleasure," 349 Mass. 69, 206 N.E.2d 403 (1965), *rev'd*, 383 U.S. 413 (1966).

tionally be declared obscene if its prurient appeal were to be commercially exploited.[66] Since the record was devoid of evidence as to distribution, the finding of obscenity was reversed. However, a new and highly important element was appended to the *Roth* standard: commercial exploitation.

Mr. Justice Douglas concurred in the reversal because (1) he found no showing of incitement to illegal action, (2) the testimony as to literary value clearly indicated the importance of the novel, and (3) the manner of advertising and distributing the book bore no relation to the book's contents.[67] Mr. Justice Clark dissented on the ground that the independent standing of the social-importance element "rejects the basic holding of *Roth* and gives the smut artist free rein to carry on his dirty business."[68] Mr. Justice White also dissented, interpreting *Roth* as holding that obscene material is unworthy of constitutional protection *because* it is without social value, not that social value is an independent element of the obscenity test.[69]

The Court modified the *Roth* standard again in *Mishkin v. New York*.[70] The defendant was found to have a dominant role in several enterprises which produced and sold sadistic and masochistic paperback books and was thus found guilty of violating section 1141 of the New York Penal Law. Over the defendant's objections that materials depicting deviant sexual practices did not appeal to the prurient interests of the "average person,"[71] Mr. Justice Brennan, now writing for a five-man majority, held:

> Where the material is designed for and primarily disseminated to a clearly defined deviant sexual group, rather than the public at large, the prurient-appeal requirement of the *Roth* test is satisfied if the dominant

[66] 383 U.S. at 420.

[67] *Id.* at 426-33. Justices Black and Stewart concurred for reasons stated in their opinions in *Ginzburg. Id.* at 421.

[68] *Id.* at 441.

[69] *Id.* at 461. Mr. Justice Harlan also dissented. *Id* at 455. Again, as in *Alberts* and *Roth*, his opinion rested on the almost totally unaccepted ground that the Constitution allows the state more freedom than the federal government to regulate individual conduct.

[70] 383 U.S. 502 (1966).

[71] Brief for Appellant 15-18.

theme of the material taken as a whole appeals to the prurient interest in sex of . . . that group.[72]

Since the evidence clearly indicated that the books in question were written and distributed in order to cater to such deviant interests, the defendant's conviction was upheld.

Mr. Justice Douglas dissented, finding it "difficult to say that a publication has no 'social importance' because it caters to the taste of the most unorthodox amongst us," and believing that freedom of expression was being denied deviant groups.[73]

In *Ginzburg v. United States*,[74] perhaps the most controversial of the three cases,[75] Mr. Justice Brennan again wrote for the Court. In a five-to-four decision upholding Ginzburg's conviction for mailing obscene material, Brennan applied the commercial-exploitation test of *"Memoirs"* to *EROS* and *Liaison* magazines and to *The Housewife's Handbook on Selective Promiscuity*. The Court assumed that in the absence of evidence of exploitation "the publications themselves might not be obscene."[76]

In fact, however, there was evidence that "[t]he 'leer of the sensualist' [permeated] . . . the advertising for the three publications," and that their aim was "titillation."

The deliberate representations of petitioners' publications as erotically arousing . . . stimulated the reader to accept them as prurient; he looks for titillation, not for saving intellectual content. . . . And the circumstances of presentation and dissemination of material are equally relevant to determining whether social importance claimed for the material in the courtroom was . . . pretense or reality . . . .

* * *

Where the purveyor's sole emphasis is on the sexually provocative

[72] 383 U.S. at 508.

[73] *Id.* at 491. Mr. Justice Black again dissented, *id.* at 476, referring to his opinion in *Ginzburg. See* text accompanying note 78 *infra.* Mr. Justice Harlan concurred on the basis of his *"Memoirs"* opinion. 383 U.S. at 515.

[74] 383 U.S. 463 (1966).

[75] *See* Newsweek, April 4, 1966, at 19 ("the Justices stunned court-watchers"); N.Y. Times, March 22, 1966, at 1, col. 8 ("lawyers expressed surprise"); Time, April 1, 1966, at 56 ("startling even Justice Department attorneys").

[76] Ginzburg v. United States, 383 U.S. 463, 465 (1966); *see id.* at 474.

aspects of his publications, that fact may be decisive in the determination of obscenity.[77]

Mr. Justice Black's dissent expressed dissatisfaction with the whole verbal formulation. In Black's view the test was so uncertain that "the guilt or innocence of a defendant charged with obscenity must depend in the final analysis upon the personal judgment and attitudes of particular individuals and the place where the trial is held."[78]

Mr. Justice Stewart's dissent emphasized that none of the material in question could be classified as hard core pornography and so could not be prohibited. Moreover, Stewart viewed the majority's affirmance on the ground of pandering as a denial of due process[79] since the defendant had not been charged with pandering. And even if the defendant had been so charged, Stewart would have dismissed the charge as invalid since no federal statute made such conduct a criminal offense.[80]

Finally, Mr. Justice Douglas dissented because he considered advertising and distribution irrelevant to the question of obscenity and concluded that none of the publications were obscene since evidence had been introduced as to their literary and scientific merit.[81]

(C) The Restatement Examined

(1) The Independence of Social Importance. If the three elements (patent offensiveness, prurient appeal, and social importance) are independent, then each element must be considered and proved separately. Neither of the first two may be balanced against social importance. This position was advanced by the

---

[77] *Id.* at 468-70.
[78] *Id.* at 480.
[79] Mr. Justice Stewart based this conclusion on Cole v. Arkansas, 333 U.S. 196 (1948).
[80] 383 U.S. at 500. Mr. Justice Harlan agreed substantially with Stewart's criticism of the majority, concluding that "[w]hat . . . the Court has done today is in effect to write a new statute . . . ." *Id.* at 494.
[81] *Id.* at 482-92.

appellant in *"Memoirs"*[82] and adopted by three justices in that case.[83] In addition, Mr. Justice Stewart indicated his adherence to independence in *Ginzburg,* with the observation that all three elements were satisfied only in the case of hard core pornography.[84] Mr. Justice Douglas viewed at least the social-importance element as independent,[85] while Mr. Justice Harlan viewed the elements as independent only when the federal government was the prosecutor.[86]

The requirement that all three elements be satisfied separately before a given work may be declared obscene clearly imposes a greater burden on the censor than does a test by which evidence of prurient appeal indicates lack of social importance. The latter test makes prurient appeal and lack of social importance almost synonymous. And if, in fact, material which appeals to prurient interests is also usually patently offensive, the latter test would often result in all three elements being synonymous.

The majority of the Court is clearly correct in its view that the most important element, social importance, is independent. To hold otherwise would surely result in the prohibition of works of true merit on the basis of the arguably more subjective elements of prurient appeal and patent offensiveness. The independence of social importance serves as a judicial restraint on those who too readily condemn works which present viewpoints different from their own. In doing so it preserves minority access to works of which the majority disapproves and thus more fully approaches the intent of the first amendment. Moreover, it achieves the goal of saving from censorship "any serious, complex piece of writing or art, regardless of the unconventionality of its candor."[87] Independence of social importance would seem a necessity if majority

---

[82] See Brief for Appellant 8-10, A Book Named "John Cleland's Memoirs of a Woman of Pleasure" v. Attorney Gen., 383 U.S. 413 (1966).

[83] 383 U.S. at 413.

[84] See Ginzburg v. United States, 383 U.S. 463, 499 (1966) (dissenting opinion).

[85] See A Book Named "John Cleland's Memoirs of a Woman of Pleasure" v. Attorney Gen., 383 U.S. 413, 426 (1966) (concurring opinion).

[86] See Ginzburg v. United States, 383 U.S. 463, 493 (1966) (dissenting opinion).

[87] Kalven, *The Metaphysics of the Law of Obscenity,* 1960 SUPREME COURT REV. 1, 13.

attitudes are not to control access to material that deals with or touches upon morality.

(2) The Relevant-Audience Problem. Clearly the Court will now look to the specific segment of the general public at which the material is directed to determine whether the material has prurient appeal. This approach reflects an increasing acceptance of the concept of variable obscenity. According to the variable obscenity theory nothing is inherently obscene, but only becomes so according to its distribution and audience.[88]

The Supreme Court used the variable obscenity concept in *Mishkin* to find sadistic publications obscene and in *Ginzburg* to emphasize evidence of commercial exploitation. How successful the Court was is open to question. Even assuming that variable obscenity is a valid concept, there are real problems of application. Identifying the factors which are to be considered as variables in analyzing commercial exploitation or delineating the relevant audience would seem to be an almost hopeless task. For instance, the Court did not consider the factor of the price of *EROS*[89] before concluding that Ginzburg's audience was composed of the sexually immature. Yet the price may well have been prohibitive to adolescents and even to most adult members of the middle class. It could be argued that *EROS* was directed at those with the money to pay for it, who in turn would be more likely to have an above-average education and who would thus be able to appreciate the artistic and literary qualities of the work, notwithstanding some obscene parts.

Mr. Justice Douglas' objections to the variable obscenity theory are more basic, challenging the very concept of the specific audience. Because "[m]an was not made in a fixed mould,"[90] Douglas argued that he should be able to reject any social mores as long as he does not interfere with the rights of others. Douglas also questioned whether rejection of the values of the socially deviant

---

[88] For the original and probably most comprehensive statement of this theory, see Lockhart & McClure, *Censorship of Obscenity: The Developing Constitutional Standards,* 45 MINN. L. REV. 5, 77-88 (1960).

[89] *EROS* was published as a hard cover magazine costing $20 for four issues.

[90] Ginzburg v. United States, 383 U.S. 463, 491 (1966) (dissenting opinion).

subgroup by censorship of material that appeals to that subgroup does not result in majority control of the meaning of social value.[91] Material that represents deviant values to the majority may or may not be pruriently appealing to the deviant group. One could surmise that deviancy is rejected by the "normal" person. If so, how is he to judge whether material is pruriently appealing to a deviant? And if the material in fact is pruriently appealing to the "normal" person, how can it be so deviant that it supports a finding of patent offensiveness because of its portrayal of deviant practices?

(3) "Close Cases" Which Make Evidence of Distribution Relevant. A further confusing factor is the Court's statement in *Ginzburg* that evidence of pandering is relevant in "close cases."[92] Immediately the question is raised of just what a close case is. One, at least, is where the work in question is found to possess the requisite prurient appeal and is patently offensive, yet has some "minimal" social importance.[93] This minimal importance cannot save the work when its distributor has emphasized its prurient appeal.

The real target of the Court in including this pandering element is undoubtedly the person who, falsely or otherwise, makes a blatant "appeal to the erotic interest of [his] . . . customers."[94] Why, then, is the degree of social importance relevant at all? If *conduct* and not the work itself is to be condemned, why can the panderer of minimally important works be punished, while the panderer of a great work who is guilty of the same conduct presumably cannot? If the answer is that in the latter case some net social good results from the distribution of great works, a claim of denial of equal protection might be valid.[95]

91 *Ibid.*
92 *Id.* at 474.
93 *See* A Book Named "John Cleland's Memoirs of a Woman of Pleasure" v. Attorney Gen., 383 U.S. 413, 419 (1966).
94 Ginzburg v. United States, 383 U.S. 463, 467 (1966), quoting from Roth v. United States, 354 U.S. 476, 495-96 (1957) (Warren, C.J., concurring).
95 The argument would be that residual "good" resulting from the *same conduct* is not a rational basis for classification if *conduct* is the evil sought to be regulated.

(4) Commercial Exploitation: A Fourth Element. The proba-
tive value of commercial exploitation in determining obscenity
is a validation of the position taken by Mr. Chief Justice Warren in his *Roth* dissent and echoed by numerous commentators
through the years.[96] Weighty objections to adding the factor of
commercial exploitation to the obscenity standard, however, came
from within the Court itself. Dissenting Justices argued that
consideration of commercial exploitation rewrites the obscenity
statutes,[97] is unconstitutionally vague,[98] and is in any case irrelevant.[99]

In *"Memoirs"* Mr. Justice Brennan intimated that *Fanny Hill,*
a book of minimal social importance according to the Massachusetts court, might constitutionally be termed obscene if it had
been commercially exploited. . . . If obscenity can be constitutionally prohibited only because it is in fact *"utterly* without
redeeming social importance," how can a work of even "minimal" importance be prohibited merely because of its method
of distribution?

The commercial-exploitation element is so grossly inconsistent
with the original rationale for finding some regulation of obscenity constitutional—namely, that obscenity was not worth protecting—that one must conclude that the phrase "utterly without
redeeming social importance" now should be read "utterly without above-minimal social importance." The addition of the element of commercial exploitation and its application to close cases
have made the standards for identifying obscenity, already vague,
now hopelessly abstruse.

The inherent vagueness of the commercial-exploitation concept
as applied in close cases will undoubtedly discourage some expres-

---

[96] *See, e.g.,* Slough & McAnany, *Obscenity and Constitutional Freedom*—Part
II, 8 St. Louis U.L.J. 449, 476 (1964). The variable obscenity theory attempts
to deal with this problem of commercial exploitation. *See* Lockhart &
McClure, *Censorship of Obscenity: The Developing Constitutional Standards,*
45 Minn. L. Rev. 5 (1960).

[97] *See* Ginzburg v. United States, 383 U.S. 463, 477 (1966) (Black, J., dissenting); *id.* at 494 (Harlan, J., dissenting).

[98] *See id.* at 500 (Stewart, J., dissenting).

[99] *See id.* at 482 (Douglas, J., dissenting).

sion which might otherwise have occurred. A finding of obscenity and affirmance of a conviction in a commercial-exploitation context would greatly discourage anyone else from distributing the same material. . . .

It might also be argued that advertisements which indicate the prurient appeal of a publication are actually valuable because they give advance warnings of the contents.[100] Such an argument is predicated on the assumption that the only value of antiobscenity laws is the removal of material which would be offensive to some members of society.[101] If this is so, condemnation of advertising which in fact does warn the reader may be a disservice.

Moreover, if advertising is emphasized, promoters of filth will simply change the labels and not the contents of their packages. Consumers who are "salaciously disposed" will probably soon learn to identify the familiar old product in the new wrapping. . . .

Finally, Mr. Justice Douglas was most likely correct when he stated that the method of distribution is irrelevant to a determination of the obscenity of particular material. Regardless of the desirability of prosecuting the commercial purveyors of smut who are the real target of the obscenity laws, the statutes in the *Ginzburg* and *"Memoirs"* cases related only to publications which were inherently obscene. No statutory mention was made of the manner of distribution. A statute reaching commercial exploitation may or may not be constitutional,[102] but some legislation directed at specific conduct would be preferable to the current practice of labeling material obscene which is not on its face obscene in order to reach those who exploit the material. For instance, if the exploitation concept were by statute limited to circumstances analogous to common-law nuisance, commercial exploitation as a limitation of distribution might be acceptable. The state can regulate nuisances and can even constitutionally

---

[100] *See* A. GERBER, SEX, PORNOGRAPHY & JUSTICE 204 (1965).

[101] *Id.* at 202-03.

[102] Any federal statute which would make pandering or titillation a criminal offense "in the terms so elusively defined by the Court would, of course, be unconstitutionally vague and void." Ginzburg v. United States, 383 U.S. 463, 500 (1966) (Stewart, J., dissenting).

regulate the time, place, and manner of distribution of religious or political literature.[103] Thus, distribution of material to unwilling recipients advertising sexual works in an erotic manner could probably be proscribed. . . .

(5) The Scope of Supreme Court Review of Obscenity Cases. The Supreme Court may find itself overburdened by review of obscenity cases, since it appears to adhere to the theory of independent review in this area. To alleviate some of the burden, the Government suggested in *"Memoirs"* that the Court limit its independent review to the question of social importance.[104] In view of this concern, do the standards set forth in the new cases help to ease the work load?

Conceivably the limitation of the commercial-exploitation element to close cases may indicate a step in the direction of Supreme Court review of only those cases which are *not* close and in which the standards clearly were erroneously applied. In the gray area where material of questionable value was commercially exploited, the lower courts would have free rein. This hypothesis, however, runs counter to the Court's own admonition in *Roth* that "[t]he door barring federal and state intrusion into this area . . . must be kept tightly closed and opened only the slightest crack necessary to prevent encroachment upon more important interests."[105] Allowing the lower courts to have free rein would seem on the contrary to open the door almost all the way.

It seems more likely the Court will continue to adhere to independent review, in which case it has certainly not eased its own burden. Now a fourth factor must be considered, a factor wholly apart from the obscenity of the publication itself. Not only must the publication be examined, but extrinsic evidence of advertising and distribution must also be considered.

Moreover, and contrary to the suggestion that review could be limited because of the exploitation element, the same publica-

---

[103] *See* Kovacs v. Cooper, 336 U.S. 77 (1949); Cantwell v. Connecticut, 310 U.S. 296 (1940) (dictum); Schneider v. New Jersey, 308 U.S. 147 (1939) (dictum).
[104] Brief for the United States 27-28, A Book Named "John Cleland's Memoirs of a Woman of Pleasure" v. Attorney Gen., 383 U.S. 413 (1966).
[105] Roth v. United States, 354 U.S. 476, 488 (1957).

tion could theoretically reach the Court an infinite number of times. Although one adverse decision based on exploitation might keep the material from being distributed at all, in an extreme case the Court would have to consider the same publication anew each time it was distributed in a different way. If the pandering concept is to be retained, the Supreme Court must either accept the lower court findings on the question or drastically restrict the meaning of the close case. Otherwise, the burden of review might be staggering.

(6) The "Community" in Community Standards. Although in *"Memoirs"* the Government contended that the scope of community standards was national,[106] the Court did not discuss the question, perhaps because of the probable division within the majority had it been considered. Of the Justices presently on the Court, only Justices Brennan[107] and Harlan[108] had previously supported the national standard. Mr. Chief Justice Warren and Mr. Justice Clark had favored a local community standard on the theory that there is no national standard.[109]

Whatever the scope of the community, an expert on contemporary community standards is hard to identify. He might be a sociologist, a psychologist, a minister, or anyone else who would rationally be thought to provide information over and above that derived from his position as an individual member of the community. A new finding in each case of the current state of community standards involves a great deal of time and effort; if some kind of expert testimony is not taken and a finding made, however, the community-standards element in operation contemplates nothing more than the subjective attitudes of the trier.

Moreover, application of the community-standards element will be paradoxical. Presumably the Government, limited in time and

---

[106] Brief for the United States 20, A Book Named "John Cleland's Memoirs of a Woman of Pleasure" v. Attorney Gen., 393 U.S. 413 (1966).

[107] *See* Jacobellis v. Ohio, 378 U.S. 184, 192-95 (1964).

[108] *See* Manual Enterprises v. Day, 370 U.S. 478, 488 (1962) (for federal prosecutions only).

[109] *See* Jacobellis v. Ohio, 378 U.S. 184, 200-01 (1964) (Warren, C. J., dissenting, with Clark, J., joining).

resources, will move only against publications it feels pose the greatest threat to society. Publications posing the greatest threat are most likely those with the widest circulation and thus the most general impact. Yet, if a publication *does* circulate widely, does this not mean that it *is* within limits which the community will tolerate?

IV. WHERE DO WE GO FROM HERE?

One solution is to do away with obscenity censorship in most instances. Obscenity could be retained as a classification, but no obscene work, absent a showing of clear and present danger of criminal conduct, could be prohibited, and no distributor could be prosecuted unless he caused the material to be distributed to an involuntary receiver who was offended by it.[110] The problem of nonobscene material being advertised as obscene could be solved by a separate statute dealing with fraudulent and misleading advertising. Emphasis on the involuntary receiver would preserve the distribution of obscenity to willing receivers in order not to inhibit the distribution of nonobscene material.

It is unlikely, however, that society would in the near future accept such a near absence of obscenity censorship. Thus, assuming censorship, some standard should be promulgated which will protect literature of any importance from censorship by lower courts and yet still relieve the Supreme Court of case-by-case disposition of obscenity litigation. With these goals in mind, the following is presented as a workable standard.

First, the commercial-exploitation element should be discarded as irrelevant to a determination of whether any given work is obscene. If a finding of obscenity is made by reference to a factor unrelated to a publication's contents, the first amendment has been violated and the public done a disservice. A statute limited to condemnation of conduct, based on theories of nuisance or the concept of the unwilling receiver, could be enacted in order to reach commercial exploitation of sex.

[110] Conceivably, such a standard could involve such related concepts as the "duty to warn" those who might be exposed to the obscene material.

Second, the means of determining social importance and the weight given to social importance must be clarified. The appellant in *"Memoirs"* suggested that expert testimony be weighed by the courts and further that the quantity of critical reviews of a work be considered highly indicative of its importance.[111] However, if serious works are to be saved from censorship, some other standard than the usual weighing of the evidence must be adopted. After all, "[t]here are among us individuals who, by training and experience, are better qualified than most to appraise the literary or artistic or other merit of a book."[112] This much is agreed—some people are better equipped to judge than courts and juries. The real question is how much weight is to be given to their testimony. There are two alternatives other than weighing the evidence of a work's social importance: (1) such evidence is conclusive if substantial, *although not predominating,* or (2) if there is a scintilla of such evidence it is conclusive.

The scintilla test is impractical because someone of at least some repute could probably be found to testify in favor of the social importance of almost anything. Therefore, expert testimony in favor of the social importance of a work should be conclusive if it is credible and substantial, although on balance definitely not predominating. "Credible" means the witness' status as a reputable expert is acknowledged. Such an evidentiary test should ensure that works of at least arguable merit would be protected, thus protecting minority access to these works. If it is true that public, and perhaps also critical, acclaim in the area of sex runs behind important expression,[113] such a test is especially important.

Third, the patent-offensiveness test should be retained, with objective evidence of widespread national circulation being conclusive of its acceptance by the community and of its inclusion within the limits of candor.

Fourth, the appeal to prurient interests test should be retained

111 Brief for Appellant 22-23, A Book Named "John Cleland's Memoirs of a Woman of Pleasure" v. Attorney Gen., 383 U.S. 413 (1966).

112 *Id.* at 22.

113 *See* Comment, *Free Speech and Obscenity: A Search for Constitutional Procedures and Standards,* 12 U.C.L.A.L. Rev. 532, 552 (1965).

THE CONTROL OF IDEAS

despite the criticism that obscenity repels rather than attracts, with the exception that evidence of shock and repulsion in a particular case may be introduced in place of the prurient-appeal element if exposure to the material was involuntary. Agreeing that in almost every case the prurient-appeal element invites the highly personal reaction of the trier, such a personal reaction will be of some utility at least in weeding out works which never should have been subjects of prosecution.

Fifth, each of the above elements should be independent of the others so that, for example, a finding of patent offensiveness and prurient appeal could be negated by a finding of even minimal social importance.

Sixth, social importance, in turn, should be negated only by a finding that the publication presents a clear and present danger of illegal action (sexual or otherwise) or of destruction of the moral fiber of society.

Seventh, the Supreme Court should treat lower court findings on patent offensiveness and prurient appeal as matters of discretion, but should make an independent judgment on social importance and clear and present danger. Alternatively, the Supreme Court could further restrict itself and limit review to two classes of cases: (1) where the social-importance element had been misapplied to prohibit a serious work and (2) where a serious and potentially provable allegation of clear and present danger had been made.

Operation of these standards should achieve the goal advocated in this Note: making censorship of any publication of even minimal social importance extremely difficult.

Free Press & Fancy Packages

A . Q . M O W B R A Y

*Freedom of the press is guaranteed only
to those who own one.*—A. J. Liebling

Although much lip service is paid in this country to the principle of an informed electorate, it seems clear that to an unhealthy degree the electorate depends for its information upon those who have a vested interest in influencing their judgments.

Any proposed legislation that promises to benefit the consumer by limiting the freedom of action of a powerful segment of industry is doomed unless it can attract widespread public support, but the process of developing this support is often long and tedious. Typically, a rising tide of complaints culminates in Congressional hearings to air the abuses. Exposure of the problem in the hearings serves the dual purpose of clarifying the need for legislation and broadcasting the issue to the people, through press reports and accompanying editorial comment. This dialogue among the people, the press and the Congress creates the substance of public awareness upon which demand for legislation must rest.

The success of this democratic procedure is assured only if the channels of communication are open. During the recent five-year

Reprinted by permission from *The Nation.* From *The Nation,* CCV (December 11, 1967), 621-623. Mr. Mowbray is the author of *The Thumb on the Scale or The Supermarket Shell Game* (J. B. Lippincott).

struggle to enact a truth in packaging law, the channels of communication were blocked, the consumer did not know what was happening, and the bill finally emerged as the Fair Packaging and Labeling Act of 1966, a highly ineffective piece of legislation that promises little in the way of reform.

The opening round of packaging hearings, in 1961, made lively copy. Newspapers reported that Senate witnesses had called the consumer a "sucker"; columnists lambasted the food manufacturers. Television screens showed Sen. Philip A. Hart (D., Mich.), sponsor of the packaging bill, holding up deceptive packages for all the nation to see. But before the mass-circulation magazines could comment, the food manufacturers collected their wits and retaliated. Paul S. Willis, then president of Grocery Manufacturers of America, the trade association for the $80-billion-per-year food industry, summoned the publishers of sixteen national magazines to "discuss with them the facts of life covering advertising-media relationships." As Mr. Willis later told it, "We suggested to the publishers that the day was here when their editorial department and business department might better understand their interdependency relationships as they affect the operating results of their company; and as their operations may affect the advertiser—their bread and butter."

Now, a persistent and dearly cherished tenet of the mass-circulation publications is that editorial policy is independent of advertising pressure. Here was a naked test of whether that separation was truth or myth. Mr. Willis "invited" the publishers "to consider publishing some favorable articles about the food industry instead of only singling out isolated cases of criticism." He pointed out that "as the readers turn the pages and come across an interesting article, they will react more favorably to the advertisement and be more inclined to purchase the product."

Some months later, Mr. Willis seemed please with the results of his persuasion. "We can point with pride," he said, "to some of the things which have happened since our visit." He then enumerated recent articles in eight magazines that were favorable to the food industry. "The articles," he pointed out, "will surely help to create a better understanding of the industry and a favorable public attitude toward it."

Two of the magazines whose publishers had met with Willis had earlier commissioned writers to prepare articles on the Hart bill. Possibly as a result of the Willis interview, these articles were never printed. While gathering material for my book on truth in packaging and the fate of the Hart bill, I wrote to nine of the leading mass-circulation magazines, asking them what they had published on the bill or on the problems that it dealt with. The replies indicated that, during the five years that the Hart bill languished in Congress, these magazines had told their readers nothing about this legislation that could have major implications for the prices paid in the supermarket. A search of *Readers'* *Guide to Periodical Literature* bore this out.

The January 26, 1965, issue of *Look* magazine contained an article titled "Let's Keep Politics Out of the Pantry," by Charles G. Mortimer, chairman of General Foods Corporation and one of the most implacable foes of truth in packaging. After charging that some vote-conscious politicians, through "headline-making innuendoes" and "emotion-charged appeals," were endangering the "machinery of free competition" by an intrusion where government did not belong, Mr. Mortimer got down to cases: "By making all packages 'look-alikes' on the shelf," he wrote, "restrictive legislation would stifle innovation and put a halter on an indispensable form of competition: the freedom to bring out packages which are easy to open, easy to close, easy to handle, easy to store." Mr. Mortimer warned his readers that "we are faced with the grim prospect of having Government officials tell the consumer what product she can buy and what kind of package she can buy it in."

This flagrant misrepresentation of his bill angered Senator Hart, who asked publisher Gardner Cowles for the opportunity to present his side of the case in the pages of *Look*. The publisher replied: "I will be interested to see how much attention the general public pays to the subject in the next several months" —the implication being that any decision to publish the Senator's rebuttal must be founded on the sound editorial basis of high reader interest. Mr. Cowles's estimate of reader interest was revealed by the fact that *Look* bought full-page advertisements in other magazines, including trade journals in the food industry, to trumpet its publication of "this compelling article." Senator Hart was never given the opportunity he requested.

Esther Peterson, then special assistant to President Johnson for consumer affairs, also wrote to *Look* as a result of the Mortimer article, offering to prepare a rebuttal. Robert Meskill, assistant managing editor, replied: "We do not plan to hold a 'debate' on this subject, but we appreciate your offering to engage in one."

At about the time of Willis' plain talk to the publishers, Senator Hart had sent background material on his bill to twenty-one magazines, hoping to stimulate articles or some editorial comment. These included twelve magazines in the grocery field and nine general circulation magazines. No articles resulted. One editor replied, "I think the bill is certainly needed but I doubt whether we can mention it editorially."

Thus did the magazine publishers and editors knuckle under to the pressure from their advertisers.

With the publishers brought to heel, Willis turned his attention to the television industry, the occasion being a speech he delivered at the eighth annual meeting of the Television Bureau of Advertising, in the Starlight Roof of the Waldorf-Astoria, on November 16, 1962, less than four months before the 1963 hearings on the packaging bill were to open.

In proud and loving detail, Willis told the television men the story of his success with the magazine men, continuing with:

I wish I could say similar nice things about the relationship of our advertisers with television. Even though the networks receive about 65 per cent of their advertising revenue from GMA members, there is lots to be desired as it applies to our relationship with their top management. We are not aware of any great amount of cooperation which television has extended to us in passing along interesting, favorable information to the public, information such as appeared in the magazine articles. The newspapers throughout the United States publish a great deal of information relating to food prices, food supplies, nutrition, and so on.

In contrast with these favorable items, we have seen some television newscasts where they seemingly took great delight in bellowing out stories that were critical of this industry.

Why should this be necessary, Willis asked, when there were

so many nice things that television could say about the food industry, its greatest source of advertising revenue? "There is plenty of interesting material available about this industry for radio/TV use, and broadcasting such information should create a better public attitude, the advertising would be more effective, and the advertiser would get more for his advertising dollar. It is something," he concluded, with all the subtlety of a pointed shotgun, "to think over."

Apparently, the television men thought it over. During the hearings held the following year, the first hearings on the bill itself, truth in packaging was mentioned on only two television shows. Further, Senator Hart's scheduled appearances on several programs were canceled. "I was told the advertisers had objected," the Senator explained.

In short, during the five-year struggle to pass a packaging bill, there was a near blackout of information on the issues in the mass media of communication. Thus it was probably true, as some opponents of the bill claimed, that the clamor of the general public for passage of the bill was notable by its absence. The voice of the food industry was strong and unequivocal; the voice of the consumer was weak and confused. The weakness and confusion stemmed from a lack of hard information on which to base a judgment. The people had not been told.

The people had not been told, for example, about "packaging to price," economically the most harmful of the deceptive practices that infest the shelves of the supermarket. Packaging to price is the technique whereby the food manufacturer, faced with rising costs, elects to decrease the contents of his packages rather than to increase the price. This practice works to the housewife's disadvantage in two ways:

First, because the decrease in contents is often accompanied by a package redesign, the housewife is often unaware that any reduction in contents has occurred, and the price is increased without her knowledge. For example, a 1-pound (16-ounce) box of breakfast cereal might be redesigned so that the box becomes higher, wider, and thinner, and contains only 14½ ounces at the same price. In this way, the manufacturer manipulates a

THE CONTROL OF IDEAS   317

10 per cent price rise that is undetected by all but the most wary shopper.

Second, the net contents of packages are reduced to quantities that no longer have any rational relationship to our system of measurement. The simple pound and quart disappear from the shelves, to be replaced by packages containing such irrational quantities as 7½ ounces, 2 pounds 5½ ounces, 1 pint 14 ounces, and so on. The great advantage of this non-system, from the standpoint of the food manufacturer, is that the shopper finds it very difficult to compare the price per ounce, per pound, or per pint of different brands or, indeed, of different sizes of the same brand.

In the bill that Senator Hart introduced in 1961, the Food and Drug Administration and the Federal Trade Commission would have been given the authority to issue regulations to standardize the net contents of those packages in which the packaging-to-price disease had resulted in chaos. As the law finally emerged from Congress five years later, the food industry is given the opportunity to clean its own house on a voluntary basis, under the aegis of the Department of Commerce. Anyone reading the thousands of pages of testimony offered by representatives of the food industry and noting their unanimous, uncompromising, unremitting hostility to any packaging legislation would entertain small hope for the success of the voluntary approach.

The Fair Packaging and Labeling Act, totally rewritten to satisfy the objections of the powerful lobbyists for the food industry, was finally signed by President Johnson in November, 1966. In view of the poor performance of the press and the broadcasting industry during its protracted passage through Congress, it may be of some interest to note the reception accorded my book on the bill, which was published the following October.

I spent the last two weeks in October on a publicity tour of Pittsburgh, Washington, New York, Philadelphia, Boston and Chicago. During those visits only two newspapers expressed any desire to talk with me about the book, and one of them canceled our appointment on the day of the interview. The other interview did take place, with the food editor for a big-city daily, who said, half jokingly, that her copy was not subject to anyone's review, and therefore it was sure to make the first edition, but she could give no guarantee about subsequent editions.

Of the six cities visited, reviews have appeared in newspapers in Boston, Washington and Philadelphia (where I live). *Newsday* published a chapter of the book in its October 21 issue.

Perhaps this limited notice in the press is all one could ask for a first book by an unknown author, even though the message in the book impinges directly on the purse of every food shopper in the nation. This reticence on the part of the press, however, was in sharp contrast to the uninhibited enthusiasm of radio and television producers.

Much to my surprise, the producers of interview and "talk" shows, which seem to be proliferating in the broadcasting industry, unhesitatingly welcomed me at every stop on the tour. During the two weeks, I was invited to appear on twenty-two shows in the six cities. Time after time, in the lobbies of the broadcasting studios, I saw proud displays in glass-enclosed cases of the products of the sponsors, many of them food packages of the very kind I was condemning in my book. How, I asked the producers, could they get away with it? The answer was always the same. "We couldn't care less about that," they said. "We thrive on controversy. That's what makes our show a success."

As I walked into one studio, a frantic bit of last-minute scrambling was under way to rearrange some of the segments that were to make up the half-hour program. I was told by the producer that someone had just noticed that there had been a commercial for a packaged food product just two minutes away from my slot in the program. Some readjustment had been ordered to insert a little more time between our conflicting messages. "Theoretically, we're completely independent of this kind of thing," the producer said, "but in practice we must be a little careful." I was totally disinclined to criticize his caution: it appeared to me commendable that I was there at all.

As more and more newspapers give up the ghost, and the power of the press becomes concentrated in fewer and fewer hands, it is heartening to find an increasing number of television and radio shows such as *Contact* in Boston, Philadelphia and Pittsburgh, the *Tom Duggan Show* and *Kup's Show* in Chicago, *Capital Tie Line* and *Panorama* in Washington, *Night Talk* and the *Murray Burnett Show* in Philadelphia, and others. The producers of many of these shows are exhibiting a degree of imagination and courage that the newspapers might well emulate, to their increased good health. It appears that islands of civilization may be forming in the vast wasteland, and that the much maligned broadcasters may be our best hope for real communication in the future.

Ethics and the Press

In Boston and Chicago, newspaper investigations into suspected hanky-panky suddenly are aborted. In one case, a subject of inquiry turns out to be a stockholder of the paper and a friend of the publisher. In the other, the investigation threatens to embarrass a politician who could help the paper in a building project.

In California, a batch of small newspapers run editorials endorsing the Detroit position on auto safety. All are worded similarly. An incredible coincidence, this identity not only of opinion but of phrasing? Hardly, for all the articles are drawn from a single "canned" editorial emanating from an advertising agency in San Francisco.

In Denver, the advertising staff of a big daily wrestles with an arithmetic problem. A big advertiser has been promised news stories and pictures amounting to 25% of the ad space it buys; the paper already has run hundreds of column inches of glowing prose but is still not close to the promised allotment of "news" and now is running out of nice things to say.

SHORT-CHANGED READERS

All this hardly enhances the image of objectivity and fierce independence the U.S. press tries so hard to project. Yet talks with scores of reporters, editors, publishers, public relations men

Reprinted by permission of *The Wall Street Journal*. From the July 25, 1967, *Journal*.

and others reveal that practices endangering—and often subverting—newspaper integrity are more common than the man on the street might dream. Result: The buyer who expects a dime's worth of truth every time he picks up his paper often is short-changed.

All newspapers, including this one, must cope with the blandishments and pressures of special interests who seek distortion or omission of the truth. And no newspaper, again including this one, can ever be positive that every one of its staff always resists these blandishments and pressures. But on some papers the trouble starts at the top; it is the publisher himself who lays down news policies designed to aid one group or attack another.

Those publishers who do strive to report the news fully and impartially—and their number appears to be growing—have been taking several steps in recent years to make unethical or questionable behavior less likely on the part of their newsmen.

They have boosted editorial salaries sharply, thus making staffers less susceptible to bribes and favors offered by outsiders and reducing their dependence on outside work—which can, and sometimes does, result in conflict of interest. And more papers are laying down rules that forbid or discourage practices they consider unhealthy.

A LONG, HARD CLIMB

All in all, there is considerable evidence that "the ethics of the American press are probably at the highest level now in the history of the press anywhere," as claimed by Russell E. Hurst, executive officer of Sigma Delta Chi, the professional journalism society. But this is not the same thing as saying they are uniformly high; the press may have come a long way in recent years, but interviews disclose it has a long, hard climb to go before reaching any summit of ethical purity.

Ideally, a newspaper is supposed to pluck out the truth from the daily maelstrom of events, make independent and objective judgments as to its importance to readers, and print it without fear or favor. Resistance to outside pressures, including those applied by advertisers, is considered a must.

It is plain, however, that a sizable minority of newspapers still are putty in the hands of their advertisers, that they allow personal as well as business considerations to flavor the news to a marked degree, that their salaries are low and that they tolerate staff practices hardly conducive to editorial independence and objectivity.

A DISAPPEARING CRUSADE

The discerning reader sometimes can tell when a newspaper is "puffing" a favored advertiser or other outsider, but it is much harder to detect the sins of omission—the legitimate story suppressed, the investigation scotched for fear of offending someone. . . .

Much the same thing has happened to an investigation by members of the "Research Bureau" of the Boston Herald. The bureau, established late last year to probe crime, corruption and social injustice, reported directly to the publisher, George E. Akerson. Three of its members—John Salin, Nicholas Gage and Jim Savage—had two-year contracts at salaries among the highest paid by the paper.

In April this year, the bureau added another staffer—Hank Messick, a noted crime reporter. Mr. Messick and Mr. Savage lost no time in getting to work. One of their first investigations involved a complicated stock transaction in Universal Marion Corp. that had attracted the attention of both the Securities and Exchange Commission and the U.S. Attorney in New York.

A CALL FROM THE PUBLISHER

The reporters had hardly begun to make inquiries when they got a phone call from Publisher Akerson, who wanted to know why they were investigating the affairs of Joseph Linsey, a well-known Boston businessman and philanthropist. The reporters, puzzled, couldn't recall that Mr. Linsey's name had come up at all in their efforts up to then, and they told Mr. Akerson so. They do recall, however, that Mr. Akerson told them Mr. Linsey was a "major stockholder" in Boston Herald-Traveler Corp., the company that publishes the Herald (now the Herald-Traveler, following its absorption of the evening Traveler July 10).

The phone call whetted the reporters' curiosity about Mr. Linsey, who has interests in a number of businesses in Boston and elsewhere, and who is a trustee of Brandeis University and a major benefactor of that school. They later discovered that Mr. Linsey's name was on a list of stockholders in Universal Marion who were parties in the transaction under investigation.

In short order they found that one of Mr. Linsey's employees at Whitehall Liquors, a Schenley distributorship he heads in Boston, is Michael (Mickey the Wise Guy) Rocco, believed by law enforcement authorities to be a leading member of the Cosa Nostra in that city. In addition, Rocco works for Dario Ford Inc., a Boston auto agency in which Mr. Linsey is a partner.

The reporters also found that one Sam Tucker, a reputed underworld figure, had an interest in the Sahara Motel, Miami, when it was partially owned by Mr. Linsey. The latter concedes this is true but says he did not sell any part of his original interest to Tucker, only met him once and remembers him as a "decent guy."

Reporters Savage and Messick were trying to run down frequent rumors that Mr. Linsey himself had spent time in jail. (Asked about this, Mr. Linsey retorts: "That's none of your business.")

A REPORTER IS DISMISSED

But the reporters were halted in their inquiries by the Herald itself. Shortly after the first phone call from Mr. Akerson, Harold W. Clancy, first vice president of Boston Herald-Traveler, told them to drop the investigation that involved Mr. Linsey. Within a week the paper then told Mr. Messick that it had decided not to keep him—a distinct shock to the reporter, since he insists that he too was promised a two-year contract, at even more pay than the other members of the bureau. Mr. Messick now is suing the company, which contends he was employed on a trial basis only.

What is Mr. Linsey's connection with Mr. Akerson and the Herald? According to Mr. Akerson, who declines to discuss other aspects of the whole affair, Mr. Linsey owns about one-half of 1% of the outstanding stock of the publishing company. Jack Anderson, columnist Drew Pearson's partner, reported earlier that Mr. Linsey denied owning any shares; later Mr. Linsey told a Wall Street Journal reporter that an interest was owned by Taunton Dog Track, of which he is president.

Mr. Linsey says he and Mr. Akerson are close friends. But when he learned that reporters Messick and Savage were asking questions, he says he called Mr. Akerson and told him that "if you write anything about me, you better be sure of your facts or face a law suit."

As for the original research bureau, it has collapsed. The three reporters who worked on it with Mr. Messick protested his discharge, but to no avail. Mr. Savage also formally requested "permission" of the Herald to interview Mr. Linsey. This petition was ignored. A few weeks after Hank Messick's firing, the others decided to quit, and all are gone from the Herald now.

Jim Savage offers a summing-up. "We certainly never accused Linsey of anything," he says, "nor did we have any evidence that he was involved in anything illegal. But we thought his apparent association with some rather well-known mobster types made him worth looking into. Things became intolerable when they wouldn't even let us interview someone about an important story. We resigned because it's clear the paper isn't interested in serving the public."

Publisher Akerson, who will not comment beyond affirming that Mr. Linsey is a stockholder, claims that "this (a newspaper, specifically The Wall Street Journal) isn't the proper forum for such a discussion."

Evidently other Boston papers seem to agree with this statement, one that probably would startle legions of journalists taught to believe that the newspaper is the natural forum for every matter of fact or opinion. Not a word about the happenings at the Herald has appeared in the other Boston dailies—even though the Drew Pearson-Jack Anderson syndicated column has outlined them twice already. The Boston Globe, which ordinarily runs most Pearson-Anderson columns, printed neither of these.

Such blackouts of news involving newspapers are quite common; hardly a working journalist could deny that one of the gravest weaknesses in coverage exhibited by the American press is its coverage of itself. This became apparent in Philadelphia recently when Harry Karafin, a prize-winning investigative reporter for the Inquirer and a staffer for nearly 30 years, was arrested on charges of blackmail and extortion. Philadelphia magazine, not a local newspaper, printed the first blast at Karafin in its April issue.

From then until the reporter's arrest earlier this month, the rival Philadelphia Bulletin carried not a word on the case—even though the Inquirer itself (which claims it had repeatedly pursued tips about Mr. Karafin's activities but could not prove anything) fired him shortly before the magazine expose and carried the whole story afterward.

SILENCE ON A COURT CASE

More often newspapers try to cover up when unfavorable news breaks about their own operations. A few years ago the Clarion-Ledger and Daily News, jointly owned papers in Jackson, Miss., were hauled into court by U.S. officials on charges dealing with violations of Federal laws governing overtime pay. The court action resulted in a permanent injunction barring the papers from continuing the offending practices. Not a word of all this appeared in the Jackson papers; staffers were even ordered to stay away from the court, and they did.

News blackouts aren't always limited to a paper's problems. Sometimes they make unpersons out of individuals who somehow have come into bad odor with the paper. On the Philadelphia Inquirer, for example, a blacklist of names not to appear in print is believed to have long existed. News executives at the paper say there hasn't been any such list, to their knowledge, but many Quaker City newsmen find that hard to believe.

So might Gaylord P. Harnwell, president of the University of Pennsylvania. Though a newsmaker by the very virtue of his position, his name was regularly expunged from the Inquirer and its sister publication, the Philadelphia Daily News, roughly from December 1963 into March 1964. All the while, his name was appearing in stories printed by the rival Bulletin. On one occasion, when Mr. Harnwell called for an extensive survey of athletics at Penn in a letter to an annual alumni banquet, the Inquirer attributed the letter to "a high university official."

This went on until Philadelphia magazine, which broke the Karafin story, drew attention to the blackout. The reason for it is still a mystery; Inquirer officials blandly deny a blackout was ordered and Mr. Harnwell's office won't discuss the matter. . . .

. . . Newspapers don't much relish losing their best talents to others, but many are liberal in their policies toward part-time outside work by staffers or don't seem to realize the extent of it. Those concerned with the ethical standards of the press suggest such outside work can seriously jeopardize the believability of many stories the moonlighters write for their papers.

In some cases, the "work" is exceptionally light—consisting mainly of being friendly in print to the interests that have the journalists on their payrolls. In New York, for example, it's known that a columnist for one of the papers that have ceased publication in recent years was on the payroll of a big liquor distiller, and a reporter for a paper still publishing has long been feeding at the trough of a powerful labor union.

CLANDESTINE ARRANGEMENTS

Discovery that a staffer is "on the take" is, of course, ground for immediate dismissal at any paper with the least respect for honesty. By their very nature, though, such arrangements between reporters and outsiders are clandestine and hard for a paper to uncover.

In the vast majority of instances, however, the reporter is honestly employed by outside interests with the knowledge of his newspaper bosses (but not the public who reads his articles). Often the reason is low pay on the paper; a reporter for the Jackson, Miss., paper says: "Almost everybody here does some kind of outside work. With the salaries they pay, you have to." Pay scales at the Clarion-Ledger and Daily News are guarded like atomic secrets, but staffers put the range at roughly $65 to $150 a week for reporters. In the past employees have labored at such sidelines as making slogan-bearing license plates and running photography studios.

There's little chance of conflict of interest in jobs like these. But there are numerous examples of outside work by newsmen that clearly could prejudice their coverage of certain stories.

On some papers, courthouse reporters have been appointed by courts as estate appraisers. Are they in a position to write critically of the courts if the facts dictate it, considering they might be risking the loss of their outside income? For the same reason, how much objectivity in rail strike coverage could have been expected from the labor reporter of a sizable East Coast Daily—who until recently had a outside publicity job with a major railroad?

Some highly respected veteran reporters are in the same position. In January, for example, Bob Considine wrote a column brushing off Detroit's auto safety critics and championing the position of the embattled manufacturers. What of it, considering Mr. Considine has every right to his own opinion? Nothing, except that he also was being paid for appearing in and narrating a Ford Motor Co. movie on its auto safety research and engineering. There's no secret about Mr. Considine's work for Ford—it was publicized—but it was not mentioned in the column.

Ralph Nader, leading auto safety critics, nevertheless calls it "a blatant conflict of interest". And in a recent issue, the Columbia Journalism Review placed the column and another article, headlined "Considine Stars in Ford Film," side by side in its "Coincidence Department."

Says Mr. Considine: "I see no conflict. I believe the (auto) industry is doing all it can do, and I've been saying that for some time. Narrating the movie for Ford was in keeping with my beliefs."

Some critics of the press believe that taking a leave of absence to perform outside duties doesn't really dispel the conflict-of-interest cloud, particularly when the outside job is for individuals or organizations regularly in the news. But this is done often.

For example, Herb Klein took a leave from his post as editor of the San Diego Union to be press secretary for Richard Nixon during his losing 1960 campaign; he took another when Mr. Nixon tried unsuccessfully to capture the California governorship in 1962. In San Francisco, it's not unusual for reporters to take leaves to do press and public relations work for candidates and return to report on their doings.

Junketing also is widely viewed as a threat to objectivity, but is widely practiced nonetheless. Junkets are trips by reporters whose travel and other expenses are paid by the news source, not the newspaper. The source often stages some "event" or shows off some facility of marginal interest, to give the reporters some excuse for going, but the real intent in many cases is to maintain good relations with the press as well as to garner some publicity in the process.

These junkets sometimes are little more than bacchanals for attending newsmen. Reporters still recall with relish a Caribbean trip staged by one big company a few years ago; the firm bank-rolled everything, including the services of a bevy of prostitutes. On one stopover during the return trip, some of the more rambunctious journalists were jailed by the police, and company attorneys used their good offices to get them sprung ("These are very important editors from New York. . . .").

FREE VACATIONS

The "news" stories that emerge from such affairs are almost always complimentary, if not gushing, and almost always have little or no intrinsic worth. Some editors frankly admit this, and say they use junkets mainly as a way to give deserving staffers expense-paid vacations.

In recent years, a growing number of papers have taken steps to end or restrict junketing, questionable outside work, the acceptance of gifts and other practices that might compromise objectivity. At the Washington Post, which past and present staffers regard as having lofty ethical standards, National Editor Laurence Stern sums up the rules: "Reporters aren't to free-load, free-ride, free-wheel. . . ."

The New York Times and The Wall Street Journal, among others, follow policies similar to the Post's. The Los Angeles Times frowns on moonlighting that would "embarrass" the paper or interfere with the staffer's regular job, and has barred all junkets except by the travel editor. It discourages gifts, too. . . .

Such measures, however, actually, do little to correct another grave fault of a good many papers: Favoritism toward business in general and advertisers in particular. Indeed, it seems apparent that a double standard exists at many papers; reporters and editors are expected to eschew practices that might compromise the paper's integrity, while the paper itself, by actual policy or common practice, distorts the news to suit advertisers or literally hands over news space to them.

At the Herald News, an 80,000-circulation daily in Passaic-Clifton, N.J., outside jobs that might constitute conflict of interest are frowned on; the paper once ordered a staffer to give up a $50-a-month job writing news releases for the Clifton Red Cross. Yet once a week the paper carries a "weekly business review" page comprised of ads and a "news story" about an advertiser—a story contracted for by the advertiser when he buys his ad space. The stories are uniformly complimentary. "Everybody's the greatest," says Managing Editor Arthur G. McMahon.

The Dallas Times Herald does much the same thing, printing each Monday from 2½ to 3 pages of "commercial, industrial news of Dallas." The "news" coverage of each company depends on how much ad space it buys; an eight-inch ad run weekly for a year, for example, qualifies for eight pictures and eight stories throughout that year, whether there is anything significant to report or not. . . .

Everyone in newspapering pays lip service to the ideal that a paper's news columns should not be for sale, and when the gap between that ideal and actual practice is bared for all to see, considerable embarrassment can result. Certainly the Denver Post was red-faced when Cervi's Rocky Mountain Journal, a weekly reporting on business and financial doings in the area, got hold of and printed an internal memo circulated among some Post people recently.

Though the Post insists it makes no such arrangements with advertisers, the memo indicates that the paper had promised to run no less than 1,820 column inches (10 full pages) of free publicity about a new shopping center because the center had bought 40 pages of advertising and was entitled to 25% of that in free space. At the time the memo was written, the Post had cranked out 826 column inches of "news" and pictures about the center, and the author of the memo foresaw little difficulty in pushing the paper's "coverage" relatively "close to the magic number."

The Post was having more difficulty meeting its obligation to Joslin's store, another advertiser promised 25% free space. At that point, it had printed less than half of the promised editorial matter and, said the memo's author, "I frankly don't see much more that can be said about them short of repetition."

On other papers, the news-advertising arrangement is less formal but still very much in evidence. The size of many, if not most, special sections on such fields as real estate, food, entertainment and travel corresponds not to what happens to be news when they are printed but to the volume of advertising each section is able to attract.

The general interests of the business community, rather than those of a specific advertiser, also affect news content. To the Sacramento Bee, for example, the weather never is hot, even when you can fry an egg on the pavement. The most the paper will concede is that it is "unseasonably warm." Anything stronger might scare off prospective new business and industry, it's felt.

Some time ago Boston papers also fudged on the weather reports; when a deluge was on the way, the papers would tell readers there was a "possibility of showers." Heavy rains, of course, are bad for the retail trade.

Among advertisers, big local retailers seem to have the most influence on papers' news coverage. One West Coast daily "blacked out" news of a housewives' revolt against high food prices in its metropolitan editions) but not in papers going out of town), though it did carry a story showing how food chains were trying to "educate" housewives about price structures. An employee of the paper says the blackout occurred after a food chain executive wrote a letter to the paper's publisher asking that the paper play down the controversy.

In another city, a department store official suggested—and got —a story in a local paper showing that a strike (at an entirely different business establishment) had resulted in the loss of jobs for all the original strikers and that the operation of the business had hardly been harmed. The union side wasn't given. The department store executive, it seems, had been restive because his own store was a target for organization; presumably he wanted to give his employees the word that no good would come of that.

There is evidence that many once-principled newsmen have been deeply demoralized by their papers' surrender to advertisers' interests. A recent survey of 162 business and financial editors, for example, revealed that 22.6% of them "indicated that as a matter of routine they were compelled to puff up or alter and downgrade business stories at the request of the advertisers." The survey found that "such pressures is most effective when it is brought to bear through the publication's own advertising department."

Prof. Timothy Hubbard of the University of Missouri, who conducted the survey, says many editors object strenuously to such attempts at distortion but often lack backing from higher management. "As a result," he says, "some seem curiously resigned to trimming their editorial sails to the edicts of the ad department, particularly on smaller dailies."

A former reporter for the Houston Post relates that he once was handed a "request" from the business office to do a story on a family picnic. The family was an advertiser's. "I thought it was a joke," says the newsman, "but it wasn't a rib—they wanted a story." He refused to do it, but the desk had little trouble finding someone else.

Bibliography for Chapter Seven

BOOKS

Berns, Walter. *Freedom, Virtue and the First Amendment*. Baton Rouge, Louisiana: Louisiana State University Press, 1957.

Blanshard, Paul. *The Right to Read: The Battle Against Censorship*. Boston: Beacon Press, 1955.

Codding, George A., Jr. *Broadcasting without Barriers*. Paris: Unesco, 1959.

Coons, John E. (ed.) *Freedom and Responsibility in Broadcasting*. Evanston, Ill.: Northwestern University Press, 1961.

Douglas, William O. *The Right of the People*. Garden City, New York: Doubleday & Company, Inc., 1958.

Downs, Robert B. (ed.) *The First Freedom: Liberty and Justice in the World of Books*. Chicago: American Library Association, 1960.

Ernst, Morris L., and Alan U. Schwartz. *Censorship: The Search for the Obscene*. New York: The Macmillan Company, 1964.

Gellhorn, Walter. *Individual Freedom and Governmental Restraints*. Baton Rouge, Louisiana: Louisiana State University Press, 1956.

Gerald, J. Edward. *The Social Responsibility of the Press*. Minneapolis: University of Minnesota Press, 1963.

Haney, Robert W. *Comstockery in America*. Boston: Beacon Press, 1960.

Lacy, Dan. *Freedom and Communications*. Urbana: University of Illinois Press, 1961.

Nelson, Jack, and Gene Roberts, Jr. *The Censors and the Schools*. Boston and Toronto: Little, Brown and Company, 1963.

Paul, James C., and Murray L. Schwartz. *Federal Censorship: Obscenity in the Mail*. New York: Free Press, Macmillan, 1961.

Schumach, Murray. *The Face on the Cutting Room Floor*. New York: William Morrow and Company, 1964.

ARTICLES

Cairns, R. B., J. C. N. Paul, and J. Wishner. "Sex Censorship: The Assumptions of Anti-Obscenity Laws and the Empirical Evidence," *Minnesota Law Review*, XLVI (May, 1962), 1009-1041.

"Censorship and the Arts," *Arts in Society*, IV (Summer, 1967), 195-444 (entire issue).

Epstein, Jason. "A Criticism of Commercial Publishing," *Daedalus*, XCII (Winter, 1963), 63-67.

Heifetz, Henry. "The Anti-Social Act of Writing," *Studies on the Left*, IV (Spring, 1964), 3-20.

Hentoff, Nat. "The War on Dissent," *Playboy*, XV (September, 1968), 155ff.

Lockhart, William B., and Robert C. McClure. "Censorship of Obscenity: The Developing Constitutional Standards," *Minnesota Law Review*, XLV (November, 1960), 5-121.

————. "Literature, The Law of Obscenity, and the Constitution," *Minnesota Law Review*, XXXVIII (March, 1954), 295-395.

Seldes, Gilbert. "The Mass Media and the Artistic Climate," *Arts in Society*, II (Fall-Winter, 1962, 1963), 150.

CASES

Burstyn, Inc. v. Wilson, 343 U.S. 495 (1952).

Ginzburg et al. v. United States, 383 U.S. 463 (1965).

Gitlow v. New York, 268 U.S. 652 (1925).

Hannegan v. Esquire, 327 U.S. 146 (1946).

Jacobellis v. Ohio, 84 U.S. 1676 (1964).

Kingsley Pictures Corp. v. Regents of the Univ. of New York, 360 U.S. 684 (1959).

Marcus v. Search Warrant, 367 U.S. 717 (1961).

Queen v. Hicklin, L.R. 3 Q.B. 360 (1868).

Roth v. United States, 354 U.S. 476 (1957).

Schenck v. United States, 249 U.S. 47 (1919).

Times Film Corp. v. City of Chicago, 81 S. Ct. 391 (1961).

United States v. One Book Called "Ulysses", 72 F.2d 705 (2d Cir.) (1934).

CHAPTER EIGHT

The Federal Government— Friend and Foe

Numerous agencies within the Federal Government find themselves both aiding the exchange of ideas and restricting the efforts of communicators to send their messages. The Post Office, for example, transmits mail and prevents the transmission of some kinds of mail. The Federal Communications Commission was established to free the channels of broadcasting in this country, yet it has done much to clog the channels with communicators of the same economic class. And the Federal Trade Commission, which was set up to help prevent unfair competition, sometimes must restrict the form that advertising messages take.

This chapter examines some of the ways in which the government very actively participates in the communication process: regulating, obstructing, and assisting the exchange of ideas. But also, running very strongly through these selections, we see the role of law against law: the Constitution invoked to prevent (or, at least, to scrutinize) bureaucratic attempts to regulate communication through administrative law.

Freedom of the Mails: A Developing Right

JAY A. SIGLER

One of the most enduring governmental institutions functioning both as friend and foe of communication is the Post Office
Department. Established to facilitate communication, the Post
Office has at various times in various ways restricted free communication by the mails. Here Professor Sigler traces in detail the
legal history of postal censorship and raises pertinent questions
regarding the wisdom of allowing the Post Office to determine
what messages are or are not mailable.*

*The United States may give up the Post Office when it sees fit,
but while it carries it on the use of the mails is almost as much a
part of free speech as the right to use our tongues, and it would
take very strong language to convince me that Congress even
intended to give such a practically despotic power to any one
man.[1]*

. . . The potential evils of postal censorship were well recognized by President Washington, who proposed at one time that
all mail be carried without charge for fear that someday someone

---

Copyright *Georgetown Law Journal*, LIV (1965), 30-54. Reprinted by permission.
* Editor's comment
[1] United States *ex rel.* Milwaukee Social Democratic Publishing Co. v.
Burleson, 255 U.S. 407, 437 (1921) (Holmes, J., dissenting), quoted approvingly
in Lamont v. Postmaster General, 381 U.S. 301, 305 (1965).

would suggest a federal power over its content. In 1835 the first attempt to censor mail was proposed by the Jackson administration. The Incendiary Publications Bill was directed at all material in postbags which might incite rebellion among the slaves of the South. The bill was defeated in the Senate by a vote of twenty-five to nineteen, but the debate among Calhoun, Webster, and Buchanan (later the fifteenth President) is of historic importance. Calhoun claimed that such a law could be passed by the states but not by Congress except in aid of a state's own laws. Webster, in agreement with Calhoun, contended that "Congress had not the power, drawn from the character of the paper, to decide whether it should be carried in the mail or not, for such a decision would be a direct abridgement of the freedom of the press." Buchanan, on the other hand, argued for a broad grant of federal authority. He said that it must be proven that freedom of the press "commands us to circulate and distribute, through our post offices, everything which the press shall publish, no matter whether it shall promote insurrection and civil war or not." Thus, the stage was set for a battle that is still being waged. The issue is the possible development of a freedom to use the mails under the protection of the first amendment.

The first successful congressional bid for censorship was the passage of the Customs Law of 1842, which prohibited the importation of pictorial art that was "indecent and obscene." This enactment, based upon the import power, did not regulate the printed word, as later statutes have done, but the use of the customs service as a censorship authority has, in itself, given rise to a good deal of litigation.

Statutory postal censorship of the printed word was begun in 1879, although the creation of this power was attended by some congressional doubt. A bill was introduced which would extend the second-class mailing privilege to "only such publications as will disseminate intelligence and be for the highest good of the whole people," a phrase which delayed passage of the bill in the Senate because it raised the issue of possible free speech violations. During the course of a companion bill through the House, Representative Springer of Illinois commented, "Under this proposed legislation [a] . . . rival publisher must go to the postmaster and submit his paper for inspection—for the censorship of the postmaster, from whose decision there is no appeal."

The notorious Espionage Act of 1917, which gave rise to the first test of the meaning of the first amendment as a limitation upon federal action, included a section permitting postal censorship. The act made nonmailable every letter, newspaper, or other publication advocating or urging treason, insurrection, or forcible resistance to any law of the United States. Circuit Court Judge Rogers, in examining the constitutionality of the statute, kept in step with the Supreme Court's limited view of the first amendment at the time. In a classic statement divorcing the first amendment from the use of the mails, Judge Rogers asserted,

[C]learly the Espionage Act imposes no restraint prior to publication, and no restraint afterwards, except as it restricts circulation through the mails. Liberty of circulation may be essential to freedom of the press, but liberty of circulating through the mails is not [essential] so long as its transportation in any other way as merchandise is not forbidden.

Although freedom of the mails is a substantial part of freedom of circulation, this position would uphold any exercise of postal censorship. However, as Mr. Justice Harlan stated in 1957, and as the most recent cases indicate, "the hoary dogma . . . that the use of the mails is a privilege on which the Government may impose such conditions as it chooses, has long since evaporated."

Currently, the postal censorship issue has been raised most frequently in connection with the obscenity problem. But as Mr. Justice Brennan observed in 1962 when considering the censorship of an allegedly obscene magazine, he did not wish to impute to Congress an intention to enter an area so "honeycombed with hazards for First Amendment guaranties." Apparently Congress has expressed such an intention, and, as discussed later in this article, the Supreme Court has recently frowned upon the application of a statute designed to stem the flow of communist propaganda through the mails.

OBSCENITY AND LIBEL AS NON-SPEECH

The basic postal obscenity statute, written in 1865, has been amended several times since. Obscene matter and many other items are deemed nonmailable (excluded from the stream of mail) and the act of depositing such mail is a criminal act. Significantly, historical research reveals no clear authorization to the Post Office to engage in a censorship program distinct from criminal law enforcement.[2]

Roth v. United States upheld the constitutionality of postal obscenity restrictions if applied according to the proper standard of obscenity: "whether to the average person, applying contemporary community standards, the dominant theme of the material taken as a whole appeals to prurient interest." According to this standard some private letters have been held to be nonmailable and their mailing a criminal offense, even in the absence of any proof of any actual effect upon the addresses. . . .

Libelous matter which appears on wrappers, envelopes, or postcards or any "delineation, epithet, term, or language of . . . threatening character" is also subject to exclusion from the mails, and the sender open to criminal prosecution. In a case in which the envelopes of the sender bore a postage stamp with a legend "in God we trust" next to a printed inscription stating that the stamp had been issued in wilful contempt of the laws of the United States, it was held that the inscription libeled the Postmaster

---

[2] Paul, *The Post Office and Non-Mailability of Obscenity: An Historical Note,* 8 U.C.L.A.L. Rev. 44 (1961). However, there does exist a separate statute, 39 U.S.C. § 4006 (1964), obstensibly as an aid to the enforcement of the criminal statute, 18 U.S.C. § 1461 (1964), which on its face appears to permit the Postmaster General to form his own judgment as to what is obscene and to deny virtually any use of the mail to the "violator." The language describing what is prohibited is the same in both statutes. Any "obscene, lewd, lascivious, indecent, filthy or vile article, matter, thing, device, or substance" is declared unlawful in both. Nevertheless, Summerfield v. Sunshine Book Co., 95 U.S. App. D.C. 169, 221 F.2d 42 (1954), *cert. denied,* 349 U.S. 921 (1955), held that the Postmaster General may only declare material to be obscene which has already been found to be so after a hearing, thus limiting a potentially broad censorship power.

General by identifying him and could not be conveyed through the mails. The statute does not appear to reach the contents of the letters, but the fact of censorship remains.

The Supreme Court has long since held that "fighting words" are not a form of speech protected by the first amendment. Both libel and obscenity may be considered as special examples of this general rule. The harm inherent in the receipt of a libelous or unsolicited obscene letter is of much the same character. Each poses a direct, immediate harm which is not controllable by subsequent regulatory action. The problem area encompasses not only the difficulty of identifying obscenity and libel but also the difficulty of determining who should pass judgment on such matters. . . .

REGULATION OF SOCIAL AND ECONOMIC MATTERS BY POSTAL CENSORSHIP

Various sections of the postal laws represent attempts to engage in regulatory or prohibitory measures through the postal clause of the Constitution. Just as the interstate commerce and tax powers have been utilized to create broad national policies, so the postal authority has been extended to control areas traditionally left to the states. Censorship has been necessarily involved since postal administrators must oversee the contents of regulated mail items, but this type of censorship is indirect because it is intended to treat a substantive problem of federal concern rather than punish a form of expression per se. The public interest in free discussion in these areas may be low when compared to the social interest in regulation of the subject matter itself. If so, the argument that the first amendment should serve as a barrier is, in such instances, a weak one.

The postal laws referring to lotteries and fraud are the best examples of regulation by censorship of socially undesirable subject matter. Firearms, poisons, and infernal machines are nonmailable. Congress has even provided punishment for the sending of political mails which do not disclose the name of the distributor, but this applies only to mail sent during a campaign for federal office.

It is clear that "the overt act of putting a letter into the post-office of the United States is a matter that Congress may regulate." It has been argued by some that Congress has inherited the postal powers of the states, including the police power. Mr. Justice Field maintained that since prohibition of circulation through the mails is not tantamount to complete prohibition of circulation, Congress is neither interfering with freedom of the press nor assuming a police power in such matters.

One case in particular, on both the appellate and Supreme Court levels, has dealt widely with the postal power to regulate. The Second Circuit in *Electric Bond & Share Co. v. SEC*[3] gave this power a most extensive reading: "[T]his power probably may be regarded as even more comprehensive than that exercised over interstate commerce for the government's interest in the mails is proprietary as well as regulatory." On appeal the Supreme Court supposedly resolved this matter with the following ambiguous statement: "While Congress may not exercise its control over the mails to enforce a requirement which lies outside its constitutional province, when Congress lays down a valid regulation pertinent to the use of the mails, it may withdraw the privilege of that use from those who disobey."

The same case illustrates how the postal power can be used in conjunction with a well-recognized power of Congress—here it was the commerce power—to avoid questions of constitutionality. *Electric Bond* makes it clear that those who refuse to register and issue a statement with the Securities and Exchange Commission can be constitutionally punished by being deprived of the use of the mails to carry on business.

However, fraud cases are not in the above category since the postal power alone is involved. Statute bars the use of the mails for the purpose of executing a scheme to defraud or obtain money or property by false or fraudulent pretenses. It has been held that the Post Office may constitutionally be given the power to prevent such schemes from being carried into effect. The stat-

3 92 F.2d 580 (2d Cir. 1937), *aff'd*, 303 U.S. 419 (1938).

ute does not impinge upon the police power of the state because it does not "purport to reach all frauds, but only those limited instances in which the use of the mails is a part of the execution of the fraud." The leading case indicates that the possibility of interference with private mail not connected with the fraudulent scheme is no reason to hold such a statute unconstitutional. The constitutionality of prohibitions on mail-lottery schemes has been upheld on a similar basis.

Congress has prohibited from the mails foreign divorce material, contraceptive and abortive materials, and, in a most dubious exercise, "any matter advocating or urging treason, insurrection, or forcible resistance to any law of the United States." The constitutionality of this last provision would seem highly questionable if normal free speech tests are applied. Nonetheless, the statute has not been recently challenged. . . .

. . . The gradations are very fine between protected and unprotected speech in the mails, but perhaps the fact that all classes of the judicially unprotected speech thus far mentioned are nonpolitical in content may account for the weakness of the first amendment as a barrier to postal censorship.

COMMUNIST PROPAGANDA

In 1962 Congress added to the Postal Code a new section entitled "Communist political propaganda." Formality was thus given to a program which had been engaged in fitfully by the executive branch ever since the beginnings of the Cold War. Foreign mail, except for sealed letters, designated by the Secretary of the Treasury to be "communist political propaganda" could be detained by the Postmaster General upon arrival in the United States. A statutory exemption was granted to "matter addressed to any United States Government agency, or any public library, or to any college . . . scientific or professional institution for advanced studies, or any official thereof . . . ." The section defines "communist political propaganda" by reference to several other statutes, rather than by any express declaration. This furthest expansion of the postal power of Congress has been challenged on first amendment grounds. Other constitutional objections flowing from the technique of censorship employed under the statute have also been raised. By entering into the area of political ideas the implications of this extension are fraught with difficulty.

General postal regulations provide that prohibited mail of foreign origin will be held for the addressee to be opened in his presence or by his authorization. If the addressee fails to appear or respond, then the letter is to be endorsed "unclaimed" and returned, unopened, to its origin. Despite the apparent simplicity of enforcing such regulations, the procedures used until last May [1965] to censor communist mail were much more complex and much less successful than the procedures used in other areas such as obscenity. This was probably the case because of the greater degree of subtlety needed to detect propaganda. In detecting communist propaganda the Post Office shook out its sacks at the point of entry, sent on the sealed letters (which are unaffected by the statute), and detained for customs inspection all mail excepting that not believed to be exempt. Working side by side, postal officials and customs inspectors sorted the mail into two piles, sending the nonpropaganda back into the mail flow and the propaganda into a file room. The Post Office then sent out notice form 21403X to the addressee asking him if he wished to receive the mail. The addressee could check "deliver this publication," "deliver similar publications," or "do not deliver." Providing the card was returned, each time a new publication from the same source arrived the postal employee checked the name file and disposed of the material accordingly. It is unclear whether postal authorities or customs personnel did the actual censoring.

Last May the Supreme Court in *Lamont v. Postmaster General* declared unconstitutional the above censorship program for communist propaganda mail. This important decision marks a long step forward toward a recognition of a freedom of the mails. The Court concluded that the program was unconstitutional because the act of returning the reply card was a limitation upon the unfettered exercise of the addressee's first amendment rights. The majority found that by requiring a request by the addressee the Government was imposing upon him an unreasonable and unconstitutional burden.

The majority sought to rest its rationale upon a narrow ground. However, a right to receive the mails is mentioned in the concurrence of Justices Brennan and Goldberg. Since the statute impeded delivery even to a willing addressee, such an individual may be said to need the protection of a right of mail receipt.

The program of customs inspection was explicitly left unquestioned. . . . It is yet to be determined whether Congress can permit other types of foreign propaganda censorship. The lack of a single dissenting vote in the communist mail propaganda cases is indicative of a new vigilance in the mail censorship area.

NEW FRONTIERS IN POSTAL CENSORSHIP

In years past, Congress has been very circumspect in its creation of new censorship areas. However, recent years have seen great pressures, brought to bear upon Congress, which encourage the proliferation of postal censorship. Bills to impose censorship on a whole range of materials, from obscenity to communist propaganda, have been dropped into the hopper, and in 1964 a broad postal censorship proposal, H.R. 319, passed the House of Representatives by a margin of 325 to nineteen, only to die in Senate committee. . . .

Representative Glenn Cunningham of Nebraska sponsored H.R. 319 and obtained bipartisan support for its passage. . . .

In 1965 Representative Cunningham introduced another version of his obscene mail bill, H.R. 980. It differed from its predecessor in requiring the Postmaster General to hold a hearing before requesting a court order for the sender's compliance with the recipient's request that the sender refrain from mailing similar material to him. Once again the House passed the bill, this time by a roll call vote of 360 to twenty-one. (*Editor's Note.* A version of this bill did become law on April 15, 1968. Titled "Prohibition of Pandering Advertisements," the law allows the recipient of what he deemed a "pandering advertisement" to notify the Postmaster General, who then will order the mailer to delete that person from the mailing list.)

THE SECOND-CLASS MAILING PERMIT

For purposes of analysis, it is possible to separate the question of suspending a mailing permit from the broad question of censorship. In the very nature of the second-class permit there are predefined conditions which must be met before the mailer may obtain what amounts to a subsidy of his mailed items. It has been argued that permit holders may be treated differently from ordinary users of the mail for this reason and for the additional reason that they still have access to first-class mail services upon the payment of a higher sum of money.

A second-class permit is issued under the Postmaster General's statutory authority. The publishers must apply for the privilege on a form prescribed by the Post Office. If the postal authorities fail to consider the publisher's application within a reasonable time, a federal district judge may pass on the application.

Statute now requires that if the published matter "is originated and published for the dissemination of information of a public character, or devoted to literature, the sciences, arts, or a special industry," it is eligible to receive a second-class permit. The meaning of the statutory language was so limited by the Supreme Court in *Hannegan v. Esquire, Inc.* that the Postmaster General has been left with little discretion. Determinations are not to be made on the basis of the "goodness" or "badness" of the contents. Treating the matter as a censorship question, Mr. Justice Douglas said that "to uphold the order of revocation would, therefore, grant the Postmaster General a power of censorship" which, he believed, Congress had not intended to grant. . . .

It must be emphasized, however, that the Postmaster General still retains the power to exclude from the mails anything which he deems nonmailable, but if it is mailable matter, he must apply the standards set by Congress for granting the permit. In addition, it is still possible for Congress to restrict the granting of a second-class permit by making it dependent upon the meeting of some special condition, such as the full disclosure of newspaper ownership and control or the labeling of paid editorials. It may be concluded that although there is no "right" to a second-class mailing permit, the Postmaster General is hedged around with many restrictions upon his discretion, and these restrictions indicate a judicial suspicion of his activities in this field of near censorship.

MAIL COVERS

On February 18, 1965, testimony before the Senate Committee on the Judiciary revealed the widespread use of the "mail cover." The Post Office provided this administrative device to assist federal agencies investigating or prosecuting criminal offenses. Without opening first-class mail the postal authorities recorded the name and address of anyone sending mail to the suspect. It was disclosed that special mail covers were in effect for up to 750 individuals at a time and that there were then about 1,000 mail covers a month. The mail cover, issued under the authority of postal regulations, was utilized, it was said, only when there was good reason to believe it might be instrumental in solving a crime. The information derived from the use of mail covers was used as a lead in investigations and not, assertedly, as evidence in court. The General Counsel of the Post Office Department testified that although there was no statutory authorization for mail covers, neither was there any prohibition. Thus, there was supposedly a legal basis for the practice in the negative inference drawn from congressional silence.

A subcommittee of the Committee on the Judiciary demanded that the Post Office produce the names of about 24,000 persons whose mail was put under surveillance during the previous two years (1963-1965). The Department resisted this directive on the ground that such disclosures could warn suspects under investigation, but Senator Edward V. Long, the Chairman, gave the Department a week to submit the lists. In March Senator Long offered to "hold in abeyance" his demand for a list of persons whose mail is under surveillance until the Postmaster General "tightened up and centralized controls."

On June 16, 1965, Postmaster General John A. Gronouski announced new regulations to limit the use of mail covers to obtain leads in investigations. Prosecutors were barred from ordering the institution of a mail cover. The authority to institute mail covers is now vested in the chief postal inspectors, and any request for a mail cover must henceforth be presented in writing and show reasonable grounds to justify its use. . . .

The use of mail covers raises the question of possible invasions of privacy, a tentatively recognized constitutional right. Many prominent individuals, including Roy Cohn and Frank Costello, have undergone this form of surveillance. For the moment embarrassing public exposure has caused the postal authorities to use the mail cover very discreetly, but abuses could lead to congressional regulation or to a constitutional challenge. In either event, use of mail covers is likely to be sharply curtailed.

FREE SPEECH AND THE STOP ORDER

For a number of years the Postmaster General has had the power to deny summarily use of the mails by persons who attempted to convey materials relating to fraud or lotteries. In 1948 this practice was held not to be an unconstitutional exercise of prior censorship, an unreasonable search and seizure, or a deprivation of a guaranteed jury trial. In 1950 a similar power was given to the Postmaster General in regard to obscene material. The practical result of this "stop order" is very sweeping. The effect, as described by a past Solicitor for the Post Office, is as follows: "They don't deliver any more mail of any kind to the particular defendant or respondent, as we call them, in those actions. In other words, he can't even get a telephone bill or he can't get a postal card from his wife or daughter or from anybody else."

A 1955 case limited the use of the stop order by permitting it to be imposed only in connection with those issues of a magazine already published and found after a hearing to be obscene. As a result Congress amended the Postal Code so that upon a showing of probable violation, the Postmaster General can get a court order from a federal district court directing the detention of defendant's incoming mail pending the conclusion of statutory proceedings. The same statute provides that the district court may also order detained mail to be opened for examination by the defendant. As to nonmailable matter itself the Postmaster General may seize or detain it, as well as dispose of it, in any manner he shall direct; he need not get a court order to do so. . . .

Post Office removal of matter or detention of mail may be viewed as a prior restraint of speech. . . .

CONCLUSION: EXPECTATIONS OF CHANGE

. . . The Supreme Court has never recognized a freedom of the mails. Congress, through exercise of its postal authority, has not been careful to protect the free use of the mails. The legislative temptation to experiment with this constitutional power may be difficult to resist, but it seems an increasingly obvious fact, which the courts and Congress must some day perceive, that the use of the mails is merely an extension of the use of the vocal cords, especially as society becomes more farflung and mobile. That the use of the mails is not a legislatively granted privilege has been observed, but that it is a constitutionally protected right has not been definitely established. This article is written in the expectation that the force of events and logic will require the recognition of a right of freedom of the mails as a necessary adjunct to free speech.

The Federal Trade Commission: Protecting the Consumer or Restricting the Advertiser?

ANN VARNUM COMMONS
DAVID G. CLARK

In 1914, the Federal Trade Commission Act established a regulatory agency designed to combat monopolistic practices by "big business." At its inception, the Federal Trade Commission was mainly concerned with anti-trust policy, in which it had a purely advisory role, except for the provisions of Section 5 of the Act, which declared "unfair methods of competition" illegal and gave the FTC authority to combat them by cease and desist orders. Aimed at trade practices injuring competitors, the law did not specifically grant the FTC power to regulate advertising.

In 1938, the Wheeler-Lea Amendment altered Section 5 to make all unfair methods of competition in commerce, and unfair or deceptive acts or practices in commerce unlawful, and granted the FTC control over advertising of food, drugs, cosmetics and therapeutic devices. From this revision of the law the FTC derives its power to restrict false or deceptive advertising.

The Commission has no power to imprison, fine, assess or

award damages. To enforce its prohibitions of deceptive acts and practices, the FTC goes through an administrative process to obtain an order that the respondent cease those practices. This order can be appealed within sixty days by the respondent. If the order is violated, the FTC can seek to impose through the Department of Justice penalties of up to $5,000 per day.

But the agency sees as its fundamental purpose guiding business rather than prosecuting violators. When the FTC was established, the hope was that the Commission would be able to put teeth into the broad terms of its basic legislation by developing ruling principles and case law more quickly than could the courts. To this end, the FTC has adopted several programs of industry guidance with rules and suggestions on how to avoid trouble. The Trade Practice Conference, oldest of the programs, provides a set of well-defined rules for a particular industry to follow, as a result of a voluntary conference of industry members and research on the problem by the FTC. Trade Regulation Rules are similar to Trade Practice Rules in their educational intent. They differ in that Trade Regulation Rules may deal with several industries at once, and are intended to carry the same force as statutes, so that a practice which is contrary to a regulation rule is, in the opinion of the FTC, against the law.

Industry guides are another method of interpreting the law for business. They, too, are strictly advisory. But they are issued without a formal conference, and regardless of the industry's attitude. They serve several purposes: to explain to businessmen how the law applies to specific aspects of their advertising, to aid the FTC staff in evaluating questionable practices, and to advise businessmen of their rights against unfair practices by competitors. Written in layman's language, they are particularly helpful to the small businessman without constant legal counsel, and their wider publicity makes them more effective for consumer education.

Advisory opinions are a recent development of the FTC which give advice on the acceptability of proposed courses of action by an advertiser. These opinions are binding on the FTC, subject to reconsideration only if necessary for the public interest.

They enable businessmen to be sure of their ground before embarking on an expensive advertising campaign.

While the industry guidance program is in constant use to prevent deception before it starts, these rules can only be enforced through investigation of individual cases.

The case of *FTC v. Colgate-Palmolive* is a good example of the procedures of the FTC. It is illustrative in that the case ran the full gamut of FTC actions, but atypical for the same reason. Most cases are settled before adjudication. According to one student of the FTC, between 1915 and 1950, of 22,830 cases in which action was taken, only 18 per cent led to issuance of cease and desist orders.

In 1959, the Colgate-Palmolive Company, with the assistance of its advertising agency, Ted Bates and Company, produced for television three commercials which purported to demonstrate that its shaving cream, Palmolive Rapid Shave, really "outshaves them all." In an impressive visual demonstration of the cream's shaving power, Rapid Shave was applied to a piece of rough sandpaper, which was immediately shaved clean by a single stroke of a safety razor. Thus the viewer was encouraged to believe that if he had a "sandpaper" beard, he could count on Rapid Shave to do for him what it had just done to the sandpaper.

Actually, Rapid Shave did not shave sandpaper at all in the commercial. It shaved a mock-up of sandpaper, made of plexiglass to which sand had been applied. Nor could Rapid Shave shave a similar piece of sandpaper (or any type of sandpaper, for that matter) in the time allowed by the commercial. It was this use of a mock-up to demonstrate what a product could not actually accomplish which became the focus of the FTC proceeding against Colgate-Palmolive and Ted Bates.

The Rapid Shave commercial came to the attention of the FTC through the Commission's television investigations in Washington, D.C. From time to time, the FTC conducts spot checking of commercials, and asks television stations for those run at a certain time of day or on a certain day. The Rapid Shave commercial was noticed by an FTC "scanner" conducting such a check. Further investigation revealed the use of the mock-up described.

On January 8, 1960, a complaint was issued by the FTC against Colgate-Palmolive and Ted Bates asserting that the use of such a commercial was "false, misleading and deceptive . . . tending to mislead members of the purchasing public" and to cause substantial injury to competition by unfairly diverting the public to Rapid Shave.

Notice was given the respondents to appear on March 21, 1960, at the FTC Building in Washington before a hearing examiner, when they would be allowed to show why a cease and desist order should not be entered as a result of this complaint. The respondents were given thirty days to reply to the complaint with their grounds for defense, and admission, denial or explanation of the charges in the complaint.

During the hearing, counsel for the FTC filed a motion to amend the complaint to emphasize that the respondents misrepresented the "moisturizing" properties of Rapid Shave as well as the sandpaper. This motion was apparently in response to the hearing examiner's finding that the only objection to the ad was to the use of a mock-up to represent sandpaper. On May 19, 1960, the Commission denied this motion to amend the complaint, stating that "the complaint . . . clearly presents an issue of whether the alleged spurious demonstration has had the capacity to mislead or deceive the purchasing public as to the moisturizing or moistening properties of Palmolive Rapid Shave, in actual use, for shaving purposes. . . ."

The hearing was finally terminated more than a year later. On May 4, 1961, William L. Pack, the hearing examiner, gave his decision that the complaint be dismissed. He reasoned that there had been no material misrepresentation of the product, as sandpaper could be shaved if adequate time were allowed for soaking. Thus, the commercial was merely "puffing" the product by employing the sandpaper sequences "simply for the purpose of emphasizing and dramatizing the wetting properties of the cream." Finally, in view of the technical problems of television (where sandpaper would appear as plain brown paper), Pack concluded that "reasonable latitude in the use of mock-ups or props should be permitted."

Although Examiner Pack's decision might have closed the case of *FTC v. Colgate-Palmolive,* Docket 7736, the Commission chose to review the case on its own motion. In so doing, it disagreed with the findings of the examiner and presented two main objections to the commercial: (1) sandpaper cannot be shaved with Rapid Shave in the manner described by the commercials; and (2) the mock-up of plexiglass and sand, which purported to be sandpaper for this "visual demonstration" or "sandpaper test" which the commercial promised, is misleading to the consumer, who thinks he is getting visual proof at that moment of Rapid Shave's moisturizing power. In accordance with these findings, the FTC issued a cease and desist order on December 29, 1961.

Contained in the order was a statement which was to prove a focal point of subsequent litigation. The Commission declared unlawful:

> Representing, directly or by implication, in describing, explaining, or purporting to prove the quality or merits of any product, that pictures, depictions, or demonstrations . . . are genuine or accurate representations . . . of, or prove the quality or merits of, any product, when such pictures, depictions or demonstrations are not in fact genuine or accurate representations . . . of, or do not prove the quality or merits of, any such product.

Thus the FTC appeared to be condemning the use of simulated props in all commercials, an extremely broad ruling in an as yet unexplored area of FTC regulation.

The Commission's ruling included another opinion of significance for future regulation. It found the advertising agency equally culpable with Colgate-Palmolive for the condemned practices. Previous to this case, the advertiser had seldom been included in prosecution by the FTC.

Respondents exercised their right of appeal to the Circuit Court of Appeals, First Circuit, which remanded the Commission's cease and desist order on November 20, 1962, stating that although it agreed with the Commission generally on the misrepresentation by respondents, the phrasing of the order was too broad in scope. Furthermore, the court suggested that perhaps the respondent Bates, as an agent rather than a principal in the deception, should not be included in the order.

In order to comply with the remand of the Court of Appeals, the Commission reconsidered the entire case and formulated a new order, issued on February 18, 1963, which it hoped would clarify the sections which the court had found ambiguous or too broad. The Commission attempted to do this by citing the precedents for its judgments and by explaining in greater detail the reasons for and meaning of its original order against mock-ups.

The respondents filed exceptions to the proposed final order on April 15, 1963, attempting to limit the order to advertising of shaving creams, where the product is represented as having moisturizing qualities it does not possess. These objections were rejected by the Commission as "ineffective and unrealistic" and the order was made final on May 7, 1963. Both respondents were to cease and desist from:

Unfairly or deceptively advertising any product by presenting a test, experiment or demonstration that is represented to be actual proof of a claim made for the product, and is not in fact a genuine test, experiment or demonstration being conducted as represented and does not constitute actual proof of the claim because of undisclosed use of a mock-up or prop. . . .

Contending that the new order failed to comply with the court's requests, the respondent again appealed to the First Circuit Court of Appeals for review. The court remanded the cease and desist order for a second time on December 17, 1963, concluding that "in the absence of an express statement that no mock-up was used, the only implied representation [made in the commercial] is that no basic dishonesty has been introduced into the picture by the photographic process."

The Supreme Court of the United States granted the FTC's petition for a writ of certiorari to consider the portion of the order dealing with simulated props, which the Court of Appeals had found unsatisfactory and refused to enforce. The respondents argued that the Court should not grant a writ of certiorari in this case, as the time for filing such a writ had elapsed. According to the FTC statute, petition for certiorari must be filed within ninety days after the issuance of judgment by the Court of Appeals. The respondents contended that the Commission had failed to seek the writ after the judgment of the Court of Appeals on November 20, 1962, had merely restated its former position in a new order, and so was barred from seeking a writ as the ninety-day time limit had expired.

The Supreme Court ruled, however, that the Commission's order of May 7, 1963, was indeed "a good-faith attempt" to incorporate the changes suggested by the Court of Appeals. Moreover, until the second appeal clarified the court's position, a writ of certiorari would have been impossible to grant. Therefore, the Supreme Court determined that "the time within which certiorari had to be requested dates from the second opinion."

Mr. Chief Justice Warren delivered the opinion of the Court, which reversed the decision of the Court of Appeals and remanded the case for enforcement of the Commission's order. The Court's ruling was two-pronged. In reviewing the substantive issues of the case, it found the Commission's interpretation of deceptive practices to be more in line with the legal precedents than that of the respondents. For this reason, and giving due consideration to the experience of the Commission in such cases of deceptive practice, the Court agreed with the FTC "that the undisclosed use of plexiglass . . . was a material deceptive practice."

Secondly, the Court upheld the final cease and desist order of the Commission as sufficiently clear and precise, overruling the Court of Appeals' main objection. It said: "We think it reasonable for the Commission to frame its order broadly enough to prevent respondents from engaging in similarly illegal practices in future advertisements." The Chief Justice reasoned that the terms of the present order "are as specific as the circumstances will permit," and respondents may ask for an advisory opinion from the FTC if in doubt as to the legality of a proposed action.

Two Justices, Harlan and Stewart, dissented on the grounds that "the proper legal test . . . concerns not what goes on in the broadcasting studio, but whether what is shown on the television is an accurate representation of the advertised product and of the claims made for it." They did, however, partly affirm the broad order of the FTC on the basis that: (1) there was a misrepresentation as Rapid Shave could not shave sandpaper as it did plexiglass, and (2) a continued pattern of similar misrepresentations by the respondents could justify such an order.

In summary, perhaps the most striking aspect of this case was the time required to pursue it to its conclusion. This case is not typical of the vast majority of cases handled by the FTC. Most are simply a matter of whether an ad violates an established ruling, and are settled quickly, out of court. Here the FTC was attempting to break new ground. For that reason, the case was litigated all the way to the Supreme Court and took more than five years. Obviously, subsequent cases falling in this area should not take so long, because the Commission will have a precedent to follow. *FTC v. Colgate-Palmolive* demonstrates the procedures of the FTC, but also points out the difficulties these procedures entail, especially in a case opening up a new area of FTC regulation. The process can be a cumbersome one.

Since in any case the offending ad may continue to run up to twenty-nine days after the order becomes final, which in this case would have been five years and four months after the original complaint was issued, the impact of such litigation is obviously not on the offending ad itself (which probably would not run more than a year in any case), but upon those which come after the final ruling. Such cases presumably will not require litigation.

Against the ineffectiveness of such a process must be balanced the right of the advertiser to defend his methods of advertising. If the FTC were to issue summary rules with no right of contest by the respondent, its regulation would obviously be more efficient, and less costly in time and money. However, such action would be considered a restriction of respondent's right of free speech or of due process of law.

Finally, there are times when such alternative solutions as the Trade Practice Rules and Guides have not deterred violators. In such an instance, the Commission must resort to adjudication, clumsy as it is, to enforce its established standards for the advertising industry.

The Federal Communications Commission: Neither Fish Nor Fowl

JOHN M. KITTROSS

For any decision-making body such as the Federal Communications Commission to make its decisions in the public interest, it must possess three things: (1) clear authority or prerogative jurisdiction over the matter in question; (2) sufficient information to be able to judge the situation, and sufficient knowledge of the subject to distinguish between and among the facts and opinions included in the body of information; and (3) power with which to enforce its decisions. Unfortunately, the FCC has possessed none of these attributes in full or sufficient measure.

The FCC's *authority* has been diffused by the virtual autonomy of the Interdepartmental Radio Advisory Committee over the spectrum used by the Federal government. The FCC also is circumscribed by many international treaties, by precedent, by technical and economic limitations, by Congressional and appellate court decisions, and by a number of "built-in" legal limitations to its efficient functioning.

In the absence of advance planning and prerequisite *knowledge,* many formal decisions of the FCC are issued on the basis of relative strength of partisan sources in adversary proceedings rather than from a basis of impartial information and analysis. Factors of immediate economic investment and dislocation often are given more weight than is national policy or the long-term public interest. It could hardly be otherwise, considering (a) that Commissioners are, by law, isolated from most legal and engineering experts on the FCC's staff when acting in a quasi-judicial capacity; (b) that the Congress has never seen fit to provide, and the Commission has never stressed the need for, an impartial technical laboratory and research staff able to "study new uses for radio," without having to rely upon the self-serving testimony of manufacturers and inventors; and (c) that the Commissioners themselves are not required to have any special skills (including legal ones) or knowledge of the technology of telecommunications.

The realities of the FCC's enforcement *power* are complex. The FCC has its budget submitted through the political administration controlling the executive branch of government, but its job priorities usually stem from Congressional wishes and ultimate control of the purse strings. The Congress always has considered the FCC as its own arm; but the Commissioners are selected and appointed by the President. The Communications Act tries to isolate the Commission from partisan politics, but manages chiefly to limit the political influence of the FCC. Under our political system, the regulated, through lobbying and other pressures often have a substantial voice in how regulations are to be drawn and enforced. The public, through elected and often publicity-conscious representatives, also influences the FCC. The effects of these pressures can seriously attenuate prestige and power.

When all of these handicaps of the Commission are considered, the record of achievements proudly presented by Commissioner Cox on the following pages of the JOURNAL becomes impressive indeed. It would be more impressive if the FCC were given additional help in securing the three attributes mentioned earlier. It already has obtained a spectrum of punitive measures to employ against rule-breaking licensees in place of the not-very-credible "death penalty" that was its sole weapon until 1960. The recent "one man-one vote" Supreme Court decisions will tend to free Congress and the Commission from a doctrinaire preference for rural areas. However, more needs to be done.

It is unreasonable to suggest, as do some broadcasters, that broadcasting needs *no* regulation, and that the FCC should be abolished. It is unlikely, in the absence of any "operating" functions, that a cabinet-level Department of Communications will be established. The "complete rewriting" of the Communications Act proposed by many may turn out to be largely change for the sake of change. Other theoretical proposals might prove interesting, and productive of longer-range philosophies and policies, but hardly necessary.

Some potentially useful changes do not require fundamental legislative alterations. For example, a number of Commissioners recently have been selected from those who already have prestige in another field, or who are recognized by the public as men "on the way up." This selection process should be continued and strengthened by the President, so that the reputation of the FCC and its members cannot again sink to the nadir of a few years ago. Also, the FCC's tiny research and technical intelligence staff should be strengthened with men and money. To do this requires only changes in an appropriations bill and cooperation between Commission, President and Congress. Finally, the provisions that prevent the FCC from making full use of its professional staff should be amended. The attempt to divorce the various roles of the Commission is a form of schizophrenia, not a guarantee of fairness and efficiency. A Commissioner is one man, whether or not he "wears three hats." A regulatory Commission is not *only* a court, or *only* a legislature, or *only* an administrative office. Under the present procedural rules, the values of partaking of the functions of all three branches of government largely are dissipated. The adversary system of deciding an issue in a complex technical field is neither efficient nor fair. If the Commission is strengthened, confidence in it as an *expert* regulatory agency may grow until the existing judicial avenues of appeal are rarely needed or used. Broadcasting has enough natural enemies in the other media without constantly attacking an agency that could, with help, act as a partner and protector.

Bibliography for Chapter Eight

BOOKS

Emery, Walter B. *Broadcasting and Government: Responsibilities and Regulations.* East Lansing: Michigan State University Press, 1961.

Here Is Your Federal Trade Commission. An FTC Orientation Pamphlet. Washington: Government Printing Office, 1964.

Minow, Newton N. *Equal Time: The Private Broadcaster and the Public Interest.* New York: Atheneum, 1964.

Paul, James C. N., and Murray L. Schwartz. *Federal Censorship: Obscenity in the Mail.* Glencoe, Ill.: The Free Press, 1961.

Self-Regulation in Advertising: A Report on the Operations of Private Enterprise in an Important Area of Public Responsibility. Submitted by the Advertising Advisory Committee to the Secretary of Commerce. Washington: Government Printing Office, 1964.

Whitehead, Don. *Border Guard.* New York: McGraw-Hill, 1963.

ARTICLES

Barron, Jerome A. "In Defense of 'Fairness': A First Amendment Rationale for Broadcasting's 'Fairness' Doctrine," *University of Colorado Law Review,* XXXVII (Fall, 1964), 31.

Benton, William. "The FCC: A Comment," *Columbia Journalism Review,* IV (Fall, 1965), 37.

Berkman, Dave. "A Modest Proposal: Abolish the FCC," *Columbia Journalism Review,* IV (Fall, 1965), 34-36.

Cairns, Huntington. "Freedom of Expression in Literature," *Annals of American Academy of Political and Social Science,* CC (November, 1938), 76-94.

Drew, Elizabeth Brenner. "Is the FCC Dead?" *Atlantic,* CCXX (July, 1967), 29-36.

"Developments in the Law–Deceptive Advertising," *Harvard Law Review,* LXXX (March, 1967), 1005-1163.

Kintner, Earl W. "Federal Trade Commission Regulation of Advertising," *Michigan Law Review,* LXIV (May, 1966), 1276.

MacIntyre, Everette, and Paul Rand Dixon. "The Federal Trade Commission After 50 Years," *Federal Bar Journal,* XXIV (Fall, 1964), 337.

Millstein, Ira M. "The Federal Trade Commission and False Advertising," *Columbia Law Review,* LXIV, 439-499.

Sigler, Jay A. "Customs Censorship," *Cleveland-Marshall Law Review,* XV (January, 1966), 58-74.

CHAPTER NINE

Protection for the Author— Copyright

THE right of an author to the fruits of his labor is never disputed, even though legal protection of that right is a form of idea control. However, this area of agreement is just about the only area in which agreement does exist in today's copyright tangle.

Incredible as it may seem, in view of the vast technological advances in the communications industry since the passage of the 1909 Copyright Act, this act (with minor variations) is still the law of the land. Since the law was passed, we have observed the life span of authors (and everyone else) increase so that more than one author has seen his works pass into the public domain during his own lifetime. We have seen the coming of elaborate machines, which can copy books more cheaply than they can be purchased. We have seen development of two new media of mass communication—radio and television—and we have watched, via satellite, the performance of artistic works in foreign countries.

One example will show the weaknesses of 1909 law applied to 1968 events. A community antenna television company was piping movies into Clarksburg and Fairmont, West Virginia. United Artists Television, Inc., held copyright on several of the movies brought in from commercial television stations in Pittsburgh, Steubenville, Ohio, and Wheeling, West Virginia. The CATV company, Fortnightly Corporation, did not obtain permission of the copyright holder to show the movies and, in fact, United Artists had expressly forbidden use of its movies by CATV systems, although it had granted permission for their use by the commercial stations whose signals Fortnightly used. The Supreme Court, when it finally received the case, was unable to define Fortnightly's use of the movies as "performance" under the 1909 definition of that term. The result: Fortnightly is able to broadcast movies, without paying royalties, piped from television stations that do pay royalties.

General relief from abuses suffered under this obsolete law was sought in 1967 when a bill seeking general revision of the law was introduced in Congress. Yet, the hearings for this bill were so lengthy and involved that revision was postponed until December 31, 1969.

When the Register of Copyrights, Abraham L. Kaminstein, was asked to contribute an article on the current copyright scene, he replied on April 1, 1968:

The copyright revision bill is in a critical stage and because of the comparatively short legislative session in an election year, I do not believe it would be possible to write such an article in 1968. We have spent 13 years on this project and the next few months will determine its fate.

Nevertheless, the general counsel for the American Society of Composers, Authors and Publishers had undertaken the task in two articles dealing with the revision bill, and the bulk of his work is included here. When the revisionists take up where they left off, they will have to concern themselves with just those problems discussed by Herman Finkelstein.

In addition, they will be looking at a test court case involving photocopying. A petition filed with the U.S. Court of Claims in Washington, D.C., February 27, 1968, charges the Department of Health, Education, and Welfare, "including but not limited to the Library of the National Institutes of Health and the National Library of Medicine," with copyright infringement.

The petition filed on behalf of the Williams & Wilkins Company, Baltimore, Md., publishers of medical and other scientific books and periodicals, cites eight counts of infringement by photocopying articles from periodicals to which the company hold copyright. The suit, brought under Section 1498(b) of Title 28, U.S. Code, which permits claims for damages to holders of copyright for infringements by the Federal Government, will be defended by the Department of Justice. Williams & Wilkins first challenged the Library's photocopying practices in April 1967, when they notified NLM that permission to photocopy from their journals would be granted "provided the person making the copies pays us a royalty of 2¢ per page per copy." Similar notification from the same publisher was recently received by the New York Academy of Medicine. The interpretation by the courts of the principle of "fair use" as applied to photocopying by libraries will have vast significance for research libraries and the scientists who use them. Expressions of interest and concern are already being heard from the nation's major library associations and many leading scholars.

The history and problems and future of copyright in our dynamically changing technological society are limned in the following pages.

Copyright Law Revision: Unilateral Federal Protection

The federal system of government utilized in the United States reserves a certain degree of sovereignty to each state. In order to provide uniformity in matters which affect more than one jurisdiction, it is often necessary for the federal government to supersede state authority. It became apparent, early in the development of the United States, that copyright protection would require such nationwide uniformity.

Since the Articles of Confederation lacked any provision for federal copyright protection, various states filled the void either by continuing the common-law doctrine of protection until publication or by enacting statutory provisions. As early as 1783, Connecticut, Massachusetts, Maryland and Rhode Island had passed copyright legislation. Since a state's authority can extend no farther than its jurisdictional limits, to protect his work fully an author had to seek protection in each state or the work could be copied in any state in which he was not protected and then circulated in competition with his copyrighted work.

The lack of efficient national protection afforded by unrelated state provisions prompted James Madison to urge that the federal government be given the power to extend patent and copyright protection.

Awarded First Prize in the 1967 Nathan Burkan Memorial Competition, St. John's University School of Law, this article appeared anonymously in the *St. John's Law Review*, XLII (October, 1967), 226-239. It is reprinted by permission of the St. Thomas More Institute for Legal Research.

371

The copyright of authors has been solemnly adjudged, in Great Britain, to be a right of common law. The right to useful inventions seems with equal reason to belong to the inventors. The public good fully coincides in both cases with the claims of individuals. The States cannot separately make effectual provision for either of the cases, and most of them have anticipated the decision of this point, by laws passed at the instance of Congress.

With the adoption of the United States Constitution, authority to act in the area of copyright protection was bestowed upon Congress:

To promote the Progress of Science and useful Arts, by securing for limited Times to Authors and Inventors the exclusive Right to their respective Writings and Discoveries.

Although Congress acted swiftly in passing the first copyright act, subsequent amendments have been infrequent; since 1790 there have been only three major revisions of the law. With minor variations, the Act of 1909 comprises the present copyright law. The existing law provides a "dual" system of protection, allowing the states to provide protection *before* a work is published but making federal protection exclusive *after* publication.

Rapid technological advances, especially great developments in the communications industry, unimagined in 1909, have resulted in the inadequacy and obsolescence of many provisions of the present law. Therefore, for a number of years, the communications and publishing industries have clamored for a re-evaluation and revision of the federal statute. An extensive program of study under the auspices of the Copyright Office culminated in a report by the Register of Copyrights urging a general revision of the law. After further study and public hearings, a bill for the general revision of the Copyright Law was introduced in the Congress in 1967.

The attempt to enact legislation capable of dealing with contemporary problems, yet flexible enough to adjust to future advances in communications and publishing, seems destined to result in the broadest copyright revision in the history of our country. Perhaps the most radical change, and the most fundamental characteristic of the proposed law, provides for the abolition of the "dual" system of copyright protection and substitutes in its stead unilateral federal protection for all copyrightable works.

The purpose of this paper is to examine some of the inadequacies of the present "dual" system of protection and evaluate the effectiveness of the proposed "unilateral" system.

COMMON-LAW COPYRIGHT

It is a generally accepted rule of law that copyright protection will not be extended to an abstract idea, but only to a tangible expression of that idea. Thus, it is the author's manner of expression which is the subject of a copyright. For example, an artist may not prevent another from viewing the same scene, utilizing the same vantage point and thereby producing an identical work. He may only prohibit his own work from being copied or appropriated. Similarly, an author who verbally describes a scene will not be given an exclusive right to the words he uses. Rather, his arrangement of the words will be protected from wrongful use. Two people arriving at the same result, through individual efforts, might each be extended copyright protection.

At common law, an author's rights in his work are in the nature of property rights. As an incident of ownership, they exist independent of statutory authority and are usually styled a "common-law copyright." That term is somewhat of an understatement, however, since the author's exclusive claim to his work permits him more than the mere privilege of copying it. The scope of these rights was settled, after much litigation, by the House of Lords in *Donaldson v. Becket*, wherein the court answered the question:

> Whether at common law, an author of any book or literary composition had the sole right of first printing and publishing the same for sale; and might bring an action against any person who printed published and sold the same without his consent?

Both issues were decided in the affirmative, the court ruling that the right to publish and print would exist in perpetuity but for statutory provision limiting it.

Sixty years later the United States Supreme Court reached the same conclusions and considered it to be "well settled" that an author had a perpetual right to the exclusive use of unpublished manuscripts, but, once published, any further rights were contingent upon the federal copyright statute.

Thus, the continued existence of common-law protection depends on state law and can be abrogated or superseded by state law. Upon publication, however, prior protection extended either under the common-law doctrine or pursuant to a state statute ceases and thereafter federal law becomes the exclusive source of copyright protection.

An author's common-law rights are basically two-fold: *first,* he has the right to the exclusive use of his work until he permits a general publication; and, *second,* he has the exclusive right to make or authorize the first general publication of his work. The protection against unauthorized use of a work is absolute; not even "fair use," the right of others to use the owner's work in a reasonable manner without his consent, is allowed. An author may use his work in any manner he wishes, short of a general publication, exploit it commercially and enjoy the profits therefrom, without fear of the work being copied or becoming part of the public domain.

PUBLICATION

Upon publication, the author's common-law copyright terminates and his work enters the public domain unless further protection is granted by federal statute. The Federal Copyright Law, which specifically recognizes common-law or state protection prior to publication, begins protection of copyrightable works after publication, if the author takes the necessary statutory steps. The importance of publication, therefore, is clear: it serves as the divider between the pre-publication protection of the common law, or state law, and the post-publication protection of the federal statute or the entrance of the work into the public domain. After publication, an author loses all exclusive right to his work if he does not qualify for federal statutory protection or if he fails to take the steps necessary to obtain that protection.

Despite the legal significance of the term "publication," its meaning has been obscured by the fact that the federal statute lacks a definition. Conflict has arisen over whether the "publication" which terminates an author's common-law rights is the same "publication" as that which qualifies him for federal protection. The conclusion that they are one and the same, although subject to strong criticism, is supported by the fact that Section 2 of the Copyright Law allows common-law protection only until federal protection begins.

It has been suggested that the definitional difficulties could be eliminated by having the federal law define the word for its purposes and the states define it for the purpose of determining the limit of common-law or state protection. The danger of conflict between the two makes this solution unacceptable. Perhaps a better solution would be a uniform federal definition.

Since the federal law has failed to assume this burden, the task has fallen to the courts to attempt to work out a definition on a case-by-case approach. A summary of the case law provides what seems to be the accepted definition of publication.

[P]ublication occurs when by consent of the copyright owner the original or tangible copies of a work are sold, leased, loaned, given away, or otherwise made available to the general public, or when an authorized offer is made to dispose of the work in any such manner even if a sale or other such disposition does not in fact occur.

A close study of this definition indicates two major problems which have arisen in connection with copyright protection. The first is that the definition speaks of *tangible copies*. Since the concept of common-law copyright originated when written and printed copies were the only anticipated means of reproduction and distribution of literary works, authors were protected only against the misappropriation of their work in those ways. The courts have strictly adhered to this "copy" requirement despite the development of new methods of distribution. It is accepted, almost without question, that the public performance or dissemination of a work other than by copies does not result in a publication of that work. For example, playing a musical composition has been held not to be a publication in the absence of the distribution of copies. Similarly, neither delivery of a lecture nor performance before a radio microphone has been held to constitute publication. Despite strong criticism, the "copy" concept of publication is still a viable principle of law. As a result, the author has the advantage of presenting his work to the public and profiting thereby without "publishing" and, thus, not losing his common-law copyright.

The second problem arising from the accepted case-law definition of publication is the requirement that the work be released to the "general public." This is contrasted to a "limited publication" which allows the author to release his work to an audience of a limited size, whose use of the work is restricted, while retaining his common-law rights.

These two inroads on the concept that publication terminates common-law rights often make it advantageous for an author to avoid utilizing the federal statutory protection and to continue the perpetual common-law protection of his work. Modern methods of communication and dissemination have made this practice even more attractive. For example, an author of a play can present it to an unlimited audience as often as he wishes and never lose the common-law protection as long as he does not distribute copies. Using radio and television, he can broadcast around the world and derive great financial benefit, while never endangering his common-law rights.

FEDERAL COPYRIGHT PROTECTION

As previously stated, common-law protection prior to publication is specifically acknowledged in the federal copyright statute. It is, in effect, a grant to the states of the power to act. Federal statutory protection, obtainable only after publication, gives the author a monopoly in his work for a limited time.

From a reading of the constitutional grant of power, it seems clear that Congress could extend federal protection at any time after the creation of copyrightable matter. By virtue of the Supremacy Clause of the Constitution, federal legislation would preempt any common-law rule or state enactment seeking to extend protection to a work which has entered the purview of the federal statute.

No state may violate the copyright policy of the United States, even though that state attempts to do so by exercising its otherwise lawful powers. For example, many states have attempted to extend protection to matter not copyrightable under the federal statute by use of unfair competition legislation. Such schemes have, however, generally been rejected. In *Sears, Roebuck & Co. v. Stiffel Co.*, the Supreme Court rejected state protection of items not patentable under the federal law by means of unfair competition laws.

Just as a State cannot encroach upon the federal patent laws directly, it cannot, under some other law, such as that forbidding unfair competition, give protection of a kind that clashes with the objectives of the federal patent laws. . . . To allow a State by use of its laws of unfair competition to prevent the copying of an article which represents too slight an advance to be patented would be to permit the State to block off from the public something which federal law has said belongs to the public.

While *Sears* involved the federal patent laws and made only passing reference to the copyright statutes, subsequent case law has held that state protection of literary property has also been preempted by federal law.

The federal concept of copyright protection places the public benefit in a position of prime importance; the author's reward, resulting from his monopoly, is only secondary. The author is given certain exclusive, enumerated rights, but the public may use the work in any other way it wishes without having to answer to the author.

By offering the author a period of monopoly in his work and the opportunity to profit from its use, the federal law seeks to provide an incentive to utilize the federal system of protection rather than to continue common-law coverage. Once an author does seek federal protection, the public benefits since the "limited times" clause guarantees that the work will eventually enter the public domain. In return for his monopoly, the author abandons all exclusivity in his work after the expiration of the statutory period of protection. Unless given an adequate period of exclusive use, an author may lack the incentive to publish his work and may continue to utilize common-law protection. Such avoidance of the federal scheme might result in public deprivation of much literary material. Therefore, the "limited time" must be sufficiently long to provide incentive for authors, yet short enough not to impair the public benefit. Under existing law, copyrightable works are protected for twenty-eight years from the date of first publication with the opportunity for renewal granted to the author, his heirs or executors for an additional period of the same length. In addition to protecting published works, the federal statute provides protection for unpublished works through a system of voluntary registration.

It is clear that the dual system of copyright protection has certain inherent problems which have been intensified with the advent of modern methods of communication. When the present copyright law was enacted, mass dissemination of literary material was accomplished mainly by printed copies. The benefits to be derived by an author who refrained from general publication were limited and it was generally more advantageous to utilize the federal protection. Present-day means of dissemination no longer make publication so attractive since an author can often benefit financially for a longer period by methods other than the distribution of copies.

As previously discussed, the extent of state protection of unpublished material greatly differs. This is compounded by the fact that modern methods of communication permit a work to be rapidly transmitted across state boundaries and, thus, become subject to the laws of more than one jurisdiction. In addition, the conflict between state and federal law is accentuated by the vague definition of "publication" which has been utilized to determine the applicability of either form of protection. A further difficulty founded in the dual system of protection is that federal protection can be provided only for a limited period while the common law can extend perpetual protection and still allow broad dissemination of a work. The author who invokes his federal right to protection may, in effect, be penalized for so doing. Thus, many authors avoid publication and the public is deprived of the use of these works. Such a result is clearly contrary to the constitutional concept of public benefit.

FEDERAL COPYRIGHT LAW REVISION

Congress, aware of the various shortcomings of the dual system, sought to entirely eliminate them in the revision. Three alternatives have been suggested.

The first proposal, and the one which would probably have been least effective, provided for the continuation of the present dual system. However, the voluntary registration provisions would have been broadened to allow registration of all types of unpublished works. Common-law protection would have continued for any work not registered. While this system had the advantage of providing protection to any work made available to the public by means other than publication, it failed in one major respect:

[U]npublished works not voluntarily registered, though widely disseminated by performance or exhibition, would continue to have perpetual protection under the common law.

The second method of revision would have retained common-law protection until "public dissemination" occurred, at which time federal statutory protection would be available. With one qualification, it was this method which the Register of Copyrights advocated.

We believe that the constitutional principle of a time limitation should be applied when a work is disseminated to the public, whether by the publication of copies or registration, as under the present law, or by public performance or the public distribution of sound recordings. We also believe that any statutory limitations imposed in the public interest on the scope of copyright protection should apply when a work has been publicly disseminated in any of these ways.

Undisseminated material, the Register suggested, should continue to be afforded common-law protection.

This proposal received widespread support since it was not a drastic change from the existing system. The transition, therefore, would be simpler and the procedure under the act would be more acceptable to those working in the copyright area. However, the fear that many of the same problems which exist under the present statute because of the failure to define "publication" would also arise with the use of a new, undefined (or vaguely defined) word "dissemination," resulted in rejection of this method of revision.

The last, and most radical, method contemplated the abolition of common-law protection for all copyrightable works. Material would be protected by federal statute from the date of creation regardless of dissemination or publication. The Register had rejected this approach as inferior to the dual system of protection, stating that there were "overbalancing reasons to preserve the common-law protection of undisseminated works until the author or his successor chooses to disclose them." The Register felt that the bulk of undisseminated material was personal correspondence, manuscripts and other private material which the author, if he so desired, should be able to keep out of the public domain. Under the third proposal, *all* works would be subjected to a statutory period of protection after which they would be available to the public. There seemed to be a danger that the author of a private manuscript dealing with a controversial subject might destroy his work rather than allow it to become available to the general public and subject himself or his heirs to public comment. The Register further objected to this system since it would require that the federal courts exercise exclusive jurisdiction in copyright matters. It was his contention that undisseminated works, usually matters of local concern, should be dealt with by the state courts.

PROVISIONS OF THE PROPOSED LAW

Despite the objections noted, the drafters of the new legislation, in seeking to attain the constitutional ends of uniformity of protection for authors and the furtherance of public benefit through the advancement of scholarship, adopted the third scheme of revision.

Under the proposed law, all copyrightable material, whether published or not, will be protected exclusively by the federal statute from the time of creation. When a work is "fixed in a tangible medium of expression" it is deemed to have been created. By extending protection from the day of creation, one major obstacle encountered in the present law will be removed. It will no longer be necessary for the courts to struggle to define publication or any similar term in order to find the division between common-law (or state) and federal protection.

The preemption section permits neither common-law nor state protection of any copyrightable work, even if that work has been *published* and fails to qualify for a federal copyright or has already passed into the public domain due to the expiration of the statutory period of protection. This is, in effect, a codification of the *Sears* line of cases, holding that the states cannot "block off from the public something which the federal law has said belongs to the public."

The proposed law, however, does not preempt the common-law or state legislation in three limited areas: (1) protection of *unpublished* materials not copyrightable under the statute (including works not "fixed"); (2) in respect to causes of action which arise prior to the effective date of the statute (January 1, 1969); and, (3) where state action is taken against activities other than violations of an author's copyright protection. The first area indicates the continuance of the *Wheaton v. Peters* doctrine that publication terminates common-law protection; the last indicates that the doctrine of the *Sears* case, admitting the states' power to prevent unfair competitive practices, has not been abrogated by the new statute.

ADVANTAGES OF THE PROPOSED LAW

The framers of the new legislation found several major advantages in a uniform system. First, the uniform system alleviates the problem of reconciling the differences between state laws and between state law and federal law. The exclusive federal provisions will only be subjected to the interpretations of the federal courts, thus minimizing the danger of conflicts. Unpublished, non-copyrightable material which is left to state control under the proposed law will generally be of an extremely local nature and the danger of such matter bringing about a conflict between the laws of two jurisdictions is minimal. For example, an impromptu, unrecorded performance before an audience would not be copyrightable under the proposed legislation and would fall within the area reserved to the states to provide protection. Since such a performance is only of a transitory nature, there is little likelihood that it could be subjected to the laws of any jurisdiction other than the one in which is was performed.

As noted, the new statute eliminates the difficulties involved in the lack of definition of publication. Since the creation of a copyrightable work would result in the applicability of the federal statute and thus federal protection, it would become unnecessary to continue to determine the point at which a work passes from the common-law sphere of protection. Of greater significance is the fact that the broad definition of "creation" gives the proposed law sufficient latitude to encompass the various means of communications present in our society.

Another advantage of the new system is that it seems to be more in accord with the constitutional concept of extending protection to authors for a "limited time." An author will no longer be able to retain maximum protection by maintaining protection under the common law. Protection to all authors will be uniform and no advantage will be gained by avoiding the statutory provisions.

CONCLUSION

The preemption provisions of the new copyright bill seem to benefit both the general public and authors. By providing exclusive federal protection, all works will eventually enter the public domain. No longer will an author be able to hide under the common law and exploit his work without endangering his exclusivity. Furthermore, the longer period of protection will make the federal statutory protection more appealing to authors.

While the public clearly benefits from the eventual release of all literary works into the public domain, one aspect of such a scheme is subject to severe criticism—the release of private papers and manuscripts. While it is true that after a sufficient period of time following an author's death the importance of privacy may decline, there is definitely a strong interest in the individual's right to protect his private work from the peering eye of the general public. There is a real danger that many documents such as private correspondence and diaries, will be destroyed, although this could be overcome by the retention of such works in libraries or archives, available to scholars, but removed from the grasp of the general public.

One advantageous change which will result from the new system is that all causes of action involving copyright protection under the new law will be within the exclusive jurisdiction of the federal courts, thus minimizing the conflicts between court interpretations of the statute.

It seems, in conclusion, that the benefits to be derived from the proposed scheme of protection greatly outweigh its shortcomings. After too long a wait, the United States seems prepared to equip itself with copyright legislation capable of meeting the needs of our technologically advanced society.

Literary Buccaneering in America

BRIAN WILLIAMS

Literary buccaneering in the United States used to be a practice that had British publishers and authors wringing hands and American book pirates chuckling all the way down to the vault.

American publishers published unauthorized reprints of the *Encyclopedia Britannica,* starting with its third edition (issued from 1777 to 1784), for over a hundred years. And while doing it, they were protected by a special clause of the 1790 U.S. Copyright law. Charles Dickens became known in the United States not only for his literary works, widely circulated by our book pirates, but also for his querulous lectures on international copyright and slavery. His *American Notes* supposedly pirated some of our worst characteristics in symbolic revenge.

Supposedly such publishing entrepreneurs went the way of all robber barons when in 1955 the United States joined the Universal Copyright Convention (UCC) and agreed to extend the same protection to foreign authors as it did to Americans. UCC membership also afforded protection abroad to books published and copyrighted in the U.S. The arrangements under the Berne Convention (the United States is not a member, although Australia and most UCC signatories are) and the Buenos Aires

This selection, reprinted by permission of the author, is part of a paper written for Professor David G. Clark at Stanford University in 1966. The author has had extensive experience working for book publishers on the West Coast.

384

Convention safeguard books published "simultaneously" in the United States and a Berne Convention country where the customary copyright notice is usually sufficient. The United States also concluded a number of treaties and exchanged copyright proclamations with foreign countries.

Yet the bootlegging of books has still gone on. Books published abroad are excluded from copyright protection here because of quirks in the U.S. copyright law. Foreign pirates publish unauthorized editions of American books either because their countries are not members of a copyright convention, or in spite of the existence of copyright law.

Piracy and infringement are different from plagiarism. Plagiarism violates no legal right and therefore has no legal redress. It's only morally wrong. Wittenberg declares, "if a work is in the public domain, subsequent use of it by another author as his own is plagiarism."[1]

Piracy and infringement, however, imply violation of legal ownership, and therefore redress is available under common law and copyright statute. An infringer under United States law, according to Harriet Pilpel, may "be enjoined from any further manufacture, importation or sale of the infringing work, his copies of the infringing work may be destroyed and he may also be compelled to pay damages to the copyright owner." The legitimate owner may also collect the pirate's profits on the unauthorized work, or a court may award him statutory damages, "the amount to be generally not less than $250 nor more than $5000." Criminal prosecution is rare, but the infringer may also be liable for imprisonment up to one year and a fine up to $1000.[2]

Despite the apparent carefulness of the U.S. copyright law, book pirates have found a license to operate in the so-called "manufacturing clause"—a section always regarded by publishers as a piece of "printers' lobby" legislation—under which a book written by an American author but published abroad could go

---

[1] Philip Wittenberg, *The Protection and Marketing of Literary Property* (New York: Julian Messner, Inc., 1937), p. 66.
[2] Harriet F. Pilpel and Morton David Goldberg, *A Copyright Guide* (New York: R.R. Bowker Company, 1963), pp. 20-21.

unprotected in the United States unless the copies first published overseas were physically manufactured in the United States. An American publisher has six months to register a foreign book written in English, and five years in which to print his own edition, during which time his book was protected by *ad interim* copyright. However, if he imported more than 1500 copies or failed to publish before the *ad interim* term expired, the work fell into public domain and copies could be freely imported.

One victim of the manufacturing clause is J. R. R. Tolkien, whose book *The Hobbit*, an overture to his fantasy-trilogy *The Fellowship of the Ring*, now popular on college campuses, was first imported by Houghton-Mifflin. Houghton-Mifflin made the mistake of importing more than 1500 copies, thus relinquishing its copyright. It thought at the time that the book was so esoteric no one else could want to publish it. Then in 1964 *The Hobbit* unexpectedly sold 3500 copies. When Ballantine Books contracted to bring it out in paperback, it suddenly found itself rivaled by Ace Books, which announced its own edition. What happened next, according to David Dempsey, was that:

> Tolkien promptly declared Ballantine's the "authorized" version; and well he might, since this publisher was treating the book as though it were still in copyright, and paying the author a royalty.
> Tolkien has written: *"Fellowship of the Ring* was the product of long labor, and like a simple-minded hobbit I feel that it is, while I am alive, my property in justice unaffected by copyright laws. It seems to me a grave discourtesy, to say no more, to issue my book without even a polite note informing me of the project". . . . (Ace states that it has since sent the polite note, via an intermediary, offering to make an arrangement; but to date nothing has come of it.)[3]

Most American authors can count on having their works protected for 56 years under the copyright law, but if their books are first published abroad, they may not even have the protection of the five-year *ad interim* copyright. *Candy* by Terry Southern and Mason Hoffberg, first published in Paris by Olympia Press, presented a curious legal dilemma. According to Dempsey:

[3] David Dempsey, "The Candy Covered Copyright," *Saturday Review*, XLVIII (October 2, 1965), 40.

. . . the authors took it for granted that *Candy* would never make it through customs, hence made no effort to register her in Washington— a case of one regulation preventing the fulfillment of another. Then came the *Lady Chatterley* case in 1959, and down went the bars. She was followed by a number of Henry Miller's books, beginning with *Tropic of Cancer,* but for all these books the break came too late; the *ad interim* period was over.[4]

One of the most enterprising reprinters to capitalize on books declared public domain under a liberalized customs law has been Greenleaf Publishers of Chicago, who, in addition to producing several Henry Miller books, brought out its own bootleg edition of Jean Genet's *The Thief's Journal.* The work of a French author, first published in the French language in France and copyrighted there (thus giving it the U.S. copyright protection under the UCC agreement), the book was translated into English by an American, Bernard Frechtman, and published by Olympia in Paris. Though licensed, the translation was not copyrighted, and Greenleaf simply photocopied the Olympia translation. The bootleg translation was distributed in the U.S. at about the same time that Grove Press published an "authorized"—and *ad interim* registered—edition of the same translation. Grove took Greenleaf to court for infringement of copyright. Though the defendant protested that the translation was in the public domain, the court ruled that "copying from a copy is no less an infringement than copying from the original copyrighted work" and that a copyright of a translation was not essential to preserving the underlying protection of a copyrighted work.[5]

[4] *Ibid.,* p. 45.

[5] " 'Thief's Journal' Copying Ruled Infringement," *Publishers' Weekly,* CLXXXVIII (October 18, 1965), 26-27.

Recent Developments in the Copyright Law

HERMAN FINKELSTEIN

During the last session of Congress, the Subcommittee Number 3 of the House Judiciary Committee, under the chairmanship of Congressman Kastenmeier of Wisconsin, conducted extensive hearings on copyright revision and reported out a bill (H.R. 4347) after hearing 150 witnesses over a period of twenty-two days. The committee held fifty-one executive sessions, and the 279-page report of the House Judiciary Committee[1] contains an exhaustive analysis of the problems facing the Committee, and the reasons for the conclusions reached on controversial subjects.

Bills in the form reported out by the House Judiciary Committee have been introduced in both houses of the present Congress.[2] House Bill 2512 has already been reported out by the House Judiciary Committee of the present Congress and is expected to reach the floor of the House shortly.[2a]

Reprinted by permission of the author and the copyright holder, Matthew Bender and Company. Originally the article appeared in 1967 *Patent Law Annual* (Matthew Bender 1967).

[1] H.R. Rep. No. 2237, 89th Cong., 2d Sess. (1966).

[2] S. 597 (Sen. McClellan), R.R. 2512 (Rep. Celler); 90th Cong., 1st Sess. (1967).

[2a] H.R. 2512 with Amendment relating to so-called CATV (Community Antenna Television) educational television and juke boxes was passed by the House on April 11, 1967.

Inventions and discoveries during the last half century, since enactment of the 1909 Copyright Law, have had a revolutionary impact on the means of communicating thought and ideas to the consuming public—readers, audiences at concerts, theaters, movies, and the whole new field of entertainment at home via radio, television, stereophonic records, and more recently, the use of computers for storage and retrieval of all kinds of information and entertainment—a field still in its infancy. . . .

[T]hese technical advances have generated new industries and new methods for the reproduction and dissemination of copyrighted works, and the business relations between authors and users have evolved new patterns."[3]

The laws defining property rights in both patents and copyrights must be viewed in an international setting. Unlike tangible forms of property, the products of invention and authorship (protected by patents and copyrights) may be used throughout the world immediately upon disclosure. A literary, dramatic, or musical work—or any work of authorship—today may be transmitted to all parts of the globe at once by communications satellites. Thus international boundaries are erased, and the author's works may be present everywhere at the instant of first disclosure to the public. It is important, therefore, that the standards of protection shall be as nearly uniform in all countries, as their respective notions of property rights permit. The pending revision bills take this into consideration particularly in dealing with the formalities (or absence of them) required as a condition for international protection of copyrighted works, and the duration of property rights in such works.

The United States is a relative newcomer among nations respecting the rights of foreign authors. Henry Clay, in a Senate report favoring international copyright in 1837, pointed out that our patent laws even then recognized the rights of foreign inventors.[4] It was not until 1891 that the rights of foreign authors

---

[3] H.R. Rep., N. 1 *supra*, at 31.
[4] Report on Senate Bill No. 223 (Feb. 16, 1837), quoted at length in Finkelstein, "The Copyright Law—A Reappraisal," 104 U. Pa. L. Rev. 1025, 1038 (1956).

were first protected in the United States.[5] During the next quarter century, we entered into certain Western Hemisphere Conventions, but it was not until 1955 that we adhered to one of worldwide scope—the Universal Copyright Convention.[6]

Most of the countries of Europe are parties to the Berne Convention, which was formulated in 1886 and which has a higher plane of protection than the Universal Copyright Convention, to which they also adhere. The Berne Convention requires its member countries to provide copyright protection without any formalities such as a notice of copyright, and provides for a term of copyright which commences on creation of the work and continues until at least fifty years after the author's death.[7] This is in conflict with our existing law, but the pending revision bills go a long way toward reconciling the differences.

Another problem is the fact that in the United States literary property rights may be protected by state law (common-law rights) until the work is published. It is difficult for foreign lawyers to understand why certain rights in literary property are enforced in the state courts, while others are subject to exclusive federal jurisdiction. The pending bills would solve this dilemma by conferring copyright upon creation of the work and transferring all rights to the federal domain [§§ 302(a) and 301].[8]

The present law provides for an initial term of twenty-eight years from date of publication, and a renewal for an additional twenty-eight years. Unless the renewal term is applied for during the last year of the original term—and applied for by the right person—all rights expire at the end of the first term. This has given rise to much litigation, particularly with respect to the persons entitled to the renewal term.[9]

---

[5] Act of March 3, 1891, Ch. 565, 26 Stat. 1106.

[6] For a discussion of our international copyright arrangements, see Garland, "Our Copyright Law in International Society," 11 *ASCAP Copyright Law Symposium* 82 (1962), and Seither "UNESCO: New Hope for International Copyright," 7 *ASCAP Copyright Symposium* 74 (1955).

[7] Fifty-four countries have adhered to the Berne Convention. See Bodenhausen, "U.S. Copyright Protection and the Berne Convention," 13 Bull. Copyright Soc'y 215, 216 (1966).

[8] All section references in the text are to S. 597 and H.R. 2512, N. 2 *supra.*

[9] See, e.g., Miller Music Corp. v. Charles N. Daniels, Inc., 362 U.S. 373, 80

The revision bills deal separately with three classes of works: (1) those created on or after January 1, 1969; (2) those previously created, but not theretofore published or copyrighted; (3) those copyrighted before January 1, 1969.

Works Created After January 1, 1969

The bills provide that the protection of such works shall commence upon creation of the work and shall continue for the life of the author and fifty years after his death [§ 302(a)]. We shall not dwell here on the special provisions for joint works [§ 302(b)] and anonymous works [§ 302(c)].

Some concern was expressed about establishing the date of an author's death. The bills provide that persons in interest may file in the Copyright Office a statement of the date of an author's death, or a statement that he is still living on a particular date [§ 302(d)]. Anyone may obtain from the Copyright Office such information as is on file. After seventy-five years from the date of publication, or 100 years from the date of creation of a work, there is a presumption that the author has been dead for fifty years if the Copyright Office certifies that its records disclose nothing to indicate that the author of the work is living, or died less than fifty years before [§ 302(e)].

Works Created, But Not Published or Copyrighted
Before January 1, 1969

Such works enjoy a term of life and fifty years, but if this term would expire before December 31, 1993, and the work is still unpublished, the copyright will expire on that date. If, however, the work is published on or before that date, the term of copyright will not expire before December 31, 2018 (§ 303).

Copyrights Subsisting on January 1, 1969

Copyrights which are in their first twenty-eight-year term when the new Act goes into effect will be subject to a renewal term of forty-seven years instead of twenty-eight years [§ 304(a)].

S. Ct. 792, 4 L. Ed. 2d 804 (1960); De Sylva v. Ballentine, 351 U.S. 570, 76 S. Ct. 974, 100 L. Ed. 1415 (1956); Gordon v. Vincent Youmans Inc., 358 F.2d 261 (2d Cir. 1965).

Those in their renewal term on the effective date will be extended to endure for a term of seventy-five years [§ 304(b)].

Under the existing law, any grant of rights by the author (except in the case of "employment for hire") terminates at the end of twenty-eight years if he has died before that time leaving a widow or children. They are entitled to the renewal term regardless of any grant or bequest made by the author in favor of others.[10] There are other instances where a grant terminates after the twenty-eighth year, but we shall not discuss them here. The present bills make very substantial changes in the conditions under which rights granted by an author cease, and as to the beneficiaries of any revisionary interest.

A distinction is drawn between grants made before the effective date of the new law and those made thereafter. Grants or transfers made previously (except by will) would be subject to termination at the end of a period ranging from thirty-five years after execution of the grant to forty years thereafter. A notice of termination must be served not less than two nor more than ten years before its effective date (§ 203).

In the case of grants under preexisting copyrights, the termination would be effective during a period of five years beginning at the end of fifty-six years from the date of copyright or on January 1, 1969, whichever is later. The notice must be served not less than two years nor more than ten years before its effective date [§ 304(c)].

EFFECT OF CHANGES ON POSSIBLE
UNITED STATES ADHERENCE TO
THE BERNE CONVENTION

Duration of Copyright

The duration of copyright, one of the major changes, perhaps the greatest, will bring the United States much closer to adher-

---

10 See 17 U.S.C. § 24 (1964); White-Smith Music Publishing Co. v. Goff, 187 Fed. 247 (1st Cir. 1911); Sweet Music, Inc. v. Melrose Music Corp., 189 F. Supp. 655 (S.D. Cal. 1960).

ence to the Berne Convention. At a conference for revision of that Convention to be held in Stockholm in June, the United States will attend as an observer. Much attention will be given behind the scenes to the possibility of an ultimate merger of the Berne Convention and the Universal Copyright Convention.

The Manufacturing Clause

A unique feature of American copyright law is the so-called manufacturing clause, which requires English-language books and periodicals to be manufactured "within the limits of the United States,"[11] if they are to qualify for copyright protection. This provision came into the law in 1891[12] through the insistence of business and labor groups who feared foreign competition in the printing industry.

If the work was originally published and manufactured abroad, it may enjoy protection for a five-year period by registration and deposit of one copy with the Copyright Office within six months after first publication abroad.[13] Full copyright protection may be secured if during that period an edition of the work is published and manufactured in the United States.[14] During the five-year ad interim term, the copyright owner is entitled to import a maximum of 1500 copies of his foreign edition into the United States.[15] Should he import more than 1500 copies, he is forced either to manufacture a United States edition or to abandon his copyright.

The new bill retains a manufacturing requirement, but in sharply abbreviated form. The requirement of domestic manufacture would apply only to "a work consisting preponderantly of nondramatic literary material that is in the English language." It does not apply at all if the author is not an American national or domiciliary or, in the case of an American national, he has been domiciled abroad for at least one year prior to importing copies into the United States. In addition, 2000, rather than 1500,

11 17 U.S.C. § 16.
12 Act of March 3, 1891, 26 Stat. 1106.
13 17 U.S.C. § 22.
14 4 U.S.C. § 23.
15 5 U.S.C. § 16.

copies of books manufactured abroad may be imported to the United States before any provisions of the manufacturing clause come into play (§ 601). Of greatest importance is the provision that failure to comply with the manufacturing clause does not invalidate the copyright; but such failure is available as a defense to an action for infringement of the right to reproduce and distribute copies of the work if defendant proves:

1. that the copyright owner has violated Section 601 by having copies imported or publicly distributed in the United States in violation of that section; and

2. that the defendant's infringing copies complied with the manufacturing requirements; and

3. that the infringement began before an authorized edition complying with Section 601 had been registered. [§ 601(d)].

Thus, under the proposed law, the author of an English-language book will not lose all copyright protection merely because his book has not been manufactured in the United States; he may protect himself against subsequent infringers by domestic manufacture of a new edition. This change goes a long way towards meeting the spirit of international copyright conventions and does not affect foreign nationals residing outside the United States.

Now for the remaining changes. . . .

JUKE BOXES

One of the quirks of the 1909 Act was a provision that the performance of a musical composition by means of a coin-operated machine, in a place where admission is not charged, "shall not be deemed a public performance for profit."[16] Almost ten years ago the annual juke box receipts were estimated at $500 million.[17] The price per play has increased since then, and it is

---

[16] 17 U.S.C. § 1(e) (1964).
[17] Hearings on S. 1870 before the Subcommittee.

common to deposit half dollars and even dollars to insure continuous play of several records.

The revision bills would replace the exemption by a compulsory license of 3 cents for each three-months period that a record of a work is in a box (§ 116).

In recommending this provision, the Committee Report comments:

> 1. The present blanket jukebox exemption should not be continued. Whatever justification existed for it in 1909 exists no longer, and one class of commercial users of music should not be completely absolved from liability when none of the others enjoys any exemption.[18]

The compulsory license will not apply unless five conditions are met. The first makes it clear that it applies only to coin machines which reproduce nothing but music. In the language of the report:

> 1. It must be used for no purpose other than the "performance of nondramatic musical works by means of phonorecords" and, in order to perform that function, it must be "activated by the insertion of a coin." The definition would thus exclude coin-operated radio and television sets, as well as devices similar to jukeboxes that perform musical motion pictures.[19]

The second makes it clear that a machine in a place that has any form of admission charge is not exempt. This would apply to "establishments making cover or minimum charges, and those 'clubs' open to the public but requiring 'membership fees' for admission."[20]

The third eliminates machines capable "of transmitting the performance beyond the establishment in which it is located."[21]

The fourth requires a prominent listing "of all the musical works available for performance on it." The Report notes that "this condition would not be satisfied if the list is available only on request."[22]

[18] H.R. Rep., N. 1 *supra*, at 108.
[19] *Id*. at 109.
[20] *Ibid*.
[21] *Ibid*.
[22] *Id*. at 110.

Finally "the machines must provide 'a choice of works available for performance,' and must allow 'the choice to be made by the patrons of the establishment in which it is located.' " The Report points out that "a machine that merely provides continuous music without affording any choice as to the specific composition to be played at a particular time, or a case where selections are made by someone other than patrons of the establishment, would be outside the scope of the definition."[23]

COMPULSORY LICENSE FOR "PHONORECORDS"

The original compulsory-license approach to resolving the juke box problem has been in the law since 1909.[24] We are told on good authority that the original compulsory-license provision for phonograph records was a "makeshift" device in 1909.[25]

The present bills would continue the compulsory-license provision, but would increase the existing statutory royalty from 2 cents per record to $2\frac{1}{2}$ cents, or $\frac{1}{2}$ cent per minute of playing time (or fraction), whichever amount is larger (§ 115).

---

23 *Ibid.*

24 17 U.S.C. § 1(e), providing that once a record of a musical composition is made with the consent of the copyright owner, anyone else may manufacture the record on paying the copyright owner 2 cents for each record manufactured.

25 Congressman Charles G. Washburn, the proponent of this provision, wrote to Thorvald Solberg, Register of Copyrights,

"That royalty clause was a 'makeshift' made necessary to get the bill through. Without it, there would have been no copyright legislation in 1909. The author should have 'complete control' of his rights. The constitutional right expressed in the provision that Congress may secure for limited times to authors and inventors the exclusive right to their respective writing and discoveries should if exercised, not be abridged by legislation—that I believe to be a sound principle."

Quoted in Hearings Before the House Committee on Patents on H.R. 10434, 69th Cong., 1st Sess. 240 (1926).

COPYRIGHT IN PHONORECORDS

The existing law does not make any provision for copyrighting the sounds recorded on phonograph records. There is a conflict in the cases as to whether such sounds may be protected independently of copyright.[26] The revision bills would protect the record against duplication of the sounds recorded on it, but would not prevent someone from independently producing and recording those identical sounds (§ 114). As the Report points out, "Mere imitation of a recorded performance would not constitute a copyright infringement even where one performer deliberately sets out to simulate another's performance as exactly as possible."[27]

EXEMPT PERFORMANCES

The existing law does not permit recovery for performances of nondramatic literary or musical works unless they are both "public" and "for profit."[28] In this respect, these works receive less protection than dramatic works, which are infringed if the performance is given in public even though it is not "for profit."[29] There has been some dispute under existing law as to when a performance is "for profit."[30] The revision bills do away with the "for profit" requirement as to all works, but rather specifically

---

[26] Cf. RCA Mfg. Co. v. Whiteman, 114 F.2d 86 (2d Cir.), cert. denied, 311 U.S. 712, 61 S. Ct. 394, 85 L. Ed. 463 (1940), and Waring v. WDAS Broadcasting Co., 327 Pa. 433 (1937). See Gamboni, "Unfair Competition Protection after Sears and Compco," 15 ASCAP Copyright Law Symposium 1 (1967); Kaplan, "Performer's Right and Copyright: The Capitol Records Case," 69 Harv. L. Rev. 409 (1956).

[27] H.R. Rep. N. 1 supra, at 94.

[28] 17 U.S.C. § 1(c) and (e).

[29] Id. § 1(d).

[30] See Associated Music Publishers, Inc. v. Debs Memorial Radio Fund, 141 F.2d 852 (2d Cir. 1944).

exempt certain performances. It will be helpful to draw a distinction between those exempt public performances which are not "for profit," and those which are.

Exempt "Nonprofit" Performances

The bills would exempt the following nonprofit uses (§ 110):

1. Performance or display of a work by instructors or pupils in the course of "face-to-face teaching activities" of a "nonprofit educational institution" [§ 110(1)];

2. Performance of a nondramatic literary or musical work or display of a work in the course of transmission by a nonprofit organization if part of systematic instructional activities, within a radius of not more than 100 miles, made primarily for reception in classrooms or by disabled persons or by government employees, and "the time and content of the transmission are controlled by the transmitting organization and do not depend on choice by individual recipients in activating transmission from an information storage and retrieval system" [§ 110(2)];[31]

3. Performance of certain works in the course of services at a place of worship [§ 110(3)];

4. Performance of a nondramatic literary or musical work "without any purpose of direct or indirect commercial advantage," without payment of any fee to the performers or promoter,

---

31 This section distinguishes between true "educational" television (systematic instructional activities), and "public" television, which present entertainment without commercial announcements. As the Register of Copyrights pointed out,

"The time may come when many works will reach the public primarily through educational broadcasting. In terms of good education it is certainly true that the more people reached the better; but in terms of the author's rights it is equally true that the more people reached the more he should be compensated. It does not seem too much to ask that some of the money now going to support educational broadcasting activities be used to compensate authors and publishers whose works are essential to those activities." H.R. Rep., N. 1 *supra*, at 71.

For a good analysis of the direction in which "public television" (as opposed to "private television") must move, see Lester Markel, "A Program for Public-TV," N.Y. Times, Magazine, March 12, 1967, p. 25.

and (a) without admission charge, or (b) when, if admission is charged, the proceeds must be used for an educational, religious, or charitable purpose. If the copyright owner has objected to the performance at least seven days in advance, the exemption does not apply [§ 110(4)];

5. Public reception of a transmission embodying a performance on a single receiving apparatus of a kind commonly used in private homes, unless a direct charge is made, or the transmission is further transmitted to the public.

6. Performance of a nondramatic musical work without any purpose of direct or indirect commercial advantage by a governmental body for a nonprofit agricultural or horticultural organization in the course of its conduct of an annual agricultural or horticultural fair or exhibition whose duration does not exceed sixteen days. . . .[31a]

FAIR USE

An important limitation on the copyright owner's rights, which exists in the present law as a judicial doctrine and which has been written into the revision bill (§ 107), is the doctrine of fair use.

By specifically listing purposes for which one may make fair use of a copyrighted work, such as "criticism, comment, news reporting, teaching, scholarship, or research," and by listing the factors to be considered in determining whether a use has been fair, that is:

(1) the purpose and character of the use;

(2) the nature of the copyrighted work;

(3) the amount and substantiality of the portion used in relation to the copyrighted work as a whole; and

(4) the effect of the use upon the potential market for or value of the copyrighted work . . .

an attempt has been made to state briefly an "equitable rule of reason"[32] that has taken over 125 years to develop.

[31a] This exemption for certain agricultural fairs was not in the original bill. It was added by the House as an amendment.

[32] H.R. Rep., N. 1. *supra*, at 58.

The first American decision dealing specifically with the doctrine of fair use is *Folsom v. Marsh*.[33] It is interesting to compare the factors listed in the revision bill with Mr. Justice Story's opinion:

> In short we must often, in deciding questions of this sort, look to the nature and objects of the selections made, the quantity and value of the materials used and the degree in which the use may prejudice the sale, or diminish the profits or supersede the objects of the original work. Many mixed ingredients enter into the discussion of such questions. In some cases a considerable portion may be fused, if I may use such an expression, into another's work, so as to be undistinguishable in the mass of the latter which has other professed and obvious objects and cannot fairly be treated as piracy; or they may be inserted as a sort of distinct and mosaic work into the general texture of the second work and constitute the peculiar excellence thereof and then it may be clear piracy.[34]

From this opinion, as from the revision bill, it is clear that each case must be decided on its own facts, based on the given guidelines. . . .

[33] 9 Fed. Cas. 342 (No. 4901) (C.C.D. Mass. 1841).
[34] *Id.* at 348.

Bibliography for Chapter Nine

BOOKS

American Society of Composers, Authors, and Publishers. Copyright Law Symposium. No. 5, 1954; No. 6, 1955; No. 7, 1956; No. 8, 1957; No. 9, 1958; No. 10, 1959; No. 11, 1962; No. 12, 1964; No. 13, 1964; No. 14, 1965; No. 15, 1967. New York: Columbia University Press.

Committee Report of the 1909 Copyright Law.

Committee Report of the New Copyright Bill. Public Law 90-416; 82 Stat. 397; Senate Joint Resolution 172; App. July 23, 1968 (Copyright: Protection Extension).

Copyright Society of the United States. Studies on Copyright. 2 vols. South Hackensack, New Jersey: Rothman, 1963.

Copyright Law Revision. Studies Prepared for the Subcommittee on Patents, Trademarks, and Copyrights of the Committee on the Judiciary, United States Senate, Eighty-Sixth Congress, Second Session Pursuant to S. Res. 240. Studies 1-34. 1961.

Copyright Law Revision. Hearings before Subcommittee No. 3 of the Committee on the Judiciary, House of Representatives, Eighty-Ninth Congress, First Session, on H.R. 4347, H.R. 5680, H.R. 6831, H.R. 6835, Serial No. 8, Parts I-III. 1965.

Drone, Eaton S. *A Treatise on the Law of Property in Intellectual Productions in Great Britain and the United States.* Boston: Little, Brown, and Company, 1879.

Hogan, John C. and S. Cohen. *Author's Guide to Scholarly Publishing and the Law.* Englewood Cliffs, New Jersey: Prentice-Hall, 1965.

Kupferman, Theodore R., ed. *Copyright Problems Analyzed.* 2 vols. in 1; South Hackensack, New Jersey: Rothman, 1966.

Patterson, Lyman Ray. *Copyright in Historical Perspective*. Nashville: Vanderbilt University Press, 1968.

Pilpel, Harriet F. and Morton D. Goldberg. *Copyright Guide*. 2nd ed. New York: Bowker, 1963.

Schnapper, Morris Bartel. *Constraint by Copyright*. Washington, D.C.: Public Affairs, 1960.

UNESCO. *Copyright Laws and Treaties of the World*. 1956. Suppl. 1, 1957; Suppl. 2, 1958; Suppl. 3, 1959; Suppl. 4, 1960; Suppl. 5, 1961; Suppl. 6, 1962; Suppl. 7, 1963; Suppl. 8, 1964; Suppl. 9, 1965; Suppl. 10, 1966. New York: Publications Center.

ARTICLES

Beelar, Donald C. "Cables in the Sky and the Struggle for Their Control," *Federal Communications Bar Journal*, XXI (1967), 26-41.

Cunningham, Dewey J. "Information Retrieval and the Copyright Law," *Bulletin*. Copyright Society of the U.S.A. XIV (October, 1966), 22-7.

Lieb, Charles H. "The Computer and Copyright: The Next Five Years." *Publishers' Weekly*, CXCII (September 18, 1967), 40-42.

"Literary and Artistic Products and Copyright Problems," *Law and Contemporary Problems*, XIX (Spring, 1954), entire issue devoted to copyright—139-322.

Netterville, Victor S. and Barry L. Hirsch, "Piracy and Privilege in Literary Titles," in *Copyright and Related Topics: A Choice of Articles*. The Los Angeles Copyright Society and the UCLA School of Law eds. Berkeley and Los Angeles: University of California Press, 1964. 273-334.

Patterson, Lyman Ray. "The Statute of Anne: Copyright Misconstrued," *Harvard Journal on Legislation*, III (1966), 223-255.

Roeder, Martin A. "The Doctrine of Moral Right: A Study in the Law of Artists, Authors and Creators," *Harvard Law Review*, LIII (February, 1940), 554-578.

Strauss, William. "The Moral Right of the Author," *American Journal of Comparative Law*, IV (Autumn, 1955), 506-538.

CASES

Barr v. Matteo, 360 U.S. 564 (1959).

Brattleboro Publishing Co. v. Winmill Publishing Corp., 369 F. 2d 565 (2d Cir. 1966).

Capitol Records, Inc. v. Mercury Records Corp., 221 F. 2d 657 (2d Cir. 1955).

Donaldson v. Becket, 4 Burr. 2408, 98 Eng. Rep. 257 (H. L. 1774).

Folsom v. Marsh, 9 Fed. Cas. 342 (No. 4901) (C. C. D. Mass. 1841).

Ilyin v. Avon Publications, Inc., 144 F. Supp. 368 (S.D.N.Y. 1956).

International News Serv. v. Associated Press, 248 U.S. 215 (1918).

Mazer v. Stein, 347 U.S. 201 (1954).

Millar v. Taylor, 4 Burr. 2303, 98 Eng. Rep. 201 (K. B.).

Nichols v. Universal Pictures Corp., 45 F. 2d 119 (2d Cir. 1930), cert. denied, 282 U.S. 902 (1931).

Nutt v. National Institute, Inc., for the Improvement of Memory, 31 F. 2d 236 (2d Cir. 1929).

Robertson v. Batton, Barton, Durstine & Osborn, Inc., 146 F. Supp. 795 (S. D. Cal. 1956).

Stanley v. Columbia Broadcasting Sys., Inc., 35 Cal. 2d 653, 221 P. 2d 73 (1950).

United Artists v. Fortnightly Corporation, 255 F. Supp. 177 (1968).

Washingtonian Pub. Co. v. Pearson, 306 U.S. 30 (1938).

White v. Kimmell, 193 F. 2d 744 (9th Cir. 1952).

White-Smith Music Publishing Co. v. Apollo Co., 209 U.S. 1 (1908).

Wheaton v. Peters, 8 Pet. (U.S.) 591 (1834).

CHAPTER TEN

Freedom for Whom To Do What? A Guide to the Future

Previous sections of this book have made clear the vital role of law in freedom of expression issues. Law acts to maintain and expand freedom: where monopoly of expression exists, law can sometimes encourage growth of diversity; where censorship is allowed, law can prevent blatant abuses; where secrecy prevents public knowledge of public business, law can cause a beam of light to be cast. Yet occasionally, through agencies that also have a responsibility to maintain freedom, law can cripple expression: the Constitution can be applied to prevent a completely open exchange of views; when the bounds of truth may have been overstepped, law may apply sanctions; sometimes, even the threat of possible new law restricts expression.

The law itself permits freedom to thrive only as those who make and enforce law wish freedom to thrive. What, then, are the proper objectives for law and the mass media in society? And where is the future taking us?

One crucial fact has been underlined and re-underlined for us as we have compiled this book: never before has there been such concern for, and attention paid to, the many areas where law and the media touch. The many problems our nation faces and the difficulty of establishing contacts among all segments of our population place great burdens on the communication media. In the future the law must work more efficiently than it has in the past to facilitate the establishment of these contacts and to maintain the media as their social functions are fulfilled. The points of contact between law and media appear to us to form the cutting edges of the future. Tomorrow's developments will be based on the successes and failures of today, of yesterday, and of the past half century.

But what guidelines do we offer for tomorrow's course? First, we present an excerpt from the writing of one of the leading students of the concept of freedom of expression, Professor Thomas I. Emerson of Yale University, on the role of law in maintaining freedom of expression. Next, we include the recommendations of the Commission on Freedom of the Press, offered nearly a quarter-century ago, relevant then but even more relevant today, when we see further results of trends that the Com-

407

mission spotted in 1947. Finally, for its value as a thought-provoking challenge to traditional ways of regarding the concept of freedom of the press, and for its practical emphasis on the central theme of this book—that freedom of the press exists for *society's* benefit and not solely for the benefit of the media proprietors— we present Professor Jerome Barron's article on the need for a guaranteed access to the press.

The Role of Law and Legal Institutions in Maintaining a System of Free Expression

THOMAS I. EMERSON

The American people have frequently been warned that they must not count too heavily upon the legal system for the preservation of democratic liberties. Judge Learned Hand, one of the most eloquent exponents of this view, has made the point in the strongest language:

> I often wonder whether we do not rest our hopes too much upon constitutions, upon laws and upon courts. These are false hopes; believe me, these are false hopes. Liberty lies in the hearts of men and women; when it dies there, no constitution, no law, no court can save it; no constitution, no law, no court can even do much to help it. While it lies there it needs no constitution, no law, no court to save it.[1]

Certainly this admonition must be taken to heart. Obviously, a perfect set of legal rules and an ideal array of judicial institutions could not by themselves assure an effective system of free

[1] Irving Dilliard, Editor, *The Spirit of Liberty, Papers and Addresses of Learned Hand* (New York, Alfred A. Knopf, 1959), p. 144.

expression. Many other factors are critical. There must be a substantial consensus on the values and goals of the society—some minimum area of agreement or acquiescence. The economic structure must provide a certain standard of material welfare, shared broadly by all elements of the population. Political institutions must have some basis in the traditions of the people, must receive some degree of acceptance, must prove reasonably effective in meeting the problems of the society, and must remain capable of adjustment and change. Other institutions, such as private corporations and labor organizations, must permit communication on a diverse scale in important areas of decision-making. There must be some feeling of security in relation to other nations or societies. The educational system, the media of communication, and similar institutions molding public opinion must have some capacity to produce mature and independent members of the local and national community. The general philosophy, attitudes and mental health of the citizenry must be favorable. In short, basic conditions for a viable democratic society must be present.

Yet surely Judge Hand has overstated the case. The legal system is not so peripheral to the maintenance of free expression as his words imply. The experience of mankind demonstrates the contrary. Wherever the principles of free expression have prevailed in a society, they have been closely supported by law and legal institutions. This is particularly true, of course, in the United States. The main elements of that role, especially as it has changed in recent years, must be kept in mind in formulating a satisfactory theory of the First Amendment.

THE GENERAL ROLE OF LAW

The legal system is, of course, one of the most effective instruments available to a society for controlling the behavior of its members so as to realize the values and goals sought by that society. Because of certain characteristics of a system of free expression, the role of law is of peculiar significance in any social effort to maintain such a system.

First, a system of free expression is designed to encourage a necessary degree of conflict within a society. To be sure, it attempts to avoid resort to force or violence by channeling this conflict into the area of expression and persuasion. And it contemplates that a longer-range consensus will ultimately be achieved. Yet, because it recognizes the right of the citizen to disagree with, arouse, antagonize and shock his fellow citizens and the government, such an arrangement of human affairs is hardly likely to be self-operating. In its short-term effects it may indeed be highly volatile. Hence the system needs the legitimizing and harmonizing influence of the legal process to keep it in successful balance.

Other features of a system of free expression likewise demonstrate the need for buttressing it through law and legal institutions. The full benefits of the system can be realized only when the individual knows the extent of his rights and has some assurance of protection in exercising them. Thus the governing principles of such a system need to be articulated with some precision and clarity. Doubt or uncertainty negates the process. Furthermore, the theory rests upon subordination of immediate interests in favor of long-term benefits. This can be achieved only through the application of principle, not by ad hoc resolution of individual cases. And it requires procedures adequate to relieve immediate pressures and facilitate objective consideration. All these elements a legal system is equipped to supply.

Further, as already observed, the theory of freedom of expression is a sophisticated and even complex one. It does not come naturally to the ordinary citizen, but needs to be learned. It must be restated and reiterated not only for each generation but for each new situation. It leans heavily upon understanding and education, both for the individual and the community as a whole. The legal process is one of the most effective methods for providing the kind of social comprehension essential for the attainment of society's higher and more remote ideals.

Finally, the principles of the system must be constantly reshaped and expanded to meet new conditions and new threats to its existence. This requires the deliberate attention of an institution entrusted with that specific obligation and possessing the expertise to perform such a function.

The function of the legal process is not only to provide a means whereby a society shapes and controls the behavior of its individual members in the interests of the whole. It also supplies one of the principal methods by which a society controls itself, limiting its own powers in the interests of the individual. The role of law here is to mark and guard the line between the sphere of social power, organized in the form of the state, and the area of private right. The legal problems involved in maintaining a system of free expression fall largely into this realm. In essence, legal support for such a system involves the protection of individual rights against interference or unwarranted control by the government. More specifically, the legal structure must provide:

(1) Protection of the individual's right to freedom of expression against interference by the government in its efforts to achieve other social objectives or to advance its own interests. This has been in the past the main area of legal concern, and it remains so, although other phases of the problem are assuming increasing importance.

(2) The use and simultaneous restriction of government in regulating conflicts between individuals or groups within the system of free expression itself; in protecting individuals or groups from nongovernmental interference in the exercise of their rights; and in eliminating obstacles to the effective functioning of the system.

(3) Restriction of the government insofar as the government itself participated in the system of expression.

All these requirements involve control over the state. The use of law to achieve this kind of control has been one of the central concerns of freedom-seeking societies over the ages. Legal recognition of individual rights, enforced through the legal process, has become the core of free society.[2]

2 Generally, on the development of constitutionalism, see Charles Howard McIlwain, *Constitutionalism: Ancient and Modern* (Ithaca, N.Y., Cornell University Press, 1958).

One must recognize, of course, that the legal system can be used to undermine or destroy freedom of expression. Often in the past, and still in the present, the judicial process has served the function of legitimizing action that is wholly contrary to the elemental principles of free expression. Indeed, even in the police state, infringements of political freedom are normally accomplished in the name of the law. Yet this fact does not lessen, but rather emphasizes, the power of law and legal institutions as an instrument of social persuasion and control. It underlines the warning that the legal system is not by itself sufficient to guarantee free expression. But it also furnishes evidence that without the support of the legal structure the values of such a system are not likely to prevail in the community. . . .[3]

[3] For an excellent account of the uses of legal process to thwart a system of free expression, see O. Kirchheimer, *Political Justice.* . . .

The Requirements for a Free and Responsible Press

If the freedom of the press is freighted with the responsibility of providing the current intelligence needed by a free society, we have to discover what a free society requires. Its requirements in America today are greater in variety, quantity, and quality than those of any previous society in any age. They are the requirements of a self-governing republic of continental size, whose doings have become, within a generation, matters of common concern in new and important ways. Its internal arrangements, from being thought of mainly as matters of private interest and automatic market adjustments, have become affairs of conflict and conscious compromise among organized groups, whose powers appear not to be bounded by "natural law," economic or other. Externally, it has suddenly assumed a leading role in the attempt to establish peaceful relationships among all the states on the globe.

Today our society needs, first, a truthful, comprehensive, and intelligent account of the day's events in a context which gives them meaning; second, a forum for the exchange of comment and criticism; third, a means of projecting the opinions and attitudes of the groups in the society to one another; fourth, a method of presenting and clarifying the goals and values of the society; and,

Reprinted by permission of the University of Chicago Press. This selection comes from Chapter II of the Commission on Freedom of the Press, *A Free and Responsible Press*, Chicago: The University of Chicago Press, 1947.

414

fifth, a way of reaching every member of the society by the currents of information, thought, and feeling which the press supplies.

The Commission has no idea that these five ideal demands can ever be completely met. All of them cannot be met by any one medium; some do not apply at all to a particular unit; nor do all apply with equal relevance to all parts of the communications industry. The Commission does not suppose that these standards will be new to the managers of the press; they are drawn largely from their professions and practices.

A TRUTHFUL, COMPREHENSIVE, AND INTELLIGENT ACCOUNT OF THE DAY'S EVENTS IN A CONTEXT WHICH GIVES THEM MEANING

The first requirement is that the media should be accurate. They should not lie.

Here the first link in the chain of responsibility is the reporter at the source of the news. He must be careful and competent. He must estimate correctly which sources are most authoritative. He must prefer firsthand observation to hearsay. He must know what questions to ask, what things to observe, and which items to report. His employer has the duty of training him to do his work as it ought to be done.

Of equal importance with reportorial accuracy are the identification of fact as fact and opinion as opinion, and their separation, so far as possible. This is necessary all the way from the reporter's file, up through the copy and makeup desks and editorial offices, to the final, published product. The distinction cannot, of course, be made absolute. There is no fact without a context and no factual report which is uncolored by the opinions of the reporter. But modern conditions require greater effort than ever to make the distinction between fact and opinion. In a simpler order of society published accounts of events within the experience of the community could be compared with other sources of information. Today this is usually impossible. The account of an isolated fact, however accurate in itself, may be misleading and, in effect, untrue.

The greatest danger here is in the communication of information internationally. The press now bears a responsibility in all countries, and particularly in democratic countries, where foreign policies are responsive to popular majorities, to report international events in such a way that they can be understood. It is no longer enough to report *the fact* truthfully. It is now necessary to report *the truth about the fact.*

In this country a similar obligation rests upon the press in reporting domestic news. The country has many groups which are partially insulated from one another and which need to be interpreted to one another. Factually correct but substantially untrue accounts of the behavior of members of one of these social islands can intensify the antagonisms of others toward them. A single incident will be accepted as a sample of group action unless the press has given a flow of information and interpretation concerning the relations between two racial groups such as to enable the reader to set a single event in its proper perspective. If it is allowed to pass as a sample of such action, the requirement that the press present an accurate account of the day's events in a context which gives them meaning has not been met.

A FORUM FOR THE EXCHANGE OF COMMENT AND CRITICISM

The second requirement means that the great agencies of mass communication should regard themselves as common carriers of public discussion.[1] The units of the press have in varying degrees assumed this function and should assume the responsibilities which go with it, more generally and more explicitly.

It is vital to a free society that an idea should not be stifled

---

[1] By the use of this analogy the Commission does not intend to suggest that the agencies of communication should be subject to the legal obligations of common carriers, such as compulsory reception of all applicants for space, the regulation of rates, etc.

by the circumstances of its birth. The press cannot and should not be expected to print everybody's ideas. But the giant units can and should assume the duty of publishing significant ideas contrary to their own, as a matter of objective reporting, distinct from their proper function of advocacy. Their control over the various ways of reaching the ear of America is such that, if they do not publish ideas which differ from their own, those ideas will never reach the ear of America. If that happens, one of the chief reasons for the freedom which these giants claim disappears.

Access to a unit of the press acting as a common carrier is possible in a number of ways, all of which, however, involve selection on the part of the managers of the unit. The individual whose views are not represented on an editorial page may reach an audience through a public statement reported as news, through a letter to the editor, through a statement printed in advertising space, or through a magazine article. But some seekers for space are bound to be disappointed and must resort to pamphlets or such duplicating devices as will spread their ideas to such public as will attend to them.

But all the important viewpoints and interests in the society should be represented in its agencies of mass communication. Those who have these viewpoints and interests cannot count on explaining them to their fellow-citizens through newspapers or radio stations of their own. Even if they could make the necessary investment, they could have no assurance that their publications would be read or their programs heard by the public outside their own adherents. An ideal combination would include general media, inevitably solicitous to present their own views, but setting forth other views fairly. As checks on their fairness, and partial safeguards against ignoring important matters, more specialized media of advocacy have a vital place. In the absence of such a combination the partially insulated groups in society will continue to be insulated. The unchallenged assumptions of each group will continue to harden into prejudice. The mass medium reaches across all groups; through the mass medium they can come to understand one another. . . .

Identification of source is necessary to a free society . . . . if the discussion is to have the effect for which democracy hopes, if it is to be really full and free, the names and the characters of the participants must not be hidden from view.

THE PROJECTION OF A REPRESENTATIVE PICTURE OF THE CONSTITUENT GROUPS IN THE SOCIETY

This requirement is closely related to the two preceding. People make decisions in large part in terms of favorable or unfavorable images. They relate fact and opinion to stereotypes. Today the motion picture, the radio, the book, the magazine, the newspaper, and the comic strip are principal agents in creating and perpetuating these conventional conceptions. When the images they portray fail to present the social group truly, they tend to prevent judgment.

Such failure may occur indirectly and incidentally. Even if nothing is said about the Chinese in the dialogue of a film, yet if the Chinese appear in a succession of pictures as sinister drug addicts and militarists, an image of China is built which needs to be balanced by another. If the Negro appears in the stories published in magazines of national circulation only as a servant, if children figure constantly in radio dramas as impertinent and ungovernable brats—the image of the Negro and the American child is distorted. The plugging of special color and "hate" words in radio and press dispatches, in advertising copy, in news stories —such words as "ruthless," "confused," "bureaucratic"—performs inevitably the same image-making function.

Responsible performance here simply means that the images repeated and emphasized be such as are in total representative of the social group as it is. The truth about any social group, though it should not exclude its weaknesses and vices, includes also recognition of its values, its aspirations, and its common humanity. The Commission holds to the faith that if people are exposed to the inner truth of the life of a particular group, they will gradually build up respect for and understanding of it.

THE PRESENTATION AND CLARIFICATION
OF THE GOALS AND VALUES OF THE SOCIETY

The press has a similar responsibility with regard to the values and goals of our society as a whole. The mass media, whether or not they wish to do so, blur or clarify these ideas as they report the failings and achievements of every day.[2] The Commission does not call upon the press to sentimentalize, to manipulate the facts for the purpose of painting a rosy picture. The Commission believes in realistic reporting of the events and forces that militate against the attainment of social goals as well as those which work for them. We must recognize, however, that the agencies of mass communication are an educational instrument, perhaps the most powerful there is; and they must assume a responsibility like that of educators in stating and clarifying the ideals toward which the community should strive.

FULL ACCESS TO THE DAY'S INTELLIGENCE

. . . The amount of current information required by the citizens in a modern industrial society is far greater than that required in any earlier day. We do not assume that all citizens at all times will actually use all the material they receive. By necessity or choice large numbers of people voluntarily delegate analysis and decision to leaders whom they trust. Such leadership

[2] A striking indication of the continuous need to renew the basic values of our society is given in the recent poll of public opinion by the National Opinion Research Center at Denver, in which one out of every three persons polled did not think the newspapers should be allowed to criticize the American form of government, even in peacetime. Only 57 per cent thought that the Socialist party should be allowed, in peacetime, to publish newspapers in the United States. Another poll revealed that less than a fourth of those questioned had a "reasonably accurate idea" of what the Bill of Rights is. Here is widespread ignorance with regard to the value most cherished by the press—its own freedom—which seems only dimly understood by many of its consumers.

in our society is freely chosen and constantly changing; it is informal, unofficial, and flexible. Any citizen may at any time assume the power of decision. In this way government is carried on by consent.

But such leadership does not alter the need for the wide distribution of news and opinion. The leaders are not identified; we can inform them only by making information available to everybody.

Access to the Press—A New First Amendment Right

JEROME A. BARRON

There is an anomaly in our constitutional law. While we protect expression once it has come to the fore, our law is indifferent to creating opportunities for expression. Our constitutional theory is in the grip of a romantic conception of free expression, a belief that the "marketplace of ideas" is freely accessible. But if ever there were a self-operating marketplace of ideas, it has long ceased to exist. The mass media's development of an antipathy to ideas requires legal intervention if novel and unpopular ideas are to be assured a forum—unorthodox points of view which have no claim on broadcast time and newspaper space as a matter of right are in poor position to compete with those aired as a matter of grace.

The free expression questions which now come before the courts involve individuals who have managed to speak or write in a manner that captures public attention and provokes legal reprisal. The conventional constitutional issue is whether expression already uttered should be given first amendment shelter

Copyright © 1967 by the Harvard Law Review Association. Reprinted by permission of the author and the publisher. From *Harvard Law Review*, LXXX (June, 1967), 1641-1678. Jerome A. Barron is Associate Professor of Law, George Washington Law School. A.B., Tufts College, 1955; LL.B., Yale, 1958; LL.M., George Washington, 1960.

421

or whether it may be subjected to sanction as speech beyond the constitutionally protected pale. To those who can obtain access to the media of mass communications first amendment case law furnishes considerable help. But what of those whose ideas are too unacceptable to secure access to the media? To them the mass communications industry replies: The first amendment guarantees our freedom to do as we choose with our media. Thus the constitutional imperative of free expression becomes a rationale for repressing competing ideas. First amendment theory must be reexamined, for only by responding to the present reality of the mass media's repression of ideas can the constitutional guarantee of free speech best serve its original purposes.

I. THE ROMANTIC VIEW OF THE FIRST AMENDMENT: A RATIONALE FOR REPRESSION

The problem of access to the press is not a new one. When the Newspaper Guild was organizing in the late 1930's, a statement opposing that organization was prepared by the American Newspaper Publishers Association. Not surprisingly that statement was given publicity in almost all the newspapers in the United States. Mr. Heywood Broun, a celebrated American journalist, prepared a two hundred word reply for the Guild organizers and asked the hostile newspapers to print it:[1] "A very large number of newspaper owners who had beaten their breasts as evidence of their devotion to a 'free press' promptly threw the Guild statement into the waste basket . . ."

Mr. Broun's experience illustrates the danger posed by the ability of mass communications media to suppress information, but an essentially romantic view of the first amendment has perpetuated the lack of legal interest in the availability to various interest groups of access to means of communication. Symp-

[1] Broun, *Those Charming People,* in ONE HUNDRED YEARS OF THE NATION 197, 199 (H. Christman ed. 1965).

tomatic of this view is Mr. Justice Douglas's eloquent dissent in
Dennis v. United States:[2]

> When ideas compete in the market for acceptance, full and free
> discussion exposes the false and they gain few adherents. Full and free
> discussion even of ideas we hate encourages the testing of our own
> prejudices and preconceptions. Full and free discussion keeps a society
> from becoming stagnant and unprepared for the stresses and strains
> that work to tear all civilizations apart.
> *Full and free discussion has indeed been the first article of our faith.*

The assumption apparent in this excerpt is that, without government intervention, there is a free market mechanism for ideas.
Justice Douglas's position expresses the faith that, if government
can be kept away from "ideas," the self-operating and self-
correcting force of "full and free discussion" will go about its
eternal task of keeping us from "embracing what is cheap and
false" to the end that victory will go to the doctrine which is
"true to our genius."[3]

This romantic view of the first amendment had its origin in
Mr. Justice Holmes's free speech opinions; a typical statement of
his "marketplace of ideas" theory is found in his dissent in
Abrams v. United States:[4]

> But when men have realized that time has upset many fighting
> faiths, they may come to believe even more than they believe the very
> foundations of their own conduct that the ultimate good desired is
> better reached by free trade in ideas—that the best test of truth is the
> power of thought to get itself accepted in the competition of the
> market, and that truth is the only ground upon which their wishes
> safely can be carried out. That at any rate is the theory of our Con-
> stitution.

The possibility of governmental repression is present so long
as government endures, and the first amendment has served as
an effective device to protect the flow of ideas from governmental
censorship. . . . But . . . our constitutional law has been singularly

[2] 341 U.S. 494, 584 (1951) (emphasis added).
[3] *Id.* at 584-85.
[4] 250 U.S. 616, 630 (1919).

indifferent to the reality and implications of nongovernmental obstructions to the spread of political truth. This indifference becomes critical when a comparatively few private hands are in a position to determine not only the content of information but its very availability, when the soap box yields to radio and the political pamphlet to the monopoly newspaper.

II. OBSTACLES TO ACCESS: THE CHANGING TECHNOLOGY OF THE COMMUNICATIONS PROCESS

The British M.P. and publicist, R.H.S. Crossman, has observed that the modern world is witnessing at present a Political Revolution as searing and as consequential as the Industrial Revolution, a revolution which "has concentrated coercive power and thought control in a few hands."[5] Power, he contends, has shifted from those who control the "means of production" to "those who control the media of mass communication and the means to destruction (propaganda and the armed forces)."[6] . . . his observations have the ring of urgency and contemporaneity. Difficulties in securing access, unknown both to the draftsmen of the first amendment and to the early proponents of its "marketplace" interpretation, have been wrought by the changing technology of mass media.

Mr. Broun's experience as representative of the Newspaper Guild in the 1930's led him to write an article in which he expressed concern about the implications of the newspapers' refusal to print his reply at a time when "[e]very day brings the news that one or two or three more papers have collapsed or combined with their rivals."[7] He has proved a good prophet, for where fourteen English language dailies were published in New York City in 1900, only two morning papers and two afternoon dailies survive. Many American cities have become one newspaper towns. This is a "disquieting" development for American Journalist J.

[5] R.H.S. CROSSMAN, THE POLITICS OF SOCIALISM 44 (1965).
[6] Id.
[7] Broun, supra note 1, at 197.

Russell Wiggins since "[t]his noncompetitive situation puts it within the power of the monopoly newspaper to suppress facts at its discretion . . . ."[8]

Mr. Wiggins suggests that the economics of newspaper publication—rising costs of everything from newsprint to labor—may be a more significant cause of the withholding of news than conspiratorial efforts of publishers. Less sympathetic to the mass media in evaluating the practical obstacles which confront the group seeking an adequate forum for its opinion is Marshall McLuhan's view that the very nature of modern media is at war with a point of view orientation.[9] McLuhan observes that each medium engenders quite different degrees of participation. The new modes of communication engage us by their form rather than by their content; what captivates us is the television screen itself. . . . The electronic media which have eclipsed the typographical age entail a high degree of nonintellectual and emotional participation and involvement.[10] We have become mesmerized by the new forms of communication to the point of

---

[8] J.R. WIGGINS, FREEDOM OR SECRECY 178 (rev. ed. 1964). Wiggins offers these statistics on the diminishing competitive character of the American press:

"The number of daily newspapers in the United States declined from 2202 in 1909-10 to 1760 in 1953-4. The number of cities with competing daily newspapers declined from 689 to only 87. The number of cities with noncompeting dailies increased from 518 to 1361. Eighteen states are now without any locally competing daily newspapers. *Id.* at 177."

But Mr. Wiggins cautions that the danger of suppressing varied viewpoints as a result of the rise of the monopoly newspaper can be exaggerated since newspapers compete not only with each other but with other media.

[9] H.M. McLUHAN, UNDERSTANDING MEDIA (1964).

[10] *Id.* at 173. The first amendment implications of this phenomenon are very great indeed. In the Supreme Court decisions we find a theory of knowledge which revolves around an outmoded conception of decision making: Information is distributed by advocates of various points of view and, after assimilation and reflection, the citizen makes his judgment. But, according to McLuhan, the media defeat this step-ladder approach to decision making: "As the speed of information increases, the tendency is for politics to move away from representation and delegation of constituents toward immediate involvement of the entire community in the central acts of decision. Slower speeds of information make delegation and representation mandatory." *Id.* at 204.

indifference to their content and to the content of the older media. The electronic media which dominate modern communications are, in McLuhan's analysis, ill suited to the problem of making public issues meaningful.

Another commentator on communications, Dan Lacy, has explained this indifference to content somewhat differently. More critical than popular obsession with the forms of technological advance is the dull emphasis on majoritarian values which characterizes all our media, old and new:[11]

> We have seen that the very technology of films and especially of broadcasting is such that their efficiency can be realized only when they are reaching very large audiences. This is a constant factor that is just as present in the BBC as in the advertising-supported networks of the United States. This technological fact predisposes all the mass media to conform to an already widely accepted taste. It also makes it very difficult for a novel point of view or a just emerging problem to gain access to network broadcasts or other mass components of the mass communications system. Let me make it clear once more that I am not talking about the ability of each of two conflicting points of view to get on the air so long as each is a well-recognized point of view about a controversy that already commands attention. It is rather the subject or point of view in which people are not yet interested, but ought to be, that finds understandable difficulty in gaining access to the mass media.

The aversion of the media for the novel and heretical has escaped attention for an odd reason. The controllers of the media have no ideology. Since in the main they espouse no particular ideas, their antipathy to all ideas has passed unnoticed.[12] What has

---

[11] D. Lacy, Freedom and Communications 69 (1961).

[12] That the media have had a cutting edge in the past, however, should not be forgotten. On the phenomenon of the political radio "voices" of the thirties it has been remarked:

"There were many opportunities in the early years for commentators to convert listeners to a point of view. None succeeded until the beginning of the second decade of radio, when the Depression made home entertainment mandatory for most families . . . . Men like Father Charles E. Coughlin and Huey Long could start a movement to bring to America a Fascist brand of social justice or to make it possible for Americans to share the wealth.

happened is not that the controllers of opinion, Machiavellian fashion, are subtly feeding us information to the end that we shall acquiesce in their political view of the universe. On the contrary, the communications industry is operated on the whole with an intellectual neutrality consistent with V.O. Key's theory that the commercial nature of mass communications makes it "bad business" to espouse the heterodox or the controversial.[13]

But retreat from ideology is not bereft of ideological and practical consequences. In a commentary about television, but which applies equally well to all mass media, Gilbert Seldes has complained that, in a time demanding more active intelligence than has ever before been necessary if we are to survive, the most powerful of all our media are inducing inertia.[14] The contemporary structure of the mass media direct the media away from rather than toward opinion-making. In other words, it is not that the mass communication industry is pushing certain ideas and rejecting others but rather that it is using the free speech and free press guarantees to avoid opinions instead of acting as a sounding board for their expression. What happens of course is that the opinion vacuum is filled with the least controversial and bland ideas. Whatever is stale and accepted in the status quo is readily discussed and thereby reinforced and revitalized.

The failures of existing media are revealed by the development of new media to convey unorthodox, unpopular, and new ideas. Sit-ins and demonstrations testify to the inadequacy of old media as instruments to afford full and effective hearing for all points of view. Demonstrations, it has been well said, are "the free press of the movement to win justice for Negroes . . . ."[15] But like an inadequate underground press, it is a communications medium by default, a statement of the inability to secure access to the

Long was stopped in 1935 by a bullet in Baton Rouge, Louisiana; Father Coughlin was silenced in 1940 by his bishop. Both had long demonstrated how magnetic a radio voice could be."

B. ULANOV, THE TWO WORLDS OF AMERICAN ART 404 (1965).
13 See text accompanying footnote 41 infra.
14 Seldes, Public Entertainment and the Subversion of Ethical Standards, 363 ANNALS 87 (1966).
15 Ferry, Masscomm as Educator, 35 AM. SCHOLAR 293, 300 (1966).

conventional means of reaching and changing public opinion. By the bizarre and unsettling nature of his technique the demonstrator hopes to arrest and divert attention long enough to compel the public to ponder his message. But attention-getting devices so abound in the modern world that new ones soon become tiresome. The dissenter must look for ever more unsettling assaults on the mass mind if he is to have continuing impact. Thus, as critics of protest are eager and in a sense correct to say, the prayer-singing student demonstration is the prelude to Watts. But the difficulty with this criticism is that . . . [its purveyors wish] to throttle protest rather than to recognize that protest has taken these forms because it has . . . nowhere else to go.

III. MAKING THE FIRST AMENDMENT WORK

The Justices of the United States Supreme Court are not innocently unaware of these contemporary social realities, but they have nevertheless failed to give the "marketplace of ideas" theory of the first amendment the burial it merits. Perhaps the interment of this theory has been denied for the understandable reason that the Court is at a loss to know with what to supplant it. But to put off inquiry under today's circumstances will only aggravate the need for it under tomorrow's.

(A) Beyond Romanticism

There is inequality in the power to communicate ideas just as there is inequality in economic bargaining power; to recognize the latter and deny the former is quixotic. The "marketplace of ideas" view has rested on the assumption that protecting the right of expression is equivalent to providing for it.[16] But changes in

16 *See, e.g.,* Weiman v. Updegraff, 344 U.S. 183, 194 (1952) (Black, J., concurring):

"With full knowledge of this danger the Framers rested our First Amendment on the premise that the slightest suppression of thought, speech, press, or public assembly is still more dangerous. This means that individuals are guaranteed an undiluted and unequivocal right to express themselves on questions of current public interest."

the communications industry have destroyed the equilibrium in that marketplace. While it may have been still possible in 1925 to believe with Justice Holmes that every idea is "acted on unless some other belief outweighs it or some failure of energy stifles the movement at its birth,"[17] it is impossible to believe that now. Yet the Holmesian theory is not abandoned, even though the advent of radio and television has made even more evident that philosophy's unreality. A realistic view of the first amendment requires recognition that a right of expression is somewhat thin if it can be exercised only at the sufferance of the managers of mass communications.

Too little attention has been given to defining the purposes which the first amendment protection is designed to achieve and to identifying the addressees of that protection. An eloquent exception is the statement of Justice Brandeis in *Whitney v. California*[18] that underlying the first amendment guarantee is the assumption that free expression is indispensable to the "discovery and spread of political truth" and that the "greatest menace to freedom is an inert people." In *Thornhill v. Alabama*[19] Justice Murphy described his view of the first amendment:

> The exigencies of the colonial period and the efforts to secure freedom from oppressive administration developed a broadened conception of these liberties as adequate to supply *the public need for information and education with respect to the significant issues of the times.* . . . Freedom of discussion, if it would fulfill its historic function in this nation, must embrace all issues about which information is needed or appropriate to enable the members of society to cope with the exigencies of their period.

That public information is vital to the creation of an informed citizenry is, I suppose, unexceptionable. Both Justices recognize the importance of confronting citizens, as individual decision makers, with the widest variety of competing ideas. But accuracy does demand one to remember that Justice Brandeis was speaking in *Whitney,* as was Justice Murphy in *Thornhill,* of the consti-

---

17 Gitlow v. New York, 268 U.S. 652, 673 (1925) (dissenting opinion).
18 274 U.S. 357, 375 (1927) (concurring opinion).
19 310 U.S. 88, 102 (1940) (emphasis added).

tutional recognition that is given to the necessity of inhibiting "the occasional tyrannies of governing majorities" from throttling opportunities for discussion. But is it such a large constitutional step to take the same approach to nongoverning minorities who control the machinery of communication? Is it too bold to suggest that it is necessary to ensure access to the mass media for unorthodox ideas in order to make effective the guarantee against repression?

Another conventionally stated goal of first amendment protection—the "public order function"—also cries out for recognition of a right of access to the mass media. The relationship between constitutional assurance of an opportunity to communicate ideas and the integrity of the public order was appreciated by both Justice Cardozo and Justice Brandeis. In *Palko v. Connecticut*[20] Justice Cardozo clearly indicated that while many rights could be eliminated and yet "justice" not undone, "neither liberty nor justice would exist . . . [without] freedom of thought and speech" since free expression is "the matrix, the indispensable condition, of nearly every other form of freedom." If freedom of expression cannot be secured because entry into the communication media is not free but is confined as a matter of discretion by a few private hands, the sense of the justice of existing institutions, which freedom of expression is designed to assure, vanishes from some section of our population as surely as if access to the media were restricted by the government.

Justice Brandeis, in his seminal opinion in *Whitney*—one of the few efforts of a Supreme Court Justice to go beyond the banality of the "marketplace of ideas"—also stressed the intimacy of the relationship between the goals of a respect for public order and the assurance of free expression. For Brandeis one of the assumptions implicit in the guarantee of free expression is that "it is hazardous to discourage thought, hope and imagination; that fear breeds repression; that repression breeds hate; that hate menaces stable government; that the path of safety lies in the opportunity to discuss freely supposed grievances and proposed

20 302 U.S. 319, 325-27 (1937).

remedies . . . ."[21] I would suggest that the contemporary challenge to this "path of safety" has roots in the lack of opportunity for the disadvantaged and the dissatisfied of our society to discuss supposed grievances effectively.

The "sit-in" demonstrates that the safety valve value of free expression in preserving public order is lost when access to the communication media is foreclosed to dissident groups. It is a measure of the jaded and warped standards of the media that ideas which normally would never be granted a forum are given serious network coverage if they become sufficiently enmeshed in mass demonstration or riot and violence. Ideas are denied admission into media until they are first disseminated in a way that challenges and disrupts the social order. They then may be discussed and given notice. But is it not the assumption of a constitutional guarantee of freedom of expression that the process ought to work just the other way—that the idea be given currency first so that its proponents will not conclude that unrest and violence alone will suffice to capture public attention? Contemporary constitutional theory has been indifferent to this task

[21] 274 U.S. 357, 375 (1927). Chief Justice Hughes made a similar reference to the connection between free speech and public order in De Jonge v. Oregon, 299 U.S. 353, 365 (1937):

"The greater the importance of safeguarding the community from incitements to the overthrow of our institutions by force and violence, the more imperative is the need to preserve inviolate the constitutional rights of free speech, free press and free assembly in order to maintain the opportunity for free political discussion, to the end that government may be responsive to the will of the people and that changes, if desired, may be obtained by peaceful means."

However, although all Justices would probably agree that there is a public order function underlying the free expression guarantee, others have pointed out that the guarantee contemplates a measure of disorder as well. Thus Justice Douglas declared for the Court in Terminiello v. Chicago, 337 U.S. 1, 4 (1949):

"Accordingly a function of free speech under our system of government is to invite dispute. It may indeed best serve its high purpose when it induces a condition of unrest, creates dissatisfaction with conditions as they are, or even stirs people to anger."

of channeling the novel and the heretical into the mass communications media, perhaps because the problem is indeed a recent
one.

(B) The Need for a Contextual Approach

A corollary of the romantic view of the first amendment is the
Court's unquestioned assumption that the amendment affords
"equal" protection to the various media. According to this view
new media of communication are assimilated into first amendment analysis without regard to the enormous differences in
impact these media have in comparison with the traditional
printed word. Radio and television are to be as free as newspapers and magazines, sound trucks as free as radio and television.

This extension of a simplistic egalitarianism to media whose
comparative impacts are gravely disproportionate is wholly unrealistic. It results from confusing freedom of media content
with freedom of the media to restrict access. The assumption in
romantic first amendment analysis that the same postulates apply
to different classes of people, situations, and means of communication obscures the fact, noted explicitly by Justice Jackson
in *Kovacs v. Cooper*,[22] that problems of access and impact vary
significantly from medium to medium: "The moving picture
screen, the radio, the newspaper, the handbill, the sound truck
and the street corner orator have differing natures, values, abuses
and dangers. Each, in my view, is a law unto itself, and all we are
dealing with now is the sound truck."

However, this enlightened view, suggesting the creation of
legal principles which fit the dimensions of the particular
medium, was probably not accepted by the majority in *Kovacs*
and appeared to be rejected by the dissenters. . . .

The dissenters, in an opinion by Justice Black, are explicit in
rejecting any attempt to shape legal principles to the particular
medium, reasoning that government cannot restrain a given mode
of communication because that would disadvantage the others—
"favoritism" would result because "[l]aws which hamper the free
use of some instruments of communication thereby favor com-

---

22 336 U.S. 77, 97 (1949) (concurring opinion).

peting channels."[23] Justice Black's theory appears to be that if all instrumentalities of communication are "free" in the sense of immunization from governmental regulations, problems of access will work themselves out. But what happens in fact is that the dominant media become even more influential and the media which are freely available, such as sound trucks and pamphlets, become even less significant. Thus, we are presented with the anomaly that the protagonist of the "absolute" view of free speech has helped to fashion a protective doctrine of greatest utility to the owners and operators of the mass communications industry. By refusing to treat media according to their peculiar natures Justice Black has done that very thing he so heartily condemns—he has favored some channels of communication.

Justice Black is not unaware of the inequality in the existing operation of the mass media, but he blurs distinctions among the media and acquiesces in their differing impacts:[24]

> Yet everybody knows the vast reaches of these powerful channels of communication which from the very nature of our economic system must be under the control and guidance of comparatively few people. . . .
>
> . . . For the press, the radio, and the moving picture owners have their favorites, and it assumes the impossible to suppose that these agencies will at all times be equally fair as between the candidates and officials they favor and those whom they vigorously oppose.

For all the intensity of his belief that "it is of particular importance" in a system of representative government that the "fullest opportunity be afforded candidates" to express their views to the voters,[25] Justice Black is nevertheless of the opinion that courts must remain constitutionally insensitive to the problem of getting ideas before a forum. That his approach affords greatest protection to mass media does not come about because of a belief that such protection is particularly desirable. Rather it results from a constitutional approach which looks only to protecting the communications which are presently being made without

---

[23] *Id.* at 102.
[24] *Id.* at 102-03.
[25] *Id.* at 103.

inquiry as to whether freedom of speech and press, in defense of which so much judicial rhetoric is expended, is a realistically available right. While we have taken measures to ensure the sanctity of that which is said, we have not inquired whether, as a practical matter, the difficulty of access to the media of communication has made the right of expression somewhat mythical.

Once again Justice Jackson was the author of one of the few judicial statements which recognizes that first amendment interpretation is uselessly conceptual unless it attempts to be responsive to the diverse natures of differing modes of communication. Dissenting in *Kunz v. New York*[26] he thought absolutist interpretations of the first amendment too simplistic and suggested that the susceptibility to public control of a given medium of communication should be in direct proportion to its public impact: "Few are the riots caused by publication alone, few are the mobs that have not had their immediate origin in harangue. *The vulnerability of various forms of communication to community control must be proportioned to their impact upon other community interests.*" Although originally made in a context of the greater likelihood that a riot would be initiated by an harangue than by a newspaper publication, the principle applies equally well to the impact which the new technology has on the informational and public-order goals of the first amendment.

An analysis of the first amendment must be tailored to the context in which ideas are or seek to be aired. This contextual approach requires an examination of the purposes served by and the impact of each particular medium. If a group seeking to present a particular side of a public issue is unable to get space in the only newspaper in town, is this inability compensated by the availability of the public park or the sound truck? . . . If ideas are criticized in one forum the most adequate response is in the same forum since it is most likely to reach the same audience. Further, the various media serve different functions and create different reactions and expectations—criticism of an individual or a governmental policy over television may reach more people but criticism in print is more durable.

[26] 340 U.S. 290, 307-08 (1951) (emphasis added).

The test of a community's opportunities for free expression rests not so much in an abundance of alternative media but rather in an abundance of opportunities to secure expression in media with the largest impact. Such a test embodies Justice Jackson's observation that community control must be in proportion to the impact which a particular medium has on the community.

(C) A New Perspective

The late Professor Meiklejohn, who has articulated a view of the first amendment which assumes its justification to be political self-government, has wisely pointed out that "what is essential is not that everyone shall speak, but that everything worth saying shall be said"—that the point of ultimate interest is not the words of the speakers but the minds of the hearers.[27] Can everything worth saying be effectively said? Constitutional opinions that are particularly solicitous of the interests of mass media —radio, television, and mass circulation newspaper—devote little thought to the difficulties of securing access to those media. . . . Creating opportunities for expression is as important as ensuring the right to express ideas without fear of governmental reprisal.

The problem of private restrictions on freedom of expression might, in special circumstances, be attacked under the federal antitrust laws.[28] In *Associated Press v. United States*,[29] involving an attempt to exclude from membership competitors of existing members of the Associated Press in order to deprive them of the use of the AP's wire service, Justice Black wrote for the Court that nongovernmental combinations are not immune from governmental sanction if they impede rather than expedite free expression:

> [*The First*] *Amendment rests on the assumption that the widest possible dissemination of information from diverse and antagonistic sources is essential to the welfare of the public, that a free press is a condition of a free society.* Surely a command that the government itself shall not

27 A. MEIKLEJOHN, POLITICAL FREEDOM: THE CONSTITUTIONAL POWERS OF THE PEOPLE 25-28 (1960).
28 *See* Lorain Journal Co. v. United States, 342 U.S. 143 (1951).
29 326 U.S. 1, 20 (1945) (emphasis added).

impede the free flow of ideas does not afford non-governmental combinations a refuge if they impose restraints upon that constitutionally guaranteed freedom. . . . *Freedom to publish is guaranteed by the Constitution, but freedom to combine to keep others from publishing is not. Freedom of the press from governmental interference under the First Amendment does not sanction repression of that freedom by private interests.*

Despite these unusual remarks this opinion reflects a romantic view of the first amendment, for Justice Black assumes the "free flow of ideas" and the "freedom to publish" absent a combination of publishers. Moreover, this was an unusual case; antitrust law operates too indirectly in assuring access to be an effective device.

But the case is important in its acknowledgment that the public interest, here embodied in the antitrust statutes, can override the first amendment claims of the mass media; it would seem that the public interest in expression of divergent viewpoints should be weighted as heavily when the mass media invoke the first amendment to shield restrictions on access. In the opinion for the trial court, Judge Learned Hand at least suggests first amendment protection for the interest which the individual members of the body politic have in the communications process itself. Identification of first amendment beneficiaries is not complete if only the interests of the "publisher" are protected:[30]

However, neither exclusively, nor even primarily, are the interests of the newspaper industry conclusive; for that industry serves one of the most vital of all general interests: the dissemination of news from as many different sources, and with as many different facets and colors as is possible. That interest is closely akin to, if indeed it is not the same as, the interest protected by the First Amendment; it presupposes that right conclusions are more likely to be gathered out of a multitude of tongues, than through any kind of authoritative selection.

Our constitutional theory, particularly in the free speech area, has historically been inoperative unless government restraint can be shown. If the courts or the legislature were to guarantee some minimal right to access for ideas which could not otherwise be

[30] United States v. Associated Press, 52 F. Supp. 362, 372 (S.D.N.Y. 1943).

effectively aired before the public, there would be "state action"[31] sufficient to support a claim by the medium involved that this violated its first amendment rights. However, the right of free expression is not an absolute right, as is illustrated by *Associated Press,* and to guarantee access to divergent, otherwise unexpressed ideas would so promote the societal interests underlying the first amendment as perhaps to outweigh the medium's claim. Nor is the notion of assuring access or opportunity for discussion a novel theory. In *Near v. Minnesota ex rel. Olson*[32] Chief Justice Hughes turned to Blackstone to corroborate the view that freedom from prior restraint rather than freedom from subsequent punishment was central to the eighteenth century notion of liberty of the press. This concern with suppression before dissemination was doubtless to assure that ideas would reach the public:[33] " 'Every freeman has an undoubted right to lay what sentiments he pleases before the public; to forbid this, is to destroy the freedom of the press; but if he publishes what is improper, mischievous or illegal, he must take the consequence of his own temerity.' "

The avowed emphasis of free speech is still on a freeman's right to "lay what sentiments he pleases before the public." But Blackstone wrote in another age. Today ideas reach the millions largely to the extent they are permitted entry into the great metropolitan dailies, news magazines, and broadcasting networks. The soap box is no longer an adequate forum for public discussion. Only the new media of communication can lay sentiments before the public, and it is they rather than government who can most effectively abridge expression by nullifying the opportunity for an idea to win acceptance. As a constitutional theory for the communication of ideas, laissez faire is manifestly irrelevant.

The constitutional admonition against abridgment of speech and press is at present not applied to the very interests which have real power to effect such abridgment. Indeed, nongoverning minorities in control of the means of communication should perhaps be inhibited from restraining free speech (by the denial of

---

[31] *Cf.* Shelley v. Kraemer, 334 U.S. 1 (1948).
[32] 283 U.S. 697 (1931).
[33] *Id.* at 713-14.

access to their media) even more than governing majorities are restrained by the first amendment—minorities do not have the mandate which a legislative majority enjoys in a polity operating under a theory of representative government. What is required is an interpretation of the first amendment which focuses on the idea that restraining the hand of government is quite useless in assuring free speech if a restraint on access is effectively secured by private groups. A constitutional prohibition against governmental restrictions on expression is effective only if the Constitution ensures an adequate opportunity for discussion. Since this opportunity exists only in the mass media, the interests of those who control the means of communication must be accommodated with the interests of those who seek a forum in which to express their point of view.

IV. NEW WINDS OF CONSTITUTIONAL DOCTRINE: THE IMPLICATIONS FOR A RIGHT TO BE HEARD

(A) New York Times Co. v. Sullivan: A Lost Opportunity

The potential of existing law to support recognition of a right of access has gone largely unnoticed by the Supreme Court. Judicial blindness to the problem of securing access to the press is dramatically illustrated by *New York Times Co. v. Sullivan*,[34] one of the latest chapters in the romantic and rigid interpretation of the first amendment. There the Court reversed a five hundred thousand dollar judgment of civil libel which Montgomery Commissioner Sullivan had won against the *Times* in the Alabama state courts. The Court created the *"Times* privilege" whereby a defamed "public official" is constitutionally proscribed from recovering damages from a newspaper unless he can show that the offending false publication was made with "actual malice."

The constitutional armor which *Times* now offers newspapers is predicated on the "principle that debate on public issues should

34 376 U.S. 254 (1964).

be uninhibited, robust, and wide-open, and that it may well include vehement, caustic, and sometimes unpleasantly sharp attacks on government and public officials."[35] But it is paradoxical that although the libel laws have been emasculated for the benefit of defendant newspapers where the plaintiff is a "public official,"[36] the Court shows no corresponding concern as to whether debate will in fact be assured. The irony of *Times* and its progeny lies in the unexamined assumption that reducing newspaper exposure to libel litigation will remove restraints on expression and lead to an "informed society." But in fact the decision creates a new imbalance in the communications process. Purporting to deepen the constitutional guarantee of full expression, the actual effect of the decision is to perpetuate the freedom of a few in a manner adverse to the public interest in uninhibited debate. Unless the *Times* doctrine is deepened to require opportunities for the public figure to reply to a defamatory attack, the *Times* decision will merely serve to equip the press with some new and rather heavy artillery which can crush as well as stimulate debate.[37]

---

[35] *Id.* at 270.

[36] This protection bestowed on the press may extend far beyond that suggested by the "public official" language of *Times*. Expansion has already been made by the Supreme Court. Garrison v. Louisiana, 379 U.S. 64 (1964) (criticism of "private" behavior which reflects on judge's fitness for office is protected by *Times*); Rosenblatt v. Baer, 383 U.S. 75 (1966) (local nonelected official may be a "public official"). Lower court cases have begun further extensions. The *Times* privilege may come to bar recovery by a private individual who is "incidentally" defamed by a criticism directed at a public official. *See* Gilberg v. Goffi, 21 App. Div. 2d 517, 251 N.Y.S.2d 823 (Sup. Ct. 1964), *aff'd*, 15 N.Y.2d 1023, 207 N.E.2d 620, 260 N.Y.S.2d 29 (1965); Note, *Defamation à Deux: Incidental Defamation and the Sullivan Doctrine*, 114 U. PA. L. REV. 241 (1965). The privilege may also be extended to protect defamatory statements about "public men." Walker v. Courier-Journal & Louisville Times Co., 246 F. Supp. 231 (W.D. Ky. 1965) ("public man"); Pauling v. National Review Inc., 49 Misc. 2d 975, 269 N.Y.S.2d 11 (Sup. Ct. 1966) ("public figure").

[37] The decision may have a direct impact on discouraging debate if extended, as Judge Friendly suggests, to protect a defamatory statement about "the participant in public debate on an issue of grave public concern." Pauling v. News Syndicate Co., 335 F.2d 659, 671 (2d Cir.) (dictum), *cert. denied*, 379

If financial immunization by the Supreme Court is necessary to ensure a courageous press, the public officials who fall prey to such judicially reinforced lions should at least have the right to respond or to demand retraction in the pages of the newspapers which have published charges against them. The opportunity for counterattack ought to be at the very heart of a constitutional theory which supposedly is concerned with providing an outlet for individuals "who wish to exercise their freedom of speech even though they are not members of the press."[38] If no such right is afforded or even considered, it seems meaningless to talk about vigorous public debate. . . .

Although the Court did not foreclose the possibility of allowing public officials to recover damages for a newspaper's refusal to retract, its failure to impose such a responsibility represents a lost opportunity to work out a more relevant theory of the first amendment. Similarly, the Court's failure to require newspapers to print a public official's reply ignored a device which could further first amendment objectives by making debate meaningful and responsive.[39] Abandonment of the romantic view of

U.S. 968 (1964). Individuals will be less willing to engage in public debate if that participation will allow newspapers to defame with relative impunity. Despite this undesirable consequence, the Supreme Court might abandon its "public official" standard in favor of protecting the publication of statements about "public issues." See Note, *The Scope of First Amendment Protection for Good-Faith Defamatory Error*, 75 YALE L.J. 642, 648 (1966); cf. Time, Inc. v. Hill, 385 U.S. 374 (1967) (right of privacy case).

[38] 376 U.S. at 266.

[39] The right of reply is commonly used in Europe and South America, constituting more than a remedy for defamation since it is available to anyone named or designated in a publication. There are essentially two approaches to the right of reply, one modelled on French law, which allows the reply to contain a statement of the individual's point of view, and one on German law, which limits the reply to corrections of factual misstatements. For a thorough study of these devices, see Donnelly, *The Right of Reply: An Alternative to an Action for Libel*, 34 VA. L. REV. 867 (1948). If either approach were to be adopted here, the French method would appear appropriate since assurance of debate is the stated purpose of *Times*, suggesting the exchange of opinion. See also Pedrick, *Freedom of the Press and the Law of Libel: The Modern Revised Translation*, 49 CORNELL L.Q. 581 (1964).

the first amendment would highlight the importance of giving constitutional status to these responsibilities of the press.

However, even these devices are no substitute for the development of a general right of access to the press. A group that is not being attacked but merely ignored will find them of little use. Indifference rather than hostility is the bane of new ideas and for that malaise only some device of more general application will suffice. It is true that Justice Brennan, writing for the Court in *Times,* did suggest that a rigorous test for libel in the public criticism area is particularly necessary where the offending publication is an "editorial advertisement," since this is an "important outlet for the promulgation of information and ideas by *persons who do not themselves have access to publishing facilities* —who wish to exercise their freedom of speech *even though they are not members of the press.*"[40] This statement leaves us at the threshold of the question of whether these individuals—the "nonpress"—should have a right of access secured by the first amendment: should the newspaper have an obligation to take the editorial advertisement? As Justice Brennan appropriately noted, newspapers are an important outlet for ideas. But currently they are outlets entry to which is granted at the pleasure of their managers. The press having been given the *Times* immunity to promote public debate, there seems little justification for not enforcing coordinate responsibility to allocate space equitably among ideas competing for public attention. And, some quite recent shifts in constitutional doctrine may at last make feasible the articulation of a constitutionally based right of access to the media.

(B) Ginzburg v. United States: The Implications of The "Commercial Exploitation" Doctrine

The *Times* decision operates on the assumption that newspapers are fortresses of vigorous public criticism, that assuring the press freedom over its content is the only prerequisite to open and robust debate. But if the *raison d'être* of the mass media is not to maximize discussion but to maximize profits,

[40] 376 U.S. at 266 (emphasis added).

inquiry should be directed to the possible effect of such a fact on constitutional theory. The late Professor V. O. Key stressed the consequences which flow from the fact that communications is big business:[41]

> [A]ttention to the economic aspects of the communications industries serves to emphasize the fact that they consist of commercial enterprises, not public service institutions. . . . They sell advertising in one form or another, and they bait it principally with entertainment. Only incidentally do they collect and disseminate political intelligence.

The press suffers from the same pressures—"newspaper publishers are essentially people who sell white space on newsprint to advertisers"; in large part they are only processors of raw materials purchased from others.[42]

Professor Key's conclusion—indifference to content follows from the structure of contemporary mass communications—compares well with Marshall McLuhan's view that the nature of the communications process compels a "strategy of neutrality." For McLuhan it is the technology or form of television itself, rather than the message, which attracts public attention. Hence the media owners are anxious that media content not get enmeshed with unpopular views which will undermine the attraction which the media enjoy by virtue of their form alone:[43]

> Thus the commercial interests who think to render media universally acceptable, invariably settle for "entertainment" as a strategy of neutrality. A more spectacular mode of the ostrich-head-in-sand could not be devised, for it ensures maximum pervasiveness for any medium whatever.

Whether the mass media suffer from an institutional distaste for controversy because of technological or of economic factors, this antipathy to novel ideas must be viewed against a background of industry insistence on constitutional immunity from legally imposed responsibilities. A quiet truth emerges from such a study: industry opposition to legally imposed responsibilities does

41 V.O. Key, Public Opinion and American Democracy 378-79, 387 (1961).
42 Id. at 379, 380.
43 H.M. McLuhan, Understanding Media 305 (1964).

not represent a flight from censorship but rather a flight from points of view. Points of view suggest disagreement and angry customers are not good customers.

However, there is emerging in our constitutional philosophy of the first amendment a strain of realism which contrasts markedly with the prevailing romanticism. The much publicized case of *Ginzburg v. United States*[44] contains the seeds of a new pragmatic approach to the first amendment guarantee of free expression. In *Ginzburg* the dissemination of books was held to violate the federal obscenity statute not because the printed material was in itself obscene but because the publications were viewed by the Court "against a background of commercial exploitation of erotica solely for the sake of their prurient appeal."[45] The books were purchased by the reader "for titillation, not for saving intellectual content."

The mass communications industry should be viewed in constitutional litigation with the same candor with which it has been analyzed by industry members and scholars in communication. If dissemination of books can be prohibited and punished when the dissemination is not for any "saving intellectual content" but for "commercial exploitation," it would seem that the mass communications industry, no less animated by motives of "commercial exploitation," could be legally obliged to host competing opinions and points of view. If the mass media are essentially business enterprises and their commercial nature makes it difficult to give a full and effective hearing to a wide spectrum of opinion, a theory of the first amendment is unrealistic if it prevents courts or legislatures from requiring the media to do that which, for commercial reasons, they would be otherwise unlikely to do. Such proposals only require that the opportunity for publication be broadened and do not involve restraint on publication or punishment after publication, as did *Ginzburg* where the distributor of books was jailed under an obscenity statute even though the books themselves were not constitutionally obscene.[46] In a companion case to *Ginzburg*, Justice

[44] 383 U.S. 463 (1966).
[45] *Id*. at 466.
[46] "The Court today appears to concede that the materials Ginzburg mailed

Douglas remarked that the vice of censorship lies in the substitution it makes of "majority rule where minority tastes or viewpoints were to be tolerated."[47] But what is suggested here is merely that legal steps be taken to provide for the airing and publication of "minority tastes or viewpoints," not that the mass media be prevented from publishing their views.

In *Ginzburg* Justice Brennan observed:[48]

> [T]he circumstances of presentation and dissemination of material are equally relevant to determining whether social importance claimed for material in the courtroom was, in the circumstances, pretense or reality—whether it was the basis upon which it was traded in the marketplace or a spurious claim for litigation purposes.

The same approach should be taken in evaluating the protests of mass media against the prospect of a right to access. Is their argument—that the development of legally assured rights of access to mass communications would hinder media freedom of expression—"pretense or reality"? The usefulness of *Ginzburg* lies in its recognition of the doctrine that when commercial purposes dominate the matrix of expression seeking first amendment protection, first amendment directives must be restructured. When commercial considerations dominate, often leading the media to repress ideas, these media should not be allowed to resist controls designed to promote vigorous debate and expression by cynical reliance on the first amendment.

(C) Office of Communication of the United Church of Christ v. FCC: A Support for the Future?

There are other signs of change in legal doctrine, among the more significant the recent decision in *Office of Communication of the United Church of Christ v. FCC*.[49] In *Church of Christ,* individuals and organizations claiming to represent the Negro

were themselves protected by the First Amendment." 383 U.S. at 500 (Stewart, J., dissenting).

[47] A Book Named "John Cleland's Memoirs of a Woman of Pleasure" v. Attorney General of Massachusetts, 383 U.S. 413, 427 (1966) (concurring opinion).

[48] 383 U.S. at 470.

[49] 359 F.2d 994 (D.C. Cir. 1966), *noted in* 80 HARV. L. REV. 670 (1967).

community of Jackson, Mississippi—forty-five percent of the city's total population—requested the FCC to grant an evidentiary hearing to challenge the renewal application of a television broadcast licensee in Jackson. The petitioners contended that the station discriminated against Negroes, both by failure to give meaningful expression to integrationist views contrary to the segregationist position taken by it and by the relatively tiny segment of religious programming assigned to Negro churches. The Commission held that the petitioners were merely members of the public and had no standing to claim a hearing since there was no showing of competitive economic injury or electrical interference. However, in an opinion which may be the harbinger of a new approach for the whole field of communications, the court of appeals reversed the Commission, radically expanding the grounds for standing by holding the interests of community groups in broadcast programming sufficient to obtain an evidentiary hearing on license renewal applications.

The court of appeals rested its decision on the FCC's "fairness" doctrine, an administrative creation[50] first adopted in 1949 and later codified in a 1959 amendment to section 315 of the Federal Communications Act.[51] The statute requires licensees "to afford reasonable opportunity for the discussion of conflicting views on issues of public importance," which in operation means that where a licensee has taken a position he must permit spokesmen for the other side or sides to reply. Of course, the defect of the statute is that, as interpreted, the obligation to provide access for ideas of "public importance" arises only after the licensee has taken a position on an issue. By avoiding controversy the licensee can evade the fairness rule—there is no duty to report the other side of silence. Beyond this, if the licensee chooses to violate the requirements of the doctrine by only reporting one side of a controversy, little can be done about it until license renewal. Formerly not much was done even at the time of renewal since a refusal to renew is an extremely harsh penalty. However, groups

---

[50] The doctrine was promulgated by the FCC in its *Report on Editorializing by Broadcast Licensees,* 13 F.C.C. 1246 (1949).
[51] 47 U.S.C. § 315(a) (1964).

and individuals representing the public now have been authorized to challenge license renewal in their own right.

Church of Christ, holding the listener's reaction to programming sufficient to furnish standing to contest license renewal, is one of the most significant cases in public law in recent years. It is unfortunate that the constitutional basis of the case, though readily discernible, was not made more explicit. The court's opinion relied on the FCC's *Report on Editorializing by Broadcast Licensees,* the document which gave life to the Commission's "fairness" doctrine. The court emphasized principally the primary status of "the 'right of the public to be informed, rather than any right on the part of the Government, any broadcast licensee or any individual member of the public to broadcast his own particular views on any matter . . . .' "[52] This statement was accompanied in the *Report* by citation to two formative first amendment cases.[53]

. . . [P]rior to the promulgation of the *Report* the alleged unconstitutionality of the fairness doctrine was vigorously asserted by industry witnesses in the hearings before the Commission. To the challenge that programming standards such as the "fairness" doctrine were violations of the first amendment, the Commission made remarks which are quite pertinent to the achievement of a healthy symbiosis between the first amendment and modern mass communications media:[54]

The freedom of speech protected against governmental abridgment by the first amendment does not extend any privilege to government licensees of means of public communications to exclude the expression of opinions and ideas with which they are in disagreement. We believe, on the contrary, that a requirement that broadcast licensees utilize their franchises in a manner in which the listening public may be assured of hearing varying opinions on the paramount issues facing the American people is within both the spirit and letter of the first amendment.

Church of Christ marks the beginning of a judicial awareness

---

52 13 F.C.C. at 1249, cited in 359 F.2d at 999 n.5.
53 Associated Press v. United States, 326 U.S. 1 (1945), Thornhill v. Alabama, 310 U.S. 88 (1940).
54 *Report,* 13 F.C.C. at 1256.

that our legal system must protect not only the broadcaster's right to speak but also, in some measure, public rights in the communications process. Perhaps this new awareness will stimulate inquiry into the stake a newspaper's readership has in the content of the press. Understanding that *Church of Christ* has a constitutional as well as statutory basis helps to expose the distinction typically made between newspapers and broadcast stations. An orthodox dictum in Judge Burger's otherwise pioneering opinion in *Church of Christ* illustrates the traditional approach:[55]

A broadcaster seeks and is granted the free and exclusive use of a limited and valuable part of the public domain; when he accepts that franchise it is burdened by enforceable public obligations. A newspaper can be operated at the whim or caprice of its owners; a broadcast station cannot.

But can a valid distinction be drawn between newspapers and broadcasting stations, with only the latter subject to regulation? It is commonly said that because the number of possible radio and television licenses is limited, regulation is the natural regimen for broadcasting.[56] Yet the number of daily newspapers is certainly not infinite and, in light of the fact that there are now three times as many radio stations as there are newspapers, the relevance of this distinction is dubious. Consolidation is the established pattern of the American press today, and the need to develop means of access to the press is not diminished because the limitation on the number of newspapers is caused by economic rather than technological factors. Nor is the argument that other newspapers can always spring into existence persuasive —the ability of individuals to publish pamphlets should not preclude regulation of mass circulation, monopoly newspapers any more than the availability of sound trucks precludes regulation of broadcasting stations.

If a contextual approach is taken and a purposive view of the first amendment adopted, at some point the newspaper must be

55 359 F.2d at 1003.
56 *See Report on Editorializing by Broadcasting Licensees*, 13 F.C.C. 1246, 1257 (1940).

viewed as impressed with a public service stamp and hence under an obligation to provide space on a nondiscriminatory basis to representative groups in the community.[57] It is to be hoped that an awareness of the listener's interest in broadcasting will lead to an equivalent concern for the reader's stake in the press, and that first amendment recognition will be given to a right of access for the protection of the reader, the listener, and the viewer.

V. IMPLEMENTING A RIGHT OF ACCESS TO THE PRESS

The foregoing analysis has suggested the necessity of rethinking first amendment theory so that it will not only be effective in preventing governmental abridgment but will also produce meaningful expression despite the present or potential repressive effects of the mass media. If the first amendment can be so invoked, it is necessary to examine what machinery is available to enforce a right of access and what bounds limit that right.

(A) Judicial Enforcement

One alternative is a judicial remedy affording individuals and groups desiring to voice views on public issues a right of nondiscriminatory access to the community newspaper. This right could be rooted most naturally in the letter-to-the-editor column[58] and the advertising section. That pressure to establish such a right exists in our law is suggested by a number of cases in which plaintiffs have contended, albeit unsuccessfully, that in

[57] This is reminiscent of Professor Chafee's query as to whether the monopoly newspaper ought to be treated like a public utility. Contrary to my position, however, he concluded that a legally enforceable right of access would not be feasible. 2 Z. CHAFEE, GOVERNMENT AND MASS COMMUNICATIONS 624-50 (1947).

[58] In Wall v. World Publishing Co., 263 P.2d 1010 (Okla. 1953), a reader of the *Tulsa World* contended that the newspaper's invitation to its readers to submit letters on matters of public importance was a contract offer from the newspaper which was accepted by submission of the letter. The plaintiff argued that, by refusal to publish, the newspaper had breached its contract. Despite the ingenuity of the argument, the court held for defendant. Note, however, that a first amendment argument was not made to the court.

certain circumstances newspaper publishers have a common law duty to publish advertisements. In these cases the advertiser sought nondiscriminatory access, subject to even-handed limitations imposed by rates and space.

Although in none of these cases did the newspaper publisher assert lack of space, the right of access has simply been denied.[59] The drift of the cases is that a newspaper is not a public utility and thus has freedom of action regardless of the objectives of the claimant seeking access. One case has the distinction of being the only American case which has recognized a right of access. In *Uhlman v. Sherman*[60] an Ohio lower court held that the dependence and interest of the public in the community newspaper, particularly when it is the only one, imposes the reasonable demand that the purchase of advertising should be open to members of the public on the same basis.

But none of these cases mentions first amendment considerations. What is encouraging for the future of an emergent right of access is that it has been resisted by relentless invocation of the freedom of contract notion that a newspaper publisher is as free as any merchant to deal with whom he chooses.[61] But the broad holding of these commercial advertising cases need not be authoritative for political advertisement. Indeed, it has long been held that commercial advertising is not the type of speech protected by the first amendment,[62] and hence even an abandon-

---

[59] Shuck v. Carroll Daily Herald, 215 Iowa 1276, 247 N.W. 813 (1933); J.J. Gordon, Inc. v. Worcester Telegram Publishing Co., 343 Mass. 142, 177 N.E.2d 586 (1961); Mack v. Costello, 32 S.D. 511, 143 N.W. 950 (1913). These cases do not consider legislative power to compel access to the press. Other cases have denied a common law right but have suggested that the area is a permissible one for legislation. Approved Personnel, Inc. v. Tribune Co., 177 So. 2d 704 (Fla. 1965); Friedenberg v. Times Publishing Co., 170 La. 3, 127 So. 345 (1930); *In re* Louis Wohl, Inc., 50 F.2d 254 (E.D. Mich. 1931); Poughkeepsie Buying Service, Inc. v. Poughkeepsie Newspapers, Inc., 205 Misc. 982, 131 N.Y.S.2d 515 (Sup. Ct. 1954).

[60] 22 Ohio N.P. (n.s.) 225, 31 Ohio Dec. 54 (C.P. 1919).

[61] *See, e.g.,* Shuck v. Carroll Daily Herald, 215 Iowa 1276, 247 N.W. 813 (1933).

[62] *See Developments in the Law—Deceptive Advertising,* 80 HARV. L. REV. 1005, 1027-38 (1967).

ment of the romantic view of the first amendment and adoption of a purposive approach would not entitle an individual to require publication of commercial material. However, at the heart of the first amendment is political speech. In this area of speech, a revised, realistic view of the first amendment would permit the encouragement of expression by providing not only for its protection after publication but also for its emergence by publication. The constitutional interest in "uninhibited," "robust" debate, expressed anew in *Times,* supplies new impetus for recognition of a right of access for political and public issue advertising generally.

[However in] . . . *Lord v. Winchester Star, Inc.,*[63] [a] Boston attorney, residing in Winchester, Massachusetts, took a position on a local matter adverse to that taken by the newspaper in town. Although the newspaper gave space to its side of the controversy, it refused to publish Mr. Lord's letter to the editor—hence debate in the only available local forum was effectively cut off. Lord petitioned the Superior Court for a writ of mandamus requiring the editor to publish his letter. The writ was denied and the Supreme Judicial Court of Massachusetts affirmed. Lord appealed to the United States Supreme Court which dismissed for want of jurisdiction and, treating the appeal as a petition for certiorari, denied certiorari. Plaintiff was unable to provoke a single court to write an opinion, illustrating the lack of recognition given to the reader's interest in "freedom of the press." Although these cases would augur ill for judicial creation of a constitutionally recognized right of access, it must be noted that the interdependence of free access and a free press was neither argued to the courts nor considered by them.

The courts could provide for a right of access other than by reinterpreting the first amendment to provide for the emergence as well as the protection of expression. A right of access to the pages of a monopoly newspaper might be predicated on Justice Douglas's open-ended "public function" theory which carried a

63 346 Mass. 764, 190 N.E.2d 875 (1963), *appeal dismissed and cert. denied,* 376 U.S. 221 (1964).

majority of the Court in *Evans v. Newton*.[64] Such a theory would demand a rather rabid conception of "state action," but if parks in private hands cannot escape the stigma of abiding "public character," it would seem that a newspaper, which is the common journal of printed communication in a community, could not escape the constitutional restrictions which quasi-public status invites. If monopoly newspapers are indeed quasi-public, their refusal of space to particular viewpoints is state action abridging expression in violation of even the romantic view of the first amendment.[65]

(B) A Statutory Solution

Another, and perhaps more appropriate, approach would be to secure the right of access by legislation. A statute might impose the modest requirement, for example, that denial of access not be arbitrary but rather be based on rational grounds. Although some cases have involved a statutory duty to publish,[66] a constitutional basis for a right of access has never been considered. In *Chronicle & Gazette Publishing Co. v. Attorney General*[67] legislation limiting the rates for political advertising to the rates charged for commercial advertising was held constitutional by the Supreme Court of New Hampshire. In upholding the statute Justice Kenison stated:[68] "It is not necessary to consider the extent to which such regulation may go but so long as it does not involve suppression or censorship, the regulation of newspapers is as broad as that over . . . private business." This decision is consistent with a view of the first amendment

---

[64] 382 U.S. 296 (1966).

[65] *Cf.* Marsh v. Alabama, 326 U.S. 501 (1946).

[66] Belleville Advocate Printing Co. v. St. Clair County, 336 Ill. 359, 168 N.E. 312 (1929); Lake County v. Lake County Publishing & Printing Co., 280 Ill. 243, 117 N.E. 452 (1917) (dictum) (statute setting rates chargeable for official notices imposed no duty to publish); Wooster v. Mahaska County, 122 Iowa 300, 98 N.W. 103 (1904) (dictum) (newspaper had no duty to publish and legislature could not impose one).

[67] 94 N.H. 148, 48 A.2d 478 (1946), *appeal dismissed,* 329 U.S. 690 (1947).

[68] *Id.* at 153, 48 A.2d at 482.

which permits legislation to effectuate freedom of expression, although the court did not uphold the statute on a theory of constitutional power to equalize opportunities for expression. However, in a dissenting opinion Chief Justice Marble pointed out that the "real purpose" of the statute was to provide for an "economical means of [political] advertising" rather than to counteract the dangers of bribery. Although clearly not put forth for this purpose,[69] Chief Justice Marble's intriguing analysis of the legislative intent is consistent with an access-oriented view of the first amendment—limiting the amount that can be charged for political advertising provides equal opportunities of access for political candidates and views not buttressed by heavy financial support.

Justice Kenison, writing for the court in *Chronicle*, thought that the legislature's failure to compel some measure of access to the press made it an easy case:[70] "The present statute does not compel the plaintiff or any other newspaper to accept political advertising." This remark at least leaves open the validity of a statute requiring access for political advertising. However, such a statute was given explicit judicial consideration in *Commonwealth v. Boston Transcript Co.*,[71] where the elegant and now vanished *Boston Evening Transcript* was charged with violation of a statute requiring newspapers to publish the findings of the state minimum wage commission. The court struck the statute down on a freedom of contract theory, the opinion bare of any

[69] I surmise that Chief Justice Marble offers this view of the statute because he believes the legislative interest in equalizing opportunities for political advertising is outweighed by the publisher's freedom of contract. Whether he would think the statute unconstitutional if it were defended on a theory that states have power to provide for "freedom of the press," so long as they do not expressly inhibit it, is arguable.

[70] 94 N.H. 148, 152-53, 48 A.2d 478, 481 (1946). Another important aspect of the case was the court's answer to the argument that regulation of political advertising rates in the press, without corresponding regulation of other advertising facilities such as job printing and billboard advertising, was unconstitutionally discriminatory: "It is sufficient answer to this argument that the 'state is not bound to cover the whole field of possible abuses.'" *Id.* at 152, 48 A.2d at 481.

[71] 249 Mass. 477, 144 N.E. 400 (1924).

mention of free expression problems. Although it was not until 1925 that Justice Sanford observed for the United States Supreme Court that freedom of press was hidden in the underbrush of the fourteenth amendment,[72] failure to discuss freedom of the press in 1924 is probably not pardonable since the Supreme Judicial Court ignored a provision in the Massachusetts constitution prohibiting abridgment of freedom of the press.

But the Massachusetts court in *Boston Transcript* stopped short of suggesting that any statutory compulsion to publish was an invasion of freedom to contract. Rather, the case clearly implies that some regulation in this area is permissible. But it did find one of the constitutional defects of the statute to be the fact that no legitimate state interest was served by the restriction on the publisher. The court was convinced that even without the statute the minimum wage board would "have ample opportunity to print its notice in other newspapers than that published by the defendant at the statutory price."[73] This less pressing need for publication contrasts with the more compelling state interest in equalizing opportunities to reach the electorate presented in *Chronicle* and the interest in access presented by the contemporary character of the mass media, illustrating the importance of a contextual approach.

Another thread common to the *Chronicle* and *Boston Transcript* cases was the concern of both courts with the increased risk of libel litigation if a duty to publish were compelled by statute. In *Chronicle* the majority did not find the objection fatal, but Chief Justice Marble relied specifically on it in his dissent; in *Boston Transcript* at least one reason for invalidation of the statute was the fear that the publisher might be exposed to libel suits. However, the treatment of editorial advertisements by the *Times* Court substantially reduces the risk of the publisher's liability for defamation. Furthermore, the statute granting the right of access could provide that the publisher would not be held for libel for publishing a statement under the statutory mandate.[74]

[72] Gitlow v. New York, 268 U.S. 652 (1925).
[73] 249 Mass. 477, 484, 144 N.E. 400, 402 (1924).
[74] In Farmer's Educ. & Cooperative Union v. WDAY, Inc., 360 U.S. 525 (1959),

A recent United States Supreme Court case, *Mills v. Alabama*,[75] places new significance on opportunity for reply in the press and thus provides by implication new support for a statutory right of access to the press. In *Mills,* as in *Chronicle,* the state legislature had regulated newspapers under a state corrupt practices act. The Alabama statute[76] made it a criminal offense to electioneer or solicit votes "on the day on which the election affecting such candidates or propositions is being held." The *Birmingham Post Herald,* a daily newspaper, carried a very strong editorial urging the electorate to adopt a mayor-council form of government in place of the existing commission form. The editor of the newspaper, who had written the editorial, was arrested on a charge of violating the statute. The trial court sustained a demurrer to the complaint, but the Supreme Court of Alabama reversed on the ground that reasonable restriction of the press by the legislature was permissible.

In reversing this decision, Justice Black's opinion for the Supreme Court was based on the familiar concept that the press is a kind of constitutionally anointed *defensor fidei* for democracy:[77]

> The Constitution specifically selected the press, which includes not only newspapers, books, and magazines, but also humble leaflets and circulars . . . to play an important role in the discussion of public affairs. Thus the press serves and was designed to serve as a powerful antidote to any abuses of power by governmental officials and as a constitutionally chosen means for keeping officials elected by the people responsible to all the people whom they were selected to serve.

Mr. Justice Black observes that insofar as the Alabama statute is construed to prohibit the press from praising or criticizing the government, it frustrates the informing function of the press. But all this is familiar theory. What makes the *Mills* case . . . in its own way quietly original, is an interesting commentary by Justice

a station was held not liable for the defamatory utterance of a candidate exercising his right to speak under the Federal Communications Act of 1934, 47 U.S.C. § 315 (Supp. V, 1964).
[75] 384 U.S. 214 (1966).
[76] ALA. CODE tit. 17, § 285 (1958).
[77] 384 U.S. at 219.

Black. In rebutting Alabama's claim that the legislature's aim was a constitutionally permissible one—to purge the air of propaganda and induce momentary reflection in a brief period of tranquillity before election day—Justice Black suggested that this argument failed on its own terms since "last-minute" charges could be made on the day before election and no statutory provision had been made for effective answers:[78] "Because the law prevents any adequate reply to these charges, it is wholly ineffective in protecting the electorate 'from confusive last-minute charges and countercharges.' "

This statement suggests a substitution of the sensitive query "Does the statute prohibit or provide for expression?" for the more wooden and formal question "Does the statute restrain the press?" It is of course clear that *Mills* did not grant a constitutionally endorsed status to legislative or judicial provisions conferring a right of access to assure debate. Quite the contrary, Justice Black prefaced his discussion of the significance of lack of opportunity to reply to "last-minute" charges with the remark that the state's argument about the reflective intent of the statute is illogical *"even if it were relevant* to the constitutionality of the law." But it is the writer's contention that the existence of adequate opportunity for debate, for charge and countercharge, is an extremely relevant consideration in any determination of the constitutionality of legislation in this area. Justice Black's inquiry into the pragmatics of debate is an encouraging step in this direction.

Evidence of an awakening to a more realistic view of the first amendment can be found in another recent case, *Time, Inc. v. Hill.*[79] Directly presented with the issue of whether the first amendment is always to be interpreted as a grant of press immunity and never as a mandate for press responsibility, a divided Court extended the *Times* doctrine by immunizing newspapers from liability under the New York right of privacy statute unless there is a finding that the publication was made in knowing or reckless disregard of the truth. But in a sensitive and thoughtful

[78] *Id*. at 220.
[79] 385 U.S. 374 (1967).

opinion, concurring in part and dissenting in part, Justice Harlan protested this "sweeping extension of the principles" of *Times*, largely because he thought an attack on private individuals was unlikely to create the "competition among ideas" which an attack on a public figure might create; the *Hill* situation was thought to be an area where the " 'marketplace of ideas' does not function."[80] I would argue that the marketplace theory will not function even in the *Times* situation without legal imposition of affirmative responsibilities. Nonetheless, Justice Harlan's words may augur well for the future, as may the attitude expressed in Justice Fortas's dissent, joined in by the Chief Justice and Justice Clark:[81]

> The courts may not and must not permit either public or private action that censors the press. But part of this responsibility is to preserve values and procedures which assure the ordinary citizen that the press is not above the reach of the law—that its special prerogatives, granted because of its special and vital functions, are reasonably equated with its needs in the performance of these functions.

The disenchantment of Justices Harlan and Fortas with the mindless expansion of *Times* discloses a new awareness of the range of interests protected by the first amendment.

Constitutional power exists for both federal and state legislation in this area. Turning first to the constitutional basis for federal legislation, it has long been held that freedom of expression is protected by the due process clause of the fourteenth amendment.[82] The now celebrated section five of the fourteenth amendment, authorizing Congress to "enforce, by appropriate legislation" the provisions of the fourteenth amendment, appears to be as resilient and serviceable a tool for effectuating the freedom of expression guarantee of the fourteenth amendment as for implementing the equal protection guarantee. Professor Cox has noted that our recent experience in constitutional adjudication has revealed an untapped reservoir of federal legislative power to define and promote the constitutional rights of individ-

---

[80] *Id.* at 407-08.
[81] *Id.* at 420.
[82] Gitlow v. New York, 268 U.S. 652 (1925).

uals in relation to state government.[83] When the consequence
of private conduct is to deny to individuals the enjoyment of a
right owed by the state, legislation which assures public capacity
to perform that duty should be legitimate.[84] Alternatively, legislation implementing responsibility to provide access to the mass
media may be justified on a theory that the nature of the communications process imposes quasi-public functions on these
quasi-public instrumentalities.[85]

... [T]he late Professor Meiklejohn did not anticipate the new
uses that the long dormant section five of the fourteenth amendment could be put in order to implement in a positive manner
the great negatives of section one of the fourteenth amendment.
Consequently, he believed that the only solution to what I have
styled the romantic approach to the first amendment was by way
of constitutional amendment. Mr. W. H. Ferry of the Center for
Democratic Institutions has made public Professor Meiklejohn's
despair at the unintended result which had been wrought by the
first amendment—freedom of the press had become an excuse
for the controllers of mass communication to duck responsibility
and to exercise by default the same censorship role which had
been denied the government.[86] Mr. Ferry says that shortly before
his death Professor Meiklejohn proposed, in an unpublished
paper for the Center, that the first amendment be revised by
adding the following:[87]

In view of the intellectual and cultural responsibilities laid upon the

[83] Cox, *Foreword: Constitutional Adjudication and the Promotion of Human
Rights*, 80 HARV. L. REV. 91 (1966). *See, e.g.*, Katzenbach v. Morgan, 384 U.S.
641 (1966); South Carolina v. Katzenbach, 383 U.S. 301 (1966).
[84] United States v. Price, 383 U.S. 787 (1966); United States v. Guest, 383 U.S.
745 (1966); Bullock v. United States, 265 F.2d 683 (6th Cir.) (by implication),
cert. denied, 360 U.S. 909 (1959); Brewer v. Hoxie School District No. 46, 238
F.2d 91 (8th Cir. 1956) (by implication). *See generally* Cox, *supra* note 83, at
110-14.
[85] Evans v. Newton, 382 U.S. 296 (1966); Marsh v. Alabama, 326 U.S. 501
(1946). Both decisions find that private property may become quasi-public
without a statute in extreme cases. The Court should surely defer to a congressional determination in an arguable case.
[86] Ferry, *supra* note 15.
[87] *Id.* at 301.

citizens of a free society by the political institutions of self-government, the Congress, acting in cooperation with the several states and with nongovernmental organizations serving the same general purpose, shall have power to provide for the intellectual and cultural education of all of the citizens of the United States.

What is especially interesting about Professor Meiklejohn's suggested addition is the depth of its criticism of contemporary first amendment theory. However, it is not necessary to amend the first amendment to attain the goal of greater access to the mass media. I do not think it adventurous to suggest that, if Congress were to pass a federal right of access statute, a sympathetic court would not lack the constitutional text necessary to validate the statute. If the first amendment is read to state affirmative goals, Congress its empowered to realize them. My basic premise in these suggestions is that a provision preventing government from silencing or dominating opinion should not be confused with an absence of governmental power to require that opinion be voiced.

If public order and an informed citizenry are, as the Supreme Court has repeatedly said, the goals of the first amendment, these goals would appear to comport well with state attempts to implement a right of access under the rubric of its traditional police power. If a right of access is not constitutionally proscribed, it would seem well within the powers reserved to the states by the tenth amendment of the Constitution to enact such legislation. Of course, if there were conflict between federal and state legislation, the federal legislation would control. Yet, the whole concept of a right of access is so embryonic that it can scarcely be argued that congressional silence preempts the field.

The right of access might be an appropriate area for experimental, innovative legislation. The right to access problems of a small state dominated by a single city with a monopoly press will vary, for example, from those of a populous state with many cities nourished by many competing media.

(C) Administrative Feasibility of Protecting A Right of Access

If a right of access is to be recognized, considerations of administrative feasibility require that limitations of the right be carefully defined. The recent case of *Office of Communication of the United Church of Christ v. FCC*[88] suggests, by analogy, the means by which such a right of nondiscriminatory access can be rendered judicially manageable. In *Church of Christ* the court, while expanding the concept of standing, did not hold that every listener's taste provides standing to challenge the applicant in broadcast license renewal proceedings. Similarly, the daily press cannot be placed at the mercy of the collective vanity of the public. *Church of Christ* suggests an approach to give bounds to a right of access which could be utilized cautiously, but nevertheless meaningfully.

The organizations and individuals requesting standing in *Church of Christ* represented the Negro community in Jackson, Mississippi, almost half of the city's population. Therefore, the court of appeal's grant of standing did not hold that all those who sought standing to challenge the application for license renewal were entitled to it. The court held, instead, that certain of the petitioners could serve as "responsible representatives" of the Negro community in order to assert claims of inadequate and distorted coverage.

A right of access, whether created by court or legislature, necessarily would have to develop a similar approach. One relevant factor, using *Church of Christ* as an analogue, would be the degree to which the petitioner seeking access represents a significant sector of the community. But this is perhaps not a desirable test—"divergent" views, by definition, may not command the support of a "significant sector" of the community, and these may be the very views which, by hypothesis, it is desirable to encourage. Perhaps the more relevant consideration is whether the material for which access is sought is indeed suppressed and underrepresented by the newspaper. Thus, if there are a number of petitioners seeking access for a particular matter or issue, it may be necessary to give access to only one. The unimpressed response of Judge Burger in *Church of Christ* to the FCC's lamentations about that enduring tidal phenomenon of the law, the "floodgates," strikes an appropriate note of calm:[89]

[88] 359 F.2d 994 (D.C. Cir. 1966).
[89] 359 F.2d at 1006.

"The fears of regulatory agencies that their processes will be inundated by expansion of standing criteria are rarely borne out."

Utilization of a contextual approach highlights the importance of the degree to which an idea is suppressed in determining whether the right to access should be enforced in a particular case. If all media in a community are held by the same ownership, the access claim has greater attractiveness. This is true although the various media, even when they do reach the same audience, serve different functions and create different reactions and expectations. The existence of competition within the same medium, on the other hand, probably weakens the access claim, though competition within a medium is no assurance that significant opinions will have no difficulty in securing access to newspaper space or broadcast time. It is significant that the right of access cases that have been litigated almost invariably involve a monopoly newspaper in a community.[90]

VI. CONCLUSION

The changing nature of the communications process has made it imperative that the law show concern for the public interest in effective utilization of media for the expression of diverse points of view. Confrontation of ideas, a topic of eloquent affection in contemporary decisions, demands some recognition of a right to be heard as a constitutional principle. It is the writer's position that it is open to the courts to fashion a remedy for a right of access, at least in the most arbitrary cases, independently of legislation. If such an innovation is judically resisted, I suggest that our constitutional law authorizes a carefully framed right of access statute which would forbid an arbitrary denial of space, hence securing an effective forum for the expression of divergent opinions.

With the development of private restraints on free expression, the idea of a free marketplace where ideas can compete on their

---

[90] *Cf., e.g., In re* Louis Wohl, Inc., 50 F.2d 254 (E.D. Mich. 1931).

merits has become just as unrealistic in the twentieth century as the economic theory of perfect competition. The world in which an essentially rationalist philosophy of the first amendment was born has vanished and what was rationalism is now romance.